ALAN CAIGER-SMITH

and the Legacy of Aldermaston Pottery

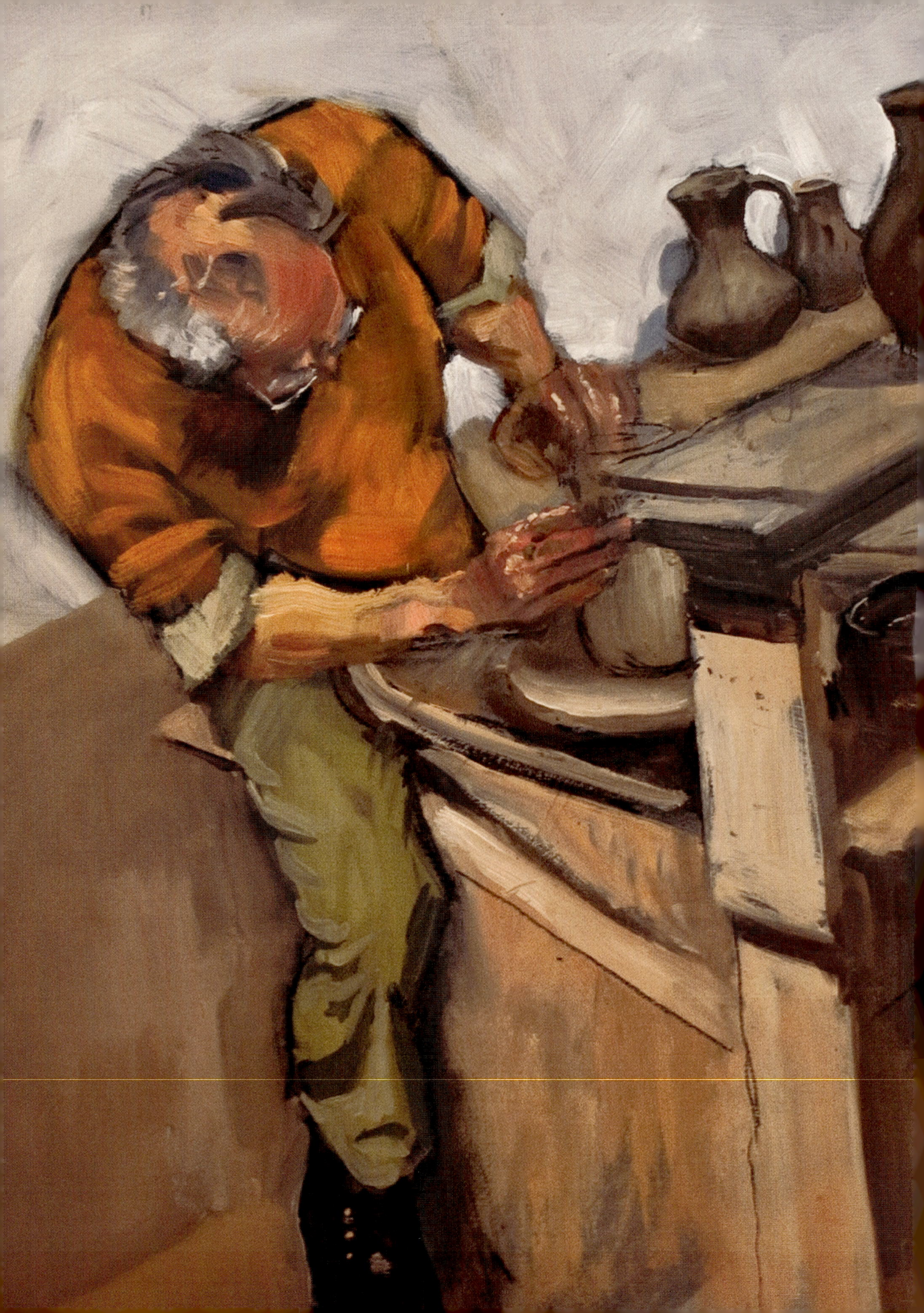

ALAN CAIGER-SMITH
and the Legacy of Aldermaston Pottery

Jane White

With photography by
Julian Bellmont

Afterword by
Alan Caiger-Smith

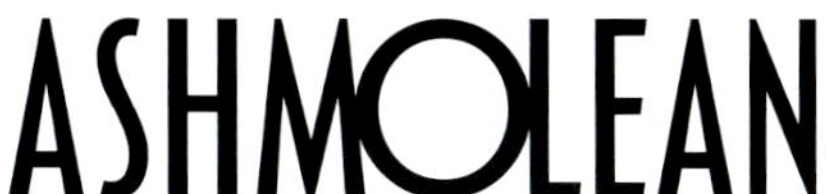

Alan Caiger-Smith and the Legacy of Aldermaston Pottery

Copyright © Ashmolean Museum, University of Oxford, 2018

Jane White has asserted her moral right to be identified as the author of this work.

British Library Cataloguing in Publications Data.
A catalogue record for this book is available from the British Library.

EAN 13: 978-1-910807-25-5

Published by the Ashmolean Museum, University of Oxford
Edited by Johanna Stephenson
Designed and typeset in Book Bembo Pro by Stephen Hebron
Printed and bound in Belgium by Albe De Coker

Frontispiece: *Alan at the Wheel* (detail) by Tom Hallifax, 1999
Great Dixter House and Gardens

For further details of Ashmolean titles please visit:
www.ashmolean.org/shop

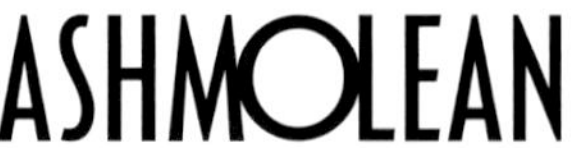

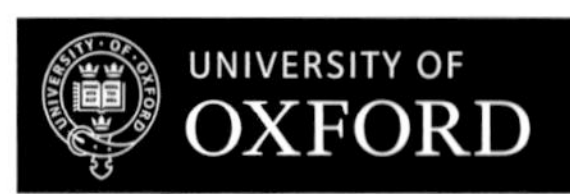

Contents

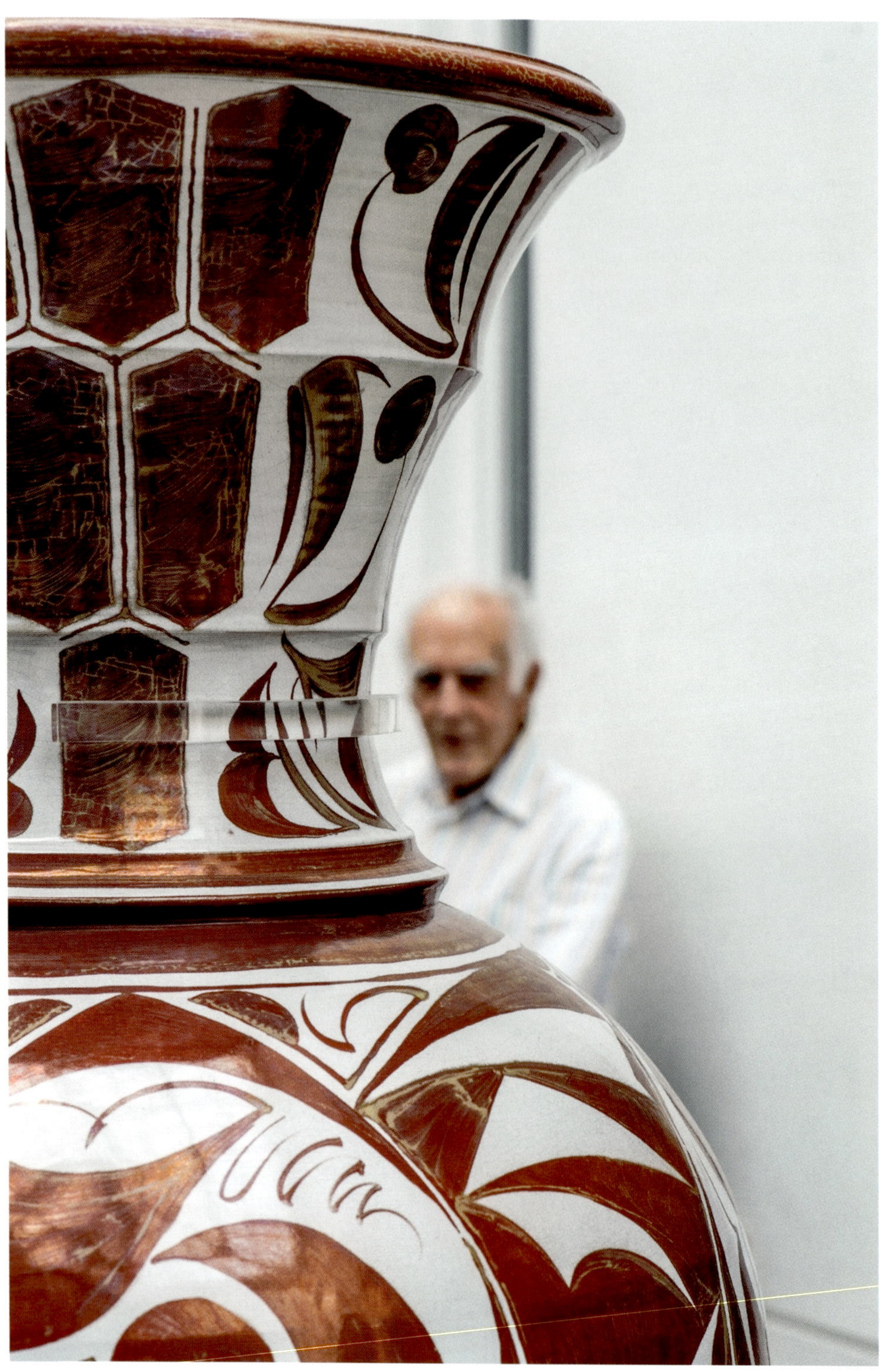

Alan Caiger-Smith with one of his large lustre pots photographed at Reading Museum in 2016

Preface

ALAN CAIGER-SMITH's Aldermaston Pottery is an inspirational chapter in the history of artistic ceramics, with a unique position in a story that has covered more than a millennium and a large part of Christendom and the Islamic world.

Tin-glazed pottery, with its complex cross-cultural heritage from Islam and resonances back to China, is not only the oldest of the European traditions of art pottery but also the best-adapted to creative brush-painting. The technology was developed in what is now Iraq around AD 800, apparently in response to the arrival from China of high-fired white-bodied ceramics. These Chinese imports were impossible to reproduce with the kiln technology and clays available to the Islamic potters, but the invention of an opaque white glaze that could cover an earthenware or other ceramic body was a passable imitation with its own aesthetic potential. Spreading westwards through the Islamic world and sometimes exploiting the mysterious technique of reduced-pigment lustre, tin glaze reached the westernmost outpost of the Islamic world, in southern Spain, where potters from Malaga made, in the fourteenth century, the monumental lustred masterpieces for the Alhambra Palace in Granada. Lustre struck contemporaries as in a real sense magical, almost the fulfilment of the alchemist's dream of making gold out of base materials.

In sixteenth-century Italy, tin glaze was transformed into a form of Renaissance painting, while Maestro Giorgio in Gubbio produced masterpieces of lustreware in which the copper reds perfectly counterpoint the silver-based golden lustres. From Italy developed, as potters travelled across Europe to where they saw opportunities, national traditions of tin glaze: 'faience' in France and Germany, 'Haban' ware in central Europe, Delft in the Netherlands, 'delftware' in England. The application of lustre became rarer and the use of tin glaze itself as a serious form of artistic expression was dealt a fatal blow in the late eighteenth century by the success of English industrial white wares, especially those made by Josiah Wedgwood. Subsequent historicist revivals of tin glaze and of lustre applied to it, especially in Italy and in the designs of William De Morgan in England, tended to be sporadic.

In 1955, when Alan Caiger-Smith bought the old smithy in Aldermaston and opened the Aldermaston Pottery in it, an entirely new chapter in the long history of tin glaze opened. In reaction to the then predominant Leachian aesthetic of 'brown pots' among British studio potters, Alan was determined to rediscover and recreate – through tireless and meticulous experimentation – the technological virtuosity of Islamic and Italian potters in painting on tin glaze, and in due course also the incomparable iridescence of reduced-pigment lustre; but in his hands painting on the raw glaze, however much influenced by the brilliance of Islamic brushwork, has always been an original medium of artistic creativity that could only be expressed ceramically.

Jane White in this book describes eloquently the special atmosphere that the community of potters, under Alan's leadership, maintained for half a century. She also brings to the fore the strong ethical aspects and indeed spiritual underpinning of the venture: in particular, Alan set his face against division of labour, so that each potter would not only have job satisfaction and a sense of ownership of the works he or she created but would also develop the range of skills needed to go out in the world and follow an individual path of artistic expression. Many, indeed most, did so and their stories are told here, often in their own words, with the consistent theme of how much their subsequent lives owed to Alan's inspiration, generosity and guidance. The geographical range covered in the narrative reminds us that this is an artist whose achievement has sometimes been better appreciated abroad – especially in Italy, the homeland of Maestro Giorgio – than in the UK.

This book had its origins in a dissertation written by Jane White – herself a talented and successful potter – for the Buckinghamshire New University in 2008. Since then she has worked intensively to assemble an extensive and precious archive relating to the potters who worked at Aldermaston, which is the

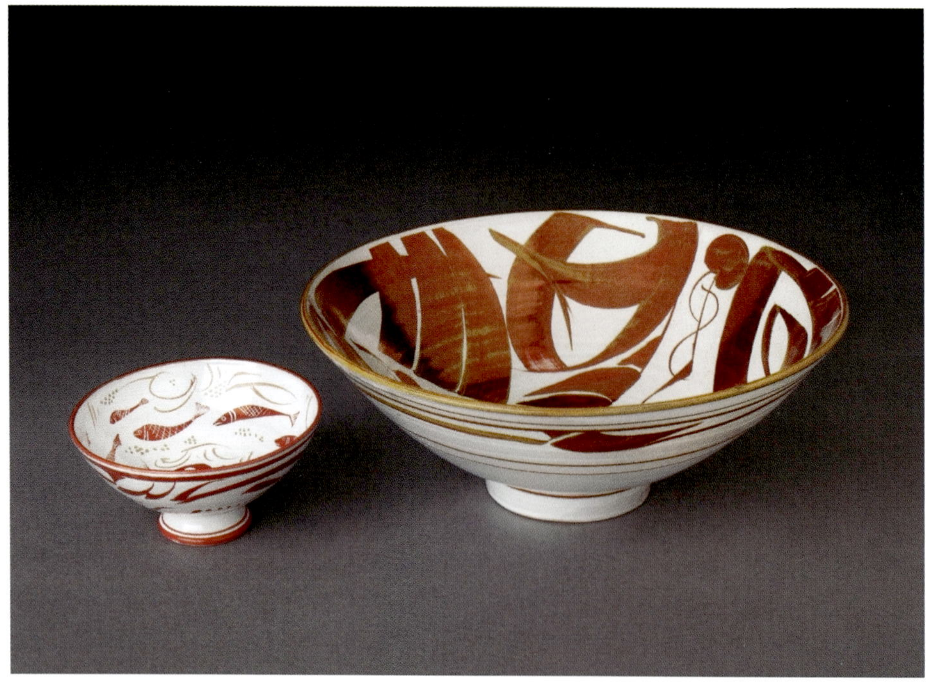

Lustred bowls by Alan Caiger-Smith from the Ashmolean Museum collection
The smaller (WA 2004.93) was made during the production (1999) of the film *Making Lustre Pottery*
with Alan Caiger-Smith, carried out in association with James Allan; the larger (WA 2005.167) is a
triumphant product of one of the last lustre firings at Aldermaston in 2005.

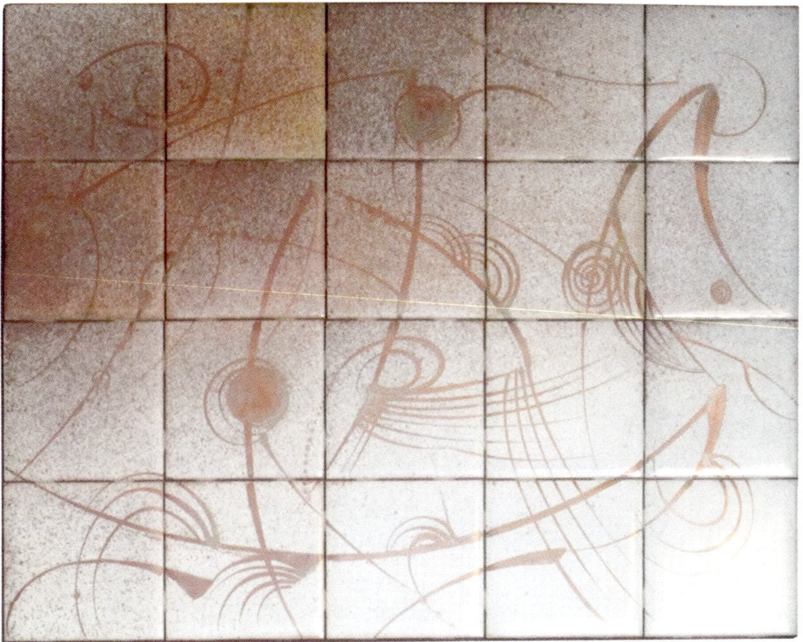

Tile panel painted in lustre by Alan Caiger-Smith, inspired by F. Capra, *The Tao of Physics*
Collection Timothy and Jane Wilson

underlying documentation for the book. It also has the inestimable benefit of input from Julian Bellmont, a sometime member of the pottery team at Aldermaston, in assembling and in great part taking the photographs.

I am personally delighted that the Ashmolean Museum is publishing this book. Both James Allan (former Keeper of Eastern Art) and I (as a curator at the British Museum, then as the Ashmolean's Keeper of Western Art) have had the privilege of Alan's friendship and counsel on matters ceramic over many decades; and the Museum has acquired fine examples of Alan's work, as well as pieces by potters who feature in the pages that follow.

The book is a sparkling and intimate record of a wonderful episode in ceramic history, the products of which will, I believe, be admired and cherished for centuries to come.

Timothy Wilson
Honorary Curator, Department of Western Art
Ashmolean Museum, Oxford

Acknowledgements

MY FIRST THANKS must go to Alan Caiger-Smith. He has been endlessly helpful and encouraging, as well as writing many interesting and invaluable pieces for inclusion in the book. To have his affirmation of everything I have written is a wonderful endorsement, thank you so much Alan.

Next I would like to thank Timothy Wilson, without whom this book would not have been written. He conceived the idea for the project, and used his supreme powers of persuasion to coax me into undertaking it. He was also there for me throughout the years of research and writing, with his expert advice, help and support. I also thank his wife Jane for reading the script many times, and always coming forward with helpful advice and observations.

I am indebted to all the potters and contributors to the story, who have sent me such wonderful descriptive pieces of writing during my years of research, as well as the images of their work. Again, without all their help there would not have been a book, thank you. Amongst these of course is Julian Bellmont, a potter himself at Aldermaston for 13 years, thank you Julian for searching out Alan's ceramics amongst collectors, and in Alan's own collection, and for photographing such a comprehensive selection of Alan's ceramics across the decades; they are a magnificent pictorial record of the work of one of our greatest potters.

The Ashmolean Museum and I would like to extend our very grateful thanks to the Ceramica-Stiftung, Basel, for their generous support of the project. We hope it will fill a gap in the story of the twentieth-century studio pottery movement, and impart to the reader, in some small measure, what it must have been like to have been a part of this interesting and dynamic time in the history of ceramics.

I am extremely grateful to my editor, Johanna Stephenson, for her sensitive understanding of the text, her professionalism, and for being a delight to work with. I would also like to thank the book designer Stephen Hebron for his invaluable input in the design of the book, working alongside Johanna. Also many thanks to the Head of Publishing at the Ashmolean, Declan McCarthy, for overseeing the project and seeing it into print.

I would like to personally acknowledge Dr Helena Chance, for her excellent tuition and inspiring lectures and tutorials while I was at university. A good teacher can change your life, as all the potters at Aldermaston found out.

Finally I would like to thank the collectors of my own work, who have been patiently waiting for me to return to making my ceramics, and all my friends and family, for their patience and understanding of my preoccupation with this book over the past three years. You can now have my full attention.

Jane White, October 2018

Introduction

So much artistic work that we appreciate today, both contemporary and historical, owes its inception to the methods and knowledge handed down by those who went before us – a kind of 'living tradition'. Alan Caiger-Smith has said that traditions are not necessarily conservative – 'they can provide grounds for innovations which in turn shape the knowledge handed down by succeeding generations'.[1] An acknowledged world authority on the history of tin-glaze and lustre pottery, he describes traditions as being like rivers: the source is often unknown, or there may be several sources; tributaries feed it, people live by it, some use it, some ignore it, and finally the river widens and merges with the sea.[2]

The maiolica heritage is probably the strongest and most enduring of all the European pottery traditions, passed on continuously and stretching back over a thousand years. For 51 years Alan Caiger-Smith and the Aldermaston Pottery contributed to and became part of that long history. He established a collaborative workshop at Aldermaston in 1955, where he shared his skills and knowledge, and over the following 38 years Aldermaston Pottery employed and trained almost 60 people. Many of these journeymen potters went on to exert their own influence across the globe, both academically and through their ceramic work. Although the Pottery stopped employing people in 1993, it continued its commercial operation for another 13 years; during this period Caiger-Smith focused on his own personal work, while sharing the workshop with several potters who stayed on to work independently.

Alan Caiger-Smith ranks among the most significant ceramicists working in the last half of the twentieth century, and is the most important living artist specialising in lustre pottery. He revived two virtually lost techniques, the use of tin-glaze and painted pigments on earthenware clay (maiolica), and the demanding and difficult technique of reduced-pigment lustre. As a writer and scholar he also made a considerable contribution to the understanding and application of the lustre technique in his book *Lustre Pottery* (1985), and to the history and knowledge of tin-glaze pottery in *Tin-Glaze Pottery in Europe and the Islamic World* (1973). In 1980 he co-translated, edited and annotated *I tre libri dell'arte del vasajo* (*The Three Books of the Potter's Art*) by Cipriano Piccolpasso, a detailed sixteenth-century description of the materials and methods used in Italian pottery making during the Renaissance. In doing so he also discovered many of the secrets of the reduced-pigment lustre technique. His work is represented in museums throughout the UK and Europe, the USA and Australia, and he was Chairman of the British Crafts Centre from 1974 to 1978. He was awarded an MBE in 1988 for services to ceramics.

Caiger-Smith has been described as 'a potter conscious of his heritage',[3] and certainly over the 51 years of the Aldermaston Pottery this was his guiding philosophy. His contribution to twentieth-century ceramics has been significant, and he has passed on his knowledge and skills to generations of young people. When commenting on the closure of the collaborative workshop in 1993 he said, 'we have all learned a great deal from each other, and my own work has been changed by almost everyone I have ever worked with'.[4] When the Pottery finally closed its doors for the last time in 2006, he wrote:

> the Pottery has seen fifty years of intense activity, some of them very good years indeed, during which many exceptional people have contributed to its work; time and change are a part of life, and the legacy of Aldermaston will live on in the pots still being used in people's homes.[5]

This book is the story of Aldermaston Pottery told mostly through the words of those who worked there. It was not possible to contact them all: some have passed away and others have disappeared into the vortex of life and left no trace. But more than thirty of the potters have contributed to this story, as of course has Alan Caiger-Smith himself, although in his modest way he was most insistent that the story predominantly belonged to the potters. They enabled an enterprise that would not be possible today: it happened when a different set of social and economic circumstances prevailed, and its legacy was without precedent. In writing down their memoirs and recording their experiences the potters have created a unique archive; a complete, unedited library of this material will be held at the Berkshire Record Office in Reading, which already retains all the historical records relating to the Aldermaston Pottery. Through its 51 years of continuous production Aldermaston Pottery has given us not only a wealth of beautiful domestic tin-glaze pottery, but also the most stunning lustreware to be produced in the last hundred years. Most importantly, it has given us a legacy that continues through the work of all the potters who contributed to its working life, and whose experience at the Pottery changed their lives forever. This legacy is now in their hands, and they are now the standard bearers of all the knowledge that Alan Caiger-Smith so generously shared with them.

Through his life and work Caiger-Smith has helped to sustain the long history of the maiolica and lustre tradition, he has fed and nourished it, used it, shared it, lived by it and let it flow on, and it is now for future generations, further downstream, to keep the water flowing.

— I —

Alan Caiger-Smith
Early Life 1930–1955

ALAN CAIGER-SMITH was born on 8 February 1930 in Buenos Aires, Argentina. His father, Christopher, an industrial chemist working for Imperial Chemical Industries (ICI), had been posted there to work in the nitrate pampas of the Chilean Desert, setting up processing plants to extract iodine from guano deposits. Christopher Caiger-Smith had married Helen Massey in March 1929, and a couple of months later the newly married couple set sail for South America, where Alan was born the following year. In 1933 the family returned to England and Alan's brother Mark was born. However their happy married life was not to last for long: in 1935 Christopher was tragically killed in a climbing accident while the family was on holiday in Cornwall. His death changed everything; Helen would never remarry, and remained devoted to her husband's memory until she died at the age of 81.[1]

Helen Massey came from a family of engineers and inventors. Her father, Harold Massey, had an engineering works in Manchester, B. & S. Massey. He was a cousin of Bernard Leach, and he designed the big oil-burning kiln at the Leach Pottery in St Ives, which was converted from a three-chambered wood kiln and installed by David Leach, Bernard's son, when he was making improvements in the late 1930s; the kiln went on to be used for over fifty years. Bernard Leach was very supportive of the family after Christopher's death, and would often come and stay. Alan remembers that there were many early Leach pots in the house when he was growing up, as his grandfather had tried to support Leach at the beginning of his career, but that his mother was not particularly fond of them.[2] In his early twenties Alan frequently visited St Ives and his cousin David became a great friend. He describes him as 'a giver', endlessly helpful, suggesting galleries and offering advice. It was David Leach who suggested that he use Fremington clay, and it was this that gave the pottery produced at Aldermaston its unique and distinctive warmth under the opaque white tin glaze.[3]

Helen had initially trained in mathematics, but at the start of the war she decided to move with her young sons from Kent to Brighton, where she rented a small house and re-trained in orthoptics. In 1941 she set up a small private practice in Newbury, and then a second one at the Royal Berkshire Hospital in Reading. So it was that the family came to live in Aldermaston, halfway between the two towns.[4] At that time the village had one main street, with as many wandering cows as cars, a pub, a smithy and a post office. There was no mains water supply until 1948, or mains electricity until 1949. One distinctive feature of the village was its solid vernacular architecture: mostly early eighteenth-century houses of warm red brick and tiles that had been made locally since medieval times, an indication of the abundant clay seams that lay just beneath the surface of the landscape. Recalling a visit from a group of American potters, Alan Caiger-Smith heard them exclaiming: 'you'd just have to work in earthenware here: the whole place is earthenware from the ground up, walls, roofs and chimneys.'[5]

In 1943 Caiger-Smith was awarded a scholarship to Stowe School, where he regarded it as a great privilege to be able to wander through Capability Brown's inspiring and influential 'landscape garden'. The temples and follies were crumbling and neglected but they invited the joy of discovery for a boy with an interest in art and architecture. The art department was run at that time by inspirational French-Canadian art teachers Robin and Dodie Watt. Stowe was one of the first schools to champion the international avant-garde, encouraging pupils to take an interest in Cubism and Surrealism, and such controversial contemporary artists as Picasso, Léger and Braque. The headmaster, J.F. Roxburgh, was devoted to the arts and vowed that no Stoic would leave the school without acquiring a lasting appreciation of beauty.[6] As well as receiving an inspiring education at Stowe, Caiger-Smith made many friends there.

In 1947 he spent a year at Camberwell School of Art studying painting and drawing. Having arrived with high hopes, he found Camberwell rather disappointing and the experience put him off painting for some time. Consequently he spent his spare time studying and preparing for the entrance exams for King's College, Cambridge, and was awarded a scholarship. To celebrate he went off to Italy, the first of countless visits he has made throughout his life; thus began a lifelong love affair with the country. Between Camberwell and Cambridge he returned to Aldermaston to work on a farm on the outskirts of the village; he describes this time as 'a wonderful experience of hard physical work shared with unforgettable local characters ... it introduced me to the pattern of rural life just before everything began to be changed by mechanised farming'. He frequently recalled this experience as seminal to the philosophy behind the working practice that he was to develop in his own workshop.[7]

As he suffered from asthma, Caiger-Smith was not conscripted and in 1949 arrived at King's College, where he studied History, changing to English in his third year. He became President of the Cambridge Society of Arts and continued to paint in his spare time, selling his work to E.M. Forster, among others.[8] It was also at Cambridge that he discovered the magnetic appeal of clay. He found a land-drain factory on the Newmarket Road where he could acquire flesh-pink clay, and was soon modelling nude figures as a diversion from his academic studies. These were discreetly fired among the drainpipes at the factory, and there developed quite a vogue for them among his friends at Cambridge. The figurines were about eight or nine inches high and included subjects such as Cleopatra, Caligula coming out of the bath, clothed figures of poets, Irish labourers, and various animals.[9] A chance meeting at a party with fellow undergraduate Julian Rea led to Caiger-Smith's first introduction to the potter's wheel. Rea, who had been taught to throw as a pupil at Bryanston, was teaching adult education classes at the nearby village college in Sawston. In spite of beginner's luck at his first attempt at throwing, and his eventual acquisition of his own wheel, over the following couple of years Caiger-Smith found the process frustrating and disappointing.[10] He also practised at the home of the influential Bohemian photographer Lettice Ramsey, friend of the Bloomsbury set; she, too, was an amateur potter, and although they would encourage each other, he soon realised that expert tuition was needed.[11]

After his graduation in 1952 he began assisting Adrian Lees, a potter working in Newbury, and it was here that he first began to learn about kiln firing and technology. That summer he went on a sailing expedition to Spain, Portugal and Tangier with three friends from Cambridge. He was captivated by the beautiful tin-glaze pottery being made and painted by potters in Triana, Seville, and by 'the variety and the richness of the pottery itself, and the ideas and assumptions of the men who made it'.[12] Walking past the street potteries in Triana, with their tin-glaze wares on display, it occurred to him that this would be the perfect way of combining his talents as a painter with his keen interest in pottery.

In 1953 Caiger-Smith was living in London, having been awarded a bursary to carry out a postgraduate study of English medieval wall painting, which eventually culminated in the publication of a book ten years later.[13] He spent much of his time working in the British Museum's manuscript room. The Central School of Arts and Crafts (as it was called then) was only a few minutes' walk away and, still enthralled with the idea of working with clay – a craft and skill that was slowly beginning to absorb him – he enquired whether there were any spaces left on the highly sought-after evening classes there; unfortunately they were already full up. Dora Billington was head of the Ceramics Department, so he decided to go and see whether she could somehow squeeze him in. After a short discussion she said she would do her best, and lived up to her word. The British Museum closed at 5 p.m. and the evening classes started at 6.30, so there was just time for a meal in between.[14]

Dora Billington had been teaching at the Central since just after the First World War. She shared the pottery teaching with Gilbert Harding Green, Richard Bateson – formerly a thrower in Stoke – and Kenneth Clark, who had recently set up a studio nearby. They all taught in different and complementary ways, and Caiger-Smith acknowledges that this offered him a wonderful opportunity:

> Sometimes Dora herself added brilliant introductory talks about the chemistry of glazes and pigments. Very few students attended them, but to me they were a godsend. It was she who told me about tin glaze and encouraged me to follow it up, at a time when hardly anyone else would have done so. She was a wonderful guide and critic and drew on a lifetime's experience of making and designing, and I shall be forever grateful to her.[15]

Caiger-Smith says he remains lastingly indebted to all his teachers at the Central – and indeed Clark remained a lifelong friend – and that he seldom used the wheel without some gem of wisdom that he had been taught by Bateson coming to mind. However, it was Dora Billington who was his true inspiration.[16] It was she who explained to him that what he had seen on his travels in Spain was painted tin-glaze pottery (maiolica), a technique that required considerable skill with the brush, and which was also at odds with the aesthetic of the time. But rather than dismiss his initial youthful enthusiasm, she actively encouraged him. So began a journey that he might never have embarked on if he had known all the difficulties that lay ahead, and undoubtedly without Billington's encouragement the story of Aldermaston Pottery might never have begun.

Dora Billington was irritated by studio potters' slavish adherence to the Leach tradition, to the exclusion of everything else, especially in the exciting atmosphere of opportunity and optimism that was developing in the art world in post-war Britain. She felt that although Leach had made an outstanding contribution to good design and excellence of brushwork, his standard style was too narrow, and that the work of his imitators was pretentious and dull.[17] Her assistant Robert Fournier, who worked with her at the Central from the late 1940s until her retirement in 1955, recalls that

> She admired Leach as a potter, but what she was against was everybody imitating the Far East. She thought that this had gone too far, and that there was a whole world of other pots which people were ignoring, and so she it made more or less her life's work to show people that there are things other than Song pots.[18]

After five years of war and post-war utility restrictions, the Government strongly encouraged the export of decorative ceramics for overseas sales; however restrictions on the sale of decorated ware to the home market were not lifted until 1952. After the years of austerity there was a pent-up demand for pottery, fabrics and wallpapers in bolder and more colourful styles. The Poole Pottery began to take advantage of this with its bright modern designs, the first of which were exhibited at the Festival of Britain on the South Bank in London in 1951. This was the first opportunity in more than a decade for the Poole Pottery to exhibit its work, although post-war restrictions meant that much of it could not yet be sold. One of the first studio potters to break the trend was Walter Cole, one of the founding members of the Craftsmen Potters Association. As soon as the restrictions were lifted, Cole, along with a small team at Rye Pottery, moved from slip-decorated wares to produce seventeenth-century-inspired Delftwares, painting fresh coloured floral and striped decoration on to unfired tin glaze. This highly successful pottery continued producing decorated maiolica until 1978, when it was handed over to the next generation; it is still in existence today.[19]

It was to Caiger-Smith's lasting advantage that Billington not only encouraged him to pursue the maiolica technique, but that she also managed to stretch the term 'evening class', allowing him to start earlier and earlier, so that he was eventually arriving when the doors opened at 8.30 a.m.:

> I had only enough money to last a few months and needed to make the best possible use of the time. I soon noticed that if I got my clay ready early before the other students stopped for tea, I could start using the wheels in their absence. In due course this extended to my lunch break, and eventually I realised that since most of them turned up late, I could get to work before they arrived in the morning. Thus I became possibly the most full-time evening student ever! The Head of School reprimanded me, but Dora and Harding Green were on my side and turned a blind eye to the situation. In this way I was able to work from 8.30 in the morning until 9.30 in the evening, and I became more and more determined to set up my own workshop. [20]

He recalls that his enthusiasm for the tradition 'simply grew out of the initial impulse to make and paint ceramic forms; it grew out of the brushes, out of the fire, out of the mood of the place and the people', adding: 'I soon began to realise that it wasn't simply a private enthusiasm but a language of form and colour shared by my co-workers and by a large number of people of very different background, far and near.'[21] As very few potters were working in earthenware, let alone painted tin glaze, Caiger-Smith's early years were a pioneering journey. A degree of naivety and the optimism and determination of youth are wonderful attributes when setting out in life. With this enthusiasm he left the Central School, determined to realise his ambitions.

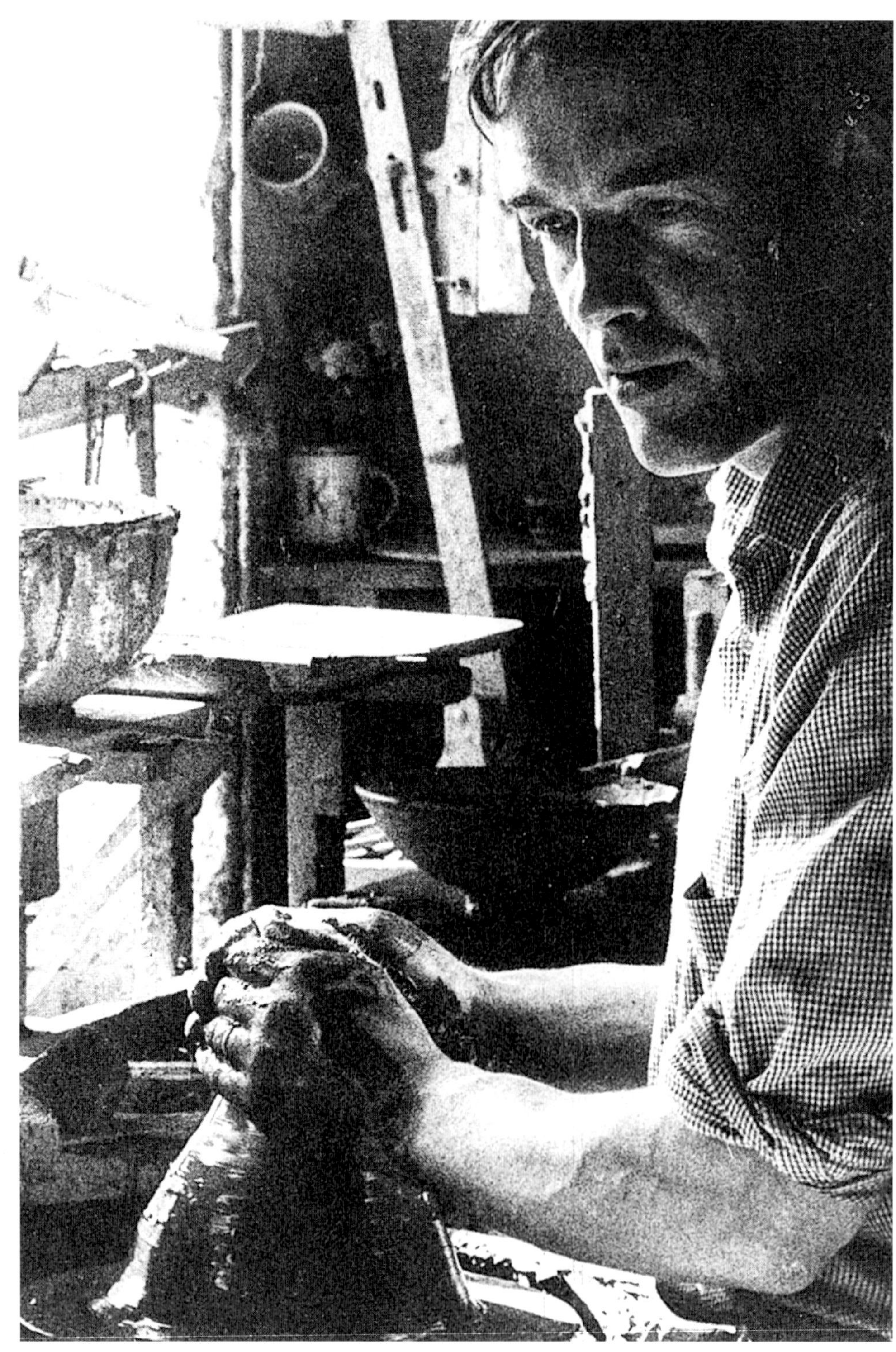

Alan Caiger-Smith throwing on the wheel
at Aldermaston Pottery, 1966

— **2** —

Early Days at Aldermaston and the Homer Street Connection
1955–1961

Inspired by his experience at the Central, when he left in the summer of 1955 Caiger-Smith knew he wanted, if possible, to make a living as a potter. Initially he wrote to all the potters he had ever heard of, offering his services as an assistant at a nominal rate of pay, but only Lucie Rie and Janet Leach replied at all, and neither of them was able to help. He began searching for possible workshop spaces in London but could find nothing even remotely affordable.[1] Around this time he became reacquainted with Anne Gordon (later Marchioness of Aberdeen); they had been students together at Camberwell. Anne was eager to learn to throw and paint lamp bases, for which she thought there would be an excellent market. However, after working for some time at the wheel she decided that she was not suited to this kind of work, so she changed to making clay figures of birds and animals, for which Caiger-Smith acknowledges she had an amazing skill. He taught her to glaze and paint them, and introduced her to the making of pigments; in the course of time her work became outstandingly good and she exhibited successfully in London and New York. They remained devoted friends until her death in 2007. Anne always insisted that Caiger-Smith had been her teacher, although in his view he had only helped her fulfil her natural talent.[2]

One day that summer of 1955, Caiger-Smith was visiting Aldermaston to see his mother, when he glanced across the road from her house and his eyes fell on the Old Smithy, where as a boy he used to watch old Bert Cox shoeing horses. It was now derelict and had been on the market for three and a half years, at the very low price of £500. Caiger-Smith thought to himself, 'What a shame no one can think of a use for it',[3] before suddenly realising that it was exactly what he was looking for. Looking back at the 51 years of work and endeavour that subsequently went on in that building, Caiger-Smith often felt that it had been lying empty just waiting for him to find it.[4]

The Old Smithy was the only building in Aldermaston that had been constructed as a place of manufacture. Once his mother had agreed to purchase it, the rest of that summer was spent restoring the building and making it ready for use:

> with the help of my friend James Sutton, a lettering mason, I cleared out a vast quantity of soot and rubble, repaired the upper floor, replaced windows and roof tiles, installed electricity, obtained the basic equipment, and then started work.

19

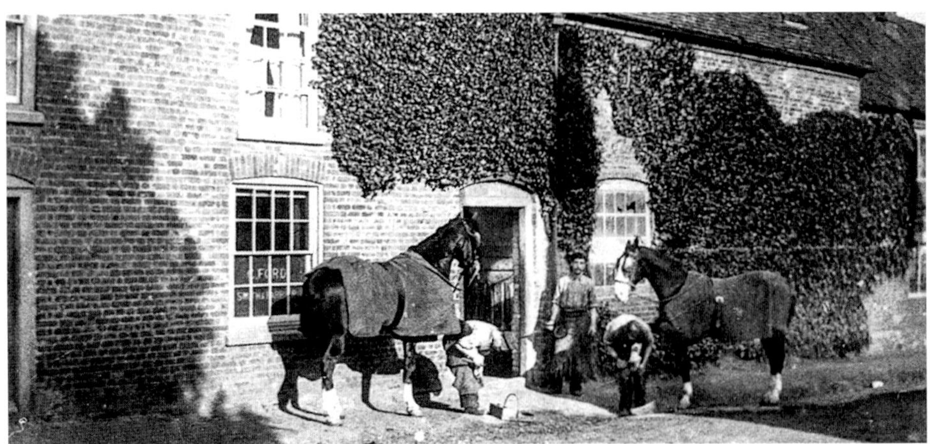

The Old Smithy, Aldermaston, 1919

> What I had learned at the Central was just enough, although I was still incred-
> ibly ignorant, and hadn't even appreciated the difference between stoneware and
> earthenware clay! Norman Bosson, from the newly established Cromartie Kilns
> in Longton, put in my first electric kiln, and helped me at intervals through all
> kinds of problems in those early years. I worked hard, but without the help of my
> mother, Dora Billington, James Sutton and Norman Bosson, nothing would ever
> have got going.[5]

The products made at the workshop between 1955 and 1956 encountered many
technical problems, and it was some time before suitable glazes, pigments, and
clays were found. The pots were very soft, and some were fired at 1060°C using
a stoneware clay that should actually have been fired 200°C higher. In Caiger-
Smith's own words, 'they had weak shapes, were poorly thrown, crudely painted,
and made with inadequate knowledge'.[6] By the spring of 1956 it became clear
that firing at or below 1100°C was essential for the kind of decorated work he was
trying to achieve. He also began to understand the language of brush decoration,
a skill that takes years of practice. He experimented with every type of brush that
he could find, handling them in various ways, including painting to music.[7]

That same year Caiger-Smith had his first exhibition of paintings and pots, at
the Parsons Gallery in London, as part of the Padworth and Aldermaston Group.
Here he met Henry Rothschild, who was to become an important supporter,
especially in the early years when Caiger-Smith was trying to establish a reputation for lustreware. It was also in the late summer of 1956 that the young Geoffrey
Eastop made his way to Aldermaston.

Eastop had seen active service for six years in the Royal Artillery, as an infantry
officer in the Low Countries, as well as serving in India and East Africa. On his
return in 1949 he began three years of training in painting at Goldsmiths School of
Art. It was during his time at Goldsmiths that an exhibition of the work of Paul
Cézanne convinced him that his future lay in becoming a painter; he describes the

exhibition as a revelation that opened his eyes, not just in an artistic sense but in his view of the world: 'suddenly seeing the world revealed as volume and space interlocking with each other suggested a powerful new direction, and set me on a course that has influenced me ever since.'[8] Eastop went on to work briefly in France and then returned to England. However, the isolation of painting alone brought about a state of mind that he soon began to find intolerable and, having studied pottery as his second subject at Goldsmiths, he sought a way he could combine working creatively and making a living alongside others. Having 'lost his way' as a painter, as he put it, in 1953 he joined the Odney Pottery in Cookham, which was run by the craftsman potter John Bew and owned by the John Lewis Partnership. This gave him the opportunity to learn to throw pots on the wheel and to experiment with painting with slips on the raw clay, which he describes as not dissimilar to painting with oil paints. When the Government lifted the restrictions on foreign imports in 1954, pots from Italy and Denmark flooded into the country, turning Odney Pottery's small profit into a trading loss and leading to its eventual closure two years later.[9] Also in 1954 Eastop married Pat Haynes, an art teacher; they went to live on a houseboat in Cookham, where they got know the artist Stanley Spencer.[10]

In an unpublished memoir Geoffrey Eastop describes the events that led him to seek out the pottery at Aldermaston two years later:

> In 1956 I went to an exhibition of painting in a gallery in Reading. There I got talking to the owner of the gallery and he told me of a young man who had just started a pottery in a barn at Aldermaston. I immediately saw this as an opening to be followed up, and one that led me to hope that I might perhaps be able to carry on as a potter after all.
>
> So I went to Aldermaston and was further encouraged when, walking down the village street, I came upon a small window displaying some impressive pots. I walked through the double stable door, into what had been the village smithy, to find a young man sitting in front of a white pot, which he was decorating with a brush. His name was Alan Caiger-Smith, and when he discovered my purpose he said that he did indeed need someone to help him in the pottery and, if I hadn't turned up just then, he supposed he would have had to advertise. He was quick to recognise that I had had more experience than he, and we came to an agreement that we would work as a kind of partnership. He would pay me seven pounds a week and I would continue with my part-time teaching.
>
> Although I was only working at Aldermaston on a part-time basis, I soon began to feel that there was an air of stability about the place. We agreed right at the beginning that there would be no division of labour, and that we would carry out the entire process of designing, making, glazing and decorating on an individual basis. The technique of maiolica involves painting with a brush on the raw, unfired glaze, and the limitations of this technique helped to create a kind of unity – the unity of style for which Aldermaston became so well known. I had the feeling that I would be working there for a long time, and so my wife Pat and I decided that we would have to find somewhere to live nearer to the pottery. Alan's mother, Helen,

lived alone with her housekeeper, Wynne Taylor [who had been nanny to Alan's brother, Mark]. Nanny was a regular churchgoer and well known in Aldermaston, and it was she who found us a charming little place to rent called Vicarage Cottage. Like most of the other buildings in Aldermaston, it dated from the same period in the seventeenth century, giving the whole village an architectural unity.

The route to Aldermaston from the Bath Road was reassuringly rural and largely unspoilt. From Padworth, just off the Bath Road, it runs over the canal bridge, through water meadows, past a magnificent mill on the River Kennet, and up into the main street of Aldermaston. Living in a genuine English village gave me a feeling of having achieved something I had always wanted. At the top end there is a grass triangle containing the war memorial and the magnificent wrought-iron gates forming the entrance to a Victorian-Gothic manor house; the road running out of the village winds, promisingly, up a hill shaded on either side by large trees. At the top of the hill, however, the land levels out into a wide-open area of stony scrubland. This is where the Atomic Weapons Research Establishment was built, known by the villagers simply as 'The Atomic'.

1956 was the year of Suez – the last fling of British imperialism. At the time it all seemed to us to be very confusing. We used to discuss it in the Pottery, wondering whether the Egyptians had any right to take over what we had always regarded as our Canal. The proximity of the Pottery to The Atomic meant that, quite suddenly and unexpectedly, we acquired a sort of fame. We received frequent visits from the representatives of the press, who liked to ask us what our feelings were about pursuing such a peaceful craft so near to an establishment conducting research into the development of the most modern and lethal weapons. By now, the campaign for nuclear disarmament had begun.

After quite a short while at Vicarage Cottage Helen Caiger-Smith offered us the use of a larger cottage, No. 29 The Street, about a hundred yards down from the Pottery itself. When the CND marches began, we offered the marchers a place to sleep on the floor of the cottage. Probably the most famous name among the protesters was Pat Arrowsmith [co-founder of the Campaign for Nuclear Disarmament – CND], and it would be quite justifiable for No. 29 The Street, to carry a blue plaque saying 'Pat Arrowsmith slept here', but I doubt whether the good people of Aldermaston would appreciate such an epitaph.

The technique of maiolica requires skill and directness with the brush. There is very little opportunity to make corrections. After quite a short time, and with the need to be able to produce repeats, Alan Caiger-Smith and I developed a method – using the shapes made naturally with the brush, either pointed or square-ended – of building up repeatable patterns which became characteristic of the Aldermaston style. Although it was necessary to be able to make repeats, much of the time I never managed to become very fluent in this. The process of repeating the same operation for quite a large number of pieces soon became rather irksome to me. There was always the desire to make one-off pieces, which was what I did whenever I saw the chance. These pieces were designed to take a broadly drawn motif in the form of an animal or a bird, treated in a formalised way vaguely reminiscent of some ancient form of decoration. My desire to become a painter was still as strong as it had ever been and this kind of work was, for me, the nearest I could get to making a painting.[11]

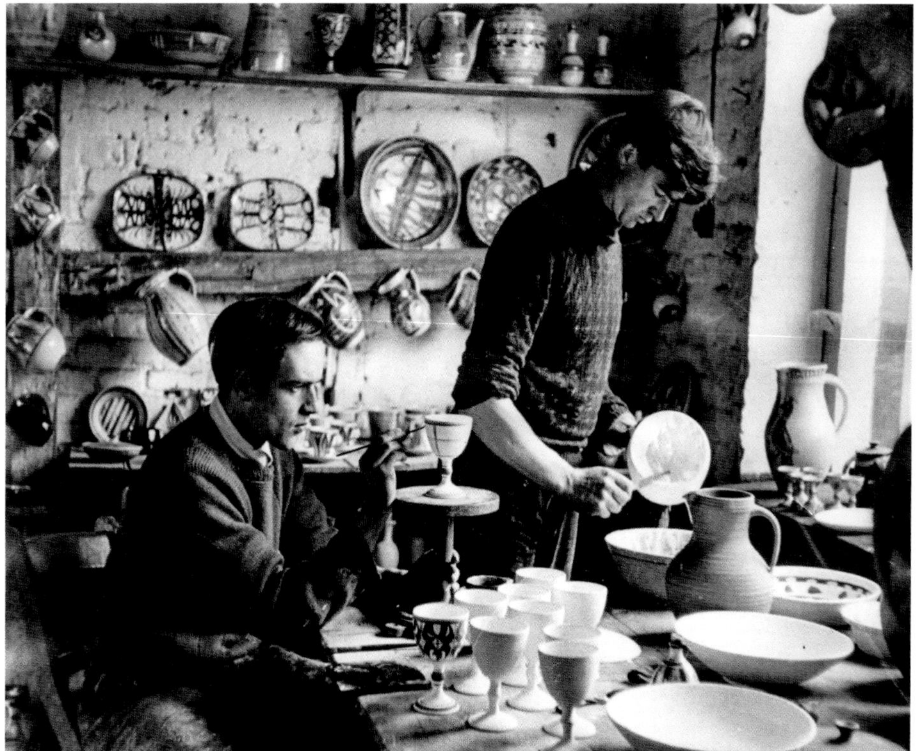

Alan Caiger-Smith (left) and Geoffrey Eastop at work in the Pottery, *c.*1961

The early years at Aldermaston were years of intense learning. When Eastop joined Caiger-Smith in 1956 they began a series of hundreds of trial tests of glazes and pigments. Decades later, Caiger-Smith described one of the resulting glazes, known as the 057 glaze, as 'one of the most versatile tin glazes anywhere in the world. It has an enormous colour range, is craze-proof, and has practically no faults at all. It is a very beautiful glaze'.[12] At the time Eastop joined him Caiger-Smith had only been working for a year, and was very inexperienced; he also had very little money. Describing his partnership with Eastop, Caiger-Smith said:

> we put together a basic repertoire of serviceable pottery and managed to sell enough to survive. His practical, methodical example was invaluable to me, and so was his company, from which developed a life-long friendship. Together we made innumerable tests of glazes and pigment recipes, and established a reliable firing schedule with the electric kiln, we began building the first wood-fired kiln, and shared a small exhibition at the Museum of Reading in 1961. It was a cordial collaboration, though we saw many things differently. Geoff's long-term interest lay not in pots that could be used, but in individual pieces as works of art. He worked slowly and thoughtfully and (to my mind) paid too little attention to the business side of the enterprise. Still, we worked enjoyably and purposefully together, and our co-operation and mutual respect enriched our whole lives.[13]

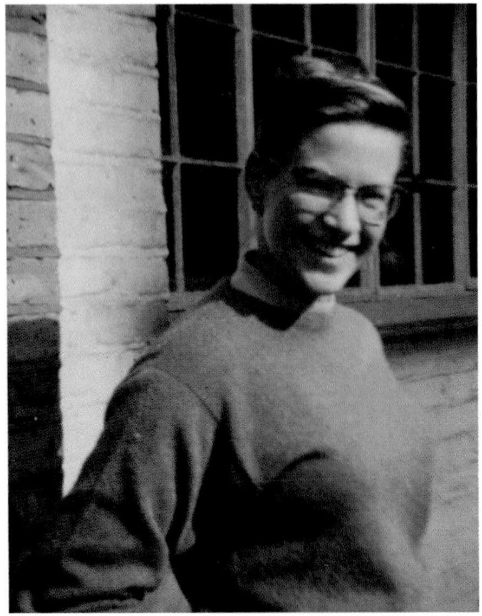

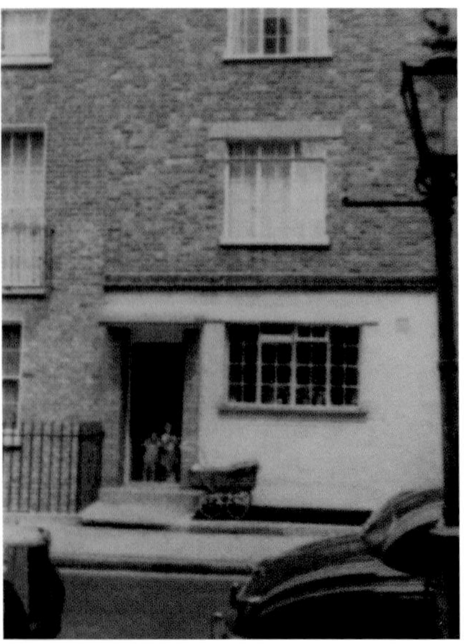

Anne-Marie Caiger-Smith
outside 32 Homer Street

32 Homer Street, Marylebone, 1960

Soon after setting up the Pottery, at Christmas 1956 Caiger-Smith married a young Swedish woman, Anne-Marie Hulteus, in Stockholm. Anne-Marie worked in London as a building engineer for the architect Sebastian Comper. Unlike her husband, she was earning a salary and the couple needed to base themselves near her work. With a small legacy from Caiger-Smith's grandmother they managed to buy a semi-derelict house, formally a plaster-caster's workshop, at 32 Homer Street, just off the Edgware Road in Marylebone. They made the small shed in the back yard, fondly known as 'the shack', into a minimal workshop space: it was so small that there was only room for one person to work in there at a time and there was also a tree growing up through the middle of it. Caiger-Smith would commute by train to Aldermaston to work at the Pottery on Tuesdays, Wednesdays and Thursdays, returning to work for the remaining two or three days in the workshop in London. Initially they lived on Anne-Marie's income, as he was earning less than £5 a week, but slowly things began to improve.

Caiger-Smith recalled their early years of marriage and life at Homer Street: 'we were wonderfully happy, and our first three sons were born there, Nicholas, Martin and Patrick. By this time, of course, Anne-Marie had stopped working, but I was earning just enough to carry on.'[14] Anne-Marie was a valuable support to her husband; her training as a designer demanding foresight and precision, both of which Caiger-Smith considered himself to be lacking. In later years she would redesign the interior of their home at Shalford, make the working drawings for the wood-fired kilns and design the new workshop, built in 1974. One of the potters who worked at Aldermaston in the late 1960s commented on their exceptional compatibility:

Alan and Anne-Marie were such a complementary couple. Anne-Marie had terrific confidence and practical abilities, and she seemed quietly aware of everything that was going on. Her steady and concentrated focus would often break, and her whole face would light up into a very warming and knowing smile, which could be very disarming.[15]

Another assistant at the Pottery in the 1970s described Anne-Marie as 'an inspiring woman, as practical as Alan was artistic'.[16] In an article published in 1961 Caiger-Smith wrote: 'My wife is my most stimulating and severe critic, she is an architect with a passion for exactitude'.[17] Many decades later one of the potters commented:

Anne-Marie was a huge part of allowing Alan to pursue all his interests. They had an incredible marriage and walked in tandem, something I admired greatly. It was extraordinary how balanced his home life, marriage, family, and time management all was, it was all in place, as well as a tremendous love and optimism in life.[18]

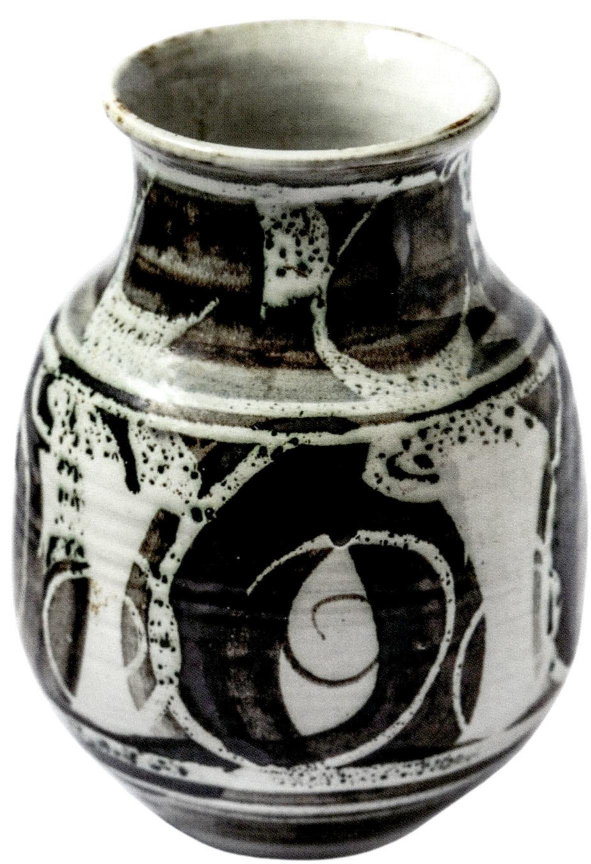

Vase with black decoration by Alan Caiger-Smith,
made at Homer Street, 1958, h. 21.3 cm, w. 15.35 cm
Collection Alan Caiger-Smith

25

By 1957 the Pottery was beginning to become known and was being discussed in magazines such as *Good Housekeeping*. Aldermaston pots were accepted for the Arts and Crafts Exhibition Society Show, *The Crafts 1957*, at the Victoria and Albert Museum; the exhibition went on to tour the USA from 1958 to 1960. But it was an exhibition at Heal's in 1958 that signalled one of the first turning points in the Pottery's fortunes.[19] All through October 1958 Aldermaston pottery was displayed in the Craftsman's Market in Heal's, and in a review of the exhibition in *Pottery Quarterly*, Murray Fieldhouse wrote: 'These pots have tone and sinew in their well thrown shapes … a great deal could happen at Aldermaston. For there is a feeling that it is a new pottery of conscientious progress, and one that will remain with us despite its difficulties.'[20]

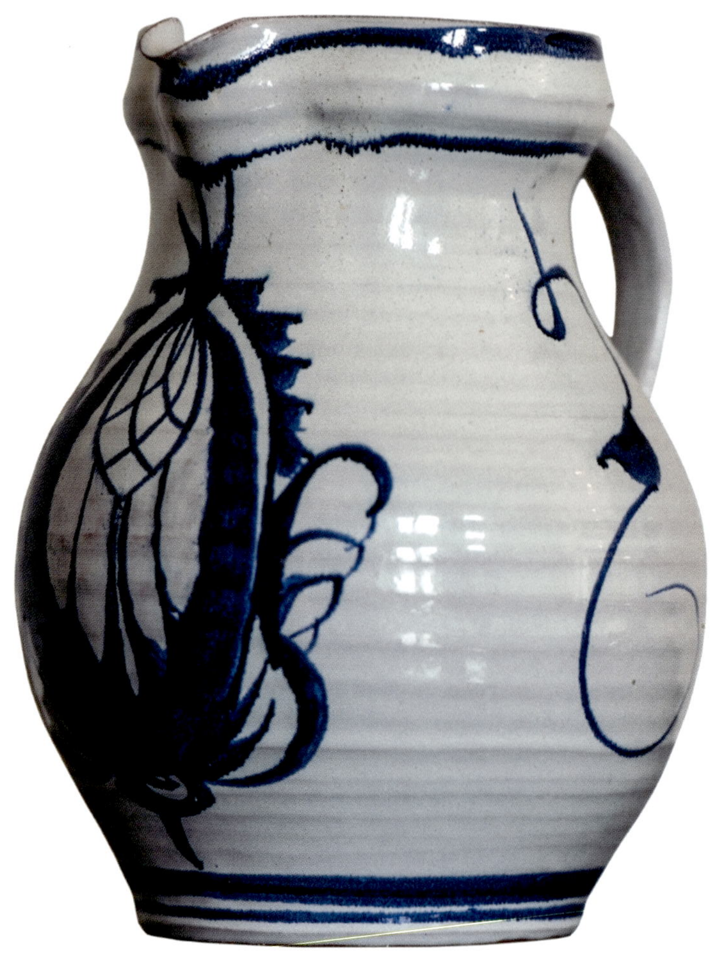

Quart jug by Alan Caiger-Smith, 1960, h. 20 cm
Collection Stephen Minchin

Towards the end of the 1950s it was becoming apparent that Eastop needed to move on and develop his own working style:

> by this time, working at the Aldermaston Pottery had begun to provide a way of life which, as far as I could see, might go on indefinitely. As well as working at Aldermaston I was teaching part-time at a technical college and earning altogether something like £14 or £15 a week, and this was what we lived on. Even in those days, this was a very low income on which to raise a family, but life then was simpler and less stressful. After five very interesting years with Alan at Aldermaston Pottery an opportunity arose to set up a small studio, and to help a neighbouring potter with her work, in the nearby village of Padworth. This also meant that I could change to stoneware, a medium of my own choosing. Stoneware has sculptural possibilities, which I felt could help me in my own quest towards painting, but on a three-dimensional surface. So I left Aldermaston to pursue my own ideas in reduced stoneware.[21]

In 1961, and now with a family of four small children, he obtained a lecturing post at the Berkshire College of Art and Design. In his Padworth studio he began pursuing his own ideas in reduced stoneware, producing work with classic celadon and tenmoko glazes, and building a kiln that was fired with drip-fed waste sump oil and water. Eastop says of this time, 'the elemental nature of this procedure completely took hold of me, hissing oil and steam, rumbling flame responding to the slight adjustments of air inside it all, the passive pots'.[22] His wife, Pat, commented that there were, however, limits to this kind of 'primitive vitality'. Eastop also began to respond more closely to the philosophical concepts of Bernard Leach and his followers. He worked on a kick wheel, but as a teacher he was also mindful of methods and materials, which were generating a new aesthetic among potters interested in design concepts. Consequently he soon chose to use a power wheel, electric kiln and oxidised firings, adopting a more Western style.[23]

In 1965 Eastop visited an exhibition at the Tate Gallery, *Painting and Sculpture of a Decade: '54–'64*, which covered the era from American Abstract Expressionism to Pop Art. He had always regretted leaving behind his ambitions to paint, and the exhibition aroused an excitement in him that he immediately wanted to translate into ceramics. So by the time of his chance encounter with John Piper in 1968 (at an exhibition of Piper's work at Reading Museum), he was already using clay slips in a painterly manner.[24] Piper had spent most of the previous decade working with stained-glass artist Patrick Reyntiens, most famously on the Baptistry window in the new Coventry Cathedral (completed in 1962), and was now ready for a new challenge. Consequently he invited Eastop to help him set up a small pottery workshop at Fawley Bottom, near Henley-on-Thames.

Piper offered Eastop the use of the pottery studio for his own work in return for technical assistance, and they soon developed a harmonious working relationship. Eastop felt that Piper saw himself as the English contemporary of Picasso and Miró, and to a lesser extent Matisse and Léger, and was exhilarated by the sense of

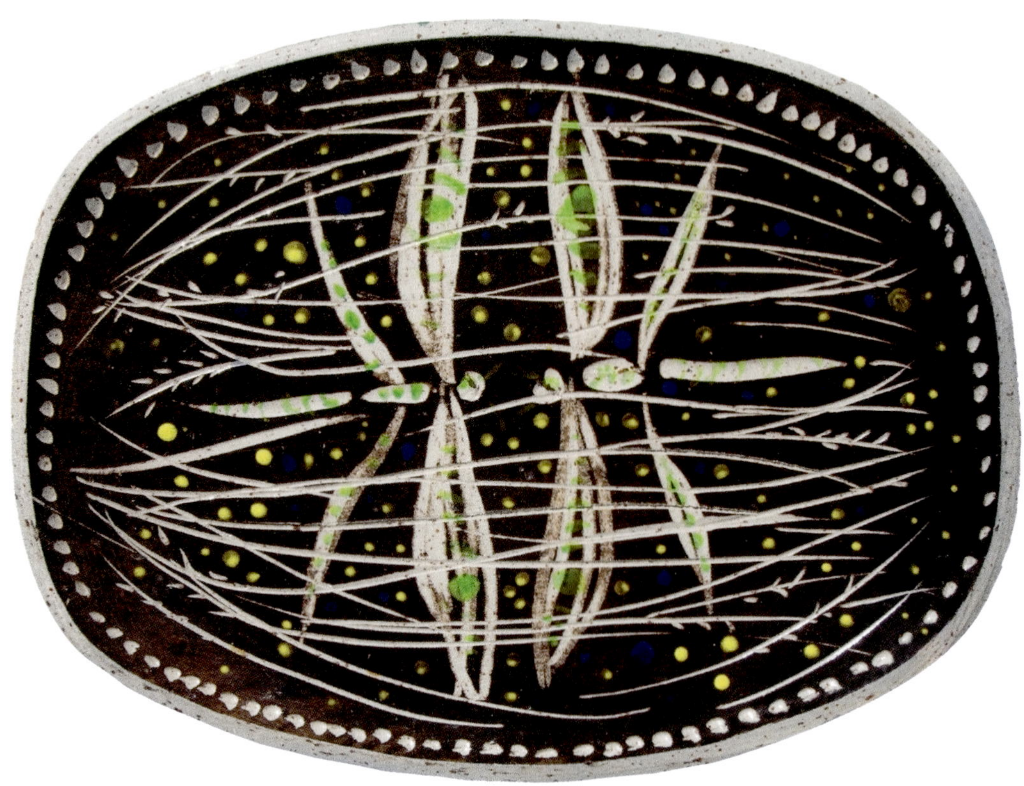

'Dragonfly' platter by John Piper assisted by
Geoffrey Eastop, 1974, 49.5 × 67 cm
Collection of Seb and Mary Piper

link with the great modern French revolutionaries.[25] He describes working with
Piper as a kind of liberation from the idea that making reduced stoneware was
somehow central to a potter's development. He wanted to free himself from the
mystique of the kiln atmosphere and of hoping that something magical might
happen in the kiln, and to adopt a technique that owed less to the uncertainties of
the kiln.[26]

Over the next 14 years they used colour boldly and on a large scale. Their
first ceramic work was shown at the Marlborough Gallery in March 1972 and
at the newly opened Bohun Gallery in Henley-on-Thames in 1973, and many
interesting commissions followed. Eastop made candlesticks for Nuffield College,
Oxford, based on an idea of Piper's, and worked with Bodfan Gruffyd on a
ceramic mural for the Maudsley Hospital in South London. He also translated a
Piper design based on the famous *Deposition of Christ* carving at the Externsteine,
near Detmold, Germany, into a ceramic wall panel for Robinson College Chapel,
Cambridge. This gained the attention of fellow painter and potter Quentin Bell,
who introduced Piper to the Fulham Pottery. A collaborative exhibition in 1982
with potters from Fulham Pottery, at Dan Klein's Gallery in Belgravia, turned

out to be a final flourish for Piper's association with ceramics.[27] Eastop's friendship with Piper continued until Piper's death in 1992; during the intervening years they would still work on the occasional ceramic project together.

In 1984 Eastop moved to the old post office in Ecchinswell, near Newbury, and converted the semi-derelict outbuildings into a studio. After retiring from teaching in 1987 he devoted his time to developing his own work, and in the mid-1990s he took the radical step of abandoning glazes and began hand-building using a technique of cutting small, ticket-shaped slices from a clay slab and pinching them together. Finally coming to terms with the fact he was more of a sculptor, the emphasis in his work became more sculptural and conceptual in character, and he began to explore natural rock forms and the human figure.[28]

Acknowledging the importance of his time with Caiger-Smith, he commented that all the periods of his working life had had a well-defined life span, and in retrospect seemed to have ended when they had served their natural time, 'however, from the point of view of development of my work, Aldermaston lasted longer'.[29]

In 1961 Anne Blakiston-Houston came to work for Caiger-Smith at 'the shack' in Homer Street. She had studied pottery at the Belfast Technical College, and then set up a small workshop in a stable loft, where she had been working for several years using a Bernard Leach kick wheel made for her by a local blacksmith, and wood-firing in a small kiln. She decided that she needed to learn more, so

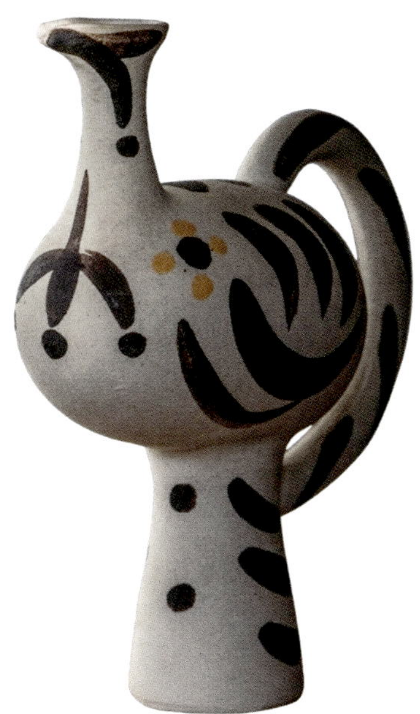

'Bird' jug by Geoffrey Eastop, 1992, h. 27 cm
Collection Jane Bellmont

she came to London to try and find a job working in a pottery.[30] She began her search for employment with a visit to the Chelsea Pottery, where she found 'awful amateur pots covered in bad decoration'.

> I then went to call on Lucie Rie, who was making delicate stoneware coffee cups. She told me she had once had a girl to help, and didn't want another one! My next call was on Alan, at Homer Street. I arrived saying, 'There is only one problem, I don't like decorated pots'. Alan's reply was, 'Well, I'm afraid you've come to the wrong place, but while you are here you had better come and have a look'. He took me to the shed, and had only opened the door a crack before I knew this was it. I think it was the 'owl' mugs lined up waiting to be dipped in tin-glaze and decorated, that caught my eye. They were all useful pots, bowls, jugs, jars, and dishes, in classical shapes, but Alan's decoration lifted them from the ordinary into something really lovely and often utterly beautiful. He used Japanese brushes with remarkable dexterity, and wax-resist, giving a much softer effect to the pattern.
>
> After my first three days working alone at Homer Street Alan came back from Aldermaston to London, where his Swedish wife Anne-Marie and their two small boys were living. I had been struggling with relearning the art of throwing again, and had very little to show for my efforts. Alan had suggested I started by throwing some simple small bowls; he held up a £1 note, my pay for three days work. I should have framed it but I couldn't afford to – my rent was £5 a week! After I had been working in the pottery for a time, Anne-Marie suggested I contribute a bit towards the cost and joined the two of them for lunch. I remember she suggested I contribute half a crown (two shillings and sixpence) and from then on we all had the most delicious Swedish-style meals. Around 4.30 every day she would open the back door and shout 'A…Anne, T…ea'. And there would be fresh bread and every spread you could think of on the kitchen table. I couldn't resist it! But the real bonus was getting to know Anne-Marie, who became a very special friend. One morning I turned up for work and was sent home. Anne-Marie had given birth to another little boy, Paddy, no. 3, had arrived; I am his very proud godmother. Alan was the kindest and nicest boss one could wish for, and I feel very, very lucky that he let me work for him. Working in the pottery was an extremely happy two years for me, in the first period of my life, I wasn't exactly changing the world, but it was, in a way, changing me. I was creating something with my hands, which I had always done, and still felt happy doing, and it was giving me time to think about life.[31]

In 1962 she married David Hallifax (later Admiral Sir David Hallifax, KCB, KCVO, KBE). He and Caiger-Smith shared a love of sailing and bought identical yachts; the two families would often go on sailing holidays together and remained life-long friends.

The pots that Anne made during the week, when Caiger-Smith was working at Aldermaston, were fired and ready for him to paint when he returned to London; she seldom worked alongside him.

Pottery made at Homer Street had a 'Made in England' mark, as well as a personal signature, and it was here that the first early experiments with reduced-lustre were carried out. Reduced-pigment lustre can only develop in a reduction atmosphere (i.e. without oxygen), and is usually obtained in a wood or gas kiln, when the kiln is starved of oxygen while the fuel is still burning. The fuel does not burn completely, and the atmosphere becomes filled with free carbon; the carbon atoms are so oxygen-hungry that they are able to break molecular bonds, reducing the oxygen in the clay and glaze molecules, and in doing so creating dramatic changes in colour and even texture. Electric kilns are unsuitable for this type of firing, however it is possible to obtain some limited reduction by pushing combustible material into the firing chamber through the spy hole during the firing, which then ignites and uses up the oxygen in the kiln. It is almost impossible to maintain reduction throughout the kiln for longer than a few minutes using this method, but an ingenious idea of making a kiln within a kiln by knocking out a section of a small saggar and placing it upside down opposite the spy hole did help to bring about some reduction in these early lustre firings. First experiments involved rolling mothballs down a slide into the saggar, and also inserting oily rags at the end of sticks, but neither were successful, with Caiger-Smith nearly losing his eyebrows in the process. Then he had a brainwave and inserted pieces of fudge on a long metal rod, these melted off the rod as soon as they started to burn, enabling more fudge to be immediately inserted, so keeping up the reduction for some time without the risk of being gassed. At last there was success: after rubbing off the clay and ochre carrier for the metallic pigments, three mugs revealed the first signs of lustre.[32] The magic of that first moment of discovery, glimpsing the velvety crimson-reds and brilliant amber-golds, meant that there was no turning back. The elusive lustre was certainly the crock of gold at the end of the rainbow, but the road to success was long; had he known the troubles that lay ahead, Caiger-Smith might never have started.

— 3 —

The Turning Point
1961–1963

Lustre is almost as old as glaze making, and of all the forms of decoration available to the potter it must certainly be the most elusive. Almost all the lustre made before 1800 belongs to the family of reduced-pigment lustre, and includes most Islamic, Spanish and Italian lustreware. After a glorious period during the fourteenth and fifteenth centuries, lustreware fell into decline, perhaps because it is such a difficult and unpredictable technique, or because of a change in taste or fashion. It was briefly revived in the nineteenth century, most famously by William De Morgan, Zsolnay and Théodore Deck, after which it virtually disappeared until Alan Caiger-Smith himself took up the thread. It was his pioneering work that eventually saw a renewal of interest in lustre.[1]

The techniques of tin glaze and lustre are thought to have originated in what is now Iraq around AD 800, where fragments of early tin-glazed pottery and lustreware have been found around the port of Basra, alongside white-bodied stonewares imported from China. It was these white wares from China that inspired the Muslim potters to develop a glaze that could in some way emulate this fine white pottery.[2] The lustre technique is thought to have transferred from glassmakers in pre-Islamic Egypt, who used copper and silver oxides to colour glass and to apply line decoration; having discovered that lustre could form on a receptive glaze, itinerant artisans then spread the technique across Persia and into Spain. The process has strong links with alchemy, and throughout its history the secrets of successful firing were confined to a small group of initiates and closely guarded for fear of commercial rivalry.

The Golden Age of Spanish ceramics began in the mid-thirteenth century in Malaga, in the Islamic kingdom of Andalucia, where the potters made a speciality of lustre and used imported cobalt to create tin-glazed pottery of exceptional quality and brilliance. Its luminous fusion of glaze and pigment raised the status of maiolica wares from an unpretentious craft to an art: good colours were rare and mysterious, and in contrast to the earthy utilitarian medieval pottery maiolica took ceramics into the realms of the exotic. Malagan lustre was greatly admired and exported throughout the Mediterranean, to Northern Europe and across the Islamic world. It was the Malagan potters who made the huge wing-handled vases in the Alhambra Palace in Granada, among the most brilliant achievements in world ceramics.[3]

In the fourteenth century, potteries in Paterna and Manises in the kingdom of Valencia on Spain's east coast started producing lustreware, probably initiated by predominantly Muslim potters who had travelled north. Together these two small towns formed the heart of the Hispano-Moresque pottery industry.[4] Between 1350 and 1370 Manises began producing pottery decorated in deep blue, with fine-quality intricate painting, and gold and silver lustreware of deep richness. Manises lustreware was regularly exported to affluent merchant families in Europe, and the sustained production of fine pieces during the years 1380 to 1480 is without parallel in the history of ceramics.[5]

It was these beautiful, luminous, iridescent pieces of Hispano-Moresque pottery produced during the Golden Age of Spanish ceramics that Caiger-Smith found so inspiring. He believed that the vitality of the Moorish brushwork had never been recaptured since, and that it had 'a magnanimity that is one of the highest achievements of ceramics in the Western world'.[6]

After his first early experiments with reduced lustre, using fudge in the electric kiln (see p. 31), Caiger-Smith was keen to build a small wood-fired test kiln; this could then be used for the multitude of tests that would need to be carried out in order to fully understand the lustre process. So in 1961 a miniature wood-fired kiln was constructed, with a 15-in square chamber, a firebox on one side and a chimney on the other. Lustre develops in a reduction atmosphere in a third firing at a lower temperature, after compounds containing copper and/or silver are painted on to the glazed surface; this small kiln could be heated to the required temperature of 600–700°C in about two hours. It took 26 tests before any reasonable silver or copper lustre was produced. Looking back, Caiger-Smith said it was difficult to comprehend the awe these first small pieces of lustre aroused, or the confidence they inspired.[7]

Fundamentally the problems seemed to be with the composition of the glaze rather than with the lustre pigments, and also, crucially, with the firing. A good lustre firing must have periods of reduction at the right temperature, of the right intensity, and maintained for the right length of time, which will in turn depend on the size of the kiln.[8] But the seeds had now been sown, and Caiger-Smith began to consider firing lustre on a larger scale. In any case a bigger kiln was needed for the regular firings, so the logical step was to build a large wood-fired kiln.

In the late 1950s he had started to employ assistants to work with him and Eastop at Aldermaston. The first of these was Maura Pender, who worked with them from 1957 to 1959. Caiger-Smith described her as a lovely person who died all too young.[9] The next assistant to arrive at Aldermaston in 1960 was Gwyn John, who went on to achieve international acclaim as a ceramicist and is better known by her married name, Gwyn Hanssen Pigott. Importantly, when she arrived at Aldermaston she had already had considerable experience of building wood-fired kilns. Having graduated with a degree in Fine Art from the University of Melbourne, Australia, she had spent two years as an apprentice with Ivan McMeekin at the Sturt Pottery in Mittagong, New South Wales, an experience that she later acknowledged was to inform her work for the rest of her life.[10] McMeekin had become captivated with Chinese Song Dynasty ware while working in the Merchant Service in the late 1940s, and his work as a potter always reflected that early influence – as, later, did Hanssen Pigott's. In 1949 McMeekin had travelled to England and served an apprenticeship for three and a half years with Michael Cardew at Wenford Bridge in Cornwall, eventually becoming a partner at the pottery while Cardew was away in Africa. He returned to Australia in 1953, and in response to his experience in England he set up the Sturt Pottery, modelled after the studio traditions of Leach and Cardew, with a small round downdraft wood-firing kiln similar to one designed by Cardew.

The Sturt Pottery had many parallels with the Aldermaston Pottery, having been set up at the same time and with a similar emphasis on small-scale production and the training of apprentice potters. Sturt still reflects its origins today, as a national centre of excellence for the teaching and promotion of Australian contemporary craft and design. During his career McMeekin was instrumental in introducing pottery to Aboriginals in Northern Territory, and in 1966 he and Cardew set up the Ceramic Research Institute at the Bagot Road Aboriginal Settlement in Darwin, and later the Tiwi Pottery on Bathurst Island under similar principles; he was also a founding member of the Potters' Society of Australia.[11]

Following in McMeekin's footsteps, in 1958 Hanssen Pigott took a long boat passage to England, carrying with her a blue celadon porcelain dish, a gift from McMeekin for Bernard Leach. She soon found herself by chance in Aldermaston, having walked 52 miles from London to the Atomic Weapons Research Establishment in Aldermaston while taking part in the very first of the Easter Aldermaston marches in protest against nuclear weapons.[12] As yet unaware that she would be working in the village some two years later, she set out to visit the major pottery workshops on her bicycle. She was first offered work at Winchcombe Pottery, where Michael Cardew had set up his first workshop in the old Gloucestershire pottery now run by his former pupil, Ray Finch. Hanssen Pigott describes the atmosphere at Winchcombe as relaxed, and she worked as part of an established team:

> I would make the clay bodies up in a dough mixer (a dusty process I never wanted to repeat) and mix up glazes in the great copper washing vessels, straining to lift them to the bench. The pot-boards were long and heavy – I could hardly carry them. But, luckily, the pots I was asked to throw were of modest size and I was happy to kick away at the wheel for most of my time there. Sometimes I would make the clay balls for Ray's throwing, hurrying to keep up with his easy, practised pace. I lived in the hut in the orchard where Michael and Mariel Cardew had first installed themselves. I raced the geese for the fallen morning apples. On weekends, I rattled off on Ray's moped to Stratford-upon-Avon and the Royal Shakespeare Company.[13]

Still cycling, with the celadon dish on the back of her bike, she arrived at the Leach Pottery in St Ives, Cornwall, where she found herself 'a member of a team made up of fellow pilgrims from far and wide … with Bill Marshall and Janet Leach organising them all, to keep the production flowing'.[14] Here she met her future husband, the Canadian poet Louis Hanssen. She left the pottery when Michael Cardew returned from Abuja in Northern Nigeria where, in his post as Pottery Officer in the Department of Commerce and Industry, he had built and developed a successful pottery training centre. On his return from Africa Cardew collected Hanssen Pigott from St Ives, and together they drove to Wenford. On the way,

> we stopped on the moor and, for our picnic, from a bundle of Nigerian cloth, he pulled out two porcelain plates from St Ives with Bernard's pigment drawings – a swallow in flight and a gannet swooping on a fish. It was the first of four months of remarkable meals together. After the austerity of student economies, the Wenford table was abundant … And with all that was Michael's conversation – and his wonderful erudition. At the time he was preparing his lectures for the famous 1959 summer school that were to be the basis for his book *Pioneer Pottery*. I could type, so transcribed the lectures from the handwritten original…
>
> There were biscuit pots from the last leave. We glazed them and prepared and packed the great, round, down-draft kiln for the summer school firing – a casually organized event that was the catalyst for friendships that were to last over the years. I first met Alan Caiger-Smith, Henry Hammond, Paul Barron, and Helen Pincombe here. A fine time, and my graduation, I guess. After that, it was all up to me.[15]

By late 1959 she and her husband were living in London. She became a library assistant, moonlighting as a thrower at Caiger-Smith's tiny workshop in Homer Street; Louis would sometimes join her, and taught himself to throw. The following year she started working all week at Aldermaston, with weekends back in London; the couple found a low-rent two-room basement flat in Notting Hill, where they had an electric kiln built on hire purchase.[16] Caiger-Smith lent them a kick wheel and some other equipment, and gave them lots of encouragement.[17] For a while Gwyn taught at The Isaac Newton Secondary Boys' Technical College in nearby Portobello Road, but once there seemed to be suitable clays and glazes and an order or two, she and Louis worked together full time in their cramped basement studio.[18]

Wood-firing fascinated Hanssen Pigott throughout her life. The Aldermaston Pottery had initially been set up with a Leach kick wheel and the small Cromartie electric kiln, but by 1960, when Hanssen Pigott arrived there, enough income had been generated to buy a bigger electric kiln, which then remained in use for over forty years.[19] It was at this time that Caiger-Smith also decided that it would make sense to build a full-size wood-fired kiln, which could be fired with the offcuts from the local cricket bat willows, since the local electricity supply was not sufficient for a second electric kiln. The woodyard at Old Village Farm in Aldermaston had been preparing and supplying clefts of wood to make cricket bats since the 1930s, and 70 trees were felled annually for this purpose. It made perfect sense to make use of their surplus material, particularly as willow was the wood best suited to the firing of tin glaze and lustre. Although pine and fir are usually the timbers of preference for wood-firing, and they are entirely suitable for stoneware and porcelain, earthenware glazes with any lead content are easily blistered by the reduction (shortage of oxygen) that is often caused by these resinous fuels. As long ago as 1557, when Cipriano Piccolpasso wrote *The Three Books of the Potter's Art*, the first major book on European pottery, it was recognised that clean, light woods such as willow and poplar are most suited to the firing of maiolica and reduced lustre. Although the thermal value of these is low, they release their heat quickly and burn with a very long, soft flame, making a kiln atmosphere that gives a pearly whiteness to the glazes and a luminous depth to most of the colours.[20] Even so, the glazes can still easily be spoiled, so in traditional kilns tin-glaze wares were often packed in saggars (clay fire boxes) to protect them from reduction and fly ash.

Caiger-Smith sought advice on the design of the wood kiln from Ray Finch. His recommendation was to use only second-hand materials, and to build the kiln so that any section could be demolished and rebuilt without taking down the whole structure. Finch told him that first kilns were seldom satisfactory, but the lessons learned from them could then be used in the building of the second kiln.[21] Caiger-Smith's first wood kiln had a four-year life, and although it turned out to be not particularly suitable for regular tin-glaze ware, it was to prove remarkably good for lustre. He knew only two lustre recipes and had not realised that the nature of the glaze was a major contributory factor. But once successful glazes were found and the lustre pigment recipes had been diversified, the results became more consistent. However, few retailers wanted this new product, and disappointingly, the lustre items were often returned.[22]

In 1961 Caiger-Smith's mother purchased the cottage next door to the Pottery as an investment: if the Pottery continued to flourish, it could used to accommodate assistants; if the business failed, it could be sold for a profit. The cottage was converted into two: Pottery Cottage, the smaller of the two, was adjacent to the Pottery; the larger cottage became known as No. 34. The garden provided the space they needed for the new 160-cubic foot wood-fired kiln and later purpose-built sheds, for the filter press and wood store.[23] In the spring of 1961 work was started on building the new wood kiln. Caiger-Smith recalls:

> It took at least four people to build the first kiln while continuing to pay our way. My wife Anne-Marie used her training as a structural engineer to convert my sketches into working drawings, and she supervised most of the construction. David Tipler and Edgar Campden joined the Pottery soon after work began – luckily they also knew a good deal about bricklaying and carpentry – and Gwyn

John spent the best part of 1960–61 working with me, contributing valuable experience gained in building and firing wood kilns with Ivan McMeekin and Michael Cardew.[24]

The kiln was completed and ready to use by the end of the summer.

By this time Gwyn and Louis Hanssen Pigott were producing tableware in oxidised stoneware and some porcelain from their basement studio, and supplying outlets including Liberty's, Heal's and Henry Rothschild's Primavera, London's premier craft and design shop.[25] Gwyn enrolled for evening classes at the Camberwell School of Art under the tuition of Lucie Rie; it was Rie's influence that injected a crisp modernity into her work.[26] During 1961 she also began a 12-year relationship with the Farnham School of Art, which only ended in 1973, when she headed back to Australia. On a visit to France in 1964 with fellow potters Warren MacKenzie and Glenn Lewis, friends from her days at the Leach

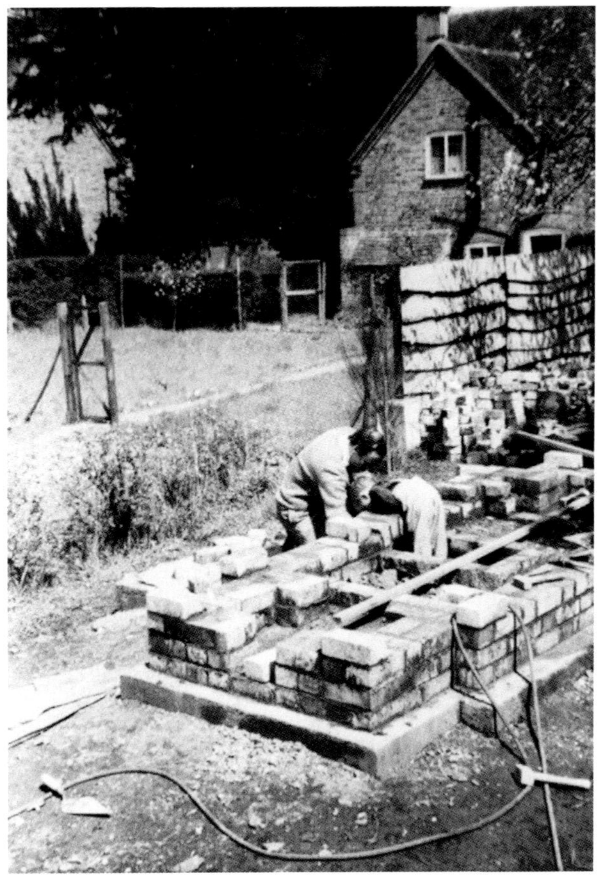

The construction of the new wood kiln in the garden of No. 34
inspected by Alan Caiger-Smith and his son Nick, 1961

Pottery, she fell in love with – and bought – a derelict 300-year-old house at Les Grandes Fougères in the Loire Valley. However she was about to leave London for Cornwall, at Cardew's invitation, to run the Wenford Bridge pottery for him while he was away in Africa, so it was 18 months before she was able to follow up her ideas for the Old Bakery in Achères. She had a lifelong friendship with Cardew, who in 1981 described her work as 'kindness in the material and loving care in the treatment of it'.[27]

She moved to France in 1966, after the end of her marriage, and remained there until 1973. The day she left England Hans Coper said to her, 'But you're too young to be a hermit!' and she remembers wondering just what she had taken on.[28] She was soon joined by students and friends, and together they spent a year restoring the house and building her first huge three-chambered wood-fired kiln, a clay storage shed, and a room to accommodate students from England, Norway and Denmark.[29] According to her autobiographical notes, written in 1991, she made some of her best work during her time in France: the clay was faultless and her work became freer, partly because of the size of the kiln. Her slip and glaze palette became paler, and for a while all she wanted to make were 'white bowls, the glaze cloudy with the salty ash'.[30]

Although Hanssen Pigott's early work reflected influences from her various apprenticeships, she will be remembered mainly for her wood-fired porcelain 'still-life arrangements', with their exciting exploration of 'negative space' and interplays of form and colour. The pivotal turning point came after she visited the Giorgio Morandi retrospective at the National Museum of Modern Art, Paris, in early 1971, where she fell in love with the work of the Italian painter and printmaker. This work, with its simple translucent glazes and soft colours, and characterised by its clarity and calm, resounds with all the meditative qualities of form so evident in the Song wares she had been exposed to at Sturt.

Arriving back in Australia in 1974, Hanssen Pigott set up a pottery in Tasmania with her assistant, John Pigott, whom she married two years later. Their partnership lasted for six years, and during her subsequent career in different parts of Australia she combined all her experiences in making the ceramics for which she was to become renowned. Australia had always regarded craft as secondary to the art of painting, but Hanssen Pigott, who exhibited all over the world, was instrumental in breaking down many of the barriers between art and craft. Caiger-Smith remembers her particularly for the 'subtle, exacting clarity of her throwing'.[31] Victor Margrie (who, with Mick Casson, co-founded the Harrow Studio Pottery course) described her as 'a potter of magical sensitivity'.[32] Her Sydney representative, Brett Stone, said that she never called herself an artist and hated the word ceramicist: 'She always regarded herself as a potter, and she liked to make ordinary things – cups, bowls, bottles, beakers – into sublime things.'[33] In 2002 she was awarded the medal of the Order of Australia, which was followed by a rare retrospective at the National Gallery of Victoria in Melbourne. At the time

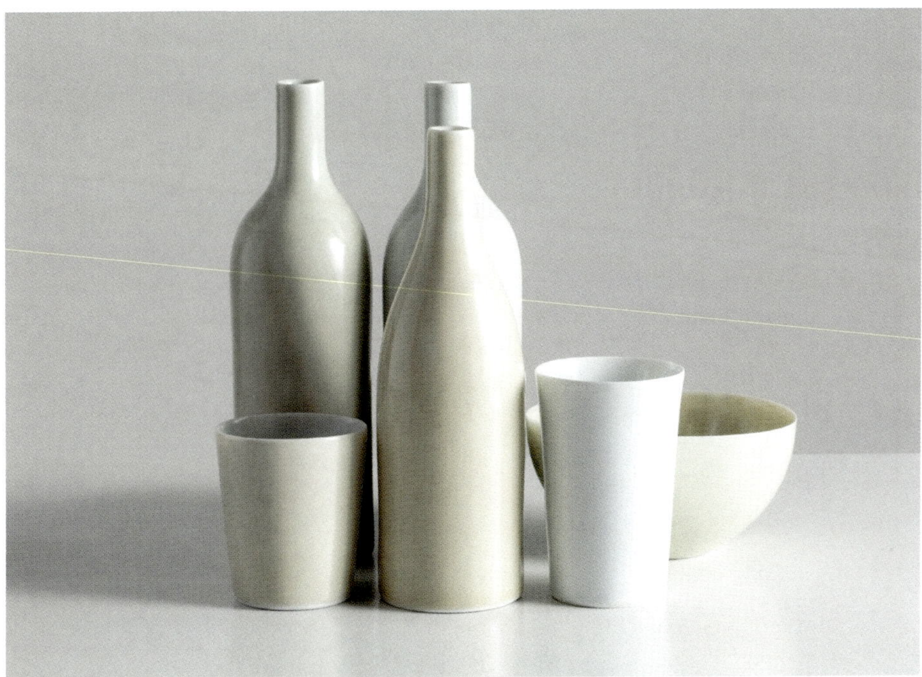

'Yellow Cluster' by Gwyn Hanssen Pigott,
various translucent porcelains, 2012, 27 × 33 × 26 cm
Private collection

of her death in 2013 she was universally regarded as 'one of the world's greatest contemporary potters'.[34]

By the early 1960s there was a steady demand for the decorated tin-glaze ware being produced at Aldermaston and people sought out the Pottery, eager to learn and explore the possibilities of the technique. Caiger-Smith believed that tin-glaze pottery was neither in nor out of fashion: it was just different from other pottery being made at that time and simply grew from the impulse to make and paint ceramic forms. He soon began to realise that far from being a private enthusiasm, it had a language of form and colour shared by his co-workers and by a large and diverse array of people.[35]

The pottery made at Aldermaston until 1961 used a dark red Etruria marl clay from Stoke-on-Trent, but with a firing temperature of 1100°C it was not really suitable for tin-glaze colours. In 1961, following David Leach's advice, the Pottery started using Fremington clay, which was supplied by Branham's Ltd of Barnstaple, where there had been a pottery and clay works since the seventeenth century. Fremington clay was a more fusible material, firing at about 1040°C, although it fired darker than Caiger-Smith would have wished and tended to bloat or warp if even slightly over-fired. The clay was stored in an underground pit, to prevent it from drying out or freezing. The potters at Aldermaston continued to

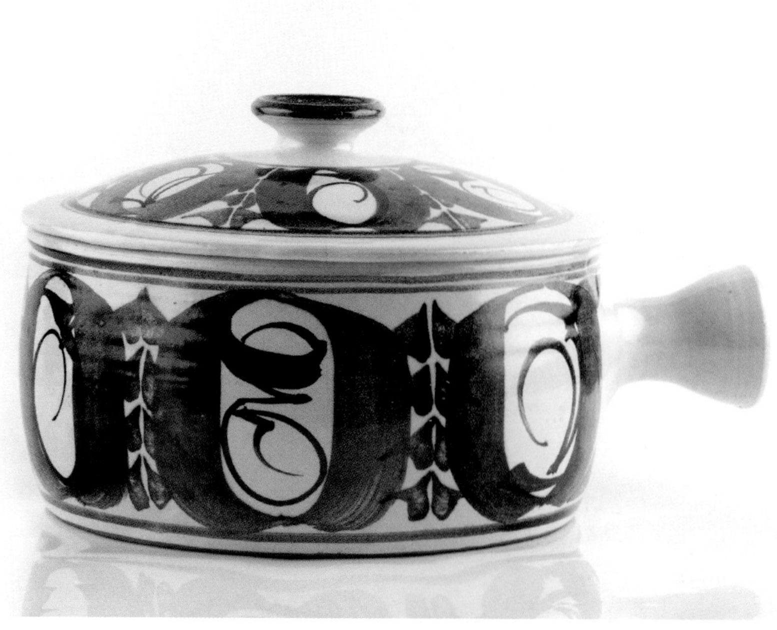

Casserole by David Tipler, date unknown, diam. 21 cm
Private collection

use Fremington clay until the Pottery closed in 1993, only refining it slightly for ovenware and large pots, and adding dolomite to lighten the colour after the filter press was installed in 1986.[36]

It was during this time that two experienced potters, David Tipler and Edgar Campden, arrived at Aldermaston. They were to work together at the Pottery for the following 15 years, enabling it to develop into a productive co-operative workshop, and they also shared with Caiger-Smith the responsibility of teaching the newcomers. Although Tipler left in 1976 to set up his own studio in Winterbourne, Berkshire, Campden went on working with Caiger-Smith until the Pottery stopped employing assistants in 1993.

David Tipler arrived at the Pottery in April 1961. Caiger-Smith remembers him as

> a bit of a loner who had been unlucky in life – he had never found a wife or a partner, and had never made the contacts that could have changed things for him … he was in his late thirties when he first started working at Aldermaston, and at the Pottery he found the only place in his life where he felt he was liked and respected.[37]

Tipler had been wounded on active service in Italy during the Second World War, and when he returned he declined to join the family business (a general store), instead training in ceramics and setting up a small workshop in the Midlands, the Kingfisher Pottery. The pottery was short-lived, however, due to an unaffordable rent, and after a brief time making honey pots at a pottery in the Cotswolds, a job he regarded as 'humiliating', he found his way to Aldermaston.[38]

According to Caiger-Smith, he was

> a versatile and reliable member of the team, and very loyal. He was largely self taught, thoughtful and remarkably widely read, and he could draw well. He did a certain amount of oil painting when on his own, although he was remarkably secretive about it. He was a good thrower and painter, and he came up with some striking and unusual ideas, but he could also be moody and abrupt with people, and from time to time he wouldn't speak to anyone for two or three days on end, yet for the most part he was a kindly, intuitive and good-humoured person. His enthusiasm undoubtedly helped the Pottery to develop in the early days.[39]

It was an irony that Edgar Campden worked with Caiger-Smith for longer than anyone else at Aldermaston: when he arrived at the Pottery in November 1961 his intention was to stay for just a few years and then set up his own pottery. He had grown up in Banbury, where he attended Banbury Art School; he then studied at

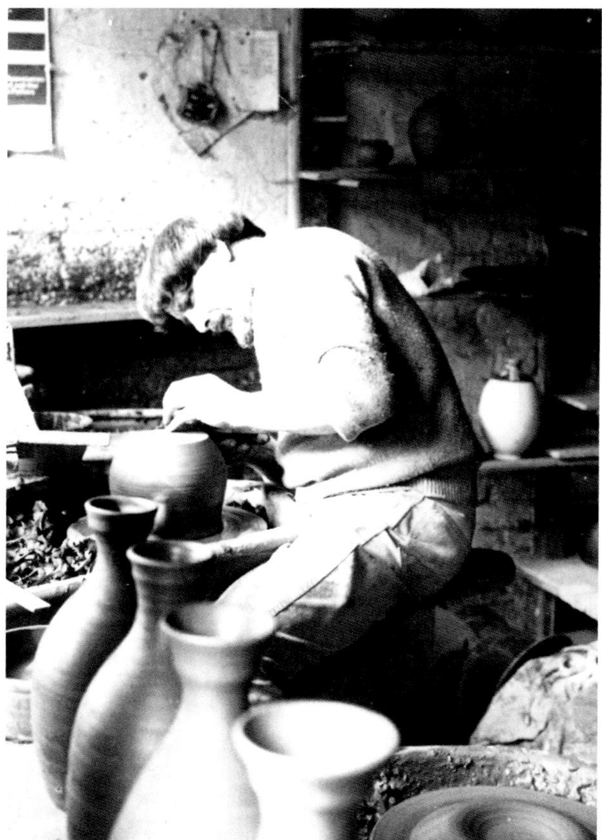

David Tipler throwing, 1969

Stoke-on-Trent College of Art (later North Staffordshire Polytechnic), gaining a National Diploma of Design in Pottery and Woven Textiles. Here he was taught by Derek Emms, later a distinguished potter and educationalist, who had spent a year at the Leach Pottery in the early 1950s. Emms was instrumental in founding a course at Stoke that followed a serious and thoughtful programme of studio pottery, in stark contrast to the design-orientated industrial processes favoured by pottery manufacturers at that time. He was also an enthusiastic advocate of Leach's philosophy that 'the making of pots involved the head, heart and hand', an approach that he was eager to pass on to his students as well as practising in his own work.[40]

After leaving art school Campden went to work with Michael Leach in North Devon, but he was not happy there and in 1961 wrote to Alan Caiger-Smith asking for a job. Caiger-Smith recalls:

> Michael regarded Edgar as a 'toper' because he occasionally drank beer in the pub, where he also smoked, as he did with pleasure all his life. He was underpaid and his ability was unrecognised. Many years later Michael asked me how Edgar was getting on, and I said that he had been throwing 21-inch platters and half-gallon jugs. Michael was amazed and told me, 'I never thought he had the makings of a thrower'.[41]

Edgar Campden was a tall, angular man with a willing and easygoing disposition. Although a good teacher, he preferred to leave that to others as far as possible. Caiger-Smith described him as a superb all-round craftsman, as good at painting as he was at throwing, and brilliant at maintaining all kinds of equipment, from electric wheels to the pug mill and the jigger and jolley; he was also a capable builder, mechanic, welder and plumber. He had a natural flair for materials, and in his own time enjoyed working in metals, leather and wood. In the late 1970s Caiger-Smith treated himself and Campden to a course in glass blowing, which he had greatly enjoyed. Although not highly imaginative, he did everything with considerable flair, encouraged by his wife Doreen, a talented sculptor and painter.[42] A number of his designs became a regular part of the Pottery's repertoire, including the soup cup with lid and stand, the faceted teapot and the 'December' pattern.[43]

Campden had met Doreen at Banbury Art School, where she had been studying sculpture, painting and English slipware. In the early spring of 1963 she joined him in Aldermaston arriving in a cattle truck with her few chattels tied together in a corner in the back, along with a blue-eyed white rabbit called Harvey and a rescue dog, Tammy, on her lap. She moved into No. 29, one of Helen Caiger-Smith's cottages, which Campden had previously shared with Tipler; their three sons, Tim, Mark and Matthew, were all born there. When Tile Cottage became available in the late 1960s they moved up The Street, and lived there for the following 25 years. Doreen was a keen gardener and Caiger-Smith offered her a small job tending the Pottery garden, enabling her to keep in touch with all the potters, which she said made her feel part of the 'pottery family'. Doreen resumed sculpture when her

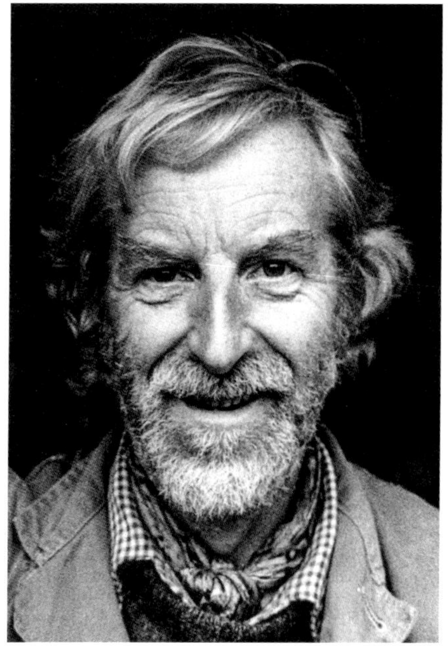

Edgar Campden, 1989

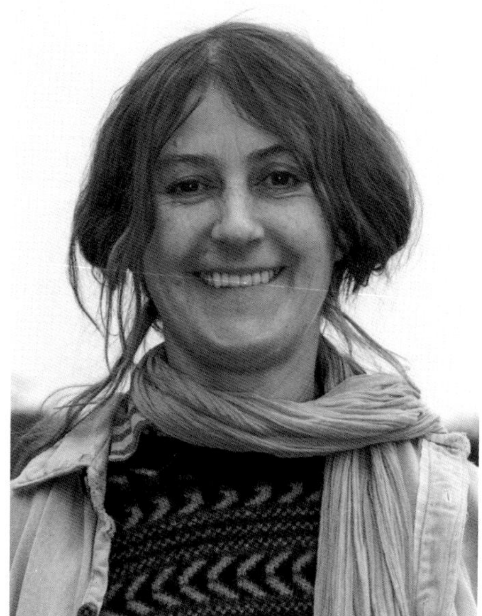

Doreen Campden, 1990

boys were older, creating small pieces using the frost-proof terracotta clay from Jim Keeling's pottery in Ascott-under-Wychwood and firing them in the electric kiln in the tile workshops behind the cottage. During the Newbury Festival she frequently exhibited her sculptures under the Open Workshop Scheme, in the beautifully kept garden she had created at the back of Tile Cottage, with the flowing stream running through it. The family had a succession of animals that shared the cottage and garden with them, including two Irish wolfhounds, cats, ducks, a pair of golden pheasants, doves, chickens, and Sabina the donkey. Sabina was very much a part of village life, her braying a familiar village sound, and she always attended the annual fête.[44] One of her ducks, Dracula, was quite ferocious, and would come in to the Pottery and stand guard at the bottom of the steps to the gallery. Visitors were really quite afraid of him, and on several occasions one of the potters had to come to the rescue and move him out of the way.[45]

Campden became skilled at packing biscuit and glaze ware in the new wood kiln, a vital job that needed experience and judgement, and usually took two or three days. For the next 20 years, with the help of an assistant, this was normally his job. Although not a natural communicator he had many friends in the village; he was kindly, humorous and supportive, and he got on well with the other potters. Caiger-Smith said he was shy with people he did not know and not very good with the visitors, often retreating down the garden or hiding in a cloud of tobacco smoke at his wheel or painting bench. Although the two men had very different temperaments, they became close friends and colleagues:[46] it was Caiger-Smith's 'enormous good fortune to work with Campden for thirty two years'.[47]

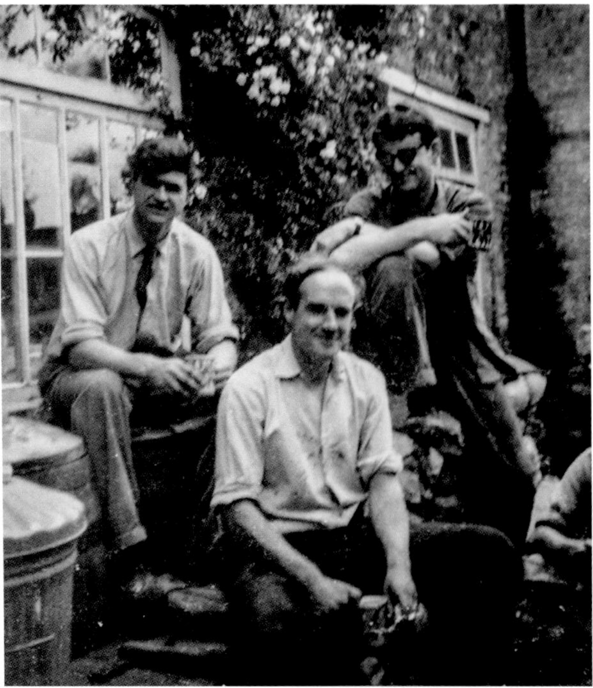

Left to right: Geoffrey Eastop, Alan Caiger-Smith
and Noel Flood outside the Pottery, 1962

The need for assistants who got on well and supported each other became increasingly important as the Pottery expanded and production increased. As well as Campden and Tipler, two more assistants joined the team in 1961: Judith Partridge and Noel Flood, followed by Sally Newton in 1962. The Pottery now began to take the form that it maintained for the next 31 years.

Judith Partridge was working at the Pottery over the cold winter of 1961 and recalls that conditions were far from luxurious, with no heating in the building except when the kiln was cooling down. The atmosphere was congenial, however, and Aldermaston was a nice environment and a most attractive village. She felt that her previous experience of teaching at art school and living on the breadline had stood her in good stead, and that although her throwing was not very good, she could draw and handle a brush, and received a good grounding in most aspects of running a business.[48] She went on to set up Rodmell Pottery in East Sussex, where she produced tin-glazed earthenware for over ten years before changing to domestic stoneware in reduced-ash glazes by 1975. Here she employed paid assistants, most notably Marshall Colman and Deborah Holpson-Wolpe. In the late 1970s she moved to County Kilkenny in Ireland, where, with her working partner Gay Latchford, she set up the Inistioge Workshops. She spent the rest of her working life combining potting with restoring derelict farmhouses.[49]

Noel Flood had come to England from Australia. Inspired by his experience at Aldermaston, the following year he found employment as a designer at the Delft Factory near Rotterdam, where he also studied at the academy of art there. In 1963 he returned to Australia and took up a lectureship at the Melbourne State College. Along with his colleagues John Teschendorff and Don Wordsworth, Flood became part of a dynamic group of teachers who nurtured an environment of experimentation, daring, excitement and professionalism, and challenged the popular conception of the division between art and craft. In 1977 Professor Flood, by now Head of the Department of Ceramics at Melbourne, and Teschendorff had a two-man show entitled *Recent Handcrafts and Other Objects* at Melbourne's Gryphon Gallery. The show made a mocking reference to the popular view of pottery as craft.[50] During a two-year sabbatical at the National College of Art and Design in Dublin in the early 1980s Flood produced a body of work entitled *The Private Parts of James Joyce's Women*. Although he did make work in functional forms, he is probably best known as a sculptor producing challenging female figures. After retiring from teaching in 1993 he continued to work from his studio and to exhibit until around 2007.

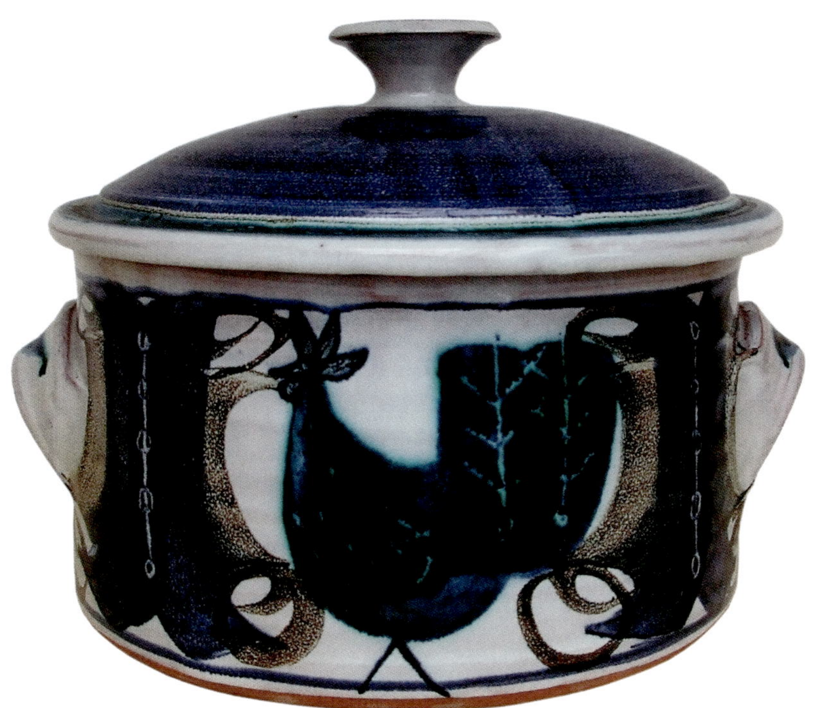

Casserole made by Judith Partridge at Rodmell
Pottery, *c.*1970, diam. 21 cm, h. 15 cm
Collection Marshall Colman

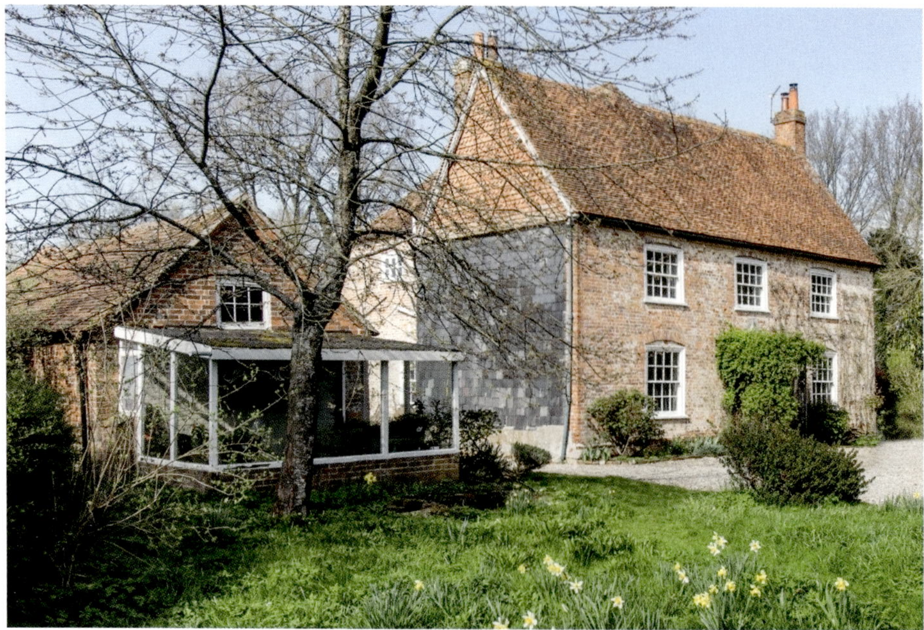

Shalford Farm House, 2017

By 1963 Caiger-Smith was spending most of the week in Aldermaston, staying with his mother in her house almost opposite the Pottery. During the school holidays Anne-Marie would bring their three young sons, Nicholas, Martin and Patrick, to stay in Pottery Cottage, travelling down to Aldermaston in a very old Morris van which smelled of fish: its previous owner had been a fishmonger. It became increasingly clear that the family would be more comfortable if they came to live permanently near the Pottery. So the house in Homer Street was sold, for £8,000. They found a suitable house near Tadley, within easy reach of the Pottery. The family moved to their new home, 'Pinnocks', in 1963, and the following year their fourth son, Daniel, was born.[52]

Two years later Shalford Farm House, just a few minutes from the Pottery, became available. Caiger-Smith recalls:

> I couldn't afford it, but thanks to a generous arrangement proposed by the vendor, Sir William Mount, who became a good friend, we were able to buy it. Shalford remained our home from then onwards, and a wonderful home it has been, enabling the work in the Pottery and family life to carry on side by side.[53]

Anne-Marie was able to put her architectural skills into practice in redesigning the interior of Shalford, and soon the family was sharing their home with a succession of assistants employed at the Pottery over the following three decades.

— 4 —

A Co-operative Workshop

In 1963 Henry Rothschild, charismatic dealer and patron of contemporary craft, offered Alan Caiger-Smith the opportunity to show his reduced lustre work in his first major one-man exhibition at the Primavera Gallery in Sloane Street, London. Rothschild's Primavera galleries here and in Cambridge were highly successful, and he was an influential figure in arts and crafts across Europe. A warm friendship developed over the years between him and Caiger-Smith, who recalls a particular exchange between them:

> Henry was an impulsive man who backed his hunches, and he could see beyond what a work was to what it might have been. Quite early on, he asked me 'Have you ever thought of using a bigger brush?' I took up the idea straight away and was thrilled by it. I have always been deeply grateful to him for this wonderful suggestion.[1]

The exhibition at Primavera was a great success and came at a pivotal time for the Pottery. The potters responded by moving beyond basic domestic ware and started to produce a variety of 'one-offs'. Freed from the constraints of the repeats, these studio pieces were made more for their aesthetic appeal than for their usefulness, with brushwork that was freer and more personal. This and other exhibitions set the pattern of work, with individual studio pieces being produced alongside the existing range of domestic ware. Caiger-Smith believed that galleries fulfilled a creative role when they offered an exhibition opportunity, which Henry Rothschild performed with great understanding.[2]

It was important to maintain a balance between regular repeat work and more personal creative output; this was vital for a workshop like Aldermaston, which supported several people and so needed to sustain a regular income. Caiger-Smith believed that repetitive work and free work were not mutually exclusive, and in the right balance each helped the other.[3] However, the need for a regular income meant that the Pottery still primarily produced objects for everyday use, with the daily work guided by a 'sample range', although few of the designs were absolutely fixed. The samples were kept behind a curtain in the showroom, where there was also 'the bible', recording the weights and dimensions of the complete range of pots made at Aldermaston. Caiger-Smith believed that using these samples gave consistency to the Aldermaston style and, more importantly, that it gave the potters time to think, enabling new ideas to develop.

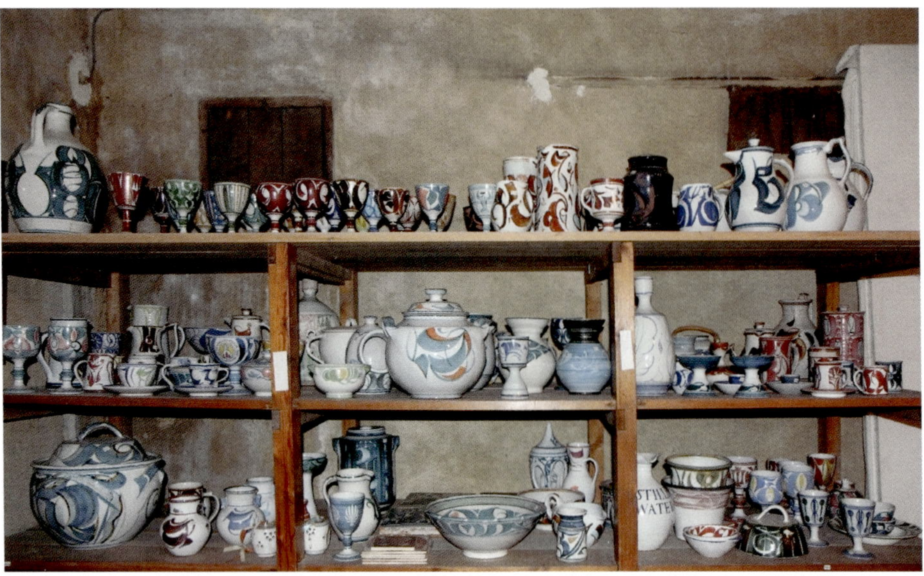

The sample shelf from Aldermaston Pottery re-created at Great Dixter House, photographed in 2018

Elizabeth Frith-Powell became an assistant at the Pottery in 1964, the year in which local builders were employed to extend the Pottery. Money was strictly limited and the extension was not a success: it was poorly built, had a leaking roof and no heating. The same year Caiger-Smith decided to demolish the first wood-fired kiln and rebuild a larger one in its place, on enlarged foundations and to a better design. Saggars were still being used for the firings in the first wood kiln, even though they took up a lot of space and had to be frequently replaced. But the results showed that it might be possible to build a kiln that could work without them, so the second kiln was designed with that in mind. The new kiln had a long entry passage for the flames, which enabled reduction to be controlled reasonably easily by opening inlets for additional air. The interior differed from a traditional up-draught and down-draught kiln, with the draught of flame moving almost in a circle, entering just below the kiln floor, rising up the rear wall, turning back under the semicircular vault, and passing down again under another part of the floor before being pulled up the chimney. Thus the flow of heat and flame was so smooth that no ash was dropped on the exposed pots.[4] Edgar Campden, who was an excellent welder, constructed the ironwork supporting the walls of the new wood kiln; he later converted them to accommodate the very large pots made in the early 1990s. This large kiln was wonderful for tin glaze; over the years it proved to be a great asset, with much of the Pottery's later success depending on it.[5] But it was less good for lustre: Caiger-Smith could not understand why the lustre firings from this second kiln were so dull, the white glazes dreary, and there was no richness or brilliance. It took him a further seven years to discover why the results were so erratic and to achieve the results he sought.

Simon Rich had always had a burning ambition to be a potter. He had been running a pottery workshop and classes at his school, when at the age of 15 he saw in the *Sunday Times* magazine a display of coffee pots featuring some of the Aldermaston pots. As soon as he left school he wrote to Caiger-Smith to ask whether he could join the Pottery.[6] Caiger-Smith could see he had potential, despite having no formal qualifications, so in 1965 Rich joined Frith-Powell, Campden and Tipler; these four worked together for the next three years.

By this time the Pottery was operating with three Leach kick wheels and one electric wheel, but by the mid-1960s there was enough income being generated to consider investing in more equipment. So in 1965 an alsager wheel was purchased from Podmores of Stoke-on-Trent, together with a pug mill. The new wheel allowed for much bigger pots to be made with less physical effort, and the pug mill was used for clay recycling and preparation; together these two labour-saving pieces of equipment allowed for more time and energy to be put to planning.[7]

As the decade progressed the Pottery became increasingly busy – so busy, in fact, that nine months had passed before Caiger-Smith became aware that the grocer's shop up the street was on the market. It was being sold together with one of the oldest cottages in the village and a collection of sheds, which were used for storing groceries behind the shop. It was too good an opportunity to miss and, having arranged a loan from a distant cousin, in 1968 Caiger-Smith bought the

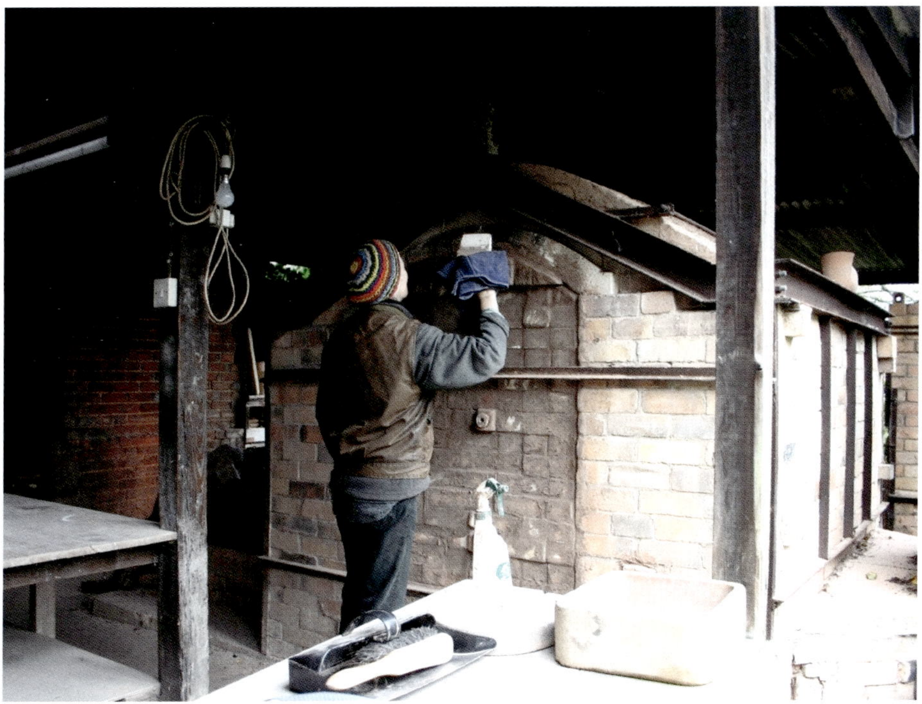

Ursula Waechter checking the flow of flames in the second wood-fired kiln, 1998

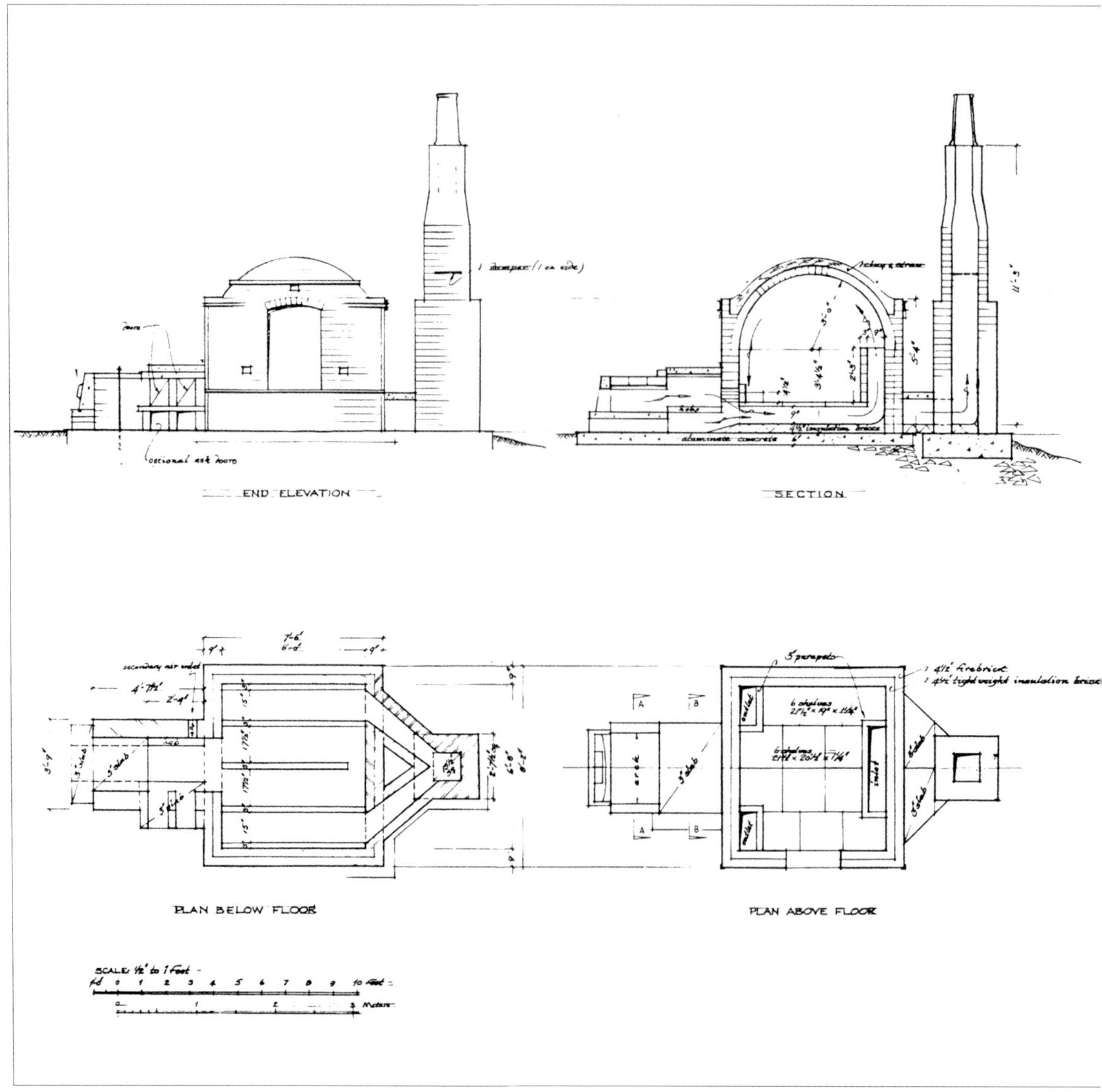

property for a very modest price.[8] The shop would become a new gallery show-room and the outbuildings provided much-needed extra space for workshops and storage. Edgar Campden and his family moved into the large cottage, known as Tile Cottage, and everyone at the Pottery got on with the conversion of the Tile Cottage workshops. After the work was completed, facilities were installed for press-moulding and the storage of the plaster moulds, together with a new jolley machine for the production of 'owl' mugs and bowls, and for making plates.[9] Later a tile press was acquired for £50, which was used for the production of thousands of lustre tiles.[10] The new showroom was refurbished with shelves and racks, and space for storing work for exhibitions, with most of the work being

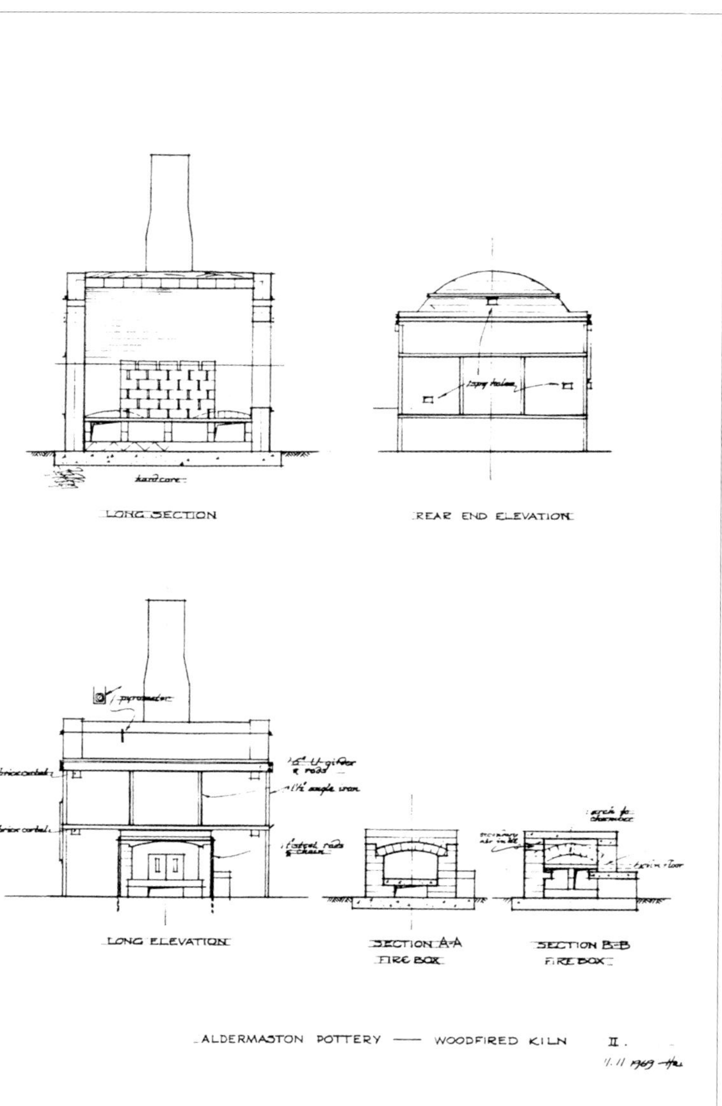

Anne-Marie Caiger-Smith's scale drawing of the second wood-fired kiln, built in 1964; drawing dated 1969

done by Anne-Marie, although willing helpers were always available. For the following 25 years this proved to be an excellent place for displaying work.

By now the Pottery was beginning to achieve a degree of recognition and success. As its reputation grew there were invitations to exhibit in Italy and Turkey, and in 1968 at the Matsuya Gallery in Tokyo, Japan. The same year two pieces of Caiger-Smith's early lustre work were exhibited in the *International Exhibition of Ceramics* at the Victoria and Albert Museum in London. Soon after the exhibition Caiger-Smith received a letter from his cousin Bernard Leach, who wrote: 'your two pots sang a solo. As you know your language is not mine, but I'm glad you're not doing what others are doing, trying to follow in my footsteps.'[11] 1968 also saw

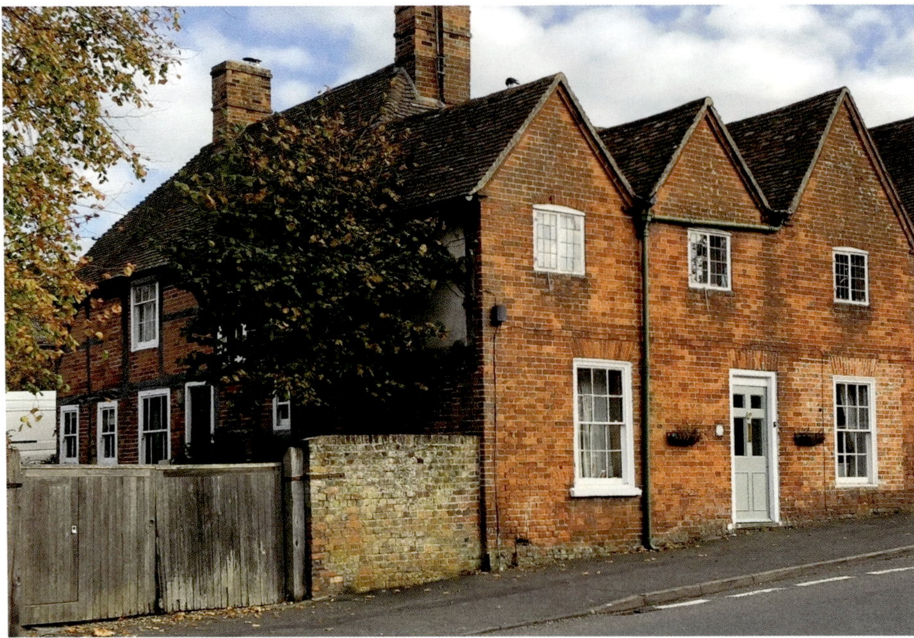

Tile Cottage from The Street: the left side opened into the
yard, garden, workshops and gallery showroom

the first of many visits to the Pottery by Alan Peascod, an influential teacher and Australian ceramicist, later considered to be 'one of the most important contributors to ceramic art in Australia'.[12] Peascod was greatly inspired by Aldermaston: as well as forming a lifelong friendship with Caiger-Smith, the experience of being at the Pottery and watching and taking part in the firings informed his whole career.

The new workshops provided additional working space for more assistants to be taken on. In 1968 six people worked in the Pottery alongside Caiger-Smith; by 1969 there were eight. One of the assistants in 1968 was Clare Cherrington. Although she only worked at Aldermaston for a year, she made a valuable contribution to the business:

> She was sure that our prices were too low and spent a good many days comparing them with the prices of industrially made ware in the shops, discovering that much of our work was being sold at under half the price of factory-produced equivalents. This was wonderfully helpful. When we raised our prices the pots sold just as well as before and only a few people even noticed. Amongst those that did, I recall one couple saying, 'We always thought the prices were rather low, but it wasn't for us to say it.'[13]

The Pottery began to settle into a daily rhythm, and it seemed that Caiger-Smith's vision of establishing a small country workshop was beginning to be realised at last. He saw this as the craftsman's natural setting, a place of learning as well as of production. Even though such workshops were already on the decline by this time, he believed that, with certain differences, the workshop pattern could survive and develop.[14] Michael Cardew, writing in 1969, explained:

> Some arts need only the powers and genius of the individual artist; others require the collaboration of a group, large or small, and a confluence of ideas from several sources…. The small unit – the team or crew – still survives in several fields of activity, and there is a good chance that the small workshop, functioning in a co-operative rather than a narrow proprietary way, will continue to commend itself to serious potters.[15]

Caiger-Smith believed that the workshop was not simply the means of increasing output, nor was it an individual multiplied by seven or eight. Naturally it permitted manufacture in larger quantities, but also the production of a variety of work that would be impossible for a single craftsman. Through its more experienced members it could follow up new ideas, while the group as a whole maintained a regular output of the staple designs.[16] Pottery had always seemed to Caiger-Smith a convivial activity and, remembering his happy days of working in a team on the farm in the 1950s, he had always hoped to establish a similar team of potters who also shared equally in every aspect of the work.[17] Besides, he said, 'three together are stronger than three times one, and in any case without congenial company I tend to fall asleep!'[18] Although he had started the journey alone, it was something he wanted to share because he said there was so much he did not understand. He believed that collaborative work epitomised one of the most basic of all human relationships, and although its structure may change, it could never become obsolete. He also believed that work was different when it was shared, the highs more effervescent, the lows less daunting, and that one learned things in unexpected ways.[19]

The steady decline in the craftsman's skills over the last few decades is in part due to the mistaken belief that craft knowledge is 'other people's rules', and denies self-expression. To quote Peter Dormer, 'to learn craft entails, for a while at least, working in the fashion of one's teachers and mentors, but in reality this is not, or need not be, a hindrance to individual creativity'.[20] In learning a craft, the role of mimicry is often essential, which means working alongside a skilled practitioner. According to Dormer, an individual in isolation does not easily acquire the skills of a craft, and although tacit knowledge becomes 'my knowledge', it is also communal.[21] Tacit knowledge – that body of knowledge gained through experience and the senses – cannot easily be articulated or described in words; this inability to describe the core of a craft becomes more acute the nearer the craft comes to being 'art'. The particular touch of a violinist, draughtsperson, surgeon or nurse cannot be described, but it can be imitated or absorbed in full by someone else.[22] This was the philosophy behind the working practice that developed at Aldermaston.

Although the traditional organisation of a pottery workshop had each individual concentrating on one activity, Caiger-Smith believed that the decorated pottery they were making at Aldermaston was best done by potters who participated in all the stages of making. Specialisation requires repetitive work and little initiative, and he believed that only by beginning to understand the relationship between form and decoration could the potter possibly progress. He saw the desire to decorate pots as 'almost as universal as the desire to dance or make footprints in the sand',[23] and painted tin-glaze pottery as not just a form with a decorated surface but as a complete entity, with the form and the painting totally belonging to each other.

So everyone had their share in the throwing, painting and firing of the pots, and each followed their own work from the thrown form right through to glazing and decoration.

> Alan saw it as fundamental that anyone making a pot should be wholly responsible for it – from taking the clay to the wedging bench to executing the last brush-stroke. So you learned from the start that every stage mattered. If you threw a lumpy pot you would later have to draw your finely chiselled sable brush over a lumpy surface. You also quickly learned that if you prepared the clay badly you wouldn't be able to centre it. You would then throw it badly, and it would be terrible to trim. If, later, you failed to stir the glaze properly and dip the pot smoothly no brushwork would later save it.[24]

Thus each person learned to be potter, painter, designer and technician, becoming a versatile member of the team, capable of covering each aspect of the work if need be, and able to stand in for others if they were ill or on holiday. 'Potting at Aldermaston was a cyclical movement', recalled one of the potters, 'with each active period being followed by a more reflective time, in a pleasing pattern of familiarity, yet always different; it was a traditional way of working and less stressful than today's hurried pace.'[25] Juliet Wilson, who worked at Aldermaston for four years from 1969, described the immense sense of satisfaction that was to be gained from working in this way:

> every potter worked on their own pieces from start to finish, so right from the start you could see your efforts through the biscuit firing (or not!) onto your own glaze shelf. It gave you such a wonderful sense of achievement as you took out those first pathetic attempts from the glaze firing which were made by *you*.[26]

But in addition to repetition and consistency, Caiger-Smith also wanted to allow for innovation and 'seizing the moment'.[27] So although everyone had to make repeat designs, they were encouraged to undertake a certain amount of individual work that could then be exhibited or incorporated in the future as a repeat design.

As there was no division of labour, inevitably learners produced a higher proportion of seconds. But there were a number of relatively simple thrown shapes with basic brush decoration, which were a useful starting-point for the beginners. As their skills developed, their range of work naturally evolved. A well-made piece could easily be spoiled by someone learning painting, but Caiger-Smith felt that this was not important: one only learns where to stop by having gone too far, and it would come right in the end. In any case by this time the individual pieces being produced, which were much more expensive than the rest of the output, easily made up for the seconds.[28]

In order for each person to participate in making, there was shared responsibility for the routine jobs that were essential for the smooth running of the workshop – preparing the clay, keeping the showroom in order, dealing with the customers and orders, or maintaining the machinery. Inevitably these jobs fell to whoever was available at the time, although a rota was always pinned up on the wall. Consequently the running of the Pottery was everyone's responsibility. In the words of one assistant,

> it was an unusual situation, but one which gave us all a sense of belonging.... The Pottery was a very nurturing environment and it had a family feel about it. Of course we were expected to work hard and to produce work to the best of our ability, but at the same time there was an atmosphere of fun and enjoyment with what we were doing. It was important that we were learning to make the Aldermaston range of pots, but we were also doing jobs that were not so skilled and helping to make the pottery run smoothly.[29]

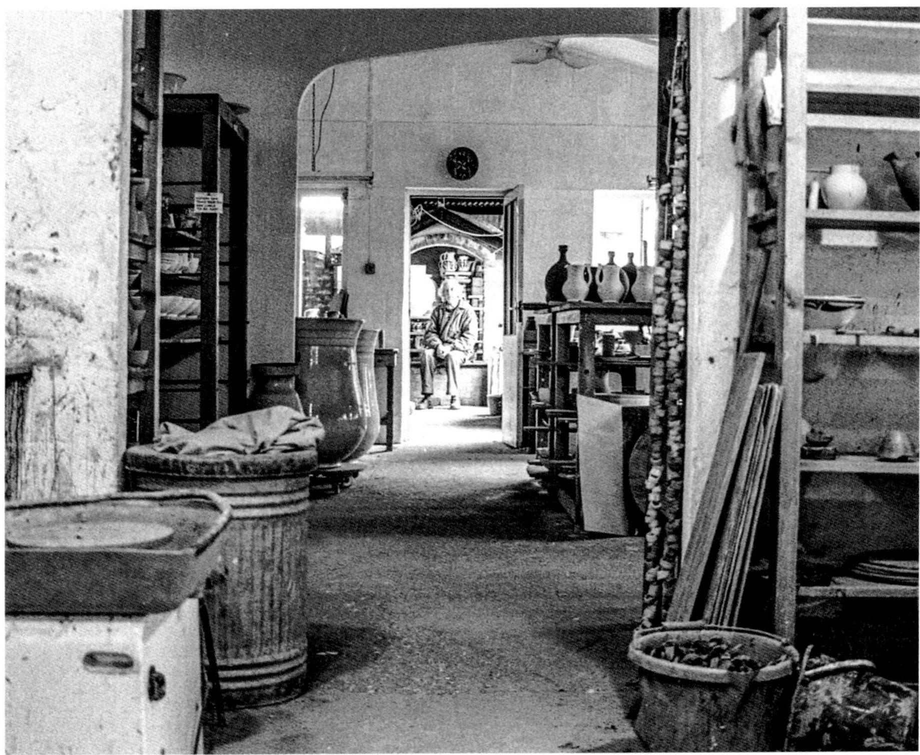

Edgar Campden sitting inside the kiln, 1991

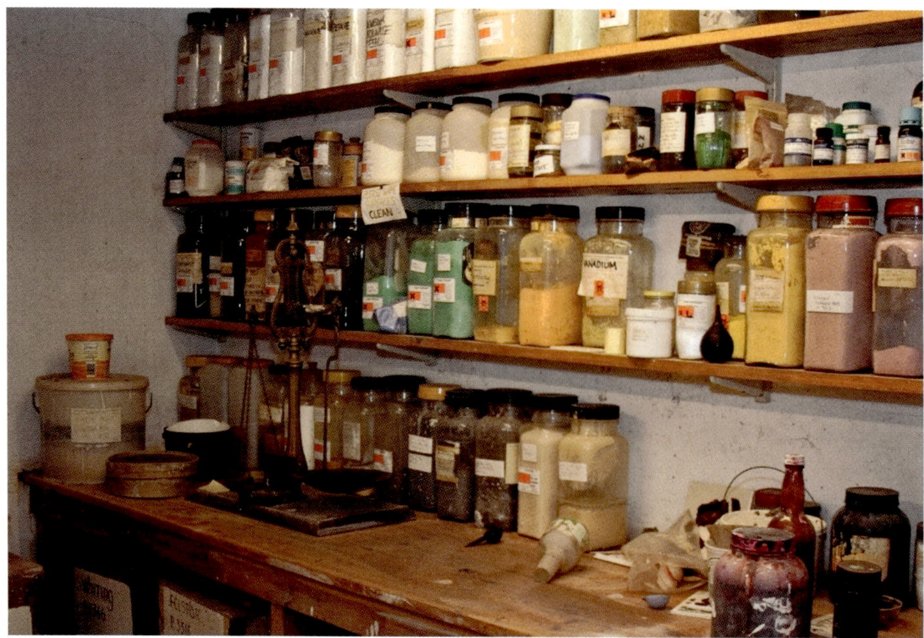

The glaze room

Caiger-Smith felt that a good team was more than a group of craftsmen, it was a system of human chemistry, with each person influencing the others, introducing a new idea, a different way of doing something, or varying a design, and that although the leader may try and set this in motion, if the atmosphere was right then it happened by simply working together. Although its members will be unequal in talent and experience, in an effective workshop everyone is always on the move and the person receiving help today is being asked for it tomorrow. This also means that the workshop is repeatedly beginning over and over again, with no gradual, steady accumulation of skill, except on the part of those who remain and maintain continuity. The danger with a system like this is having too many learners and too few experienced and productive potters, so the balance must be kept just right in order for profitability to be maintained.[30]

This type of working environment was in complete opposition to the economic philosophy advocated in Adam Smith's classic book *Wealth of Nations*, published at the beginning of the Industrial Revolution, which reflected on what builds a nation's wealth. Smith's ideas encouraged the rise of new business enterprise in Europe, based on the division of labour: giving each worker a specific job enabled the individual to become more skilled at that job, thus saving time. Although Smith stated that human welfare was on balance increased by the division of labour, he did acknowledge that there were social costs, and that human beings given repetitious and monotonous tasks become dehumanised by the repetitive tasks of the production process.[31] Fortunately Caiger-Smith did not believe in

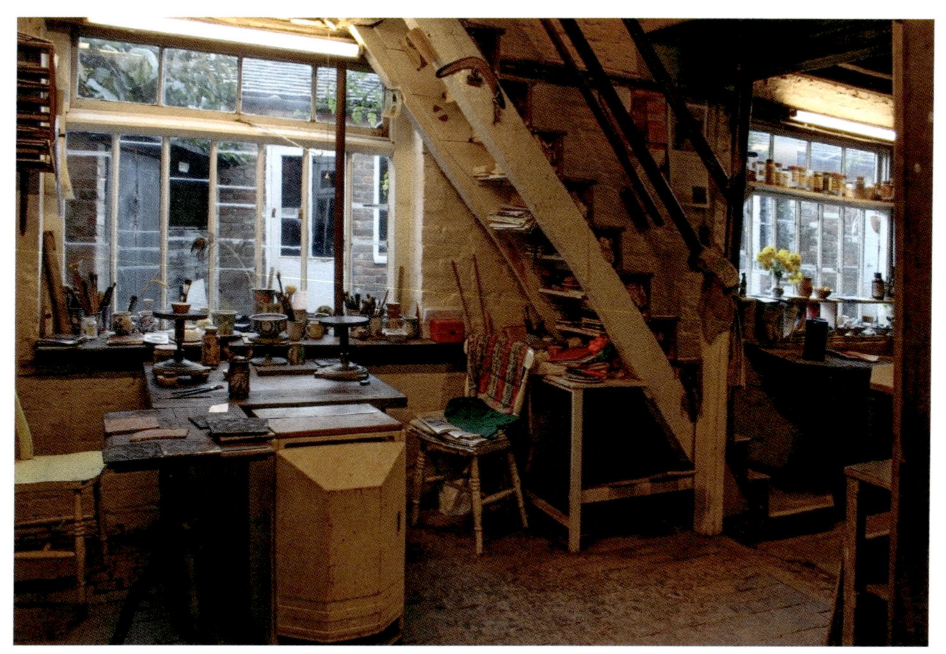

The painting area in the front workshop

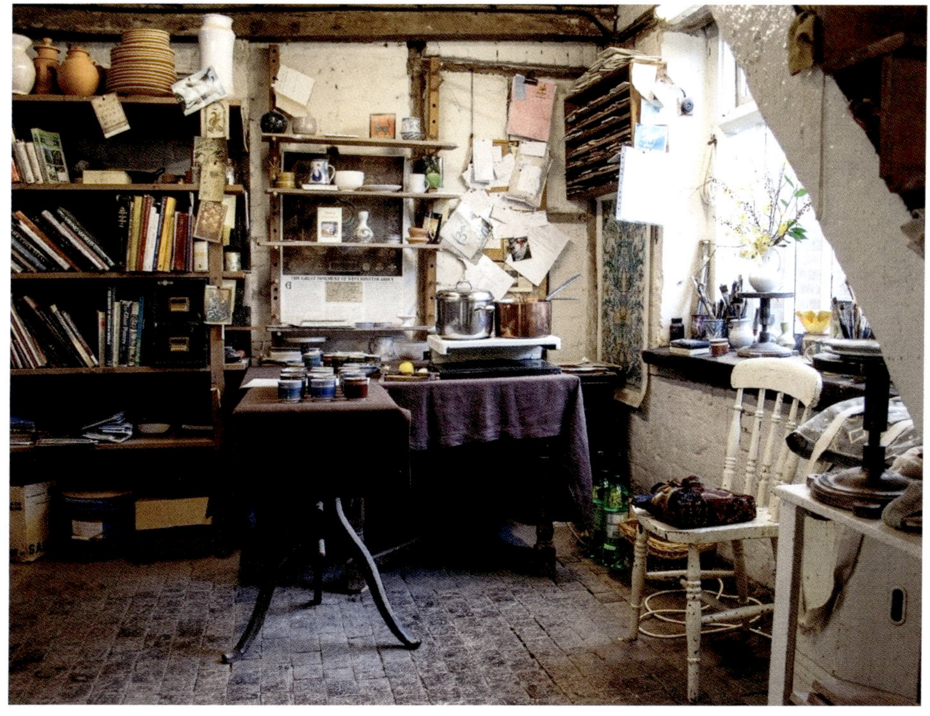

The front workshop

specialisation, and his working philosophy ultimately enabled many of his assistants to set up potteries of their own after leaving Aldermaston.

Even the seemingly mundane jobs had their rewards. Graham Adamson, who joined the Pottery in the late 1960s, described the benefits accruing from one such job, which is often shunned in a smaller studio set-up:

> My task was to reclaim and recycle the waste clay, and then prepare it and bring it to a suitable state of use again. Such a pleasing and satisfying activity gave me the opportunity to learn about the qualities of clay – allowing me to appreciate what an amazing elemental substance it is. I learned how it is necessary to 'rest' the clay, and how much kneading was required to bring back the 'life' of the body. The red clay used at Aldermaston was Fremington, from North Devon. This clay, a substance full of life, was very forgiving and flowed smoothly between hand and fingers, but was able to hold its shape even though it was very plastic. I chose to use this clay when I moved to North Wales, to use for my slipware, for I loved its malleability, and respecting its particular character was so rewarding.[32]

When a new assistant arrived at Aldermaston the expectation was for them to work there for at least two years, after an initial probationary period of one month. This informal contract was for the benefit of both the potters and the Pottery, and because many of the people who arrived without much experience were not able to make a reliable contribution until about a year after they had started.[33] The work alternated between three weeks at the wheel and three weeks doing brush decoration. The Pottery was open to the public from 8 a.m. until 5 p.m. six days a week, and all the potters worked from Monday to Friday. There was a rota for Saturdays; as well as welcoming and helping the visitors, this was also the day when the workshop was cleaned. The potters could make objects to their own design in their free time after work and, having covered the cost of materials and kiln space (they would be fired with the standard production), could take them away.

By the end of the late 1960s the 'sample range' of repeats (standard forms with specific dimensions) had become unsustainably large. The collection of prototypes for repetition was not very organised: although in theory there was a shelf with an example of every repeat shape or brush design, as the repeat shapes amounted to about a hundred, and each shape could be painted in several ways, with permutations of some ten or twelve colours on any of five regular glazes, the possible combinations were highly confusing. As a consequence, unless a customer provided an example of an original, it proved very difficult to repeat an order.[34]

While she was an assistant at the Pottery, Juliet Wilson introduced Caiger-Smith to Oliver Roskill, an industrial consultant who lived nearby at Beech Hill. Roskill became a great friend of the family, as well as giving invaluable advice over the years on improving the viability of the business.[35] He pointed out that the Pottery would be more manageable if the variety of repeats were smaller and the potters specialised in a more limited aspect of production. Caiger-Smith felt that however much sense this made logically, in human terms it did not always get the best out of people, and that an apparently less efficient system could actually produce better all-round results by allowing for greater job satisfaction and encouraging creativity. He said that he would be ashamed to ask anyone who came to work to do one job only, and tried to make the work as satisfying as possible; he never wished the potters to be forced into a secondary role of producing his designs exclusively.[36] In 1970 he wrote:

> for ten years we have received far more orders than we can cope with and had we responded properly to them all then we should have been directed from the outside, not by ourselves, and the whole place would have been turned into a limited company with semi-factory conditions and a rigid routine which none of us would have liked to work in. So in fact it would by now have stopped.[37]

Juliet Wilson had hoped to study sculpture at St Martin's College of Art, but the college lost her portfolio. However, Anthony Caro, who was teaching there at the time, gave her a piece of advice which has stayed with her ever since: 'Learn how to work through acquiring a skill, any skill … I think an apprenticeship might suit you better than art school.' Although she was later offered a place at St Martin's, and £50 compensation for her lost portfolio, she turned down both. She had been a frequent visitor to the Pottery at Aldermaston all through her childhood, where her mother would stop en route to her boarding school nearby in order to buy more pottery to add to her collection. Caiger-Smith had even fired Wilson's hand-built A-level pots for her, as they were too big for the school kiln. Her first memory of the Pottery was the unmistakable smell, so evocative that she can still smell it nearly fifty years later: 'clay dust, the cooling kiln, and a tinge of Alan's pipe'. She was upset when Caiger-Smith turned down her request to join the team, saying that he had no space for a beginner, so she decided to 'scamper off to Italy to do a summer job and to think about life'.[38] She was therefore greatly surprised to receive a letter from Caiger-Smith shortly before she left, asking her if she happened to be going anywhere near the Bargello Museum in Florence, and if so, could she possibly get him some slides for the book he was writing on tin glaze, and there might then be an opening for her at the Pottery when she returned at the end of the summer. Unable to contain her excitement, she hastened to the Bargello.

Wilson started at Aldermaston in the late summer of 1969 and describes her three years there as a proper apprenticeship. Caiger-Smith would always arrive at the Pottery an hour later than the assistants who lived in the village, as he would first do administration and make phone calls; he would also usually stay on for an hour after they had all gone home. Wilson stayed with the family at Shalford for her first year, and acknowledges that going with Alan to the Pottery from 9 a.m. to 6 p.m. every day except Sundays was a great privilege:

I think I was only half aware of how lucky I was. I know I was so happy to be working so hard every day. I wasn't like the other members of the team, who had a mass of accumulated experience, vast knowledge and skill in throwing, turning, glazing and glazes, and all the other aspects of being a potter. I was a complete novice and could barely centre a pot. However, I've always been a hard worker and enthusiastic, so getting stuck in with all the processes, and learning so many new skills was bliss for me. And what a lot of teachers! Of course at the head was Alan, who was so generous with his time and took an immense amount of trouble showing me what to do and guiding me in the way the pottery worked.[39]

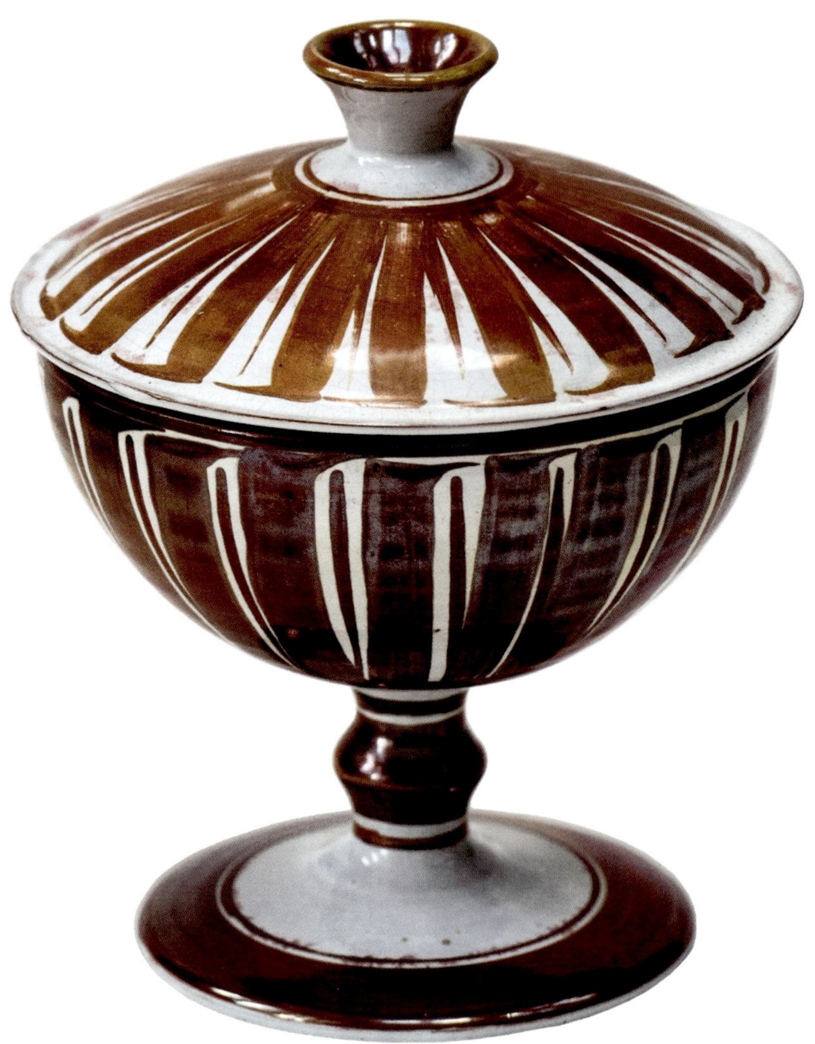

Lidded chalice with silver and copper lustre by
Alan Caiger-Smith, 1965, h. 24 cm, w. 21 cm
Collection Sarah and Adrian Dixon

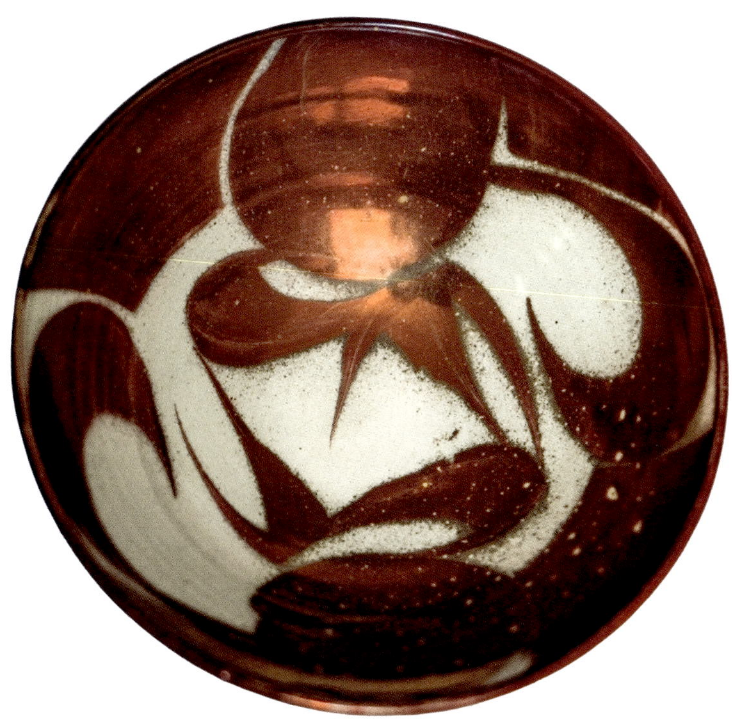

'Swallow' bowl with copper lustre by
Alan Caiger-Smith, 1967, diam. 18 cm, h. 6.3 cm
Collection Alan Caiger-Smith

As well as a potter, Caiger-Smith was also a scholar with an inquiring mind. In the late 1960s he had begun work on a complete volume of the history of tin-glazed earthenware in Europe and the Islamic world, which Michael Cardew was later to describe as a monument of erudition and scholarship and a masterpiece of perceptive writing.[40] The book took up a great deal of Caiger-Smith's time and he would often work late into the night. One assistant remembers wondering how he survived with so little sleep, although he always had a short nap after lunch – sometimes only three or four minutes – but this seemed to set him up for the rest of the day.[41] By a stroke of good fortune, while he was researching the book Oldrich Asenbryl came to work at the Pottery, and there followed a fruitful collaboration that resulted in the chapter on Central Europe. Caiger-Smith says, 'to my mind the chapter on Central Europe is one of the most worthwhile in the whole book: without Olda it could not have been written'.[42]

In 1968, with £2 in his pocket, Asenbryl had left Czechoslovakia under the brief reign of Alexander Dubcek, the leader whose bold attempt to give his country 'socialism with a human face' was crushed by an invasion of Soviet-led Warsaw Pact troops. Being a gifted draughtsman and cartoonist, Asenbryl was able to support himself by drawing in the streets of France before eventually

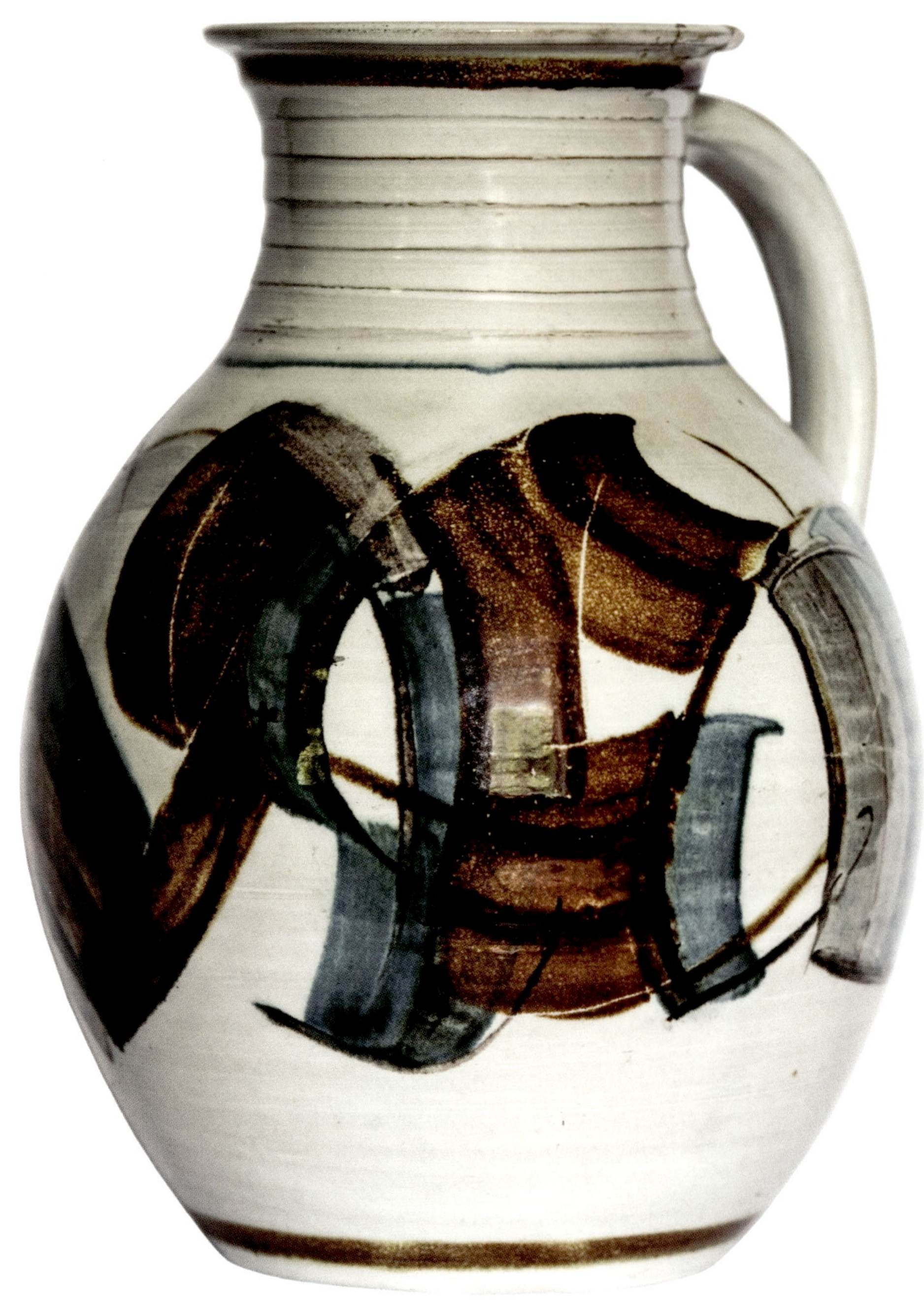

Pitcher with bronze and blue-green decoration by
Alan Caiger-Smith, 1967, h. 25.5 cm, w. 17.7 cm
Collection Alan Caiger-Smith

making his way to England. A journalist who was trying to find work for escaped Czechs contacted Caiger-Smith to see if he could accommodate one of them. Although Asenbryl was not a trained potter, he had attended the Bechyne College of Ceramics in Czechoslovakia and also had some experience of clay sculpture. As he was unable to speak English, on his first visit to Aldermaston he came with Dorotá Sebestová, a young Slovak woman who acted as an interpreter. Caiger-Smith remembers:

> I had no wish to take on any new people, but Olda's quality was irresistible. He lived in our home for several months, learning our language and familiarising himself rapidly with the work of the Pottery, soon becoming a strong thrower and versatile painter, and appreciated by all of us for his charm and resolute character. He had many other talents which I was unable to make use of, and he was in every way a wonderful presence in the workshop.[43]

Asenbryl introduced Caiger-Smith to the writings about the then little-known Haban wares once produced in Central Europe, and translated many passages for him. Later, with Dorotá Sebestová as interpreter, Caiger-Smith and his wife visited Slovakia. Here he met the potter Herman Landsfeld of Straznice, from whom he gained valuable knowledge about Haban kiln design and clay compositions, and together they visited many of the old Habaner sites.[44]

When Graham Adamson joined the Pottery during a very cold and wet autumn in 1969 he shared a caravan with Asenbryl, about 3 miles from the Pottery:

> Olda and I would cycle on our very ancient bikes to work. How fortunate I was to have met him, the source of much good humour and inspirational ideas and artwork, which was coloured very much by his experiences in Czechoslovakia. His world and background were very exotic to me, a former resident of Penge in South London. Later Olda and I moved into one of Alan's cottages in the village, and we were very happy at No. 29, The Street. This also allowed us to be on hand for any parties and meals that were on offer, and No. 29 was the location of some great celebrations, inspired by the music of the 60s and 70s.[45]

Great friendships were kindled in the welcoming and congenial atmosphere of the Pottery, through sharing the convenient and affordable accommodation available in the village, and through the generosity of Caiger-Smith when he invited potters to live with his family in his own home. Many of the potters described living and working in Aldermaston as a holistic experience: it was so much more than just a job, especially during the 1970s when the atmosphere was relaxed and fun, profitability was good, and life reflected the best of that particular era. Adamson recalls that

> the potters at Aldermaston were a very sociable lot, and always willing to share and support each other. We shared some quite strong emotional ties. An 'out of work hours retreat' and gathering place was in the cottage of Doreen and Edgar

Campden and their three young sons. They were a delightful couple, very warm and generous, who surprised us with their constant creative skills and artistic abilities.[46]

Jane O'Connor remembers her time at the Pottery in the late 1970s:

Alan was very generous to his potters. People would have no doubt paid good money to work at Aldermaston for the experience and training, but Alan believed that they should be paid a fair wage according to their experience. He provided subsidised accommodation for all his potters, having gradually acquired property in Aldermaston over the years. This meant we all lived very close to each other and the pottery, so it was a community as well as a job that we shared.[47]

Jenny Jowett, who came to work at the Pottery in 1971, also commented on this aspect of the Aldermaston experience:

Aldermaston was like an extended family. When I first joined the Pottery Alan had four cottages and a flat where potters lived; his mother lived opposite the Pottery, and then there was 'Nanny', who kept house for his mother, and lived with her. She did the washing of the aprons, and was always cross that the strings were left on! There was also Olive Ford from next door who did the packing of the pots. All the potters often met up after work and had many parties to which I was always invited. Alan was always there, but he never got too involved in the potters' personal problems, which was just as well. Anne-Marie did all the repairs to the pottery and the cottages. Alan's personal comfort always seemed immaterial to him, consequently the potters' living conditions were quite Spartan, but all this seemed unimportant beside the enthusiasm and knowledge that Alan gave them, never holding back how he achieved his results.[48]

The villagers too were part of life for the potters. Doreen Campden recalls her welcome when she and Edgar moved to Aldermaston:

After a few days a knock came at the door and I was presented with a lovely bouquet of flowers. These were from the Aldermaston and Wasing Young Wives' Group welcoming me to the village … our first-born, Tim, was born in the cottage in November 1964. Our neighbour Eileen Evans helped with the birth. She was so thrilled. She and her husband had not been able to have a family. She said she always felt a closeness, something special, towards Tim. Lovely neighbours.[49]

There were weekly meetings of the Kennet Folk Club, which was held upstairs in the Hind's Head pub at the bottom of The Street. Popular in the 1970s, the Folk Club hosted some well-known groups and musicians. Sometimes a folk dance was held on a nearby farm. There was also an active local cricket club. These occasions gave an opportunity for the potters to mix with villagers, and lasting relationships were formed. It was on one such occasion that Adamson met his future wife, Fay;[50] he was not the only one who met their future partner while working at Aldermaston Pottery.

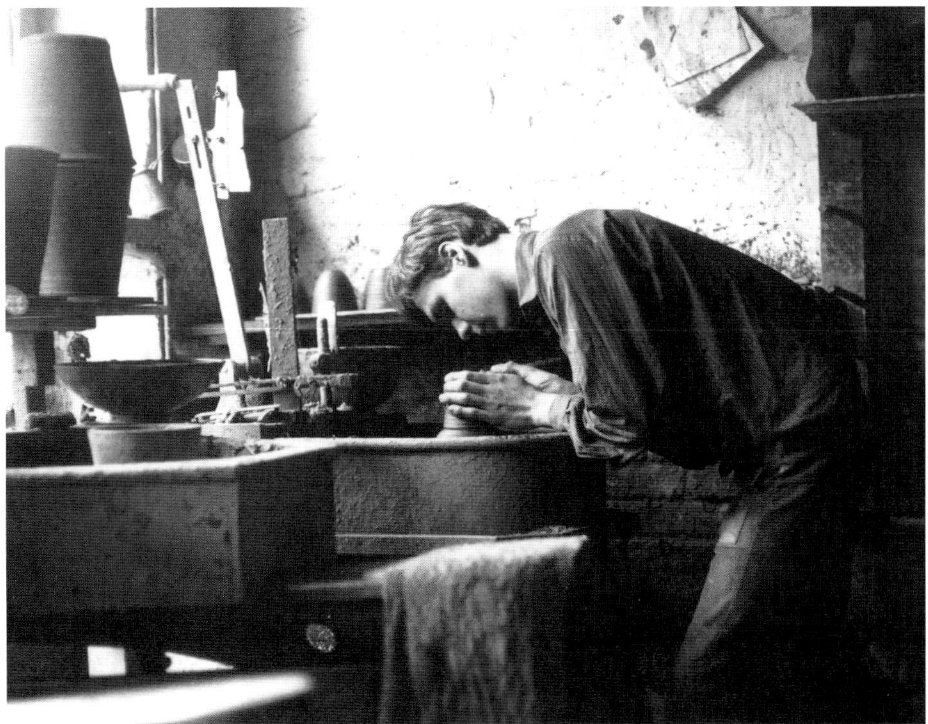

Simon Rich at the wheel, 1967

Caiger-Smith had little need to research his market; the public came to him and he responded to their requests as far as possible. He felt that one of the advantages of working as they did was that the potters were able to react to new ideas proposed by their visitors, and that this aspect of making and designing was often overlooked. Making things for people was very different from making for the market. People did so much more than just pay, and their ideas, criticisms, suggestions, and above all their enjoyment, were part of the workshop's lifeline.[51]

One unusual request he received around this time was to make tandoori ovens, which were to be supplied to a local charcoal maker for use in restaurants. These 'pots', which were 4 feet high, were made with thick coils of unfired clay; as they were so bulky and heavy, they were prohibitively expensive to import from India. This particular project was assigned to Adamson and Asenbryl, who first had to make a large plaster of Paris former in which to make the ovens. Adamson always enjoyed being able to use old skills in new projects. He had worked previously at the British Museum, mainly on archaeological digs and the restoration of objects, but one project came in very useful for this assignment: he had been involved with mixing seven tons of plaster by hand for the casting of the Sutton Hoo ship burial. At Aldermaston, the clay tandoori ovens were made in the outbuildings behind Tile Cottage.[52]

By 1970 there were six or seven full-time or trainee potters, plus a part-time clerical assistant and a part-time packer. This number seemed just right, making reasonably light work of the preparation of materials, trials and tests of various kinds, the loading and unloading of the kilns, the business of selling and the general jobs. The 24 kw kiln was fired almost continuously at this time and the ambient heat generated helped to dry out the pots, enabling orders to be completed quickly; it also prevented everything from freezing up in winter. The wood-fired kiln was fired every five weeks. Caiger-Smith felt that a team of this size could undertake all these jobs satisfactorily, while at the same time allowing the potters to undertake more ambitious projects than could be sustained by one person alone. The person in charge was still able to keep in touch with everything that was going on, and in the space available a team of seven provided the greatest freedom and possibilities.[53]

The mainstream of studio pottery produced in Britain at this time still followed the Leach tradition of Japanese-inspired high-fired stoneware. In spite of this, invitations to exhibit the pottery produced at Aldermaston were starting to come in from all over the country, and as early as 1970 the uniqueness of the set-up at Aldermaston was being recognised. In a review of the exhibition *Alan Caiger-Smith and Members of Aldermaston Pottery* at the Peter Dingley Gallery, Stratford-upon-Avon, in March 1970, Richard Dunning describes the team of six potters, led by Alan Caiger Smith, as 'unique in making maiolica pottery of the kind of which Piccolpasso wrote, for in addition to decorating their pots with raw

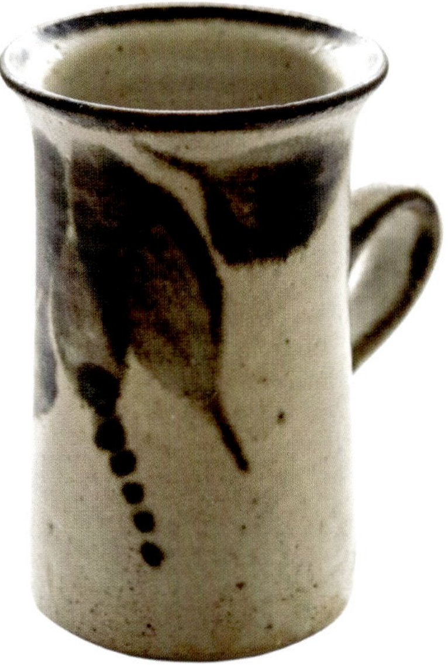

Stoneware mug made by Oldrich Asenbryl and Simon Rich
at Tisbury Pottery, 1970, h. 11 cm, w. 7 cm
Collection Jane and Bob White

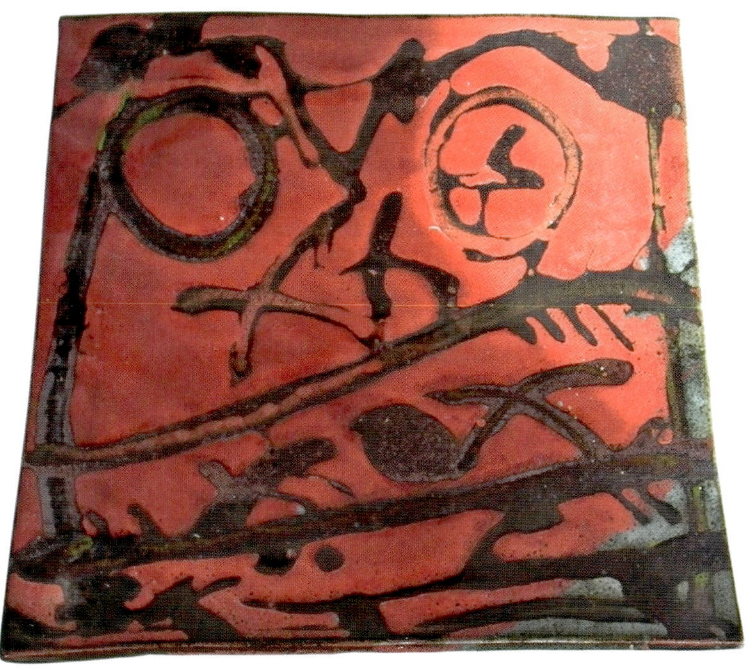

Square stoneware platter with Tenmoku, Chun and copper/red glaze, fired
to 1320°C, made by Oldrich Asenbryl at Sarn Pottery, 2012, w. 46 cm
Collection Oldrich Asenbryl

pigments on unfired opaque glazes they are also now exploring smoke-reduced
lustres'.[54] Dunning also recognised that by working as both potters and painters
there arose an integration in the pots, while the potters simultaneously gained
both strength and richness in their forms by making personal pieces as well as
producing domestic ware as a team. He said that while the integrity of the team
was obviously evident, the sensitive humanity of its co-ordinator should not be
undervalued.[55]

1970 also saw the beginning of a long and fruitful connection with Faenza in
Italy. At the *International Exhibition of Ceramics* in Faenza that year, Caiger-Smith
was awarded the 'Lions' prize of 100,000 lire awarded by the Lions Club of Faenza
for decorated maiolica.[56] The following year, also in Faenza, he was awarded the
prize of the Ministero della Pubblica Istruzione for decorated maiolica, in honour
of Gaetano Ballardini.[57] He was now also travelling more frequently to Italy to
undertake research for his book, and always returned inspired and eager to put
new ideas into practice.[58]

Oldrich Asenbryl and Simon Rich left Aldermaston in 1970 to set up a workshop together in Tisbury, Wiltshire, making oxidised stoneware. Caiger-Smith
writes that 'they were too different for the enterprise to last long, and in due
course Asenbryl moved to North Wales where he set up the Sarn Pottery, and

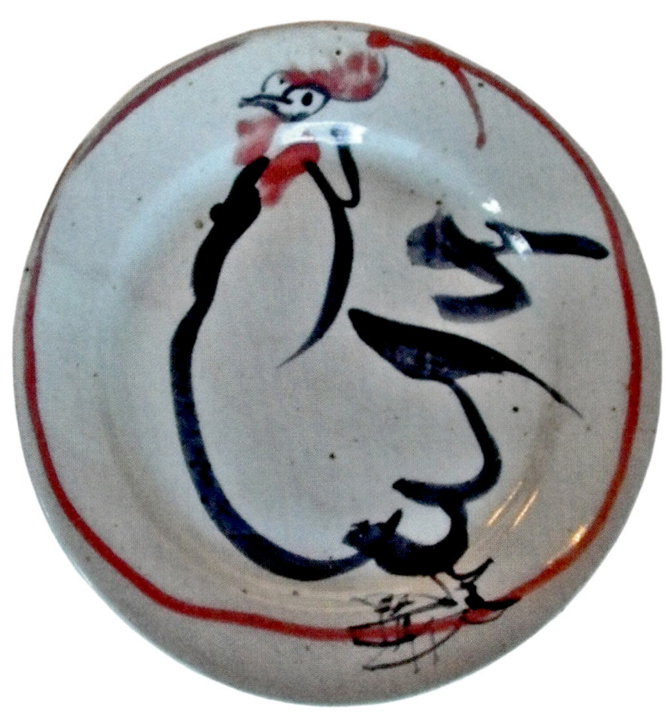

Porcelain bowl with barium glaze, fired to 1320°c, made by
Oldrich Asenbryl at Sarn Pottery, 2007, diam. 17 cm
Private collection

Rich set up Narberth Pottery in Pembrokeshire'.[59] The business they had built up
in Tisbury proved successful enough to enable them both to start up on their own.
Both the Sarn and Narberth Potteries are still working today, and both Asenbryl
and Rich have made a continuous living from making and selling ceramics for the
past 45 years, without needing to supplement their income by teaching.

Rich had always been drawn to the scenery of Pembrokeshire, and bought an
eighteenth-century bakehouse in the small town of Narberth, with the requisite
space for a workshop and gallery. Together with his wife Catherine, and latterly
with their daughter Bryony, they have built up a distinctive range of ceramics
with exciting glazes that have been sought out by collectors around the world. He
is best known for his ceramics with crystalline glazes, a technique that he has been
perfecting for the past 25 years. The zinc crystal glaze applied to porcelain is made
by melting sand, soda ash, alumina, zinc and flint into a glass compound, which
is then ground to a fine powder. Before glazing, an exact amount is weighed out
for each pot, and metal oxides are then added to produce a variety of colours. The
pieces are fired to 1270°c, and when the kiln temperature has cooled to 1140°c, that
temperature is held for up to five hours to allow the zinc oxide to form crystals.
Catherine Rich's primary interest is lustre work, with gold, platinum, copper and

mother-of-pearl lustres applied and fired on to the surface in up to four firings, over a soft ivory crackle glaze. Simon Rich has also explored other techniques, including terra sigillata and raku, along with glazed ware ranging in colour from azurite-blue to deep rich reds; his daughter, Bryony, continues this work.[60]

Bryony studied art, fashion and textiles and after travelling extensively around Thailand and Sri Lanka, she returned in 1998 to work alongside her father, while also working as a chef. In 2009 she took over the management of the pottery

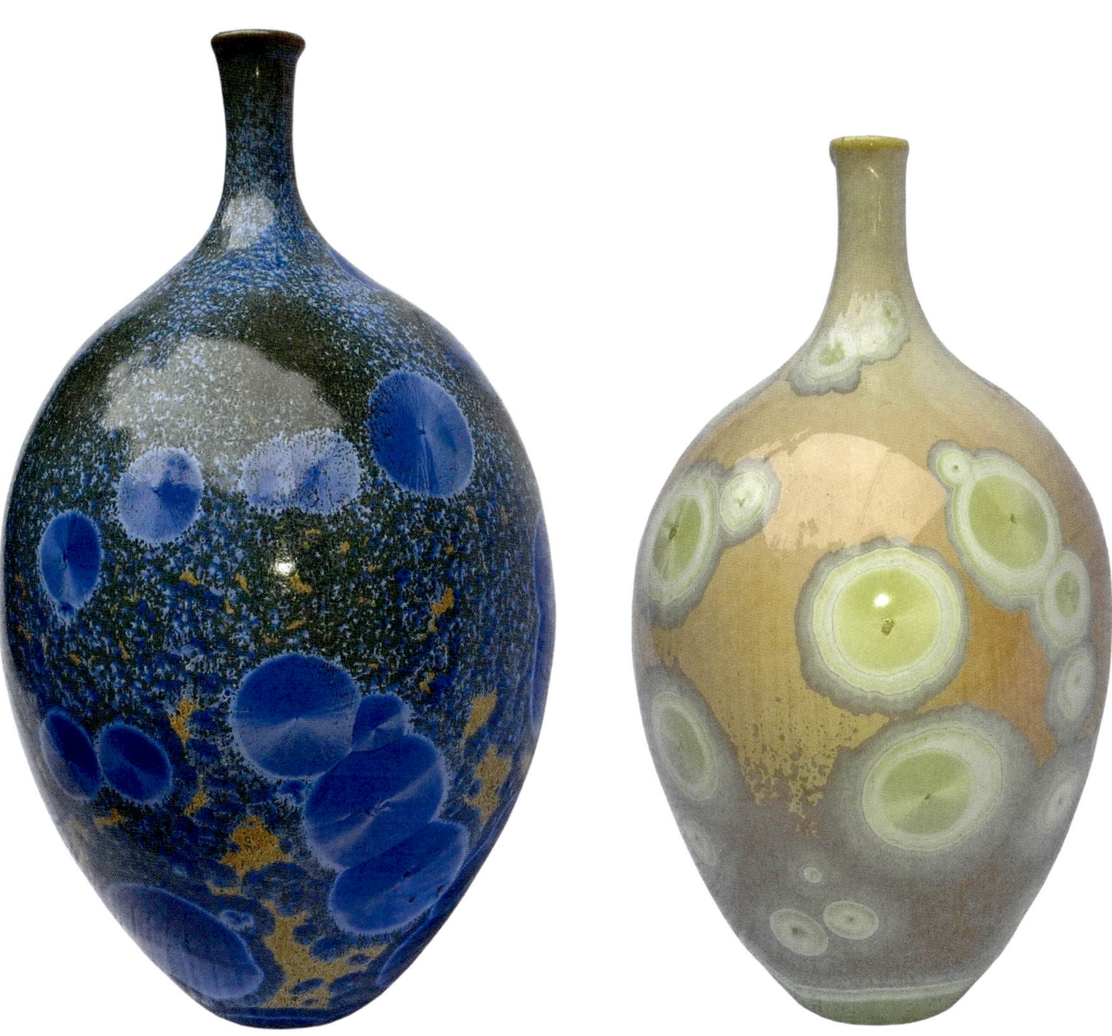

Vases with crystalline glaze made by Simon Rich at Narberth Pottery, 2017,
left: h. 26 cm, w. 15 cm; right: h. 17 cm, w. 8 cm
Private collection

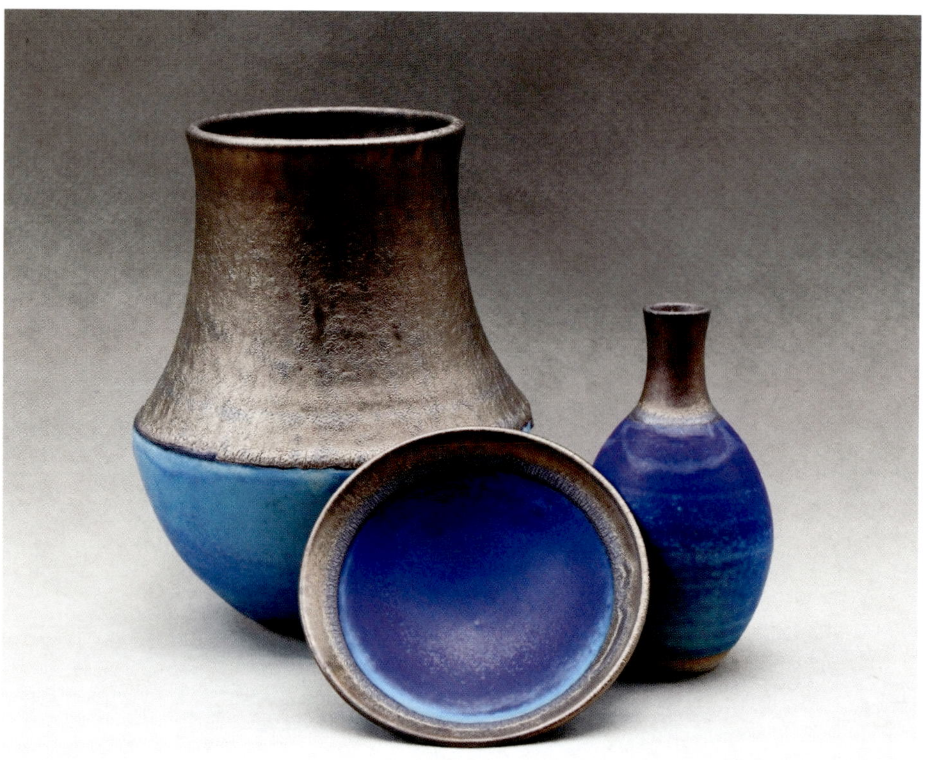

Lapis lazuli blue stoneware with bronze rims made by Bryony Rich at Narberth Pottery, 2017,
large vase h. 30 cm; bowl diam. 10 cm; small vase h. 15 cm
Collection Bryony Rich

studio and gallery, where she has carried on developing her father's legacy. Bryony
has had exhibitions all over England and Wales and is currently supplying over a
dozen galleries.[61]

Graham Adamson had introduced Asenbryl to the Bible while they were sharing No. 29. Caiger-Smith recalls Asenbryl saying that 'it was forbidden to read
that book in Czechoslovakia; the Communists said it was all lies, but the book
has many interesting ideas'.[62] In due course Asenbryl began to pray regularly, and
this helped him a great deal when at the age of 41 he suffered a stroke that left
him paralysed down his left side. Although he was told he would have to spend
the rest of his life in a wheelchair, he believed that by praying and doing exercise
he would find a way through, which he did. He remained partially paralysed but
courageously taught himself to make pots, decorate them and fire the kiln, all
with just one hand. He also went on to have a successful second marriage, and he
and his wife Jenny brought up his two daughters from his first marriage and her
two daughters from a previous marriage, at the pottery in Sarn Meyllteyrn on
the beautiful Llyn Peninsula.[63] He and Jenny are still creating high-fired reduction

stoneware and porcelain sculptures nearly fifty years later, using glazes mixed from locally found materials such as wood ash and red clay from nearby Hell's Mouth beach, as well as their Sarn red glaze, achieved with the use of copper oxide. They use cobalt, iron, vanadium and chrome oxides for on-glaze decoration. Sarn ceramics have been exhibited and continue to be collected all over the world.

Harriet Owen and Jenny Jowett both joined the Pottery in 1971, at a time when there were plenty of orders to keep everyone busy. Owen had been living on a kibbutz in Israel and had returned to London but was eager to get away again. She saw an advertisement for a job at the Pottery and loved the idea of making pottery and living in a rural village, although she had never made a pot in her life. Unfortunately the vacancy had been taken, but she was invited to come down to Aldermaston to have a look round. She recalls her utter delight when she received a letter from Caiger-Smith saying that although the initial position had already been filled, 'I like you so much that I've decided to make room for you too!'[64]

Owen was another of the potters who was welcomed to live with the family at Shalford Farm House. After six months she was invited to share No. 29, where Graham Adamson was now living with David Anthony (who was also known as 'Little David) after Asenbryl had left. Owen remembers earning £8 a week, with 3 guineas going on rent, 10 shillings on gas and 10 shillings on electricity, which left very little. There was no telephone and no television in those days, but none of those things mattered. She said they made disgusting home-made wine and fed themselves from the village shop opposite the cottage; on Friday evenings they would all pile into the back of 'Big David' Tipler's old postman's van and invade the local supermarket in Tadley, becoming known as 'the hippie lot from Aldermaston'. Owen worked at Aldermaston until 1975, when she left to work in London for the Craft Potters Association; she describes her years at Aldermaston as the happiest of her life.[65]

Visitors to the Pottery would often comment on its special atmosphere, which seems now to exist only when a place has hardly changed over the years, and retains the peace of past lives, the ghosts from a time when life was slower and more rhythmical, and people held different values. Aldermaston village had also changed very little since the early 1940s, and apart from the gradual increase in traffic over the decades, the whole scene had remained virtually unchanged for centuries.

Myra McDonnell remembers:

the lovely old brick-built buildings that were clustered either side of The Street greatly enhanced a visit to the Pottery. Looking up the hill from the old Hind's Head pub and the village shop at the bottom of The Street were the grand gates and lodges to Aldermaston Park, and beyond the gates and further up the hill was the Atomics Weapons Research Establishment (AWRE), a surprisingly regular collector of Caiger-Smith's pots over the years, with several reportedly even going out to Los Alamos National Laboratory! The Pottery itself only showed a blank brick wall from the street, with only a small kiln-fume etched window. Beyond the old stable doors, by the back of the electric kiln, there were racks of terracotta biscuit pots on shelves nearby. It was always a surprise for new visitors to find themselves in this charming old workshop, stepping back into the past, as many said. Alan loved objects that work aesthetically or practically, so the pottery was littered with objects, some in use well beyond their natural life, which added to its charm. There was a much-mended Victorian enamel washing up bowl from the workshop, which was just the perfect depth and shape to wash pots in! The pottery was just another layer on top of the blacksmith's shop. The thick slab of wood and the shallow game sink recycled from somewhere. The windows that Anne-Marie had glazed with glue overlapping the old glass panes, diffusing and spreading the light, and outlining the jars and pots of oxides. The beautiful wood-blocked floor of the original stable, which smelt of horse urine when it was cleaned! The hayloft gallery, which was up perilously steep stairs, and all kitted out in a 60s Scandinavian style. Outside was the gravel laid courtyard, and the orchard of mistletoe-hung apple trees, where we all collected for coffee breaks in the summer months. There was the modern workshop where Alan and Edgar worked, sometimes with one of the more senior potters, and of course the wood-kiln, with its attractive store of wood stacked in great symmetrical piles. It was a picturesque place of harmony, and a place to escape to. Alan recognised this and he often housed people in their times of woe, to allow the environment to soothe them.[66]

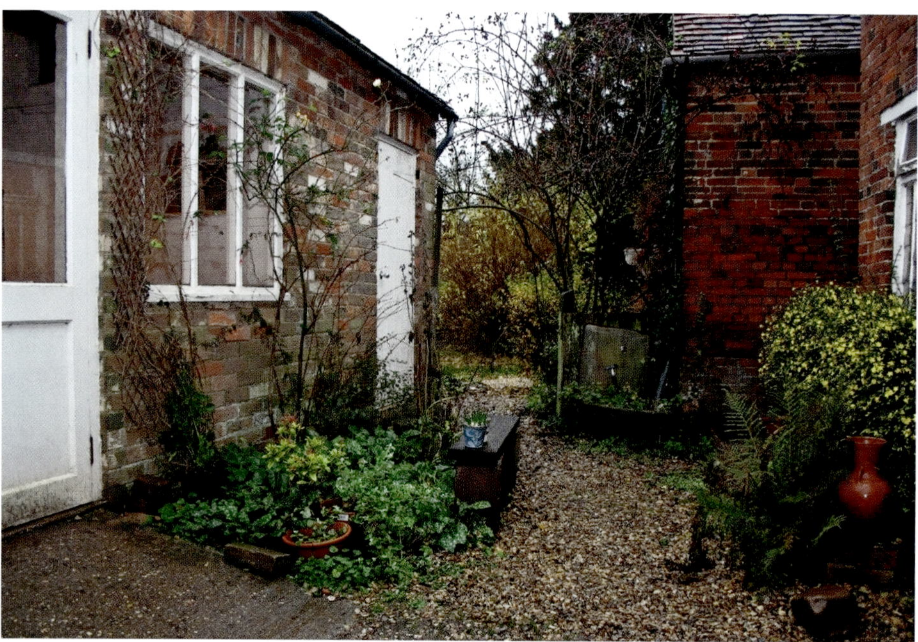

The gravel courtyard at the back of the Pottery

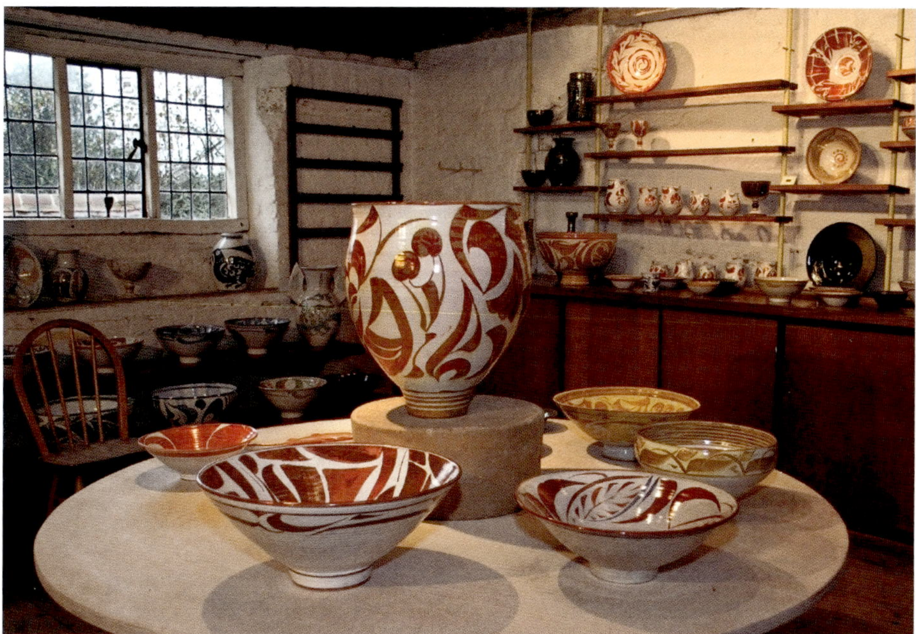

The hayloft showroom upstairs at the Pottery

Gill Bent, another assistant, writes:

> once inside the pottery it was like escaping into another world, the unchanged interior of the old forge making it all the more atmospheric. Everything about the pottery seemed to be from a different era and Alan was proud of the fact the building had changed little since he turned it into a pottery.[67]

Jaki Rothery, who came to work at Aldermaston a few years later, describes the warm and welcoming atmosphere:

> As I did not live in the village, I generally cycled to Aldermaston, and was often the first to arrive in the workshop, so in winter it fell to me, more often than not, to light the stove. It was lovely to come into an empty, quiet workshop – even if the weather was inhospitable, the pottery never was. It had a warmth and cosiness about it, which I often felt was due to it originally being a forge. I've been in many as my partner is a blacksmith, and they are invariably permeated with a particular atmosphere that I can only assume derives from a long history of heat; hard, skilled, physical toil; and the silent spirit of powerful but acquiescent animals.[68]

For Rungwe Kingdon, whose father, Jonathan, was a great friend of Caiger-Smith's, the smell of the Pottery remains an overriding memory of his visits:

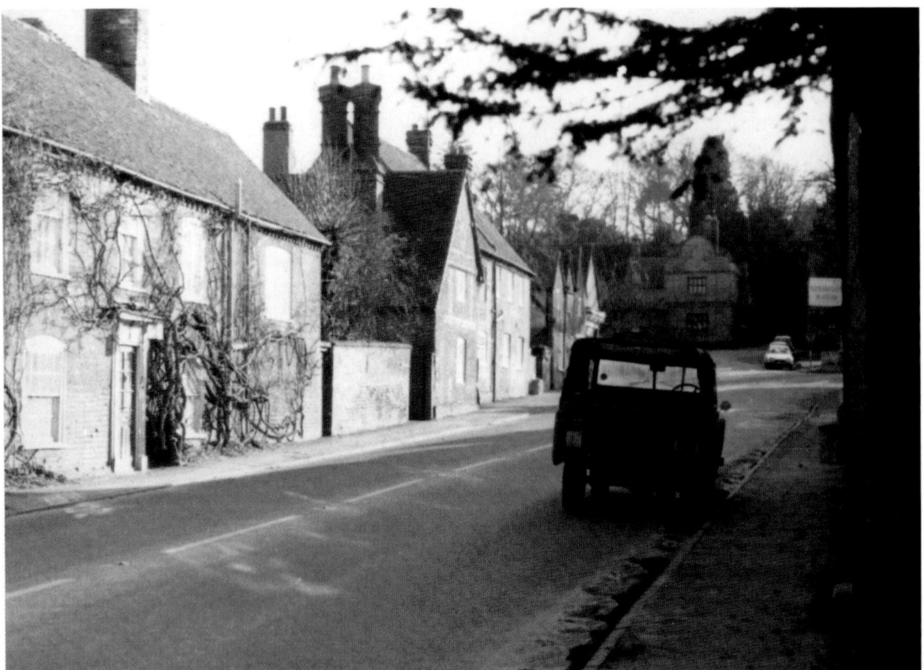

The Land Rover parked in The Street, outside the Pottery, 1978; Helen Caiger-Smith's
house (with pitched roof) is across the road, with Tile Cottage beyond it

> It smelt of dryness and damp, of wood-firing and the lustreware burning, the
> willow wood drying, and then there were the glazes, the clay, the smell of the
> processes… The smell of a place is very enticing and attractive, it sums up and
> evokes a sense of past and present at the same time.[69]

He recalls the Pottery's highly creative and industrious atmosphere. It was a
dynamic group of craftsmen working towards one goal, with an artist and master
craftsman, Caiger-Smith, at the head of it all, just as workshops had been struc-
tured in past centuries. Kingdon could see that a group could achieve so much
more than one person working alone. He was so impressed by the working prac-
tices at Aldermaston that when he and his wife Claude established the Pangolin
Foundry at Chalford near Stroud, now the largest bronze foundry in the UK, he
modelled it on what he had seen at Aldermaston.[70]

In one of several attempts to collaborate with industry, in 1972 Caiger-Smith
began an association with Denby Pottery to develop a range of tableware decorated with Aldermaston-style brushwork. He has described the challenges of
working in a factory, where it was difficult to replicate the softer pigments used at
the Pottery and to train decorators in the subtleties of the brushworked designs.
Although studio potters often toyed with having a working relationship with
industrial ceramics in those years, it was hard to come to a happy arrangement.[71]

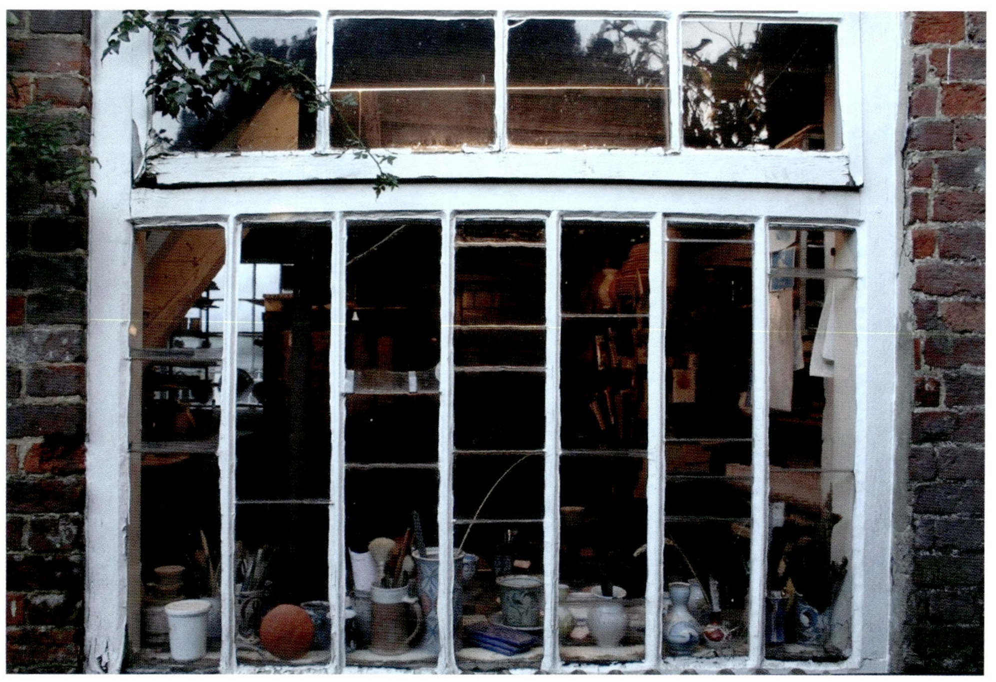

View through the window into the front workshop

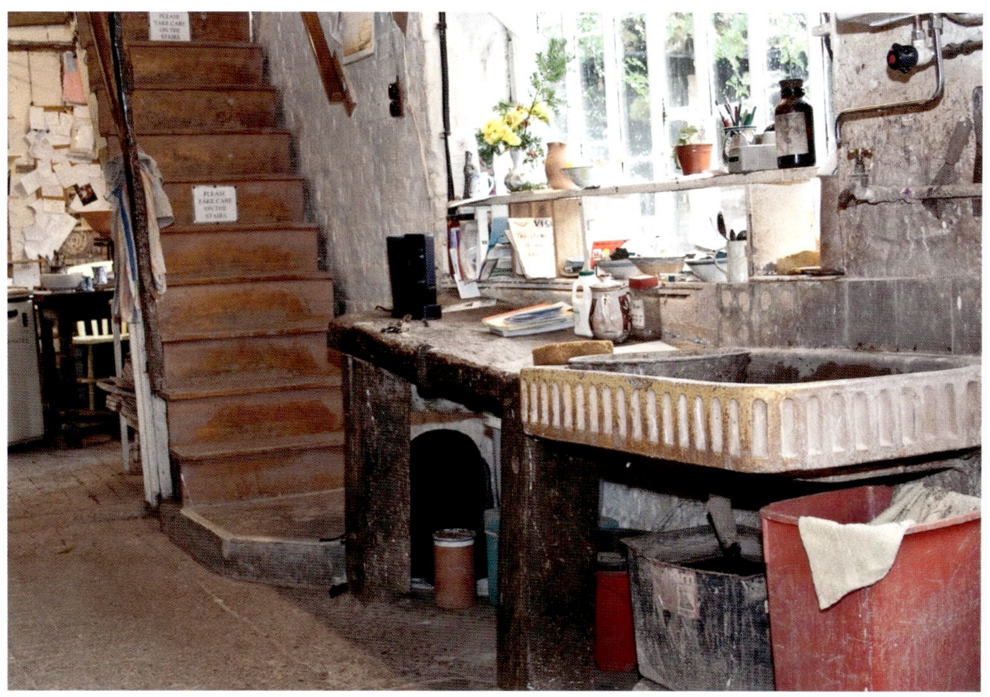

The stairs leading up to the showroom

Another attempt to work alongside industry was when Caiger-Smith designed a small range of wares for Honiton Pottery in Devon, and subsequently went to the factory to train the painters in the brushwork. However, it was not a great success: the range was mainly sold in Barcelona and was eventually discontinued. It seemed that Caiger-Smith had been over-optimistic in believing that a small workshop could collaborate with industry.[72]

Jenny Jowett was the only person ever employed on a part-time basis at the Pottery, and also the only one to have had a specific job. She was a botanical painter and had no ambition to be a potter. In 1971 she was teaching an evening class and looking for a part-time job to supplement her income. One day she was in Aldermaston leaving some pictures to be framed when she saw the Pottery. When she got home she phoned up to see if there were any part-time vacancies, to which Caiger-Smith replied that he did not take part-timers but she was welcome to visit the Pottery. When they met he conceded that she could come for one day a week – on a Friday. She then said Friday was no good, so he capitulated again, and said she could come on Mondays. Jowett only ever worked as a decorator and became known as the painter of the 'owl' mugs, with their distinctive brush pattern that when viewed from a certain angle could be said to resemble an owl. She also decorated the lustre tiles, which were becoming very popular. Although Caiger-Smith resisted piecework in principle, painting on the mugs and tiles was not dependent on the form of the piece, and although the work was repetitive Jowett painted creatively in her own right:

> I had four small children and thought how great it would be to be part of a workshop. Alan agreed to 'give me a go' as I'd never painted on tin glaze, and so I became the 'Monday Girl'. I joined a very happy 'family', and was immediately included. It took a while to really get the hang of the brushes (so different from watercolour, which was my medium). Alan was always so encouraging. I don't think anyone had thought about me long-term. For the first year or two I had a packed lunch with Juliet (Wilson), who has remained a friend to this day, and when she left Alan said, 'Why don't you come and have lunch with Anne-Marie and me', and so for twenty years that was my Mondays. They became like a second family, as their four boys were a similar age to my four.[73]

Caiger-Smith later admitted to Jowett that he had only expected her to stay for a few months; she worked at the Pottery for 22 years until it closed in 1993.

In 1974 Jowett began painting full-time as a botanical artist alongside her Mondays in the Pottery, and Caiger-Smith helped her with her first exhibitions and wrote pieces for her catalogues. She became an artist of world renown, her work appearing in many public and private collections including the Royal Botanical Gardens at Kew and the collection of the late Diana, Princess of Wales. She was a founder member of the Society of Botanical Artists, President of the Society of Floral Painters, and her work is also included in the Highgrove Florilegium. Now in her eighties, Jowett still teaches and paints. She says that the experience of

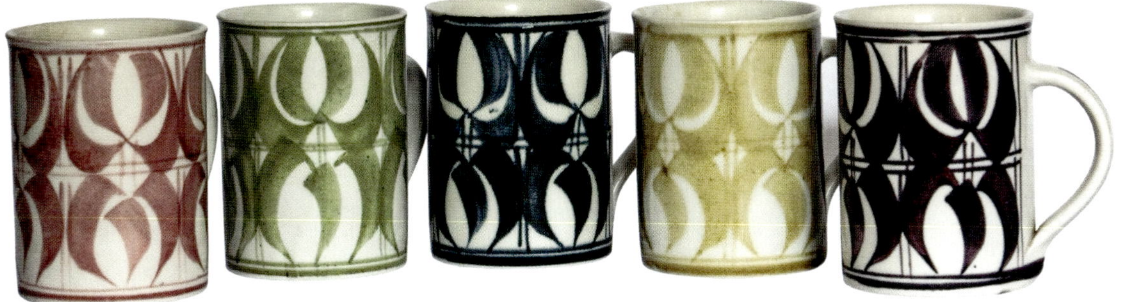

'Owl' mugs decorated by Jenny Jowett, 1979–86, h. 9.5 cm, w. 6.9 cm
Collection Alan Caiger-Smith

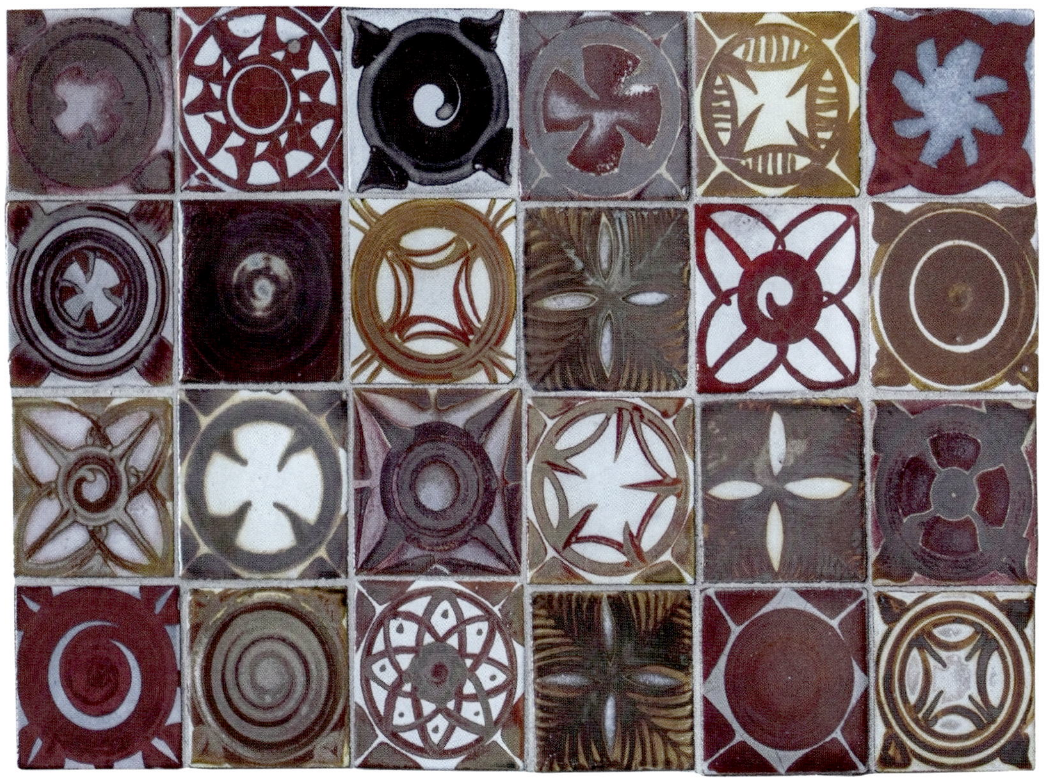

Lustre tile panel decorated by Jenny Jowett, 1980, 32 × 39 cm
Collection Nick Caiger-Smith

working at Aldermaston enriched her life enormously, and that she felt privileged to be the only person employed there part-time over all those years.[74]

Juliet Wilson left Aldermaston in 1972 to pursue her own career, teaching pottery at her old school, Downe House, and then pottery and drawing at Marlborough College. She went on to set up her own studio in the Quantock Hills, where she still works today, making clay relief panels, often depicting the surrounding countryside, as well as painting. She believes that what she took from her time at Aldermaston was much deeper than technical knowledge: although it gave her a skill, more importantly it taught her 'how to work'. Now retired, she spent most of her professional working life as designer and co-performer in 'Brog Puppets', a travelling puppet theatre run jointly with her husband:

> we developed our Puppet Theatre Company from nothing into a successful small business that lasted for 25 years. Looking back, I'm sure that the things I learned about belief in artistic purpose and hard graft encouraged me to take risks, and believe that however small our income was, or however tough it was at times, we had confidence in our work because actually it *was* good. Alan has never suffered from false modesty and he has every right to feel proud, and I am so grateful to him for giving me that strength too.[75]

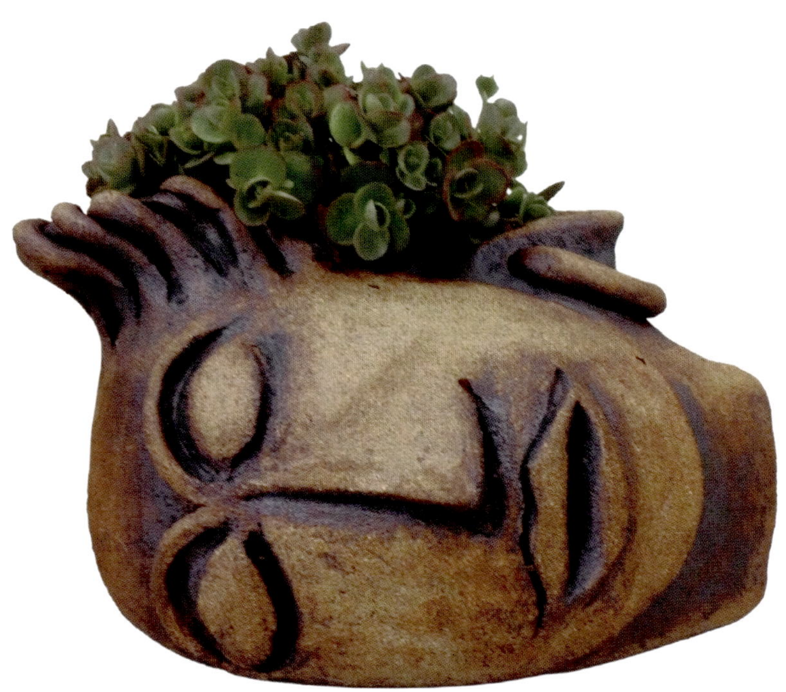

'Reclining Head' by Juliet Harkness (née Wilson), 2017, h. 23 cm, w. 39 cm
Collection Mr and Mrs Paul McGrath

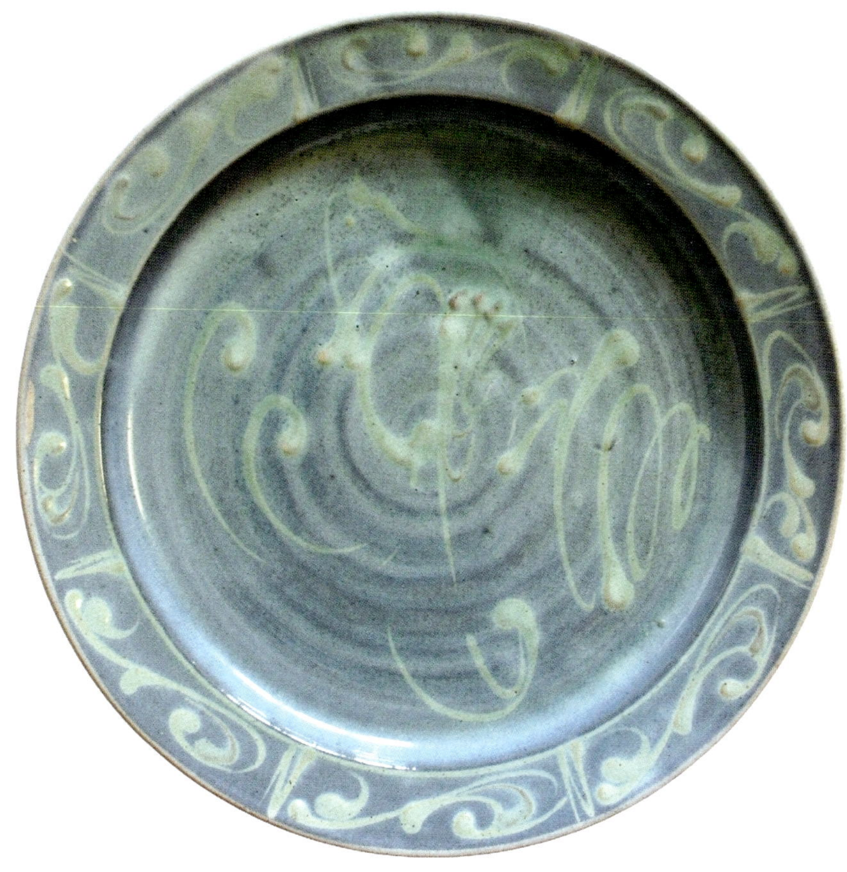

Plate with white glaze over white slip-trailed decoration on blue-slipped
background by Graham Adamson, 1993, diam. 33 cm, h. 4.4 cm
Collection Graham Adamson

In 1973 Graham Adamson moved to North Wales, where he set up a workshop
in one half of an eighteenth-century farm labourer's cottage and lived with his
wife in the other. He continued to work as a potter for 12 years, and then for
over twenty years as a teacher of crafts, including ceramics and printmaking, at
a local residential college for young adults with special needs. In retirement he
continues pursuing his fascination with ceramics, his experiments with ash glazes
inspired by a distant memory of Aldermaston, where he first saw 'the beautiful
jade green glaze on the inside of the firebox arch, where the willow ash had settled
and combined with the clay of the brickwork'.[76]

— 5 —

New Beginnings and Discovering Lustre
1973–1975

In 1973 Alan Caiger-Smith was appointed Chairman of the British Crafts Centre,[1] a post he held for five years. It was also in 1973 that the book on which he had been working for many years, *Tin-Glaze Pottery in Europe and the Islamic World*, was published, to wide acclaim. This was a busy time for the Pottery: with eight employees plus one part-time assistant, it was becoming increasingly obvious that more space was needed. So it was decided that a new building should be erected behind the main Pottery, on land occupied by sheds. Caiger-Smith recalls:

> Everyone understood that working in the Pottery involved a lot more than making pots. When it began the premises were almost derelict and they had to be put into working order and made 'visitable' … The most extensive alteration was the demolition of the old buildings behind the yard and the construction of the new workshops in 1973. Anne-Marie and I worked out a general plan, and she specified the details in a set of drawings. We then had to decide whether to engage builders, which would entail considerable expense and disruption, or to do as much of the work as possible ourselves. The whole team agreed without hesitation on the DIY option. We spent most of the summer excavating, laying concrete, collecting materials with the Land Rover and trailer, laying foundations, building brick courses, and erecting roof trusses, helped by a local joiner and a builder. It was a dry summer and the work progressed rapidly. The only setback was Anne-Marie's fall when she was constructing the roof. This led to several weeks in hospital with a broken spine, which was totally repaired by expert medical treatment and never troubled her again. Everyone worked even harder to make up for the accident, and Anne-Marie and I were amazed at what they had achieved when we returned after her convalescence. Harriet [Owen] told me later, 'We loved what we were doing and we got on much faster once the boss and his wife were out of the way!' Only a small quantity of pots could be produced while all this was going on, but the place remained open and the visitors' comments encouraged us.[2]

Campden and Tipler proved to be excellent bricklayers and carpenters, and by August 1974 the new extension was completed, having been built almost entirely by the potters. For the first time there was adequate space to store biscuitware and to stack and store wood for firing; it also provided a packing area, and the building was dry and warm in winter. But most importantly, it created space for the

80

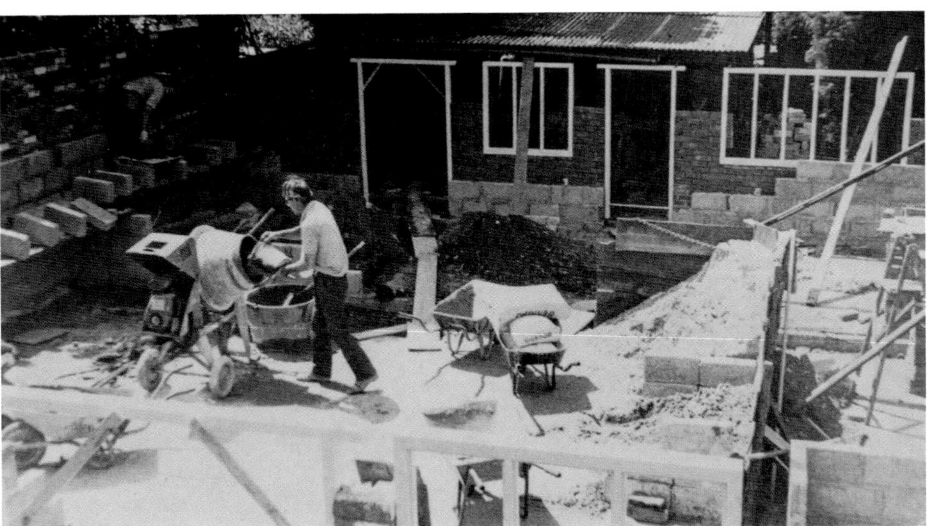

The construction of the back workshop behind the main pottery building, 1973

potters to compare and consider their work, to think more clearly, and to make bigger pots.

The 1970s were good years for the Pottery, and although its output was still very different from the dominant aesthetic at that time, it had widespread public appeal. The pottery was a fresh contrast to the predominant browns and greys of the high-fired reduction stoneware that was being produced by the majority of potteries at the time, and Aldermaston pieces were starting to reach a public that appreciated the beautiful iridescent reduced lustre. By 1974 the lustreware was at last beginning to emerge from firing in the second wood kiln with some consistency, after a decade of trial and error.

The predominant characteristics of lustreware are colour, movement and light. Caiger-Smith believed that 'the sensation of light, its meaning and associations, belongs to all lustre, old or new … and according to the nature of the mind that perceives them these lustres are as full or empty of meaning as the dawn or the moon or the dusk, sunlight over water … the moon half hidden by clouds or the iridescence hidden in a sea shell'.[3] Writing about the extraordinary vitality of the old Moorish brushwork on fifteenth-century lustred Hispano-Moresque wares, he has said that 'its roots are deeper than matters of technique or stylistic convention or skill. They lie in what people are in themselves, and in what they feel about what they do, and they are as deeply hidden as the roots of all poetry, whether of word or line or colour.'[4] For him a living tradition passed down through the centuries was more than just the sum of its technical processes and skills; it enabled deep feelings to come to the surface through what were after all merely lines and shapes painted on a simple glaze, giving one piece an inner content while a similar piece may be simply decorative.[5]

Graham Adamson recalled Caiger-Smith's unique approach to decoration, and in particular his brushwork on the lustreware:

> The contrasting formality of pattern and the lively energy of Alan's brushwork seemed to me to be inspired by an element of statement and storytelling (Alan was very fond of telling stories in our coffee breaks – particularly stories from the East), and the strength and character of the lettering on the pots of Spanish and Islamic craftsmen. Alan's very personal vision and understanding of the Hispano-Moresque pottery gave the tradition new life. His decoration, particularly on the lustreware, was obviously the result of protracted and challenging research and imaginative experimentation, with little to refer or relate to in the work of modern potters. Alan persevered, and his hard work began to pay dividends. Even so, the practical difficulties of the reduced firing procedure, especially for lustres in a wood-fired kiln, did not give time to relax or take things for granted. Though the results were amazingly rewarding, not all the often complex patterned pots were successful – although the majority of the pots had some redeeming characteristics, even if not to Alan's liking. They were still imbued with an organic and lively sense of enjoyment. The rhythms of shape and colour blended so well, and to such a high degree of harmonisation, that the pots were charged with a life of their own.[6]

It was not until some years later that Adamson realised that many of his own shapes and decoration were informed and influenced by what he had learned at Aldermaston:

> Although I used various slips under mainly honey glazes, rather than a tin glaze and oxides as at Aldermaston, my brush strokes and slip-trailed shapes drew very much on the energetic 'dance' movement that I believed was the inspiration for Aldermaston designs. Alan would describe the flow and the movement of the wonderful Japanese brushes as a 'series of breaths'. Providing the stroke began from a still and centred point, and confidently moved to a natural end, the expansion and contraction of the brush between the two points would take care of itself. Alan had managed to purchase a highly prized stock of these brushes, and they were valued for their particular 'flow and energy'. They were used in a combination with Western 'square-ended' brushes, and the behaviour of the two different brushes was complementary, the square-ended type giving the suggestion of solidity and latent energy, and the Japanese brushes the movement of dance, counter moves being very important. The decoration of the pots at Aldermaston built up a very animated vocabulary.[7]

The problems with the lustre had begun after the installation of the second wood-fired kiln in 1964, and for the following seven years the rate of loss from the lustre firings was about 70% but no one could explain why. This was especially frustrating as the first wood-fired kiln had actually produced some very beautiful lustre; but however much Caiger-Smith pored over his meticulous records, he was still at a loss to understand what was going wrong. There were, however, enough good pieces coming from the firings to sustain hope to persevere, and it was these that held the clue. The good pieces, whiter with a stronger lustre, seemed to come from the area in the kiln from which the test rings were extracted. These rings of fired clay had the same glaze and lustre pigments applied to them as the rest of the work in the kiln, and were positioned so that they could be removed towards the end of the firing, being hooked out on a long, thin iron rod, in order to check the progress of the lustre development; when the lustre had developed sufficiently, no more wood was added to the kiln and everything was shut down. In order to access the test rings a small brick in the door had to be removed, which allowed some air into that part of the kiln. Although Caiger-Smith would do this as quickly as possible, supposing that the air would spoil the lustre by re-oxidising it, this airing was in fact the clue.[8]

During the mid-1970s he had begun work co-editing and translating (with Ronald Lightbown, Keeper of the library at the Victoria and Albert Museum, where the original was held) a facsimile of Piccolpasso's *I tre libri dell'arte del vasajo* (*The Three Books of the Potter's Art*), written about 1557. Here Caiger-Smith confirmed what he was already beginning to suspect, which ultimately proved to be the key to the successful firing of lustre. In the book, having discussed lustre firing with Vincenzo, son of master lustre potter Maestro Giorgio Andreoli, Piccolpasso wrote:

> The fuel for it should be straw or else willow-branches, well dried and free from damp: keep up the fire with these for three hours, after which, and already the kiln will be beginning to show a certain glow, take broom or spartium, as Dioscorides calls it, well dried and seasoned, and leaving off the willow give it an hour of fire with this.[9]

Caiger-Smith realised that as broom is a bulky material, it could only have been added if the previous charge of fuel had died down to allow sufficient space for it, so there must have been a period of oxidation or relatively clear burning before the next period of reduction. This all made sense, and also explained why the best lustre pieces came from the part of the kiln nearest to the spy hole where the test rings were withdrawn. What it showed was that the lustre was dependent on alternating periods of reduction and oxidation in the later stages of the firing. So in subsequent firings a full minute of clear burning was allowed between each spasm of smoky, reducing fire. This was repeated seven or eight times over a period of about an hour, and was enough to develop the lustre throughout the 160 cubic feet of the kiln.[10]

Once this vital piece of knowledge was understood, at long last the lustre firings became more reliable. During the following 30 years some outstandingly beautiful pieces were to emerge from the kiln, including some of the largest pieces of lustre to have been made since the fourteenth century. The journey to success had certainly been a long one; anyone else would surely have given up many years before. It is interesting that this 'new' knowledge was in fact centuries old, but with the shortage of documentation in the intervening years there had been little to go on. Written knowledge is a valuable resource: knowing this, Caiger-Smith would write the definitive book on the subject, *Lustre Pottery* (1985), in the hope that his own journey of discovery would help those wishing to work with this difficult medium in future.

A mark of the Pottery's success during the 1970s was the number of people it was able to employ: of the 138 listings in the 1974 *Directory of Potters* of the Craftsmen Potters Association, Aldermaston Pottery was given as employing no fewer than seven assistants; in fact at some times during that year there were nine, plus Jenny Jowett, working part-time. The only potters to employ more assistants at this time were Walter Cole and Reg Southcliffe, with nine and ten respectively. That same year Bernard Leach was employing five assistants, Ray Finch and Robin Welch four, Marianne De Trey and Alan Wallwork three, and David Leach and Michael Cardew, two.[11] Many of the potteries that did employ assistants had very poor working conditions, the majority of assistants either poorly paid or unpaid. Southcliffe, at Creigeau Pottery in Wales, for example, had no running water or sanitation, and very poor health and safety with regard to silica dust; one apprentice potter recalled that one could not see from one end of the workshop to the other for the clouds of dust produced from the fettling process.[12]

Although working conditions at Aldermaston were not luxurious, they were definitely more than adequate, especially after the new extension had been completed. Everyone was paid and described their experience at the Pottery as not only life-changing but also hugely enjoyable. Catherine Bennett, who came to work at the Pottery in the late 1970s, remembers:

> Alan provided accommodation for most of his employees in houses he owned in The Street, and also paid a weekly wage so that we were able to live comfortably, something quite rare at that time when many young people working for master potters were expected to finance their own apprenticeships.[13]

Caiger-Smith was also very careful to maintain the right balance of skilled workers and learners, and also the right number of assistants. He strayed from this path at his peril. Over the years the team had increased from four to eight, and then in 1975, encouraged by the Pottery's success, he increased it to ten, plus two part-time workers. Although more pottery was made and sold, the quality of the work declined, the overhead costs increased, and he found that he was spending more and more time sorting out misunderstandings, leaving little time for new projects or to do his own work. Around this time E.F. Schumacher's *Small is Beautiful* was published, and Caiger-Smith found the book a profound reassurance as Schumacher confirmed what he already felt: that for every activity there is an ideal size and number, that some things can only be done on a small scale, and in some areas of work enthusiasm, trust, experience, and the qualities of individuals, were more important than technology and expansion.[14] Just in time, several people left the Pottery, reducing the full-time team to eight, and the crisis, made

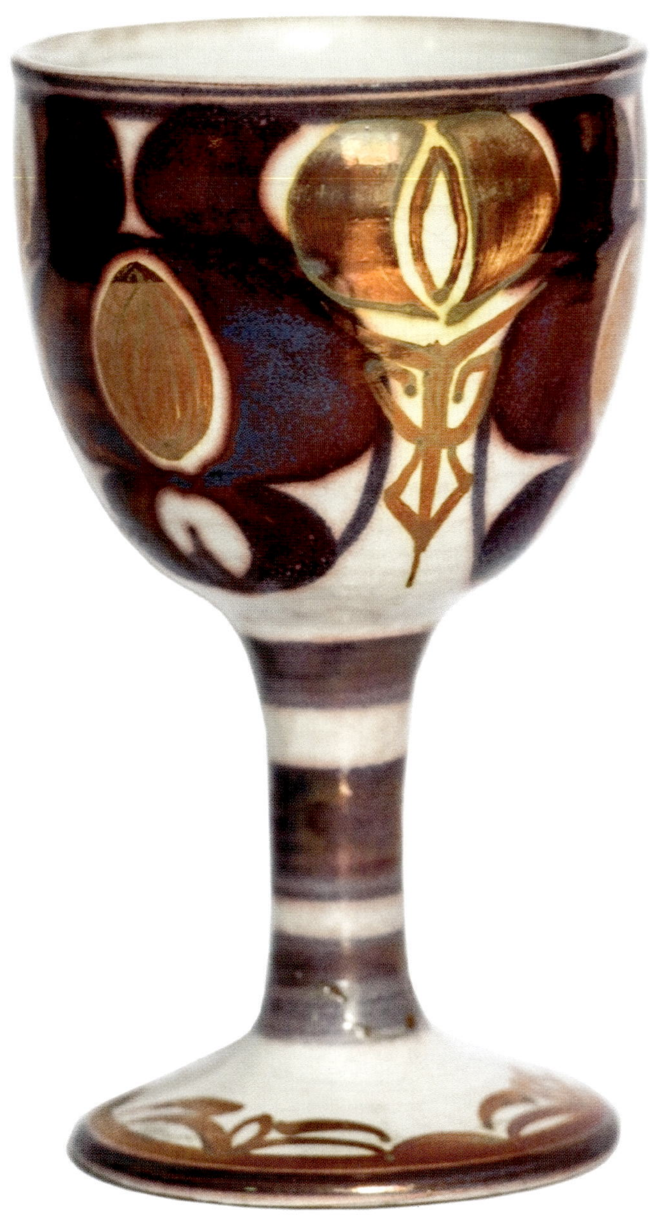

Tall lustre goblet by Alan Caiger-Smith,
1973, h. 15.25 cm, w. 8.6 cm
Collection Alan Caiger-Smith

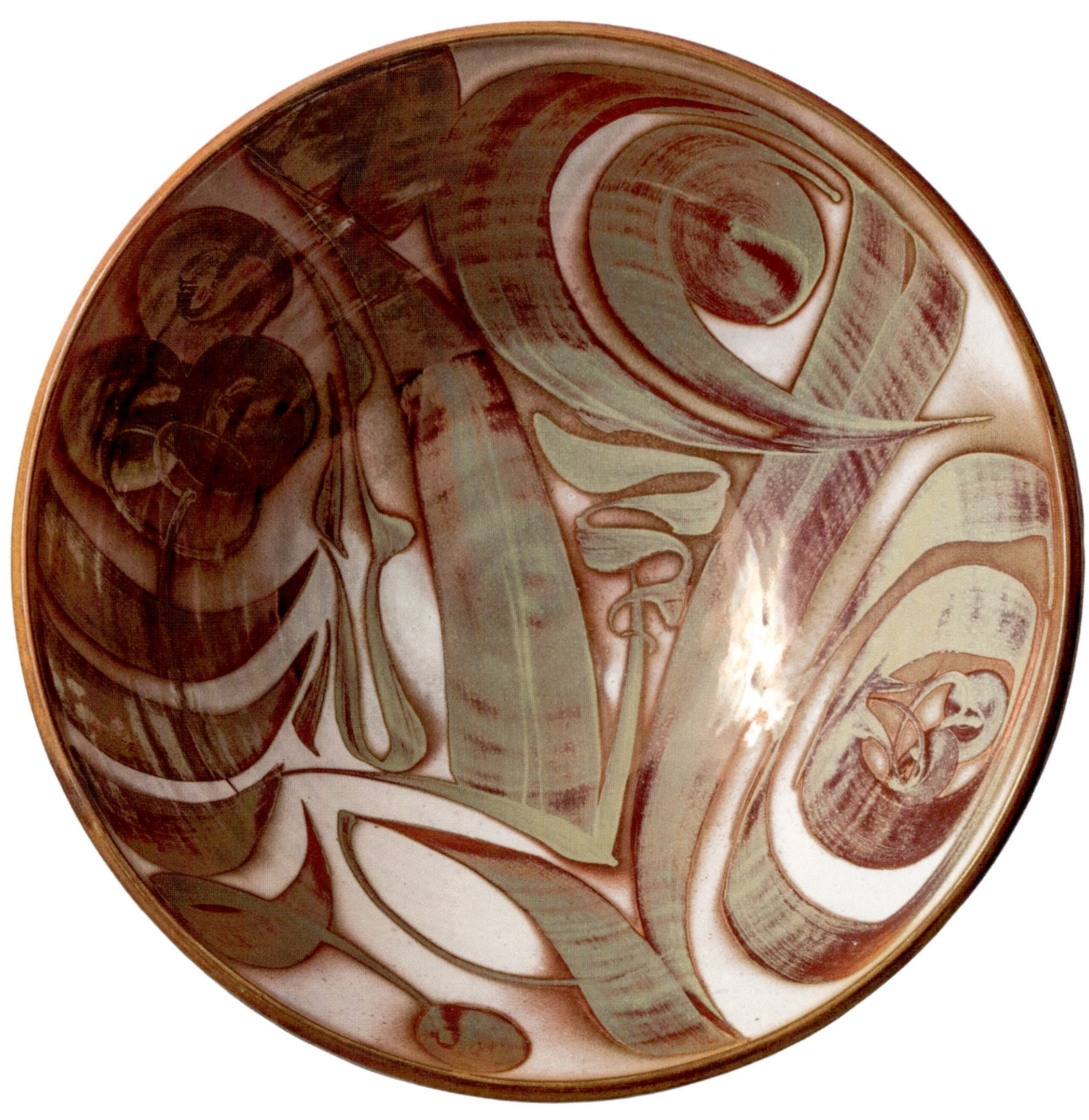

Large lustre bowl by Alan Caiger-Smith, 1977, diam. 49.5 cm, h. 16.75 cm
Collection Alan Caiger-Smith

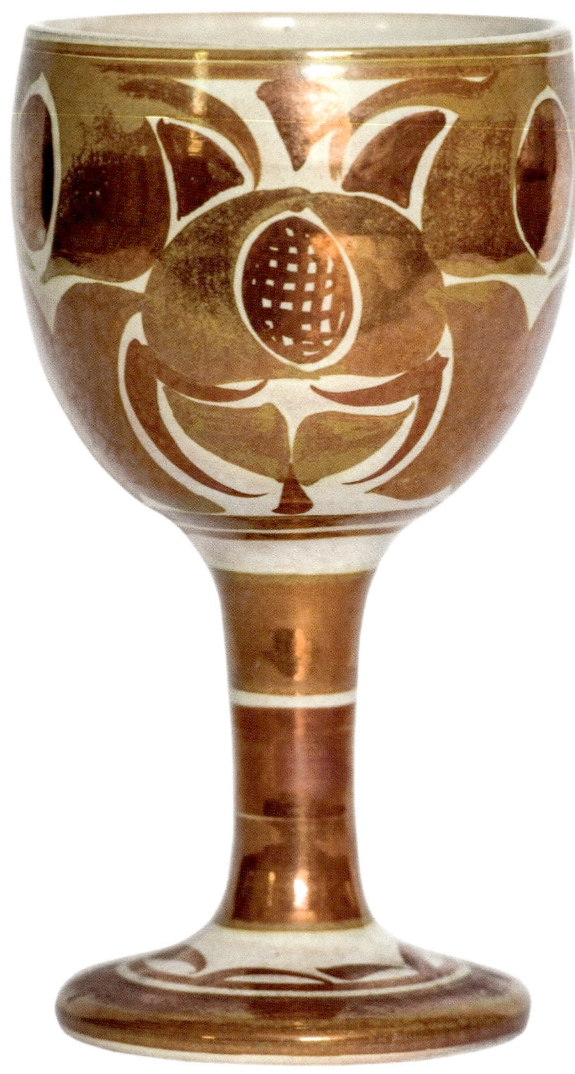

Tall lustre goblet with 'Smiling Pattern' by
Alan Caiger-Smith, 1978, h. 15.6 cm, w. 8.6 cm
Collection Alan Caiger-Smith

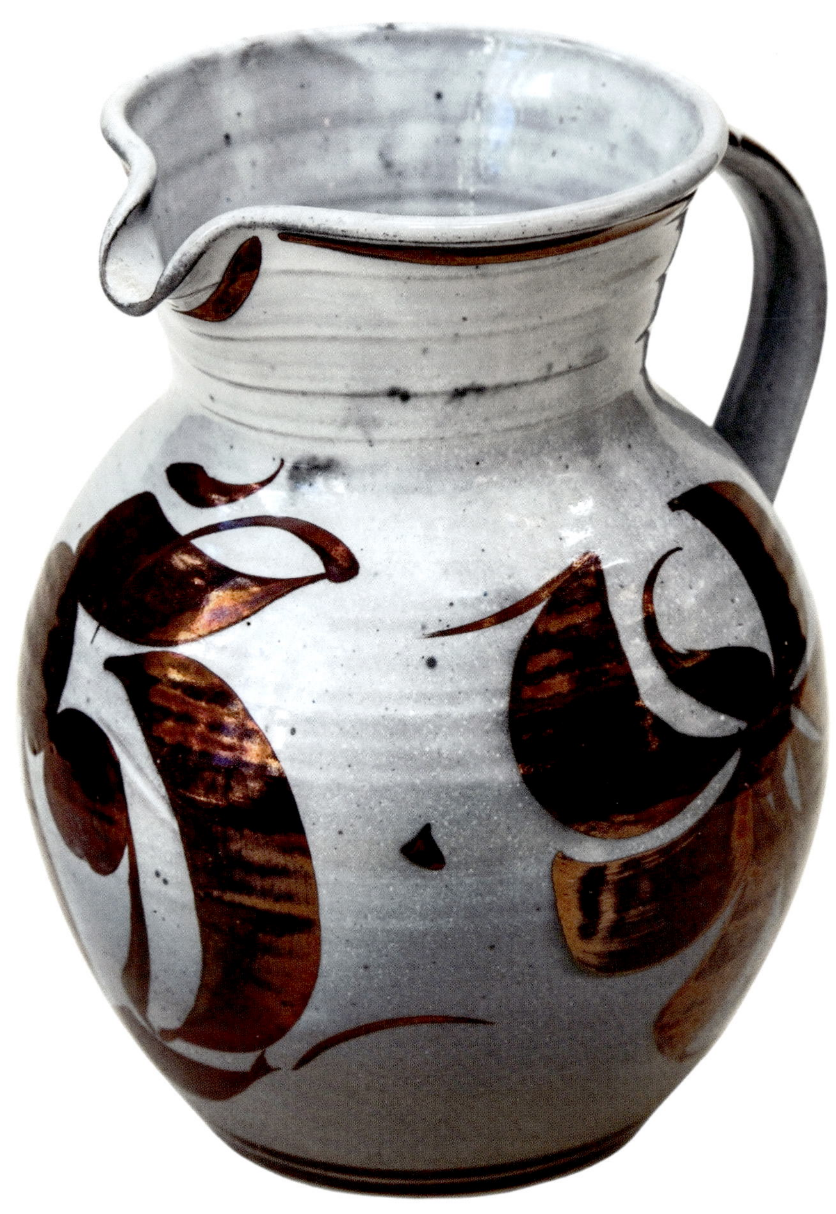

Gallon jug with copper lustre decoration by
Alan Caiger-Smith, 1979, h. 28 cm, w. 22 cm
Collection Sarah and Adrian Dixon

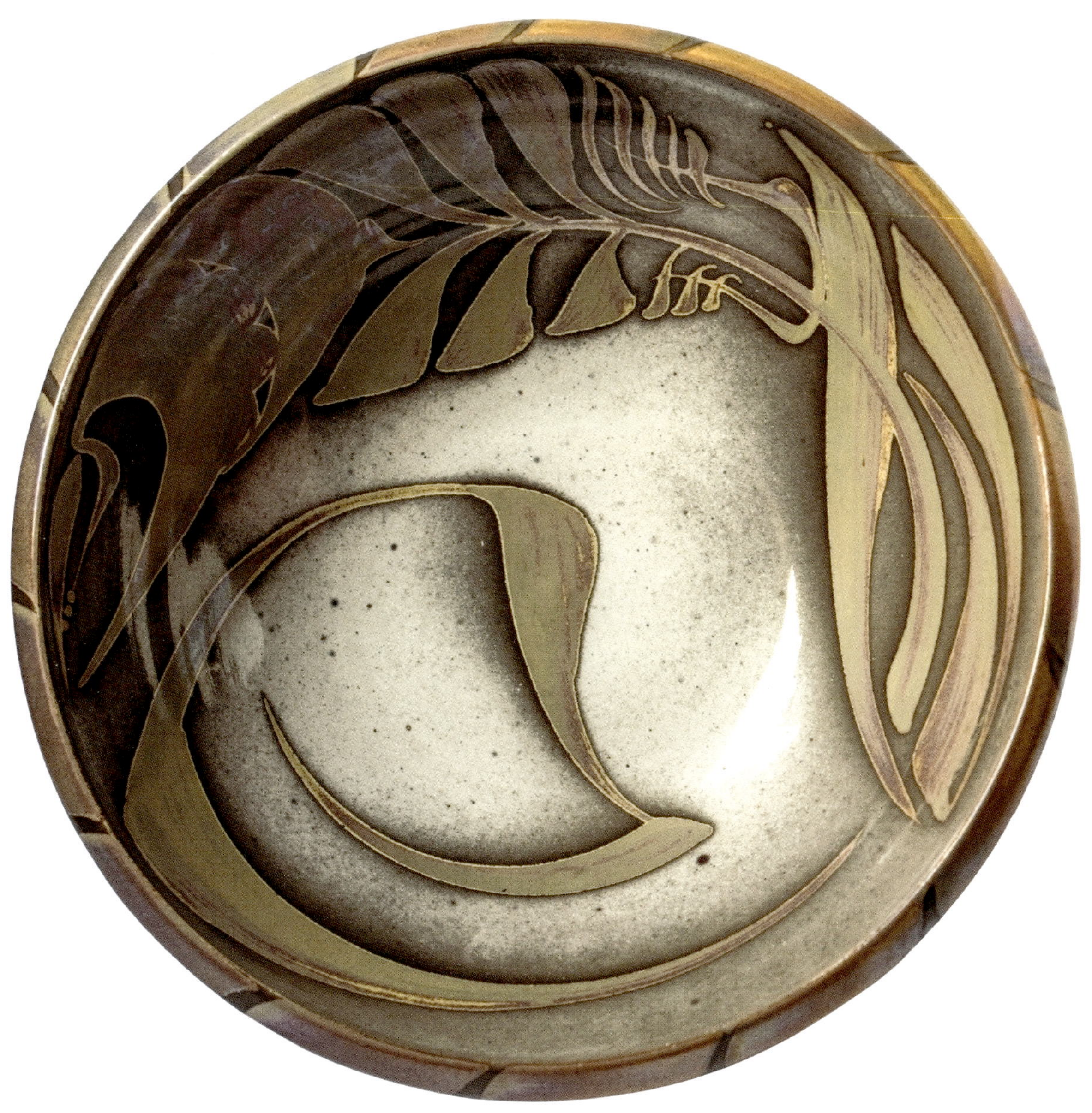

Lustre bowl decorated with silver on a reduced glaze
by Alan Caiger-Smith, 1979, diam. 28 cm, h. 8.8 cm
Collection Alan Caiger-Smith

worse by the onset of rapid inflation, was averted. Caiger-Smith was never again tempted to increase the working group above eight.[15]

Few of the larger potteries employing people at this time shared Caiger-Smith's philosophy with regard to the training of assistants in every aspect of working as potters. Walter Cole, for example, had become disenchanted with training assistants in all the necessary potting skills as early as the beginning of the 1960s, just a decade after setting up Rye Pottery, preferring instead to have employees whose job related to one particular element of the production.[16] It was Caiger-Smith's lasting legacy that he never gave up working in the way he believed was right, so everyone continued to participate in all aspects of running the Pottery.

One of the jobs that almost everyone enjoyed participating in was the collecting of willow wood as fuel for the wood-fired kiln. As Jaki Rothery, a young assistant working there at the time, recalled,

> just off The Street itself, suddenly you found yourself in something of a rural idyll, with the Kennet and Avon Canal just a few fields away, where flocks of Canada geese would come in daily during autumn and graze after the crops were taken, and hares could be seen frolicking in spring;[17]

It was here that the wood collection took place. Wood was collected at various times throughout the year, but during the late summer and early autumn, when the terrain was driest and most accessible, the job came into its own. Caiger-Smith describes the sheer joy of working outdoors until sunset on an exquisite autumn day, beside the silvery waters of the Kennet:

> When the leaves are just turning colour and come fluttering down in the sunlight into the wide fields on either side like flakes of gold … swans glide down-river … water hens, coot and mallard feeding and now and again disputing with loud squawks, and from time to time one caught sight of the dark back of a trout idling rhythmically against the current.[18]

He felt that working in such a place brought a special kind of companionship: words are seldom spoken, nor do they need to be, and the experience is absorbed gradually, to remain with you always.

Along the banks of the River Kennet, where felling willows for cricket bats took place, Caiger-Smith and his assistants were allowed to take any wood with a diameter of less than 9 inches. They were also permitted to take all the offcuts from the sawmill just behind the Post Office. Here wood with a diameter of more than 9 inches was cleft into four quarters, sawn, stacked and seasoned for making cricket bats.[19] So on sunny autumn days a group from the Pottery would set off with Caiger-Smith's Land Rover and trailer, plus chainsaw, axes and wedges, across to the water meadows where trees had just been felled, and they would saw the offcuts to length, split them to portable size, and eventually split them again before leaving them to dry. Caiger-Smith remembers:

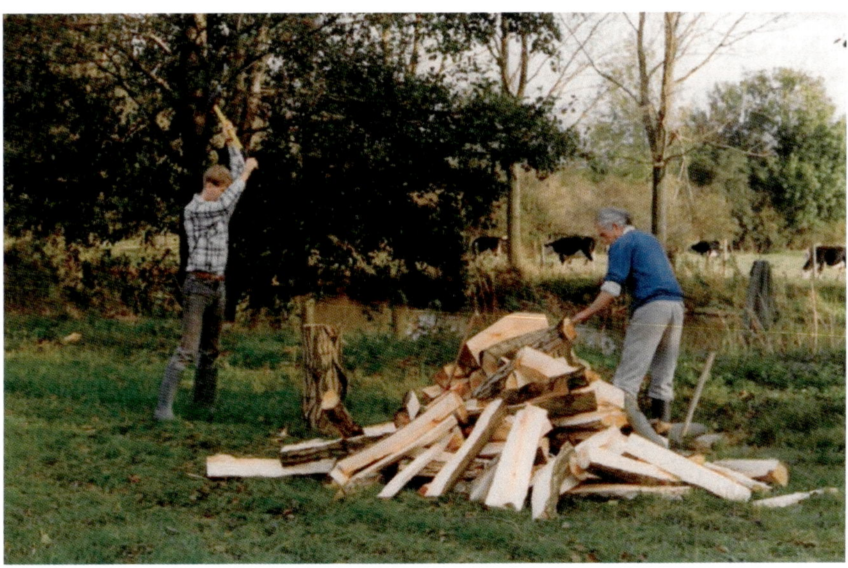

Andrew Hazelden and Alan Caiger-Smith splitting
willow on the bank of the River Kennet, *c*.1995

It was an energetic activity enjoyed by everyone who did it, even when, as happened to Mo Hamid and Andrew Hazelden, the vehicles got stuck in mud and had to be pulled out by the local farmer with a tractor. Many people would have complained that this kind of thing was not what they had come for, but no-one held back from any of the activities, and the success the Pottery enjoyed would not have been possible without this all-round co-operation.[20]

Adamson describes the willow wood as

a wild, hot timber, wayward and sinewy, liable to explode in the intense heat of the firebox. It was ideal for its heat value, but was so unsuitable for an open fire, and what tremendous heat and fireworks it gave off when dry. However it had to be split and cut when still green, for as it dried in the seasoning shed it became so tight and knotted, a devil of a wood.[21]

The split wood was stacked in an open shed behind the Pottery, where it was dried for a year before it could be used for firing the big kiln. Exposed to sun, wind and frost, in time it lost nearly half its weight as the moisture was drawn out of it.[22]

Caiger-Smith believed that firing with wood produced better results than either electricity or gas, and even allowing for the cost of labour it still compared favourably with both; but more importantly, it had a positive effect on morale:

Everyone had something in each wood-firing and everyone took their turn in fuelling it, and this was a cohesive, unifying factor for each member of the workshop, very different from turning on switches and adjusting gas pressure. It could of

course be tiring, but you must set aside from that the experience of the transformation of material, that is one of the most basic appeals of ceramics, and, unless
the firing is poor, this gives back more energy than it takes.[23]

He saw wood-firing as 'a wonderful, convivial, unifying activity':

> it's not just a process in the manufacture, it's a sort of climax, you feel the kiln as a
> sort of living being, and you are working with it. You have to know how the kiln
> is going to work, its habits, how it behaves in different weather, and it's a really
> wonderful instrument to work with.[24]

Adamson remembers often having the privilege of beginning a firing early in the
morning, first using a gas burner to gently warm and dry the kiln and pots. When
a certain temperature was reached, small pieces of willow kindling were ignited;
their size and frequency were increased during the day, ending with a final soak
at maximum temperature to end the firing in the evening. There was a meditative
quality to the firings: Adamson describes 'the stillness of those mornings, with the

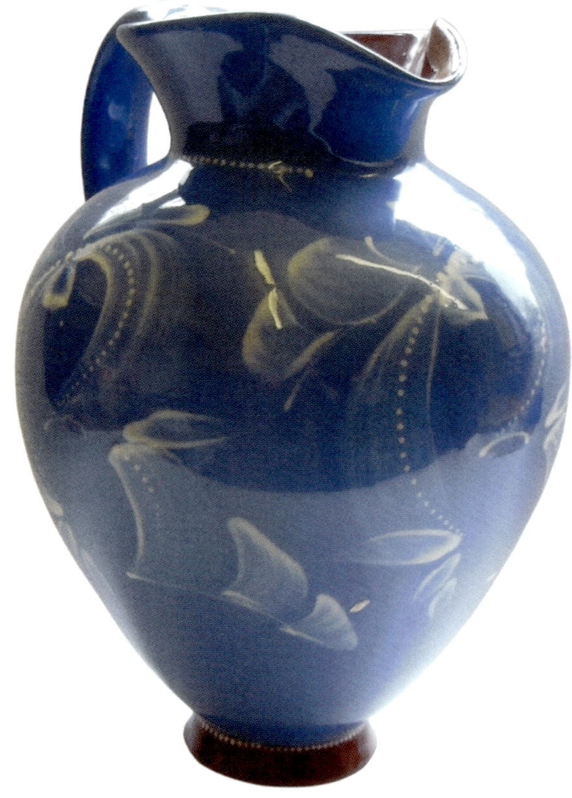

Slip-decorated Fremington earthenware
jug by Jaki Rothery, 2008, h. 26 cm
Collection Jaki Rothery

changing colours of the dawn over the fields of mist, and the changing song of the fire, which made it such a satisfying experience – one of meaning and quiet joy'.[25] Jaki Rothery recalls this shared experience:

> After cycling into the village in the early morning I would turn into the yard from the road to hear the crackle of burning willow. I would then take over from whoever had started the firing before dawn, feeding the fire to edge up the temperature. I can still feel the simultaneous winter cold at my back and fierce heat on my hands and face. On the other hand, during a hot summer day, it could be exhausting, but the rewards of opening up the lustre kiln for the first time, and seeing those iridescent colours blooming out from the pot surface as the clay deposits were rubbed away, was close to magical![26]

Rothery was a young girl from a village 5 miles away who in the autumn of 1974 volunteered to work at the Pottery on Saturdays, helping with visitors and other duties, in order to gain experience of making pots. By the following spring David Tipler had convinced Caiger-Smith that she had more than earned her place as a permanent member of the team. At Aldermaston she found herself in a world of which she had no previous conception:

> Alan allowed me into a world I would never have otherwise had access to – ultimately, a profoundly enriching experience, and included in that was going to Europe for the first time. I had been let down in a plan to travel, and Alan generously invited me to accompany Anne-Marie and himself on their visit to Italy to research background for the book he was writing. Knowing him was an education in itself, but in the most practical sense it gave me the tools to earn a living for the rest of my life, along with a deep appreciation for the aesthetics and necessity of craft.[27]

Always keen to expand and extend the experiences and knowledge of his assistants, Caiger-Smith's invitation to Rothery to join him and Anne-Marie on their trip to Italy was entirely in character: he was very different from other employers running potteries at the time. That difference was noted by almost everyone who worked with him over the 38 years of the Pottery's life as a collaborative workshop. The experience of working at Aldermaston was life-changing for nearly all the assistants. For Rothery,

> the key to the whole thing was Alan's generosity both personal and professional, his optimism, and his belief in the ultimate goodness of people. He was able to deal with just about anyone from any walk of life in a very positive way … I learned such a lot about life, people and pots, that I believe it changed my life in ways that I simply can't recognize now.[28]

Rothery worked at Aldermaston from the mid- to late 1970s and continued her career in the West Country. She went on to work in several West Country potteries, including working as a thrower for Colin Kellam at his Lion Brewery

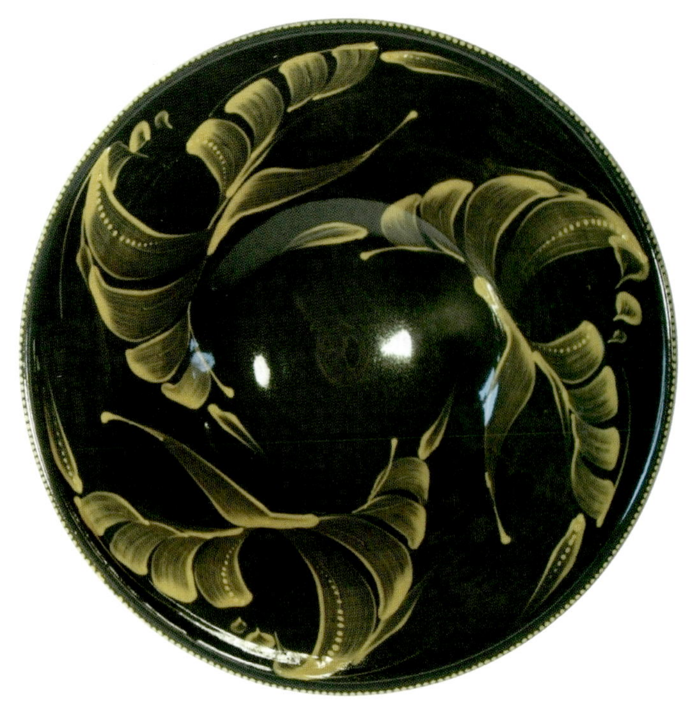

Slip-decorated Fremington earthenware bowl
by Jaki Rothery, 2010, diam. 26 cm, h. 11 cm
Private collection

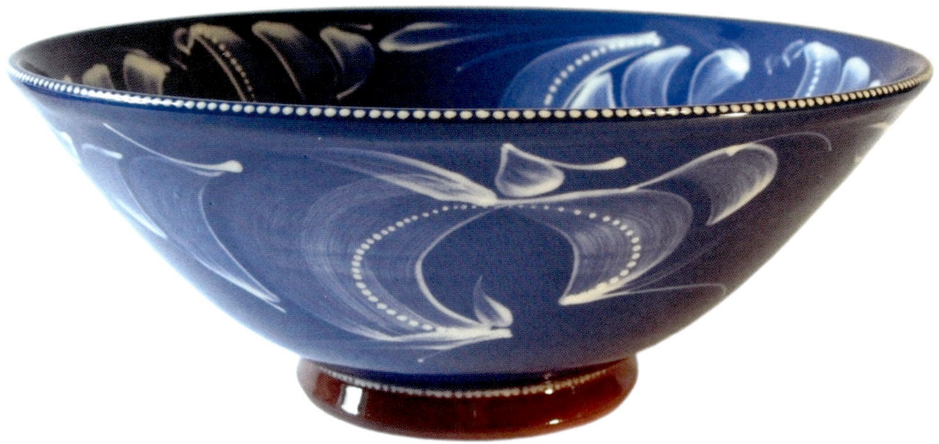

Slip decorated Fremington earthenware bowl
by Jaki Rothery, 2009, diam. 31 cm, h. 13cm
Private collection

Pottery in Totnes, Devon. She became a talented thrower. Even after setting up her own small studio in St Cleer in Cornwall in 1999 she still continued to throw pots for Kellam, as well as making her own slip-decorated earthenware, with the same Fremington clay used at Aldermaston and with brush decoration echoing the skills she learnt there. By 2008 she was supplying over ten outlets, and also demonstrating at Pressingoll Pottery in Bodmin, where she helped teach visitors to throw pots. Of the skills she learned during her time at Aldermaston, she said:

> All the learning occurred as intrinsic to the work, and there seemed to be an unspoken ethic wherein anyone learning could expect to receive assistance and instruction from any other more experienced person. When I was learning at Aldermaston I personally found Edgar Campden an incredibly wise and knowledgeable presence, and it hardly ever occurs that I don't think of him and his quiet observations when I'm throwing; he taught me about throwing dry, and the world of difference it makes, an invaluable gift.[29]

Caiger-Smith believed that through teaching one learned all over again, because it is only possible to pass on what you yourself understand. He saw giving or accepting help as more than just a technical matter: 'Learning goes by jumps; a person sometimes struggles for ages without seeming to improve, then suddenly everything comes together. It's exhilarating, and to see it happen to your own pupil is best of all. It creates a bond between people.'[30]

Between 1971 and 1981 Caiger-Smith had a series of near sell-out exhibitions in Australia, which were more successful than any of his exhibitions in England. There was a positive reaction to his strong tin-glaze colours, especially the lustres. In 1975 he was invited to undertake a lecture tour around New Zealand, which kept him away from the Pottery for the longest period so far. The tour gave him space to think afresh about the Pottery's entire character – what it made, the techniques it used and what it offered people working there – and he returned with fresh vigour to develop new ideas.[31] One such idea involved trial projects experimenting with porcelain, which he notes 'was eventually given up because it requires a different cast of mind from earthenware, and also because porcelain clay is ruined by any admixture with earthenware clay'.[32]

Sheen Sinclair worked with Jaki Rothery for three years from 1974 until 1977. She came to work at Aldermaston because she says:

> At the time Alan was probably the only potter that worked with the colours that tin glazes inspire, the rich, warm lustres that Alan had developed over the years brought such energy, exuberance and excitement to every pot, dish and vase that he made. I wanted to learn as many different skills as I could at Aldermaston so that one day I could start my own pottery, which I duly did in East Sussex.[33]

One of the youngest assistants at the time, Sinclair lived with several other potters in No. 29. She recalls that Caiger-Smith, sensitive to her needs, would often invite her to join his family for a Sunday lunch or afternoon tea in the orchard, and she has fond memories of riding their family pony and mucking about with the boys.

The training that all the assistants received at Aldermaston was absorbed and assimilated into their lives in so many unexpected ways. Sinclair was no exception: she later became a professional garden designer, and she acknowledges the enduring influence that her time at the Pottery had on her later career:

> Years later, it was Alan's use of colour and different brush strokes that certainly inspired me in my work as a garden designer. I am convinced that what I learned from working at Aldermaston was the keystone to the understanding of colour, movement and texture that I bring to my garden designs; infinitely better than time served at horticultural college! When it came to brushwork, one of the most important things Alan imbued upon me was the importance of 'knowing when to stop'. Yes, it's easy to remove plants from a border that is cramped, whilst it is impossible to remove a brush stroke of pigment from a dish, but it's the understanding of space, and when to fill it or leave it, that Alan's designs influenced in my planting schemes in later years. So definitely Alan gave me a creative and inspirational foundation from which to embark on a love of gardening and garden design.[34]

Many lasting friendships were formed in this working environment. Having recently moved to Cornwall, with potters, tin mines and clay pits in abundance – though sadly the latter now lie dormant – Sinclair is constantly reminded of her days at Aldermaston. On a positive note, she has been able to renew her friendship with Rothery some forty years after they first met.[35]

As the lustre firings became more reliable and consistent, one of the most rewarding jobs in the Pottery was opening the kiln after a lustre firing and gently removing the china clay, ochre, or more usually a combination of both, that had been used as a carrier for the metallic compounds of silver or copper. If the firing had been successful a sheen of silvery, golden or red lustre would be shining like treasure within the glaze, underneath the blackened ochre or clay. Lustre develops more easily if the metallic compounds are diluted, and mixing them with some sort of clay is the easiest way of doing this. The clay medium performs several useful roles: first it dilutes the pigment, and in so doing it makes the metallic compounds more sensitive to reduction; secondly, it protects soluble ingredients from being dissolved by steam during the early stages of the firing; and thirdly, iron-rich clays also protect the lustre film from re-oxidation. Historically, some kind of diluting medium was used for all lustre pigments, although not necessarily clay or ochre; combustible pastes or oils would have performed some of the same functions. However, a clay medium was certainly used by lustre potters in Spain and Italy, and probably also in the Middle East, since all European methods were ultimately derived from them.[36]

The pigments mixed together with the medium are then applied as decoration, most commonly with a brush, to the glazed surface. A few drops of gum arabic or sugar water can be added to ease application, with gum having the added advantage of hardening as it dries, making the pieces easier to handle. The pots are then packed fairly openly in the kiln, so that the reducing gases can surround them, for their third firing. The pieces with applied copper pigments are placed in the hotter positions in the kiln, and the silver pigments in more sheltered places. The kiln is always preheated before being packed so that the pots are warm, since otherwise moisture released from the burning fuel will condense on them, dissolving some of the pigment and causing dribbles of colour. Although lustreware can be fired in as little as two hours, it is advisable to fire larger objects more slowly, as pottery that is already glazed is easily cracked by a rapid firing. But once red heat is reached and the glaze begins to soften, the firing should be as quick as possible since the longer it continues, the more the film of reduced metal is absorbed into the glaze instead of simply adhering to the surface, and the sheen becomes dulled.[37]

The kiln at Aldermaston was fired up to a temperature of 660°C in about six and a half hours for the lustre, and that was then followed by eight or nine periods of reduction, each followed by a period of clear combustion, lasting altogether about an hour. By starving the atmosphere of oxygen and causing a reducing atmosphere in the kiln, the metallic compounds are broken down and become deposited as a thin metallic film in the surface of the glaze. If the temperature has been judged correctly, the clay or ochre does not adhere to the glaze surface. The trial rings were removed at intervals during the reduction to see how the lustre was progressing; once these showed that the reduction had been effective, the kiln was sealed up and left to cool. The pots themselves would frequently come out lighter and brighter than the rings, because some re-oxidation occurs during the slow process of cooling.[38]

The lustre firings were usually on Fridays, with the big opening reserved for a Monday. With such fine margins for error and so many factors affecting the quality of the finished lustre, this was always a tense moment. When the firing had gone well, the cleaning and polishing of the pots was an unforgettable experience. Jane O'Connor, who worked at the Pottery in the late 1970s, recalled the excitement surrounding this event:

> As well as the standard maiolica ware there was the whole beautiful and mysterious business of the lustre firings. We were encouraged to develop our own designs in this, and painted with special precious metal mixtures and ochre onto the white glaze of the second firing, before the third low temperature firing. This meant you painted on a glazed surface, very different from the usual powdery surface of the unfired glaze. Alan and Edgar, or maybe one of the other potters, would spend a few days filling the wood-fired kiln with its precious load. Then the firing would begin, and it was incredibly finely tuned, with pieces of wood and numbers of seconds being counted at critical points in the cycle of reduction and oxidation.
>
> A few days later there was an excited buzz in the pottery, and as the kiln began to be opened up other people began to gather: Granny, Nanny, Mrs Duck Eggs, Anne-Marie, Jenny Jowett, the wives or partners of the potters, and maybe one or

two of Alan's collector friends, they were all drawn to the great unpacking. At the tables we had bowls of powdered pumice and bags of sheep's wool. The ochre had protected the pigment in the firing, and when the pots came out of the kiln this had gone black, so we needed to gently remove it by rubbing it with the dampened wool dipped in pumice. It was like magic painting as the beautiful sunrise and sunset colours, pinks, reds, apricots, blues and golds, all began to emerge. What joy! What a privilege to see the world's greatest living lustre potter reveal a world-class pot in front of my eyes![39]

Miranda Thomas was an assistant at Aldermaston during the early 1980s. She describes the privilege of being able to take part in the firings:

What I remember most working with Alan was helping him prepare and pack the lustre kiln. I knew he held the secrets of this incredible technique and I wanted to learn it all. Realistically it was really above my head in so many respects, but I boldly asked if I could help. I was in awe of the incredible deep knowledge Alan had about both tin glaze and lustres. I understood that he had spent years and years deciphering the so-called 'code' of secrecy of lustres in history. As well as having a scholarly mind, and use of languages, he had the added advantage, first and foremost, of a potter's working insight into the technique. This is where he was way ahead of art historians. It was his lifelong passion. As well as an author, he also was a scientist. He kept systematic notes and did miles of tests. Yet he was mystical enough to understand the symbolism and gesture of the work.

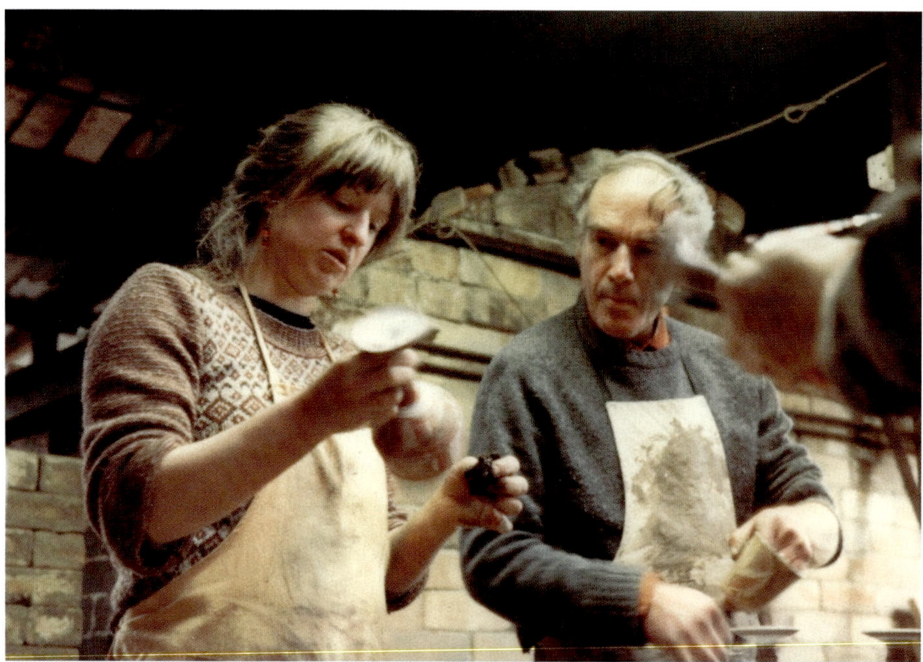

Gill Bent and Alan Caiger-Smith cleaning lustre, 1979

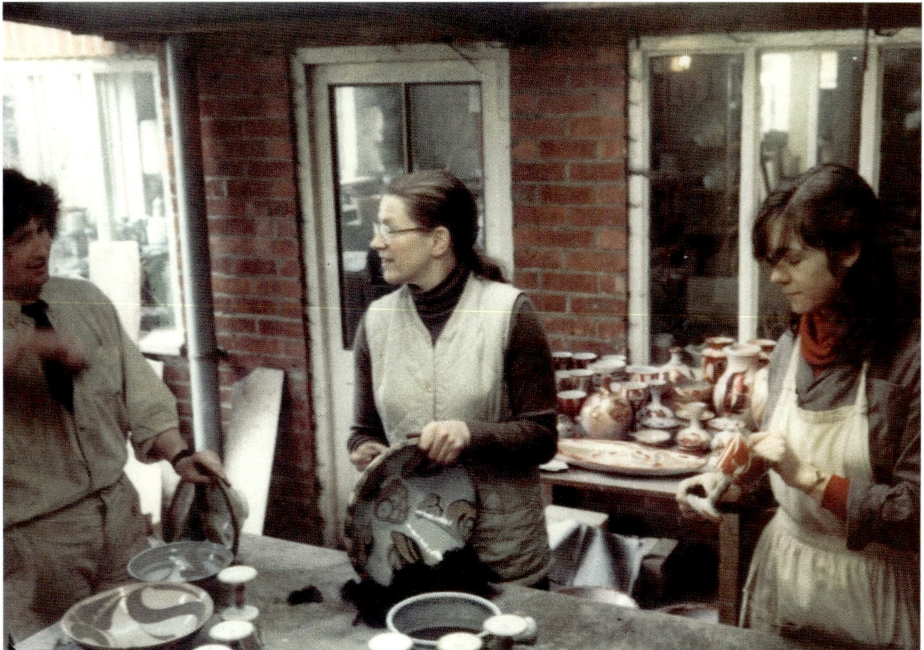

Julian Bellmont, Anne-Marie Caiger-Smith and Ruth Bennett
cleaning off ochre pigment to reveal lustre, 1981

The excitement of the lustre firings was intense, and rightly so. It took hours of concentration packing the kiln, like laying a house of cards. Alan knew all the cool and hot spots, where the best colours and reduction flowed best. I often just watched and passed him pots, allowing him to concentrate; I was like a surgeon's nurse. We both had respect for one another. He was as patient as he could be with me, and enjoyed my help. The lustre firings were very hit and miss. Not enough wisps of oxidation during reduction could make the colours dull and uninteresting; too cold, and the lustres wouldn't mature, and would rub off the surface. Too hot, and the lustres would volatilise and disappear up the chimney. Condensation had ruined many of his early firings. Hours of work could be easily destroyed.

Unpacking the lustre kiln was always an exciting event. Often that was when visiting potters and customers would come by and join in the excitement. It was everyone's job to rub away the ochre coating crusted on the pots, to reveal the shining, almost ethereal, glistening colours … these kiln unpackings were the most magical events I have ever been part of in my pottery career. Alan only fired the lustre kiln about four times a year. I realise now, with the stress of often looming exhibitions, how terrifying these firings must have been. But Alan stayed extremely calm, kept a twinkle of his eye, and remained excited![40]

—6—

Community and Friendship
1975–1979

Now that Caiger-Smith had mastered the lustre technique, invitations to exhibit started to come in from all over the world. During the late 1970s he exhibited in Holland, Norway, Germany, and the USA, as well as continuing to have a growing following in Australia and New Zealand. The Pottery was also kept busy with exhibitions across Great Britain.

During this period a number of assistants joined the team, all of whom had successful careers after leaving Aldermaston. One of these was Jason Shackleton, who arrived in 1975. He has been variously described as free-spirited and flamboyant,[1] and as unconventional in every way: loud, talented, warm and huge fun,[2] he brought the place alive with his energy, eccentricity and his passion for making pots.[3] He was certainly a major character and influence on the potters during his five years at the Pottery, with many of them reflecting Gill Bent's sentiments that Aldermaston would not have been the same had he not been there. For Bent, Shackleton was always fun to be around and she admired his own work, which he made at Hayling Island in his spare time. As he had been at the Pottery for some time when she arrived, he helped her to master the throwing and decorating techniques, and influenced her ideas about decoration. When Bent left Aldermaston, it was partly Shackleton's influence that inspired her to work with slips and sgraffito, as he was doing similar work at the time. Until she went to work at the Pottery she had never met anyone quite like Shackleton – and has not met anyone else quite like him since.[4]

Shackleton had been brought up in an inspirational household. His father, Keith, was a distinguished artist and naturalist and co-presented the BBC television series *Animal Magic* during the 1960s,[5] and his mother, Jacqueline, was a painter and sculptor; both parents were to have a great influence on their son. Jason grew up in London, but at every opportunity the family would pile into their old van and drive to Hayling Island. Here the children's grandfather had a holiday cottage near a brickworks, where they played on the tidal creek making objects from the natural clay, while their mother carved mermaids from pieces of driftwood. Later, when he was working at Aldermaston, Shackleton would hitch back to Hayling Island on Friday nights, throw pots all night, dry them on Saturday, decorate them until late on Sunday, and return to Aldermaston ready for work at 8 a.m. on Monday. On alternate weekends he would fire the pots he had made the previous weekend in the wood-fired kiln he had built in the woods on the island, starting at 5 a.m. and firing all day, and all too often he would be unpacking the shattered results with a shovel before setting off back to Aldermaston on Sunday. Undeterred, he would simply get back on his wheel and start again the next time he was on the island. He eventually found the formula – using different woods, 'soft to start with, then you throw in the hard, and hear the hum as the temperature rises'.[6]

Father and son would go on expeditions into the woods to collect snakes, which they would put into milk churns, load into the back of their van and take up to London Zoo. Together they travelled to the Seychelles and St Kitts, where they would swim with squids and turtles. All these experiences and their associated imagery would emerge many years later in Shackleton's very personal work. For him the catalyst for a lifetime of pottery was the day his elder sister returned from Dartington School with some pots she had made: at that moment his future was decided.[7]

When he was old enough to go to Dartington himself, Shackleton headed straight for the pottery room, where he then spent most of his time. He thought of himself as extremely fortunate to have had two talented and inspirational teachers at Dartington, Bernie Forrester, who had worked with Bernard Leach, and Colin Kellam. Forrester showed him how to design kilns, and together they built a kick wheel from scratch, incorporating and learning many skills in the process, including woodwork, metalwork, and welding, all regarded by Shackleton as essential parts of an education. Kellam channelled Shackleton's boundless energy into the practicalities of pottery: making pots and mixing glazes, pugging clay and loading kilns – in fact all the rudiments of running a pottery workshop. Having spent so much time in the pottery room, Shackleton left school with no formal qualifications, which proved to be a barrier when he applied to the Central School of Art. He brought to his interview some pots that he had thrown on a kick wheel and fired in a wood kiln, both of which he had built himself. When asked to explain the 'significance' of his 'rather amateurish pots', he realised that art school was definitely not for him. Enraged, he was now determined to succeed and show them how wrong they were. Michael Cardew, one of Shackleton's heroes, once told him that art school should be renamed 'art hospital', as that was where you went to be 'made better'.[8] Caiger-Smith shared this sentiment:

> an art school training can give a wide spread of knowledge and ideas but it seldom teaches people how to use time economically, or how to sustain the effort … Potters like Jason and me, who never had much formal training, tend to look down on people who have been systematically taught but haven't yet adjusted to a practical workshop that has to pay its way.[9]

Most of the assistants who worked with Caiger-Smith came to understand the wisdom of this statement. Gill Bent echoes their experience:

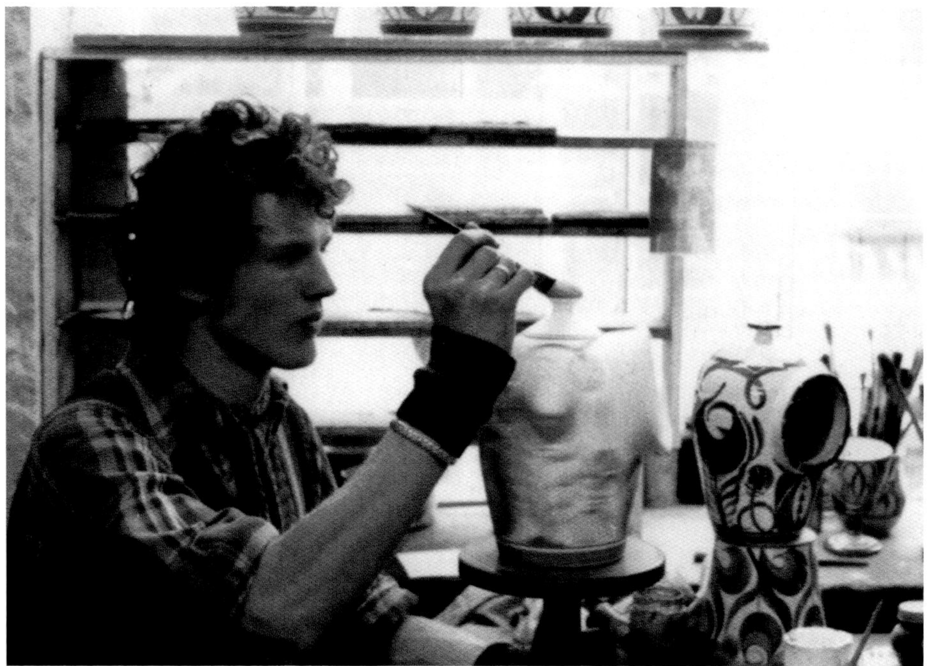

Jason Shackleton decorating, 1978

> With time and patience Alan and Edgar taught me skills that would set me up for a
> life of making pots, with a sensitivity to shape, form and colourful brushwork that
> surpassed anything I had learned before, both at art college and other potteries.[10]

On a visit to the Craftsmen Potters Shop in Soho in 1974, Shackleton saw an advertisement on the noticeboard for a potter's apprenticeship with Mary Wondrausch at her Wharf Pottery in Godalming, Surrey. He applied and got the job, and spent the following year making slipware and slip-trailed sgraffito ware, much of it commemorative and made to order, and living with Wondrausch at Brickfields, her seventeenth-century house, which they shared with an assortment of animals, including monkeys. He was paid £12 a week and charged £6 for board and lodging.[11]

Towards the end of his time with Wondrausch the pottery was commissioned by the BBC to make slip-trailed plates with the lettering 'Craft of the Potter' around the rim, and a central design depicting throwing, decorating, and firing. The plates were to revolve in the opening titles of the television series *The Craft of the Potter*. Staff from the BBC came to collect the plates one Friday, Shackleton's last day at the Wharf Pottery; the following week he was to start at Aldermaston:

> Imagine their surprise when on the Monday the same BBC team arrived at
> Aldermaston, with Mick Casson, to film Alan demonstrating painted brushwork,
> and they saw me working there. Doing a double-take they exclaimed, "You get
> around a bit don't you?"[12]

At the time Caiger-Smith had numerous employees but, eager to redress the balance of skilled assistants and learners, he was looking for an experienced thrower, preferably someone who was willing to commit to staying for five years. One of the main reasons that Shackleton wanted to work at Aldermaston was the wood-fired kiln. Bernard Leach's *A Potter's Book* (1945) had inspired him, and after experimenting on his own with the small wood-fired kiln he had built on Hayling Island, he wanted and needed to find out more. He sent Caiger-Smith some slides of his work and was consequently invited for an interview. Despite nervousness, and running a '4-minute mile' twice, after discovering to his dismay that Aldermaston Station was in fact a long way from the village, he demonstrated his throwing skills with shaking hands and was given the job. He was elated and, true to his word, he remained at Aldermaston for five years. Shackleton regarded himself as 'extremely lucky' to be working for Caiger-Smith; he found that Aldermaston had a very high standard of pottery making, painting and manufacturing, and that it was a wonderful place to work.[13]

A free spirit, nonetheless Shackleton acknowledges that the skills and the discipline instilled in them all at Aldermaston gave them everything necessary to set up on their own:

> If you couldn't throw pots when you went to work at Aldermaston, you sure as hell could when you left. The standard was incredibly high. No matter what pot we were throwing or painting we referred to the 'Samples Shelf' – enough to strike the fear of God into a free spirit like myself. Every shape of pot and the patterns that went on them, in the full range, were there, and this was backed up by 'The Bible', a clay-splattered book, well thumbed, with all the clay weights and measurements for those pots. Height, width of belly, base, rim, lid sizes … all was there. There was no escape. We were given a demonstration and left to it and the ones that didn't make the grade were scrapped. You soon learned that if you couldn't pull the pot up to its full height then the clay needed was in the base, and to use less water.[14]

Shackleton recalled one instance when Michael Mosse, 'a true workhorse and a precision thrower' who worked alongside him for two years, had just spent the day throwing storage jars:

> One day Michael had made one hundred and fifty storage jars and their lids, and then Alan walked in and said, 'Oh Michael, those aren't right'. Michael quick as a flash whipped out his ruler and calipers and the measurements were checked. All were exact, bang on; Alan stood back and looked at them, and said, 'Well Michael, it's more a feel than a measurement'. I think Alan was right, and Michael wrote a song about it![15]

Mosse was another of the potters who had had some training before joining Aldermaston Pottery. Caiger-Smith had been advised by his old friend Oliver Roskill that continually training up novice potters who then moved on was costing him too much time and money. Mosse was to be part of a new intake with previous experience. He had been working in a Welsh pottery, mass-producing souvenirs for the tourist trade. Bored with his job, he decided to halve his wage and come to work at Aldermaston, arriving one cold winter's day at the end of 1975. The subsidised housing Caiger-Smith provided was cheap and there was ample opportunity to make up his wage by doing piecework after hours. Mosse and his wife, Jo, moved into Pottery Cottage, next door to the Pottery, with their two Welsh sheepdogs. The dogs, which had Polish names, were fed on waste from the local slaughterhouse and only answered to commands in Polish. Next door at No. 34 lived Shackleton, who remembers one of their first meetings: he opened the door to their shared coal shed to find Jo chopping up a sheep's head with a full-size beheading axe![16]

Technical problems were never far away. Mosse remembers that during his first winter at the Pottery, in an attempt to cut down the crazing in the lustre glaze, Caiger-Smith decided that they should experiment with adding Kent Gault clay to the standard Fremington clay:

> Midwinter had Jason and me sieving away, unable to tell ice from the sea urchin fossils that threatened to gash the gauze. Jason even mounted some up in silver for jewellery. The resulting slip was hung up in cloth bladders to de-water by freezing. In the event the tests showed no improvement, rather an increase in crazing, and Alan reverentially laid the results to rest in the dustbin. I pounced and grabbed one of the test bowls, saying the other should be put up on the decorating room wall, as they would in Spain. So that is what happened, and the bowl stayed there right up until the Pottery closed, when Alan very generously sent it to me, together with a lovely goblet. I have both bowls out of the way of grandchildren in our pot cupboard. They look lovely. Who cares about crazing anyway?[17]

Shackleton talked Caiger-Smith into building a Continental kick wheel similar to the one he had built at Dartington, and the wheel remained in use in the Pottery from then on. It was also while Shackleton was working at Aldermaston that a commission came in from the Property Services Agency[18] for two very large lustred pots, about 45 in high, for the British Embassy in Washington. This was their first commission for such large lustre pieces. They made the decision to hand-build each jar from coils of clay on a turntable, but this proved to be slow work: the lower part of the piece had to be stiffened before adding the weight of more clay further up, and the coils had to be carefully smoothed as the vessels grew. It was particularly difficult to control the clay as the form widened, as even the slightest irregularity tended to increase as it extended upwards and outwards.[19]

Caiger-Smith had always recognised that coiled forms had a unique beauty: as the symmetry of a coiled form could never be precise, due to the basic form being softened by the method of construction, the result was an extremely subtle profile that 'felt' different to a thrown form. This ancient way of constructing vessels has given us some of the finest pots ever made, such as the Neolithic funerary jars from Kansu in north-west China, of which Caiger-Smith said: 'in the presence of vessels such as these one can only stand in awe. The forms radiate the inner silence'.[20] With all this in mind they started on the commission, knowing that they had little experience of making coiled forms, and certainly none approaching the size required.

Not surprisingly, the problems of making large coiled jars started to become evident almost immediately. The first jar warped so badly as it dried that it was scrapped. The second and third jars, although they had been slowly dried for some considerable time, both blew out their bases in the biscuit firing. The fourth and fifth jars were dried on a perforated base in an attempt to overcome this problem; although they fired successfully, and even went on to have a third firing with lustre, Caiger-Smith felt that their forms were not good enough for the Embassy, and they were sold to a private customer. Shackleton, Mosse and Campden were the assistants who devoted most of their time to this assignment, and Mosse recalls that they 'dried the pots by hanging a light bulb in them', and that they glazed them on a banding wheel 'turned by pulling a loop of string, while Edgar poured glaze from a height'; 'necessity is ever the mother of invention and Alan left us to it'.[21] And so to jars six and seven. These were considered to have good forms; both survived the first biscuit firing perfectly, so they were put to one side to have their glaze and lustre firings.

Around this time preparations were under way for Shackleton's 21st birthday, for which Caiger-Smith offered the use of the Pottery workshop as a venue. He also offered the large ceremonial platters, bowls and jugs to be used for the food and drink, and most of the bowls and plates from the showroom for serving. So everyone set about decorating the space into what Caiger-Smith described as 'a night-club with ethnic overtones'. A wonderful time was had by all – too good, in fact, because in the early hours, after the older generation had retired to bed and the younger generation had drunk far too much, the two large jars suffered a calamitous end. The next day, along with anguished apologies from the potters, came a promise that they would be replaced, in their own time, with two more that would be even better than the two that had been broken. Caiger-Smith said they were true to their word, and the two new jars were indeed much better than the originals. He already knew from his years of experience that first attempts were seldom right, that the larger the scale the more difficult it is to get it right, and that it is only by doing something again and again that confidence builds. Small details – the consistency of the clay, the timing, the pressure of the hand – all become clearer with practice, and as the scale of the form becomes physically familiar you get a sense of the object as a whole, and the confidence shows. There are no short cuts.[22]

In due course two beautiful lustre jars were shipped to the British Embassy in Washington to take their place on either side of the grand staircase. So the repetition forced on them all by accident turned out to have been fortuitous, and by the time the ninth pot in the series was completed, the potters found it hard to remember why the first ones had been so difficult, and had taken so long to complete.

The development of the range of pots was ongoing, with the famous 'gypsy bowls' being a good example. In 1975 Venetia Sieveking, the daughter of a family friend, worked for a brief time at the Pottery, before taking up a Churchill Scholarship to study mosque architecture in Isfahan, Iran. Sieveking was primarily a painter, but while she was at Aldermaston she introduced unique and original painted designs for the gypsy bowls. The form had its origins in the unusual request from a gypsy who had been passing the Pottery one day with his horse and painted cart. He wanted a pair of deep rounded bowls that could hold half a gallon of water, for his wife to collect rainwater on the steps of her caravan. They were to be decorated with brightly coloured designs inside, outside and under the foot ring, 'to keep them safe'. It was this particular remark that captured Caiger-Smith's imagination, as he had always believed that the patterns and emblems on decorated pottery in the past were not simply aesthetic ornament but invocations of happiness and prosperity, talismans to keep the vessel and its contents free from harm, and that the pots belonged to a way of living in which everything had a meaning. He wanted his own painted designs and colours to develop the resonance and conviction found in pots from the past. The gypsy called by some two years later to collect his bowls and was extremely pleased with them; in the intervening years they had attracted considerable interest, and so began to appear as a more regular line.[23]

Sieveking had been finding it difficult to adapt her painting technique to the calligraphic designs in the Pottery's repertoire, and the row of biscuit-fired gypsy bowls seemed to offer the perfect solution. Regarding the bowls as an abstract painting in the round, she would take a favourite poem as a starting point to suggest colours and motifs as the underlying theme for the design. She had found her niche; her designs extended around the bowl without any repetition, outside and inside, a continually changing sequence of shapes and colours, varying in scale and detail, all brought together by the unifying theme of the poem. It would be difficult to guess what the poems were, but they gave the bowls a slightly mysterious aura. Caiger-Smith said he had never seen anything like these colourful, elaborately painted, semi-abstract compositions, and they sold unexpectedly well, so he regrets only having kept one of them.[24] The gypsy bowls remained a regular form in the Pottery's repertoire, although following Sieveking's inspirational designs they became one of the few shapes that was never assigned a fixed pattern, allowing freedom for the decorator to respond to the form as he or she wished. Caiger-Smith especially enjoyed decorating them as they inspired brushwork that often told whole stories.[25]

Sieveking returned to her home town of Newcastle, New South Wales, Australia, where, as a single parent, she continued with her art as well as writing about the subject, alongside teaching and lecturing, although she eventually had to seek a more regular income. However, encouraged by her daughter, Amelia

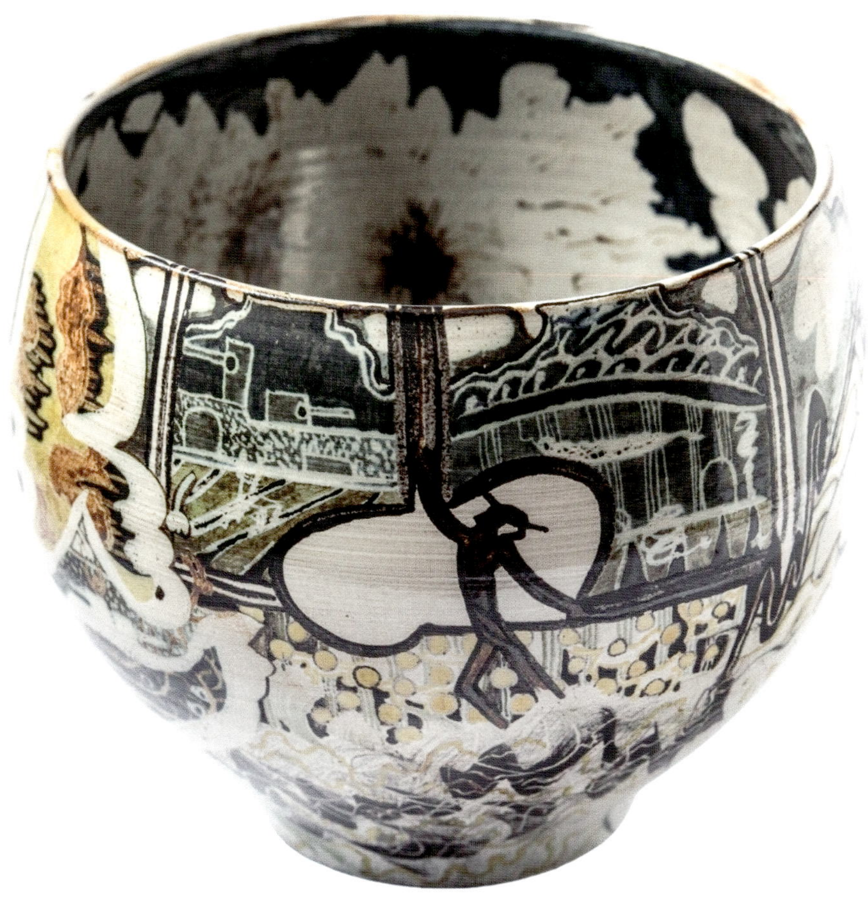

Gypsy bowl by Venetia Sieveking, 1978, h. 16.5 cm, w. 21.6 cm
Collection Alan Caiger-Smith

Filmer-Sankey, she eventually returned to painting, which resulted in a successful mother and daughter collaborative exhibition of oil and watercolour paintings, screen prints, photography and poetry, at Newcastle's ARThive, in 2010, entitled *The V&A Exhibition*. The exhibition depicted 'the magic and beauty of the small, intangible, the unseen beauty in the mundane and that which is taken for granted; work based in and around that which slips between the footpath's cracks of the Newcastle and surrounding regions'.[26]

The next assistant to arrive at the Pottery was Laurence McGowan, in 1976. Following earlier careers as a cartographer and a gamekeeper, he had by chance found himself working for Pru Green at Alvingham Pottery near Louth in Lincolnshire; but it was on one of his frequent journeys south to see his family that his imagination had been captured. The window in the Pottery always had an alluring appeal from The Street, aglow night and day with ceramics on display,

107

the gold and silver lustre shining enticingly like treasure. McGowan said that it was a wood-fired, bronze-brown gallon teapot sitting in the window that caught his eye one day, with decoration unlike anything he had ever seen before: indeed, he has been able to visualise that teapot ever since. Later, when looking through magazines and books, it was the pottery produced at Aldermaston that appealed to him above everything else being produced at the time. So when he saw an advertisement for an assistant to join the team there, he eagerly applied, thinking that at least if he was offered an interview, he would meet the hands and the mind behind the teapot in the window. He was offered an interview: in retrospect he felt sure that his indifferent throwing prowess did not impress, but concluded that it must have been his detailed sketchbooks that got him the job. The decision to work at Aldermaston completely changed the course of his life:

> Alan not only gave me the means to earn a living in an honourable, gratifying way, in the second great division of my life, but he also enabled me to experience the world in a completely new and immensely satisfying way. Not just for me, but for my wife Jackie and daughter Cate as well.[27]

Just as Shackleton, Mosse, and the younger members of the team seemed to gravitate together, so other distinct friendships and partnerships developed between the potters. McGowan soon found a connection with Edgar Campden:

> I got on with Edgar, and felt most at ease with him. We were both grammar school boys from similar backgrounds. I had had an interest in lettering and calligraphy ever since my school days, reinforced during the early years by my mapmaking training. Finding out that I could make a reasonable fist of inscribing pots, I soon found myself doing many of the one-off lettered orders. Sometimes Edgar and I joined forces on pieces, he deploying his better graphic skills, me the lettering. We had our minor triumphs, but also made a few ignorant blunders. One I remember was a plate, which was to be given to someone from a local flying club, and it had to depict a Tiger Moth aircraft that Edgar 'flew' across the middle of the plate, and on which I inscribed the rim. However our relief that it fired so well was short lived, when the person who collected it pointed out that when flying solo in such biplanes the pilot always sits in the rear of the two cockpits. So … start again.[28]

Mosse also recalls their similarities:

> Alan didn't generally encourage innovations from the shop floor, saying that when it didn't work he got left with the result, and that could be as many as the potters who went through the place. That was certainly my experience, but Edgar was a very worthwhile exception, and he could turn his hand to any sort of decorating too. Amongst various commissions he once decorated some vases to match someone's curtains! Laurence could do the same. I could never emulate these two, but I think that there is a lot to be gained by being aware of a different approach.[29]

Mosse left Aldermaston at the end of 1978 and went back to Llanbrynmair in North Wales, where he worked at Cambrian Stoneware in Llanidloes for 18 months while he was building a wood-fired kiln in preparation for starting his own pottery. Here he and his wife, Jo, specialised in producing wood-fired salt-glazed pottery. They sold their work through galleries and shops, including Primavera, as well as direct to the public at craft shows, the most important of which was the annual *Art in Action* show at Waterperry in Oxfordshire. Mosse believed that Caiger-Smith's approach worked well: simply employing people, as he himself had done, was less satisfactory, as people took the job to fit with family commitments rather than to learn the potter's craft. Eventually financial constraints forced him to seek a regular wage, as a care worker: both the pottery and his house needed expensive repairs, and he was also his mother-in-law's carer. However, after a long gap he is about to return to making pots again, with renewed enthusiasm for the future. Although he will not be employing anyone else to work with him, he will adopt Alan's approach when he returns to the clay.[30]

Not everyone who came to the Pottery found their vocation, however positive their experience. Stella Bigage, who has lived in France for most of her life, came to visit her sister, Jackie McGowan, in 1977. Attracted to 'the creative life', she stayed for nearly a year and learned to make pots. During this period Caiger-Smith was working with Ronald Lightbown on their edition of Cipriano Piccolpasso's *I tre libri dell'arte del vasajo* (*The Three Books of the Potter's Art*; see p. 83). Bigage had discovered that making pots was not really the life for her, so she spent most of her time typing out Caiger-Smith's manuscript – not what she had intended to do, but nonetheless a rewarding and worthwhile occupation. She returned to France and a career as an international civil servant, and took up painting once more in her retirement.[31]

Now that Caiger-Smith's work with reduced lustre was gaining recognition, the long years of effort began at last to reap the rewards of success. Prestigious commissions started to come in: in 1977 a lustre dish was made for presentation to the Queen Mother. The following year Simon Middleton joined the team of potters and worked with them for two years before leaving to pursue a career as a teacher. Some thirty years later his niece, Catherine Middleton, married Prince William.

The Tile Cottage workshops across the road were enabling the potters to take on commissions that would not have been possible before, and 1978 saw the completion of a large mural of relief tiles for Redland Roof Tiles in Leighton Buzzard. This project was originally conceived as an ethical form of industrial sponsorship of the arts. It arose from conversations between Caiger-Smith and the managing director of the company, David Lyon, which resulted in Lyon's conclusion:

> The best form of sponsorship occurs when all the elements are relevant and harmonious, when self-interest and altruism both point to the desirability of some work of art. Then they make possible a work which owes something to them both,

but which is essentially different from either of them, and it may remain long after the circumstances that prompted it are forgotten, its qualities of form and colour (or sound, or imagery, or language) being valued in their own right, in addition to its original purpose, date and location. Many works of art in the past came about in this way, and it is up to industry to spot the opportunity and for the artist to rise to the occasion.[32]

This concept would lead to another collaboration with industry 12 years later that resulted in the Pottery's biggest commission in its 51-year history.

In 1978 Redland was building a new roof tile plant in Britain, to be the flagship of its 130 plants across 22 countries. As the proposal to include a mural was agreed at an early stage, its size and siting could be incorporated into the architects' plans. The mural was to represent the worldwide family of Redland roofing companies, each of which would be sending staff over to the British plant for training. Caiger-Smith made several visits to the roof tile works in Leighton Buzzard to sketch equipment and people working. The final design was on a larger scale than anything the Pottery had produced before, and without the new Tile Cottage workshops it could never have been considered. As usual there were the initial problems to be overcome, such as the shrinkage and warping of large slabs of clay, but new techniques resulted. Caiger-Smith cut miniature impressions based on Redland tile profiles for texturing certain areas within the design, and he used lightly sprayed colours and glazes to emphasise the relief modelling of the imagery in a way he had not done before.[33]

The final assembly and installation required Anne-Marie's expertise. It has been a continuing source of pride to both Caiger-Smith and David Lyon that those who work at the plant enjoy and admire the mural, and enthusiastically explain the details to visitors.[34]

During 1978 two young women, Jane O'Connor and Gill Bent, came to work at the Pottery, and formed a firm friendship. Bent had graduated with a degree in ceramics from Bath Academy of Art: the course had concentrated primarily on slip-casting and work made in moulds, so she was now eager to acquire the skills of throwing. To this end she gained employment at Alvingham Pottery in Lincolnshire, but, finding the location too isolated, moved to Surrey to work with Chris Otway at Shere Pottery, making functional high-fired stoneware. She then discovered the decorated ceramics being produced at Aldermaston. As soon as she walked through the door of the Pottery she felt at home, and remembers staring in amazement at the rows of perfectly thrown pots in delicious chocolate-brown clay and wondering whether she would ever be able to make anything like them. One of the most exciting days of her life was when her suitably impressed landlady at Shere announced that there was a charming man on the phone wanting to speak to her: it was Alan offering her the job. Once at the Pottery she was struck by the diversity of the tasks she was expected to undertake, so unlike the other potteries she had worked in, but she felt sure that this led to the great sense of belonging and camaraderie that was felt by everyone who worked there.[35]

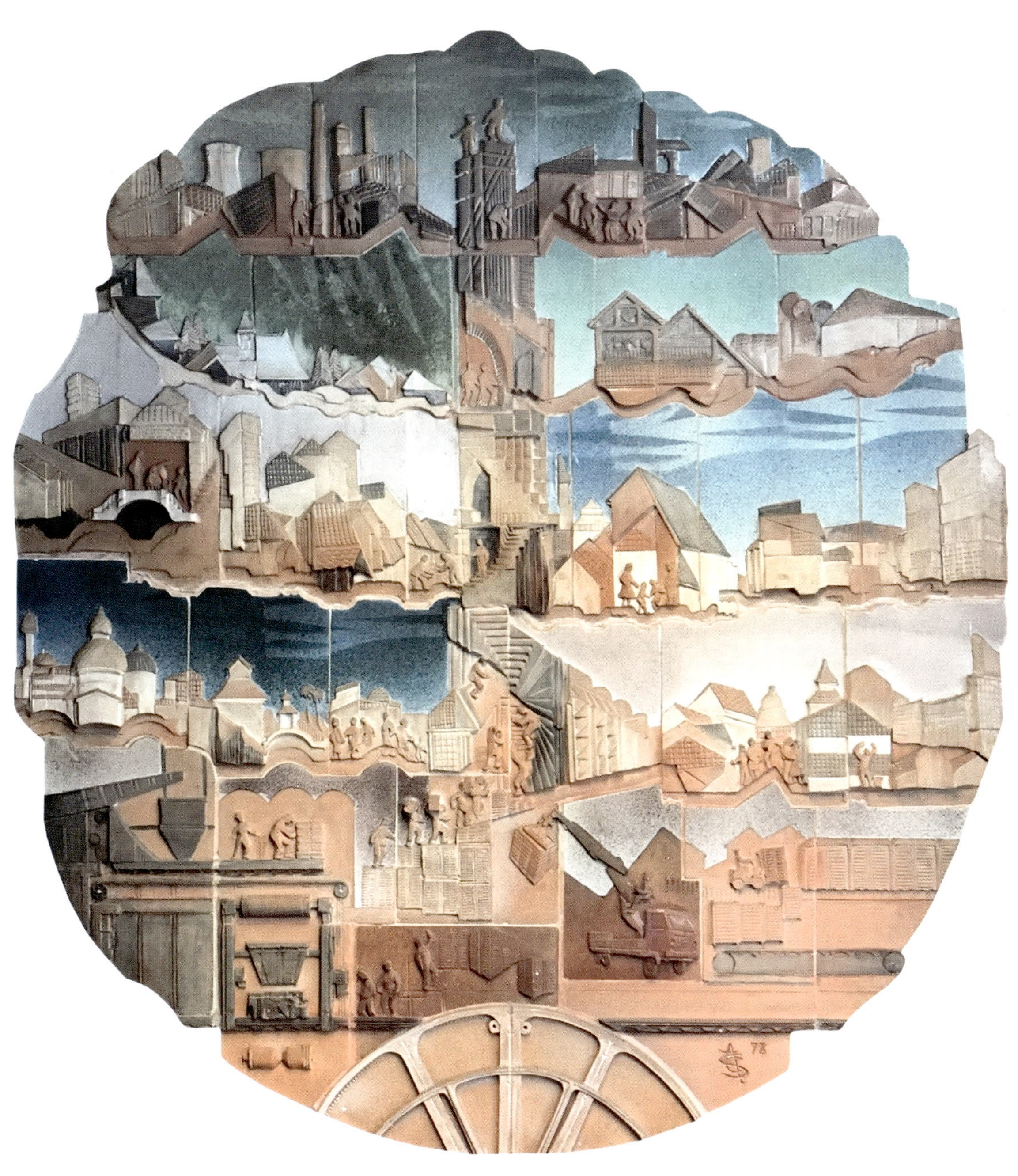

Tile mural at the Redland roof tile plant, Leighton Buzzard, 1978, 193 × 175 cm
Collection Redland Roof Tiles Ltd

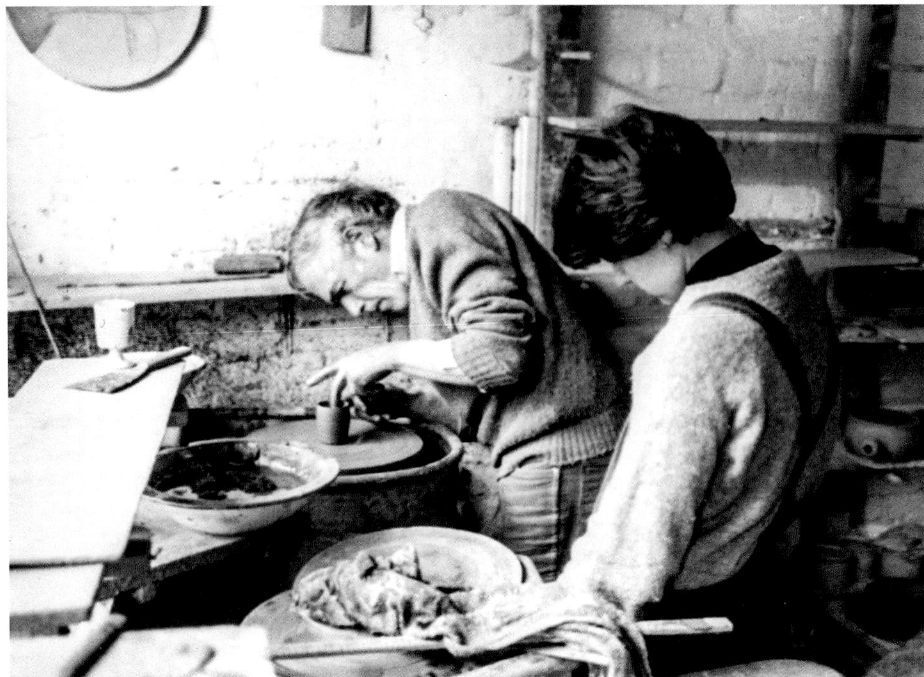

Alan Caiger-Smith demonstrating to Jane O'Connor, 1979

Jaki Rothery was still working at the Pottery when Bent arrived and made her feel at home from the start:[36]

> Jak cut another eccentric figure with her love of motorbikes, tomboy looks and
> long curly ginger hair, and she made us laugh with all her antics, amongst which
> was swinging from the beams. She was a good potter and worked hard and always
> seemed to know what needed doing around the pottery, which was a huge help to
> me in learning the ropes.[37]

Four years later, Bent herself was to be described by a new recruit as 'the most senior potter', with certain privileges, being allowed to work in the back workshop and even to make work for her own show.[38]

Jane O'Connor, who started work soon after Bent in the late summer of 1978, had just finished a three-year teacher-training course at Bretton Hall, now the Yorkshire Sculpture Park. She had specialised in art and pottery in her primary teaching syllabus, and considered herself extremely fortunate to have had Jim Robison as her ceramics tutor. Before going to college O'Connor had spent a year working with Mildred Slatter at her pottery in Fulmer, Buckinghamshire, doing her clay and glaze preparation, and in turn learning to throw, but with her limited experience she felt cheeky phoning up Alan to see if there was a vacancy at the Pottery when she left Bretton Hall. Her fiancé had just got a job as a civil engineer near Aldermaston, so the Pottery seemed the obvious place to extend

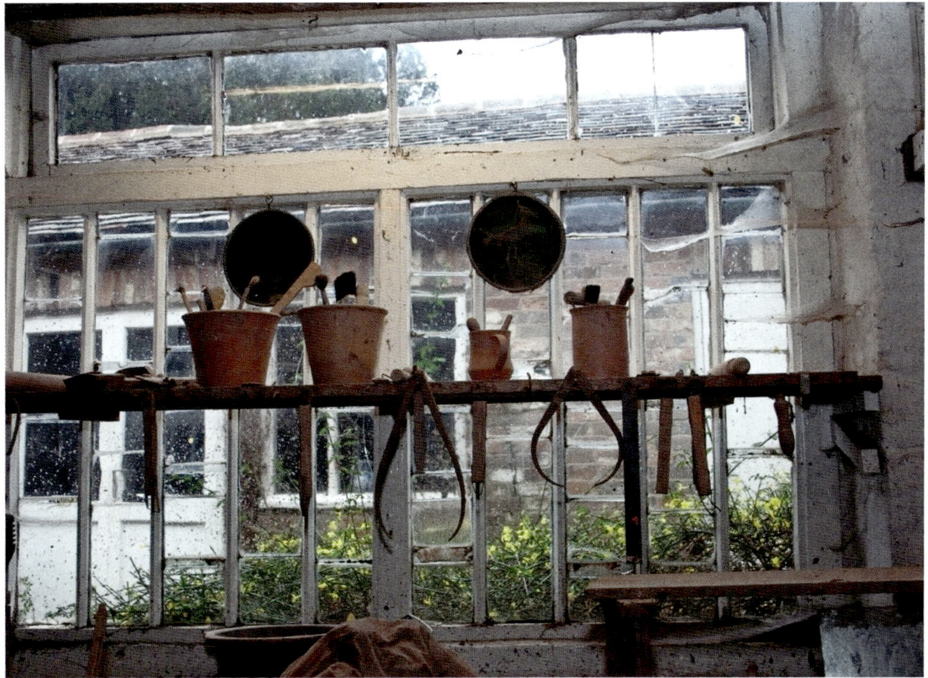

The view from the pottery wheels

her knowledge – although she knew Alan was already a well-known and highly regarded potter. To her amazement, he took her on.[39]

Thus Bent and O'Connor became the two 'learners' in the team. Not long after they had started working together they were given the task of packing up an order for a gallery. Bent, remembering the incident that followed, said that under any other employer she felt sure they would have been sacked:

> We had been used to wrapping any pots we sold from the showroom in newspaper (this was a long time before bubble wrap became the norm), and no one told us any differently. So we carefully wrapped the pieces in newspaper and packed them in a tea chest, and the work was duly sent off to the gallery. A few days later the gallery called the pottery to say that most of the pots had broken in transit. Jane and I were mortified! However I never remember Alan getting very cross (although he must have been) and he was very forgiving of our stupid mistake. Wood wool was the right packing material, we found out.[40]

For four happy years Gill Bent lived across the road from the Pottery, in No. 22b. Helen Caiger-Smith's goddaughter, Melody Cooper, lived in a flat above the cottage and spent much her time typing and retyping Caiger-Smith's book *Lustre Pottery*, published in 1985.[41] Bent acknowledges Caiger-Smith's generous and open-minded attitude, particularly in 1978, in allowing her to co-habit with her partner, Allen. She recalls that the winter of 1978–9, at the end of their first year, was so cold that the privy at the back of No. 22b froze. The village looked beautiful under a blanket of thick snow, and there was no traffic. Sir William Mount, who lived nearby at Wasing Park estate between Aldermaston and Shalford, invited some of the potters to skate on one of the small lakes on the estate: 'We jumped at the chance and my husband Allen remembers Lady Mount coming down to the lake whilst we were skating with tea and cake to warm us up. A very lovely and magical memory.'[42]

Almost everyone who worked at the Pottery at that time lived in a tied cottage. They often had suppers together or went to the local pub, and if anyone was doing overtime or went back to the Pottery after hours there was always someone about; the back door of the workshop was never locked. A culture of trust had developed within the workplace: assistants were even allowed to use the

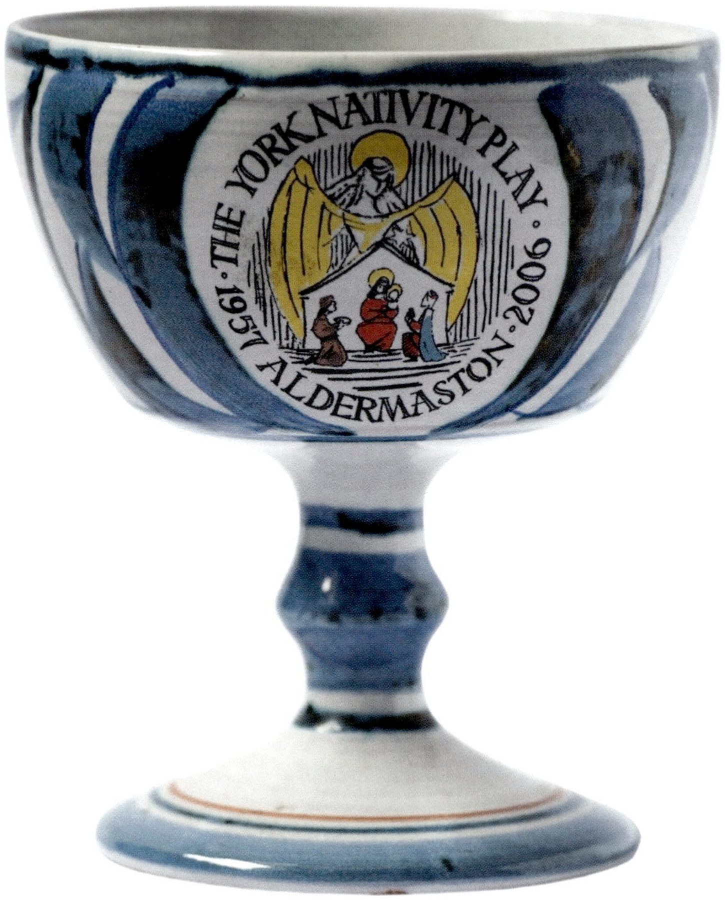

Nativity Play chalice by Alan Caiger-Smith,
2006, h. 14 cm, w. 12.7 cm
Collection Charlotte Davis

clay-spattered telephone for private calls (there was an honesty box beside it for payment). In many ways working at the Pottery was an extension of student life, with young people working and learning together.[43]

Village life continued to be an important part of the experience for all the assistants. With five cottages available for them to live in, plus Tile Cottage where Campden and his family lived, they constituted quite a big part of the community and the Pottery was very much at the heart of the village. O'Connor said she enjoyed being part of it all: she took on the local Brownie pack when there was a call for a 'Brown Owl', and even took the role of Mary in the York Nativity Play when there was great consternation as Avril, the villager who always played her, was unable to do so as she was about to give birth to her sixth child.[44] The Caiger-Smiths had been involved in this annual event since its conception by Pat Eastop (Geoffrey Eastop's wife) and the vicar of Aldermaston, in 1957, and Pat directed the medieval play for 57 years. Her dedication was recognised when she was awarded an MBE in 1998. Alan played one of the Three Kings, a role he eventually passed on to the next generation, and plates and goblets commemorating the York Nativity were often displayed in the Pottery showroom.

Gill Bent recalls the important part played by the wider community in the life of the Pottery:

> There were Bill and Olive Ford, who lived next door and supplied the Pottery with gas canisters for the heaters and paraffin for the heater in our cottage, and Olive also used to come and expertly wrap parcels for the orders that had to be sent by post. And almost next door to Alan's mother lived Nicola Brown and her family. Nicola's contribution to the Pottery was to pay our wages, and her arrival on a Tuesday morning was always eagerly awaited.[45]

There were also all the regular visitors to the Pottery:

> 'Mrs Ducks Eggs' – Julia Porter, who lived up the road and popped in to see if anyone wanted any eggs; 'Granny' (Alan's mother), who lived opposite and came over when there were a few clues in *The Times* cryptic crossword that were challenging her; and from time to time came Sir William Mount, who might chuck a brace of pheasants over the lower part of the door and ask us to give them to Alan.[46]

For Jason Shackleton,

> Aldermaston Pottery and the village was like a magnet for interesting people … I met Richard Burton and his beautiful princess Elizabeth Taylor at the village shop, their Rolls Royce parked out front, and one day Hans Coper came in a Mini to see Alan and we potters all came out to meet him; another great master.[47]

Another important figure in the village was the poet and novelist Paul Roche, also known for his 32-year relationship with Bloomsbury painter Duncan Grant. The pair had met in 1946 and remained friends until Grant's death in 1978, aged 93, at Roche's home in Aldermaston. In 1961 Roche and his wife and young family had been living in the West Indies and Mexico, but came back to England after an anguished request from Grant following the death of Vanessa Bell. They settled at the Old Stables in Aldermaston.[48] Shackleton remembers Roche as 'an eccentric character with his green and orange dyed hair and beard':

> Paul and his wife Clarissa lived in The Stables, just over the road from the Pottery, with their three angel-like daughters, Cordelia (Mitey), Vanessa and Pandora, and their son, Martin. Budgerigars would fly free in their conservatory, and it seemed as though they lived in another world, it was wonderful … Duncan would often come and stay with them, and he would always ask to go to the Pottery so he could spend time with the potters. He would be pushed up the road in his wheelchair, wearing a fine wide-brimmed straw summer hat, with his long white beard glowing, and he would sit and watch and we'd talk; he loved the energy, as did we all.[49]

Gill Bent recalls that 'Clarissa often came into the pottery just to chat, but she also acquired a good many pots. She had a black Labrador called Persephone, and together they would roam the Aldermaston Street in the early hours. They were a very eccentric family.'[50] On one visit to the Pottery Grant declared that he could never have been a potter because his thumbs were not big enough.[51]

Duncan Grant had himself been involved with decorating using maiolica pigments on tin-glaze pottery some fifty years earlier, during a brief revival of the technique by the Omega Workshops. Founded in 1913 by Roger Fry with Duncan Grant and Vanessa Bell as fellow directors, the Omega Workshops' aim was to promote 'a new movement in decorative art' that promoted the unity of art and design. Fry also sought life-enhancing colour and pattern as a foil for the dinginess of the British home interior, so his simple modernist designs and his choice of maiolica, with its Mediterranean colour associations, followed naturally.[52] This desire for colour and a certain 'joie de vivre' in decorated ceramics was the same reason that Caiger-Smith sought to revive the maiolica technique some 35 years later. He writes of Duncan Grant:

> He appreciated the processes we used all the more because of the colourful pottery he and Vanessa Bell had produced in the Omega Workshops and at Charleston. Duncan had a great love of life and he and Paul could be extremely funny together. One Christmas Eve we were all playing charades at Shalford, and they came in as Apuleius and the Golden Ass. Paul was on hands and knees on the carpet. He had turned his party hat into donkey's ears and was 'eeyoreing', while Duncan sat astride him trying to make the ass move by frantically beating its backside with a rolled copy of *The Times*. Late in Duncan's long life, Paul accompanied him to Paris for the opening of the big Cézanne exhibition. Hearing of the presence of the distinguished, elderly English painter, the Minister of Culture invited them both to the preview of the opening, when the works could be comfortably enjoyed, and they were also invited to the grand dinner that followed. They enjoyed the banquet, and their glasses were attentively refilled with vintage wine all through the evening. In the morning Paul was alarmed to find that Duncan had fallen out of bed and was lying on the floor, coughing, and very cold. He brought him back

to Aldermaston, tucked him up firmly and called the doctor. I visited him the next day and found him in bed, shakily sketching flowers with crayons in his drawing book. He said the exhibition had inspired him. After a while he asked me to get the half bottle of whisky from the desk near his bed. After one or two glasses he suggested getting some cigarettes from the drawer. We lit up. Duncan coughed, but was clearly enjoying himself, and we chatted happily for half an hour or so. Then I left him to doze. He died two days later. He loved living with Paul in Aldermaston, and I think he was not sorry to end his life there.[53]

In the last year of the decade a young Australian, Catherine Bennett, was drawn to the Pottery by her keen interest in brushwork and surface decoration and Caiger-Smith's burgeoning reputation as a master of both. Bennett's passion to become a potter had begun when she spent a year as the first school exchange student in Nara, Japan, in 1971–2. She lived with the Takase family and attended school with their daughter; because of her interest in pottery, it was arranged that she could work one day a week at a historic pottery nearby that made tea-ceremony ware. Later she worked at the pottery of one of the apprentices where, under the guidance of the senior potter, the elderly patriarch Grandfather Oisho, the eighth generation to pot there, she learnt to throw by sitting beside him and following his hand movements:

> It was the most marvellous way to learn, virtually no language at all, it was just purely demonstrating and me sitting beside him and doing it … If he said to make a bowl, he would make a bowl, and as he was making it he would pause and let me catch up with what he was doing, and gradually I learnt in that way. There were very definite rules and regulations about having women in the pottery. I was not to go anywhere near the kilns. It was supposed to be bad luck to have women around kilns – Japanese women as well – so they were packed by the pottery men, and then fired by itinerant firers who would all be men.[54]

Bennett returned from Japan to finish her formal schooling and then studied ceramics at East Sydney Technical College before setting up a pottery at Kinross Wallaroy School in Orange, where she also taught ceramics. Deciding that she needed to advance her brushwork skills, she wrote to Caiger-Smith and sent him slides of her work; she was delighted when he accepted her as an apprentice at Aldermaston. She travelled to England with her sister Jane, stopping over in Japan for six weeks on their way, where they visited the Takase family and went back to the potteries where she had worked and studied some eight years previously. Bennett acknowledges that 'the help and encouragement I had to do pottery in those early days is what has formed my life… it has probably been one of the very strongest influences'.[55]

Soon after she arrived in England, in spring 1979, and before starting work at the Pottery, Bennett chanced to meet Caiger-Smith at the Dartington Craft Camp. When he said to her with some relief that he felt it was going to be all right, she realised that he had been just as anxious about taking on a student from so far away as she had been about beginning a new venture. After she had been at the Pottery for a while she discovered that he received many letters from young potters wanting to work for him, and realised how fortunate she had been to be accepted as an apprentice:[56]

> After many years of employing potters he knew how important it was to have a team that interacted well. He was a very thoughtful employer, constantly observing and monitoring his employees, assessing their good and bad points and fitting their various skills around the work that was needed to make the workshop run happily. He made sure our work was varied and chose the right moments to demonstrate a new type of brushwork, a different thrown shape, explain a new idea, or encourage us to try our own designs, so that we were able to learn new skills and

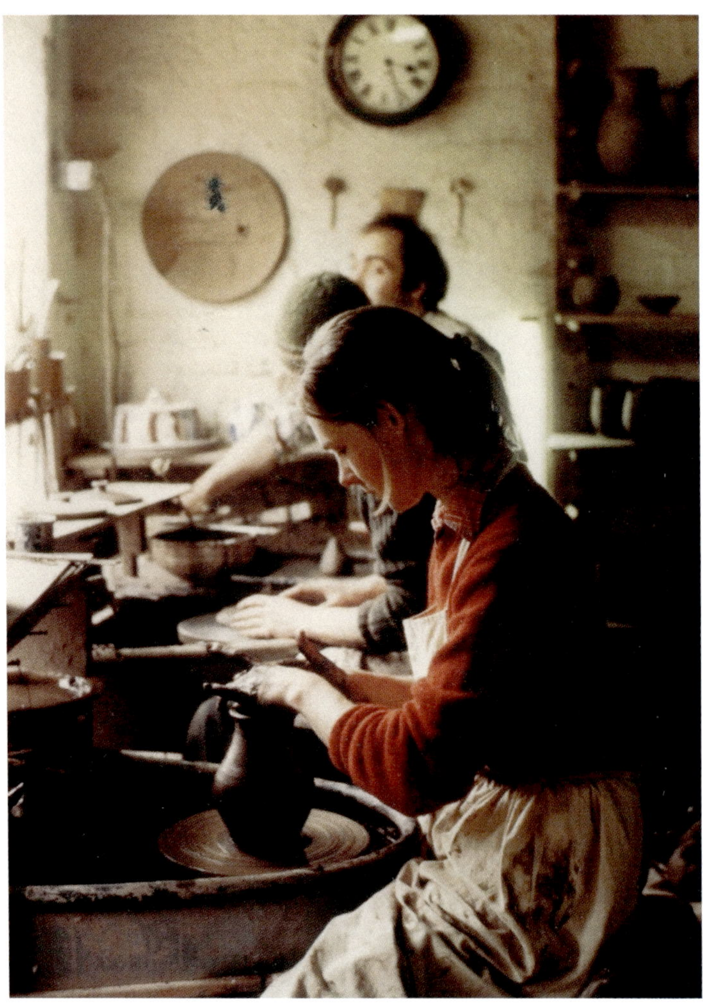

Catherine Bennett throwing a pot, 1979; Martin Wright
and Simon Middleton are in the background

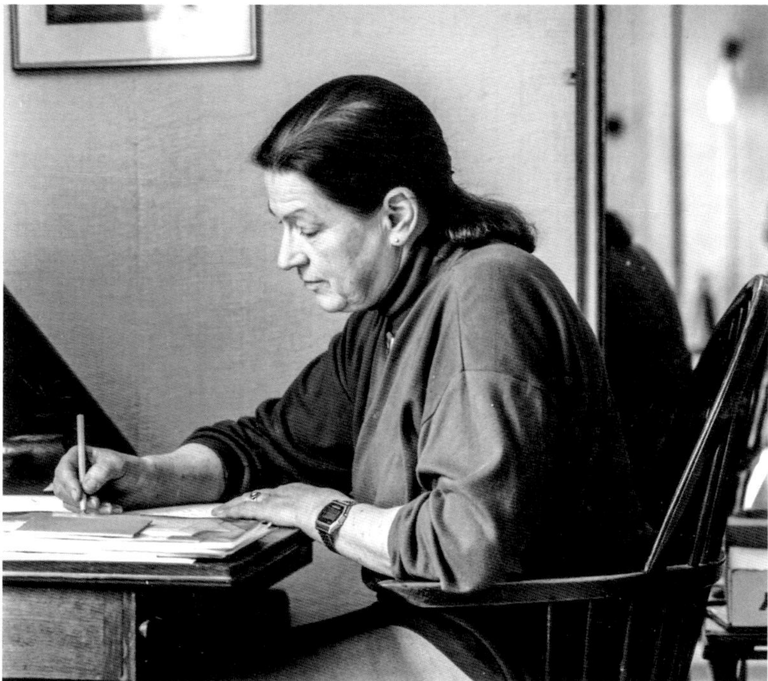

Anne-Marie at work in Shalford Farm House, 1993

gradually become useful members of the team. Hopefully we would then come to understand something of Alan's own ideas on the nature of creative work. Alan put enormous effort into teaching his apprentices, always aware of their needs and well-being, and at the same time somehow managing to make time for his own work. He would often stay on into the evening, after we had all gone to back our houses, as it was only then that he was able to concentrate on his own creative work without the interruptions.[57]

The knowledge and skills, particularly in brushwork, that Bennett acquired during her three years at Aldermaston, combined with the throwing skills she had learnt in Japan, were to set her up for a lifetime of making:

of all the work at Aldermaston, perhaps the brushwork was the most exciting. Alan always demonstrated the various brushstrokes and designs carefully – the unique language of each brush, the importance of negative space, the balance of the design, brushstrokes that touched or 'kissed', the subtleties used in applying colour, the familiar blue-green, 'old red', bronze-green, cobalt blues, soft manganese-browns, and the beautiful silver and copper lustre pigments.

Alan told the story of finding just the right Japanese brush. Years before, he had finally had made a bamboo-handled brush with a long flag, made of a combination of soft bristles to hold a good load of pigment, and harder bristles so that the brush maintained its shape once the stroke was made. He eventually needed more brushes, and so he wrote to the maker of the brushes in Japan. Months later he was

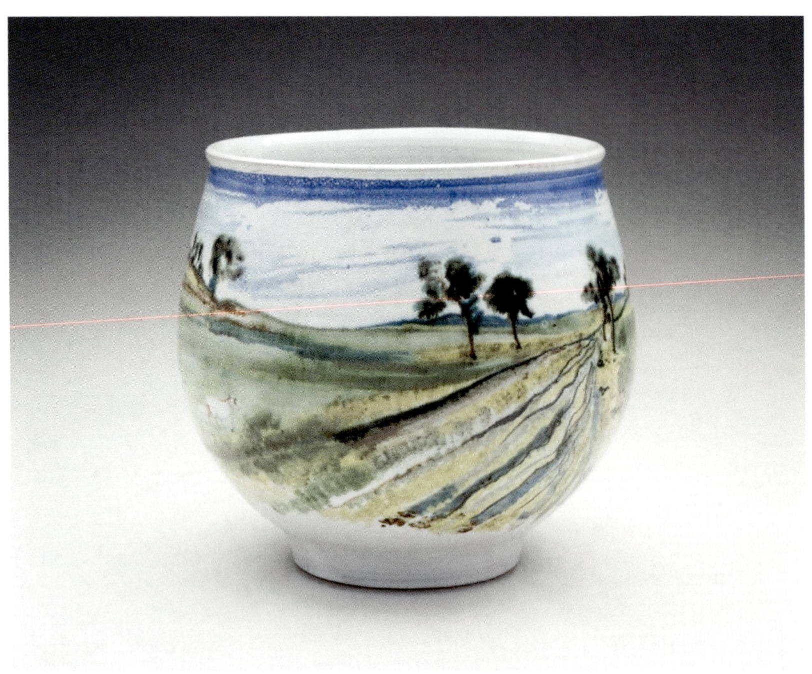

Tin-glazed earthenware gypsy bowl by Catherine Bennett,1981, h. 18 cm, w. 20 cm
Collection Catherine Bennett

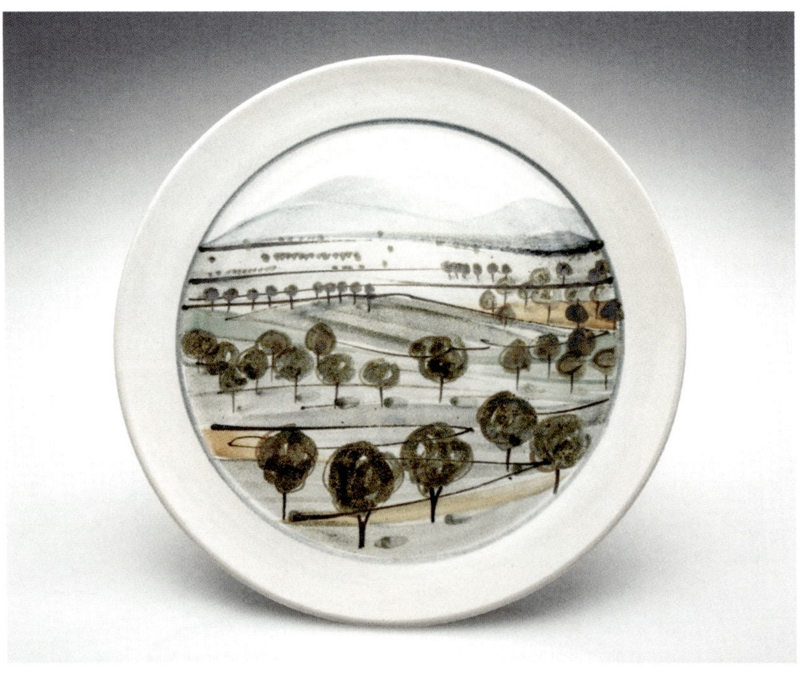

Stoneware platter by Catherine Bennett, Cowra, 1996, diam. 35 cm
Collection Catherine Bennett

pleased to receive a reply explaining that the suitable bristles had been procured, and that there were enough to make 378 brushes (or a similar number which I can't remember exactly). Alan was so delighted with the thought of the bristles being laid out to come to such a particular number that he chose to order all of them, although he probably didn't need quite so many.[58]

At first Bennett lived with Alan and Anne-Marie, and their two youngest sons, Paddy and Danny, who went to school locally. She describes this period as

> a lovely few months, not only with the challenge of learning new pottery skills, but learning about English life in general – the plants and trees growing in the Shalford garden, the history of the house and its yew tree avenue, flowers and vegetables that I had only known from literature, learning about the stars in the northern sky, and learning many practical skills from Anne-Marie – sewing, renovating furniture, re-caning a wooden stool, making lampshades for the lamp-bases made at the Pottery. The meals at Shalford were always times for fascinating conversations, ideas, stories and cheerful differences of opinion. Alan spoke beautifully, was a great raconteur and I think he enjoyed good company.[59]

She went on to live in Pottery Cottage: being part of the Pottery and village life, including getting to know all the families in The Street, was quite a novelty after a relatively isolated farming life in Australia. As none of the potters had televisions in the cottages they would often be invited to watch special programmes with Helen Caiger-Smith and Nanny. One particularly memorable occasion was 29 July 1981, the wedding day of Prince Charles and Lady Diana Spencer: everyone gathered in the Caiger-Smiths' garden to enjoy a summer picnic and watch the ceremony on the television, which had been carried outside for the occasion.[60]

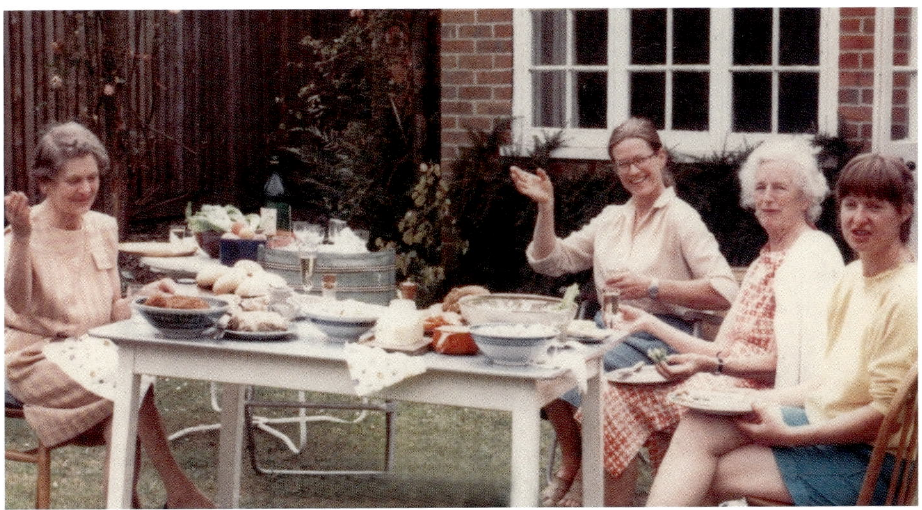

Nanny, Anne-Marie and Helen Caiger-Smith and Gill Bent
watching the Royal Wedding in Helen's garden, July 1981

Bennett had three happy years at Aldermaston. On her return to Australia she was asked to help design and establish a pottery workshop in the Japanese Garden in Cowra, New South Wales, where her family had lived for generations. Cowra had a unique wartime history: a prisoner of war camp had been built there to hold Japanese prisoners from the Pacific War. This later led to a long-lasting relationship with Japan, marked by the creation of a Japanese Garden in the 1970s.[61]

Bennett worked with the architect who had designed the Cultural Centre (part of the first stage of the Japanese Garden) to create a pottery that fitted in with the Japanese Garden aesthetic. The pottery workshop was built in recognition of Japan's long ceramic history, and provided an active workplace to complement the more passive viewing of the Garden by visitors. Bennett worked in the pottery for about ten years, first with a local man, and later a potter from Uganda joined them. The three of them produced high-fired tableware decorated with Aldermaston-inspired brushwork. Bennett also taught pottery making and decorating to adults and children locally, and in many workshops around Australia.[62]

Her three years spent at Aldermaston had reinforced Bennett's belief in the value of creative work and its importance to a balanced life. During her many years of teaching adults and children from all walks of life, she has always enjoyed seeing in so many people the sense of satisfaction when they are able to make a pot that is useful and beautiful, a painting that tells a story, or a mosaic to place in a garden.[63]

Ever since her years at Aldermaston, Bennett's life has largely revolved around the making of pottery. She had a family with the Australian potter Greg Daly, and for most of her life she and her family have been almost continuously involved with pottery and the arts world in general, working from their studio near Cowra, and teaching in Australia and abroad. She still returns occasionally to England to visit her sister Jane, who married Alan's eldest son, Nick. Although the Pottery has now gone, Shalford Farm House remains reassuringly the same as it was when she first came to live there, nearly forty years ago.

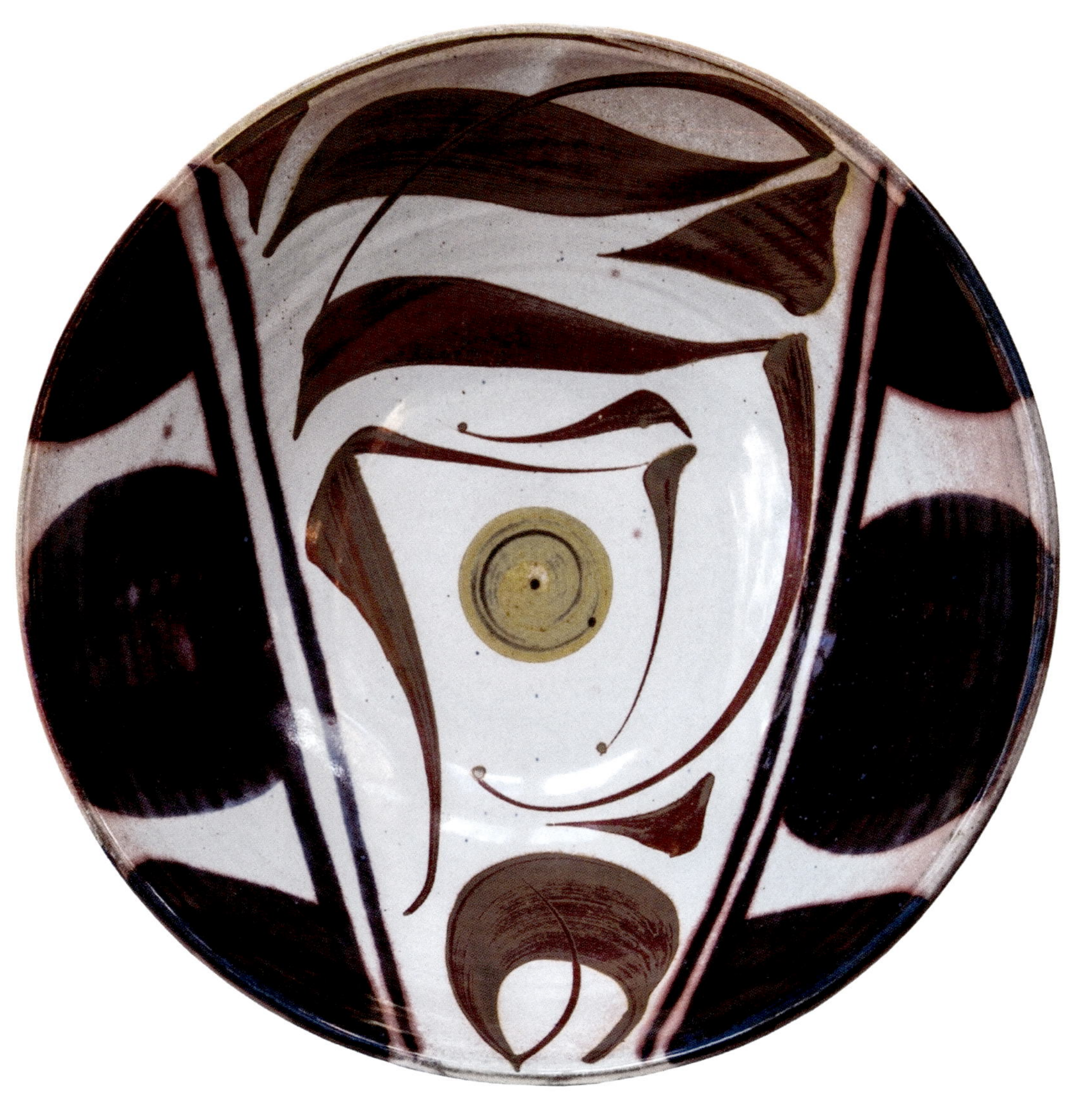

Medium bowl, copper and silver lustre, by
Alan Caiger-Smith, 1981, diam. 25 cm, h. 9 cm
Collection Sarah and Adrian Dixon

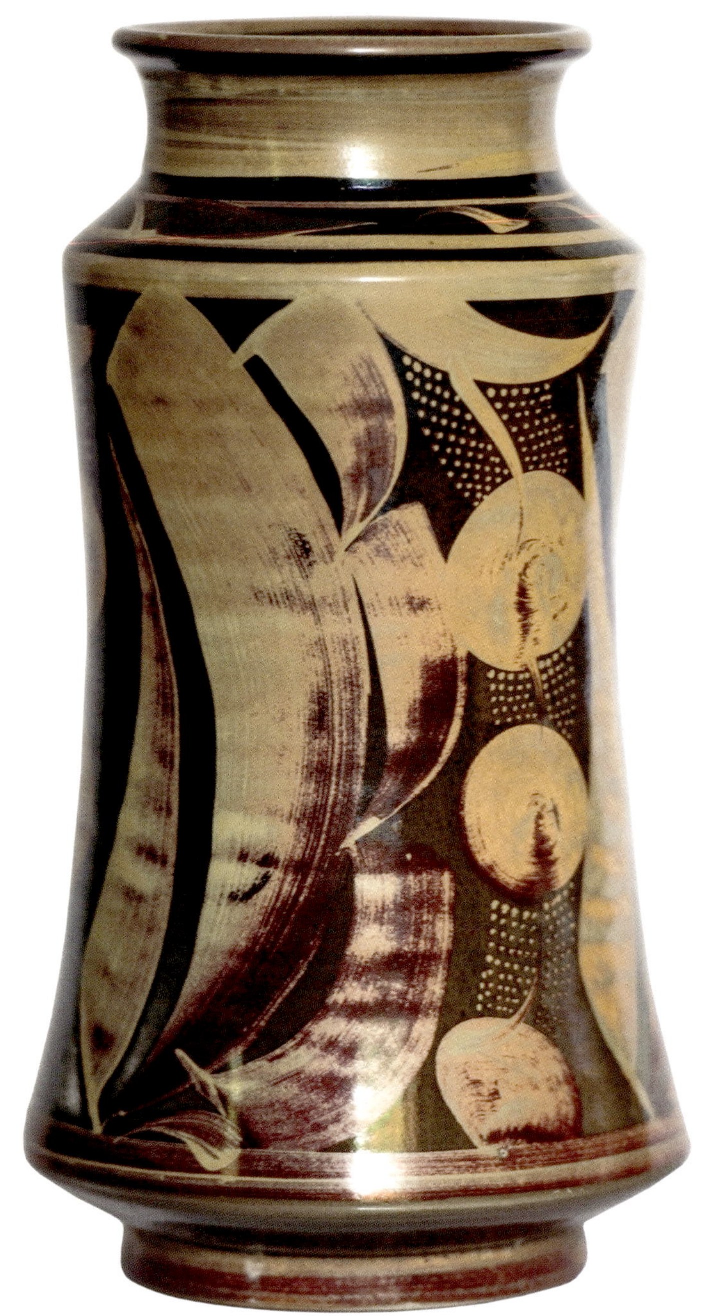

Albarello, dark lustre, by Alan Caiger-Smith,
1981, h. 25.5 cm, w. 14.6 cm
Collection Alan Caiger-Smith

124

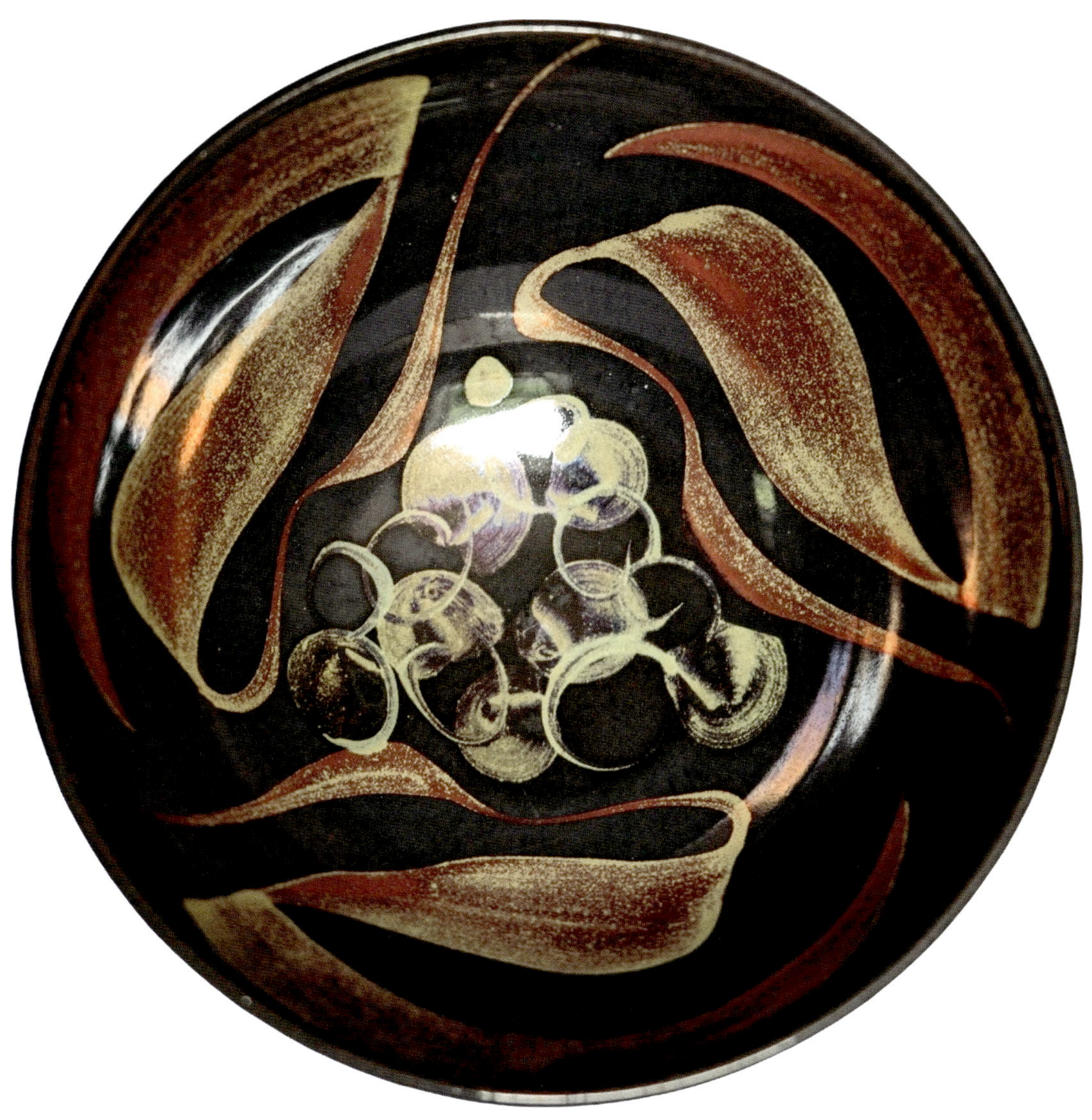

Serving bowl, copper and silver lustre on clear glaze over blue slip,
by Alan Caiger-Smith, 1982, diam. 21.5 cm, h. 8.8 cm
Collection Alan Caiger-Smith

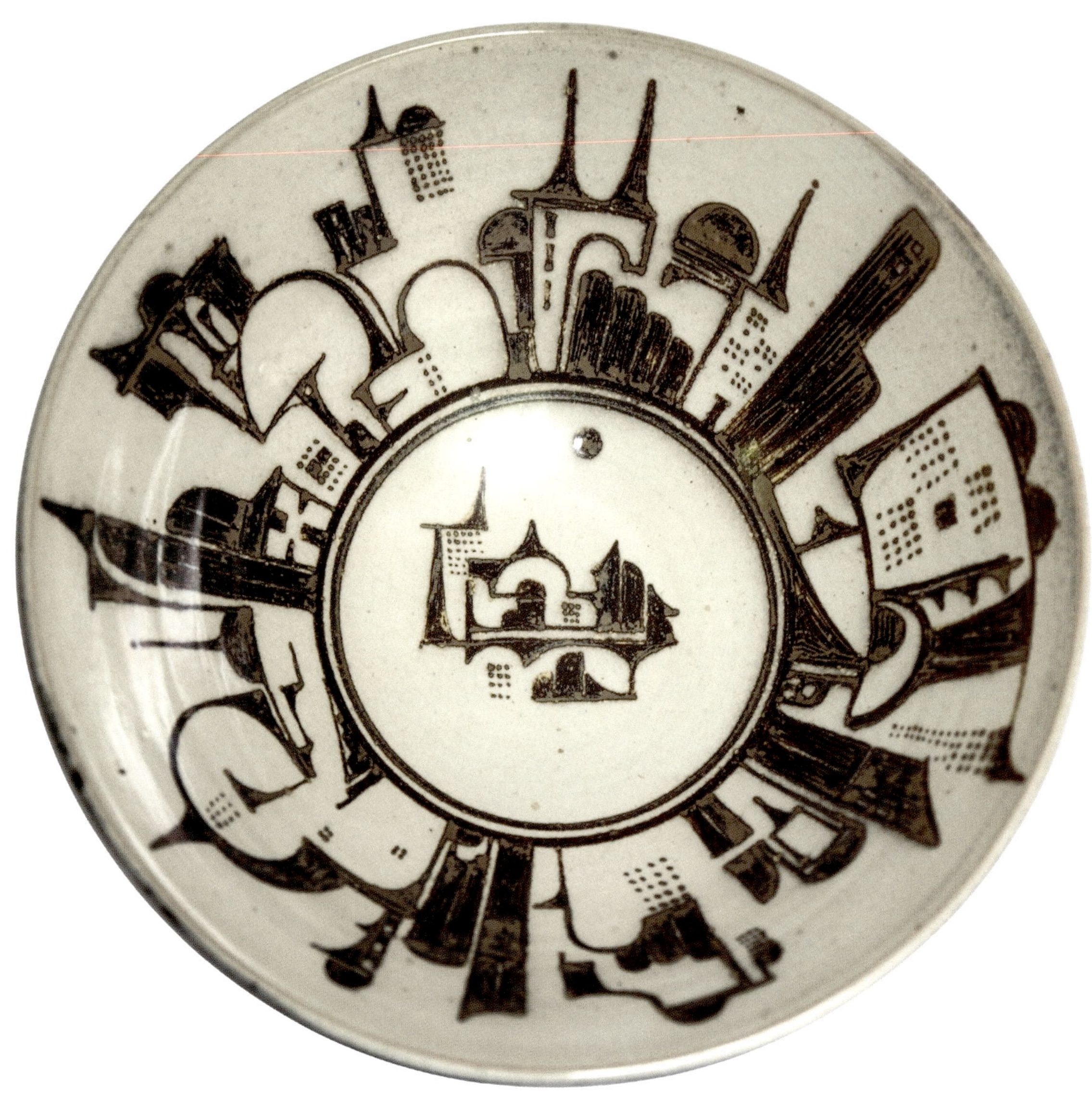

Medium bowl with Cairo theme by
Alan Caiger-Smith, 1982, diam. 28 cm, h. 9.5 cm
Collection Alan Caiger-Smith

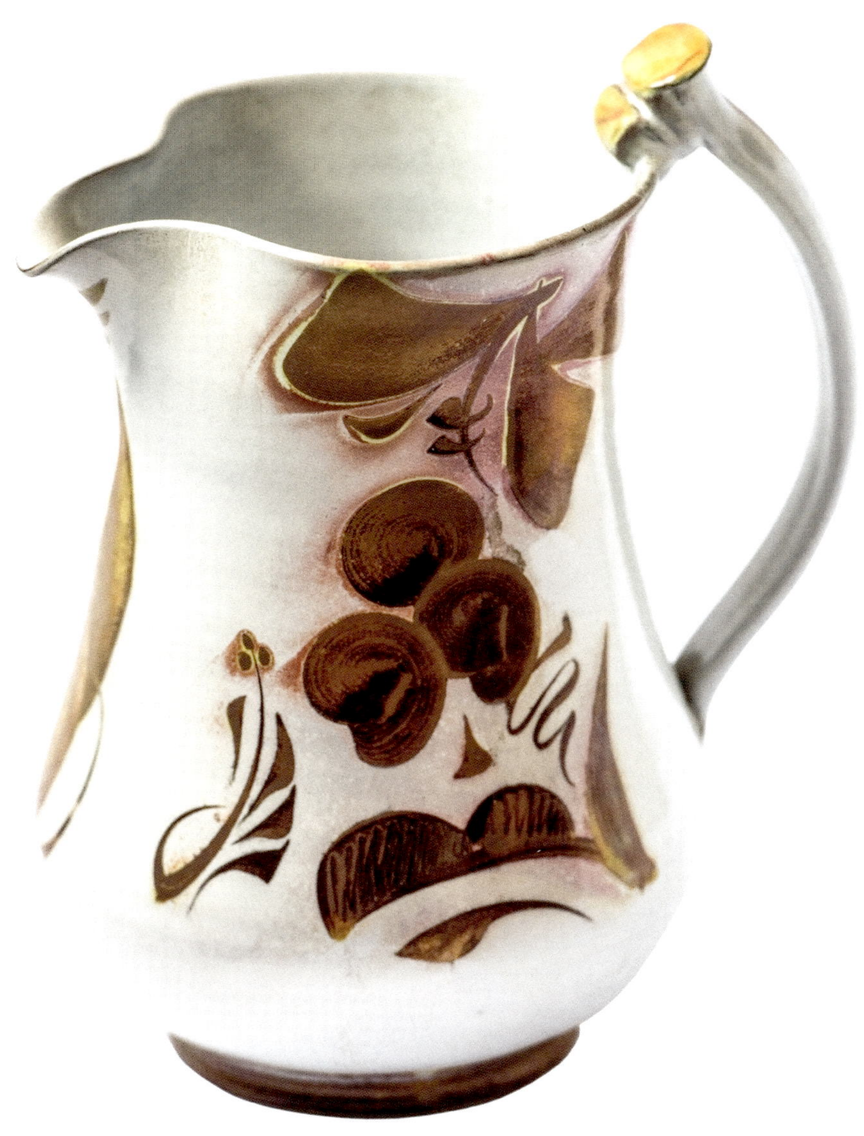

Lustre jug by Alan Caiger-Smith, 1982, h. 22.9 cm, w. 14 cm
Collection Alan Caiger-Smith

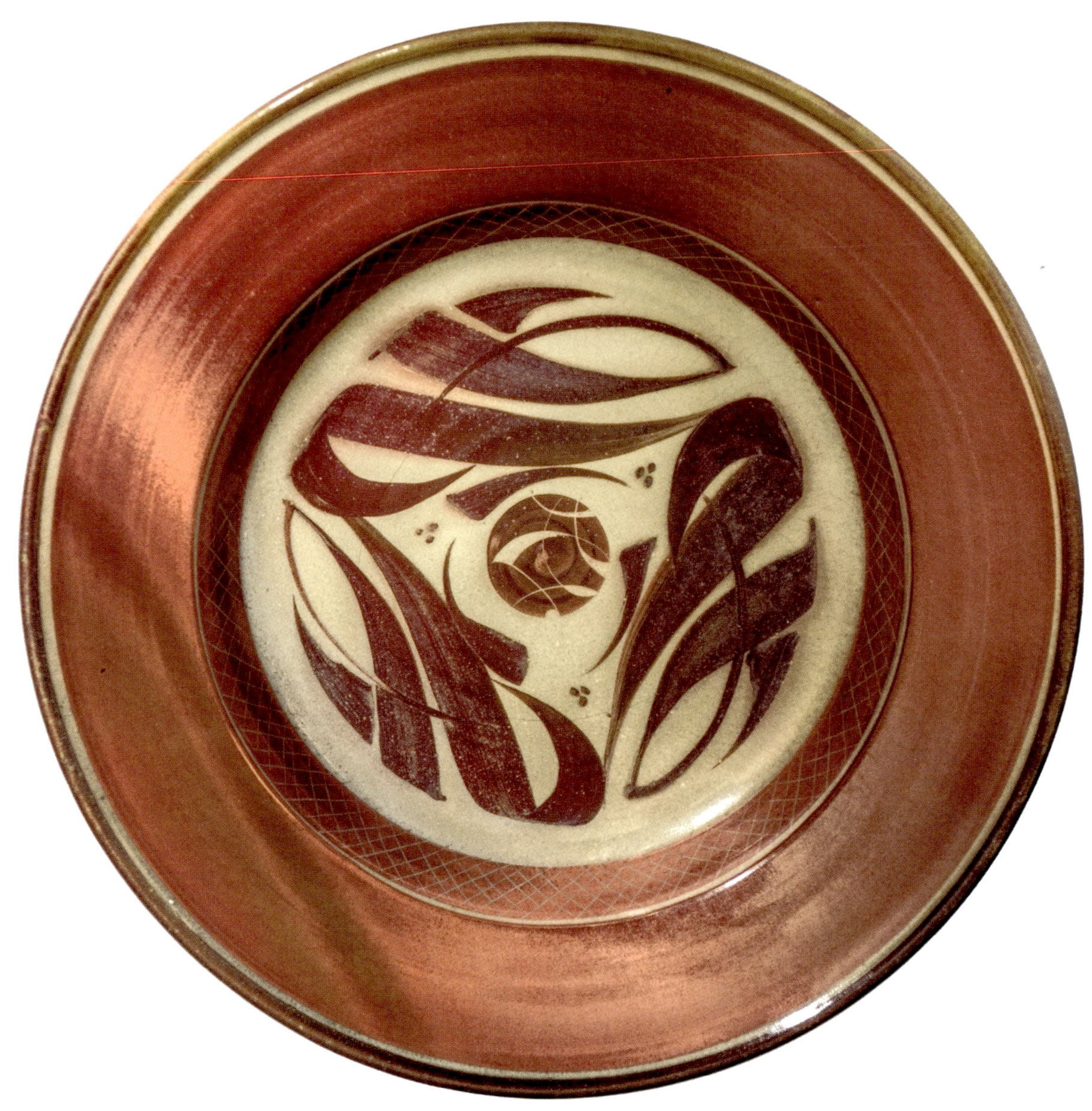

Large platter with copper lustre by Alan Caiger-Smith, 1983, diam. 41 cm, h. 6 cm
Collection Alan Caiger-Smith

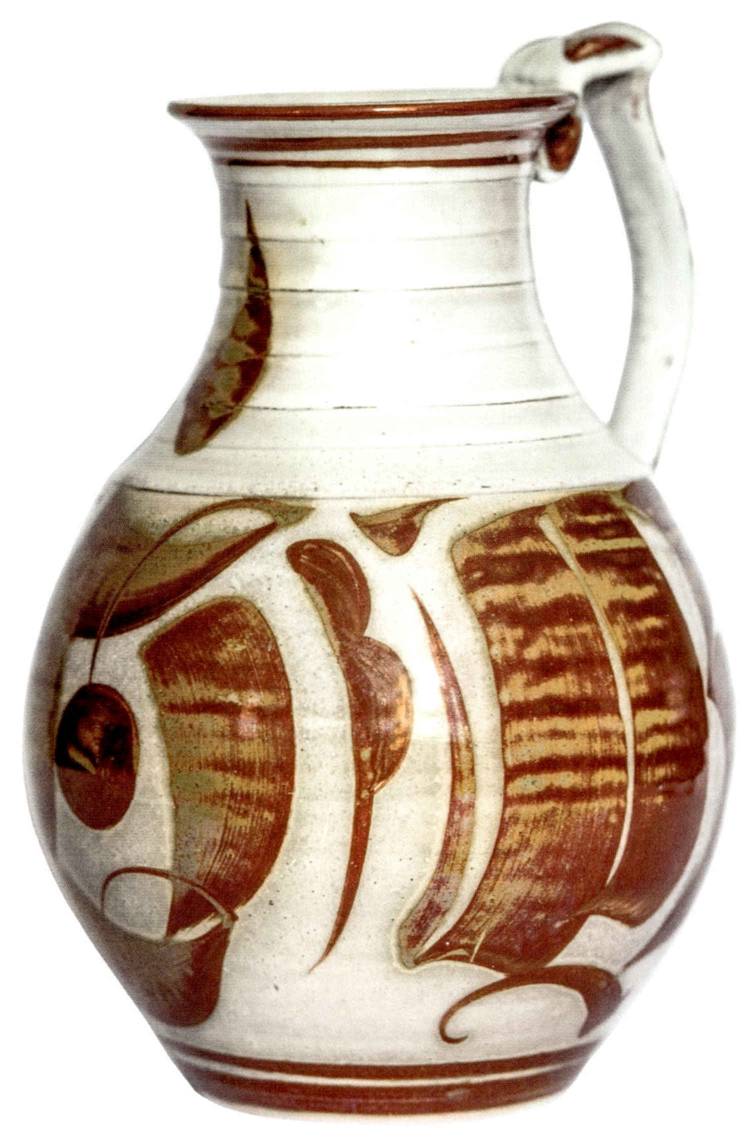

Pitcher with lustre by Alan Caiger-Smith, 1984, h. 25.5 cm, w. 17.8 cm
Collection Alan Caiger-Smith

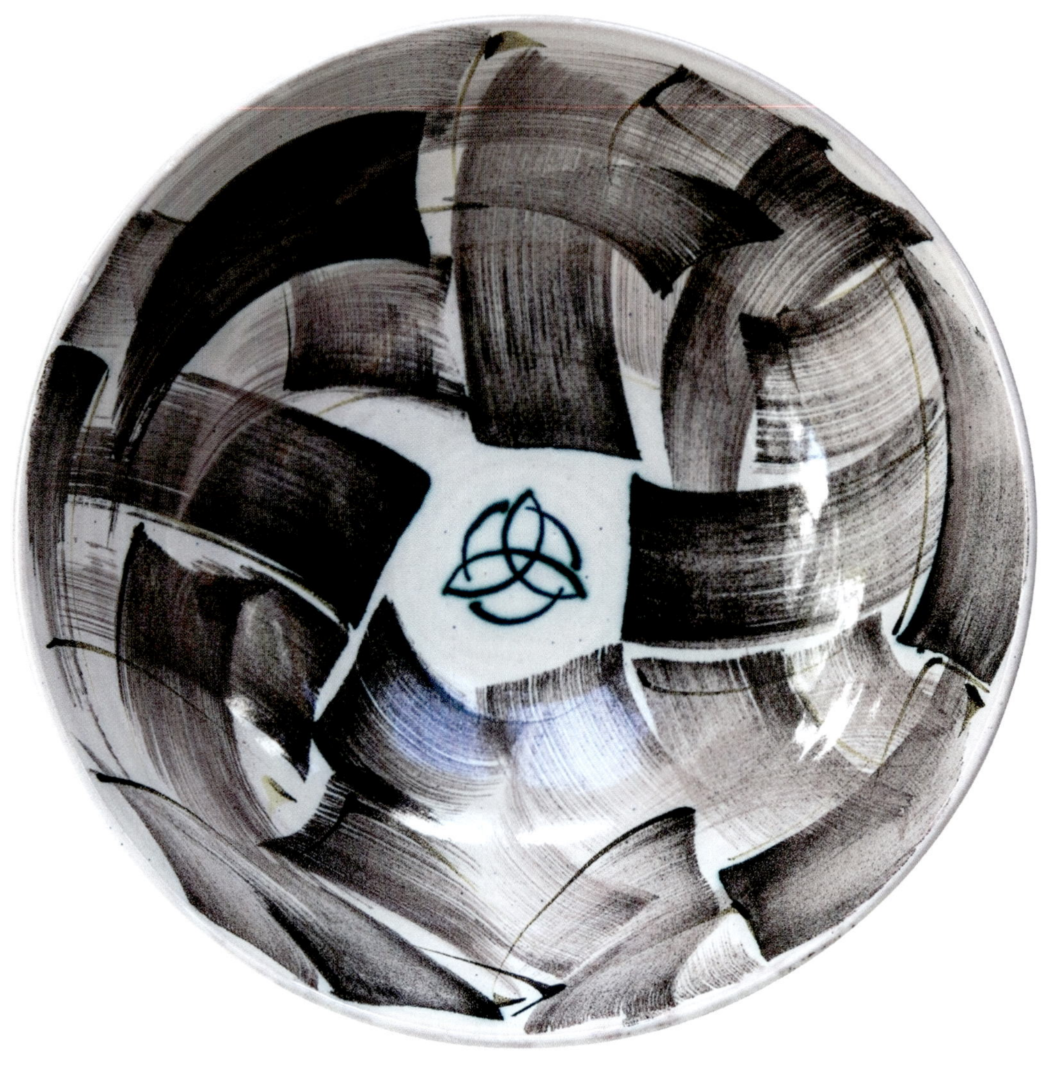

Medium bowl with copper grey and blue-green decoration
by Alan Caiger-Smith, 1984, diam. 27 cm, h. 8 cm
Collection Sarah and Adrian Dixon

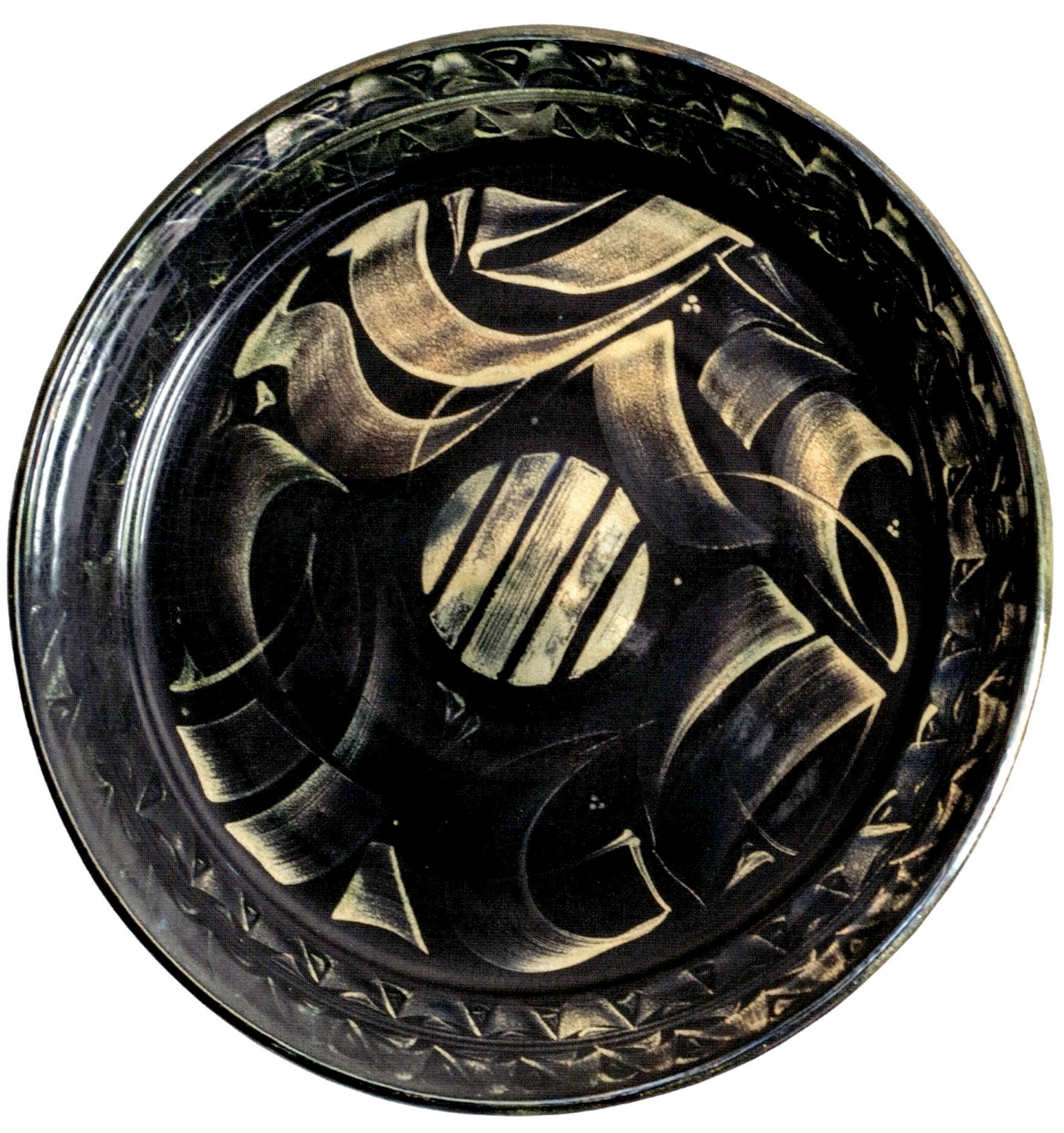

Blue platter with silver lustre on clear glaze over blue slip
by Alan Caiger-Smith, 1984, diam. 53 cm, h. 3.8 cm
Collection Alan Caiger-Smith

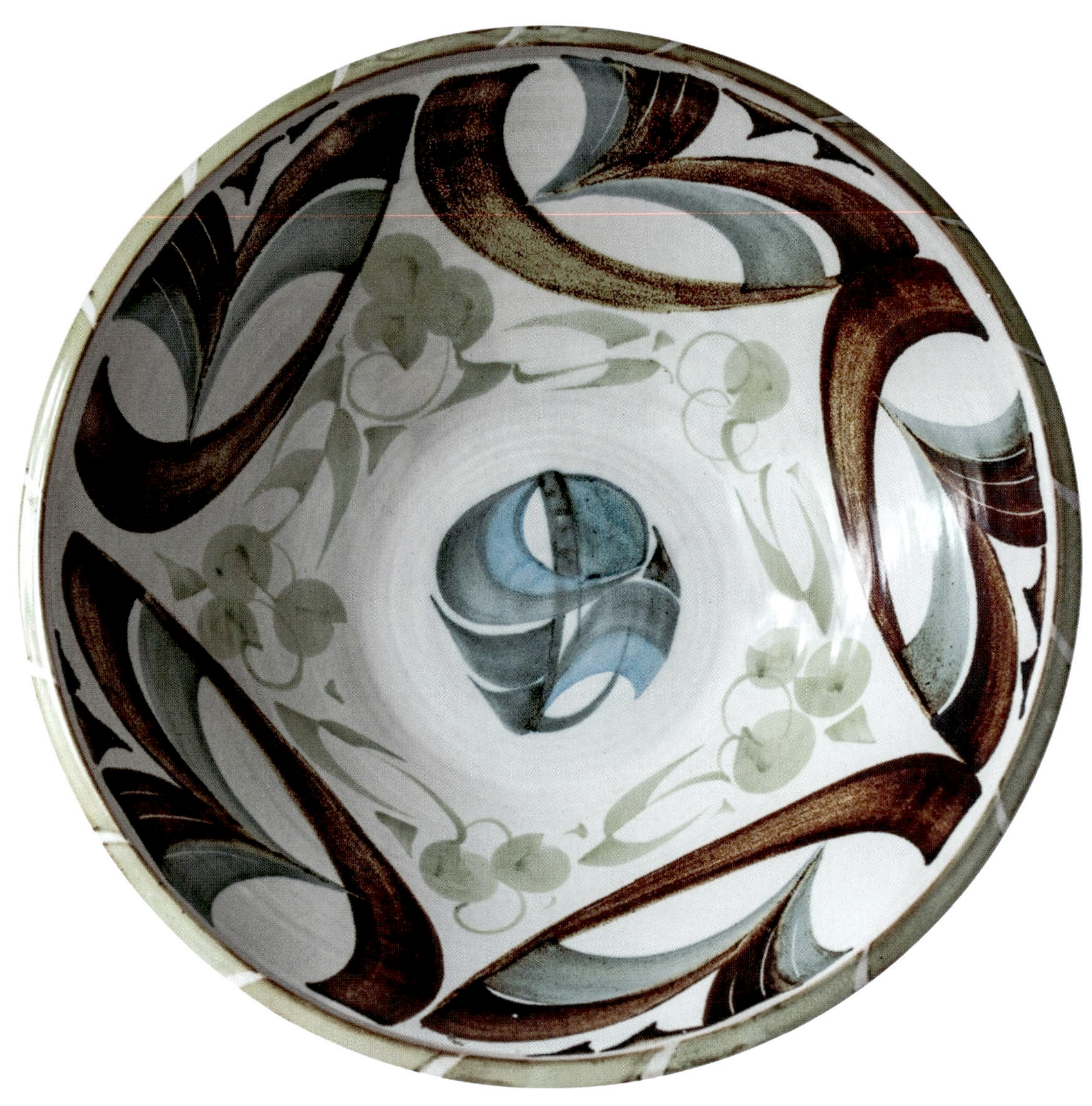

Charger with bronze, new bronze-green, lime green and celestial blue decoration
by Alan Caiger-Smith, 1986, diam. 46 cm, h. 16 cm
Collection Julian Bellmont

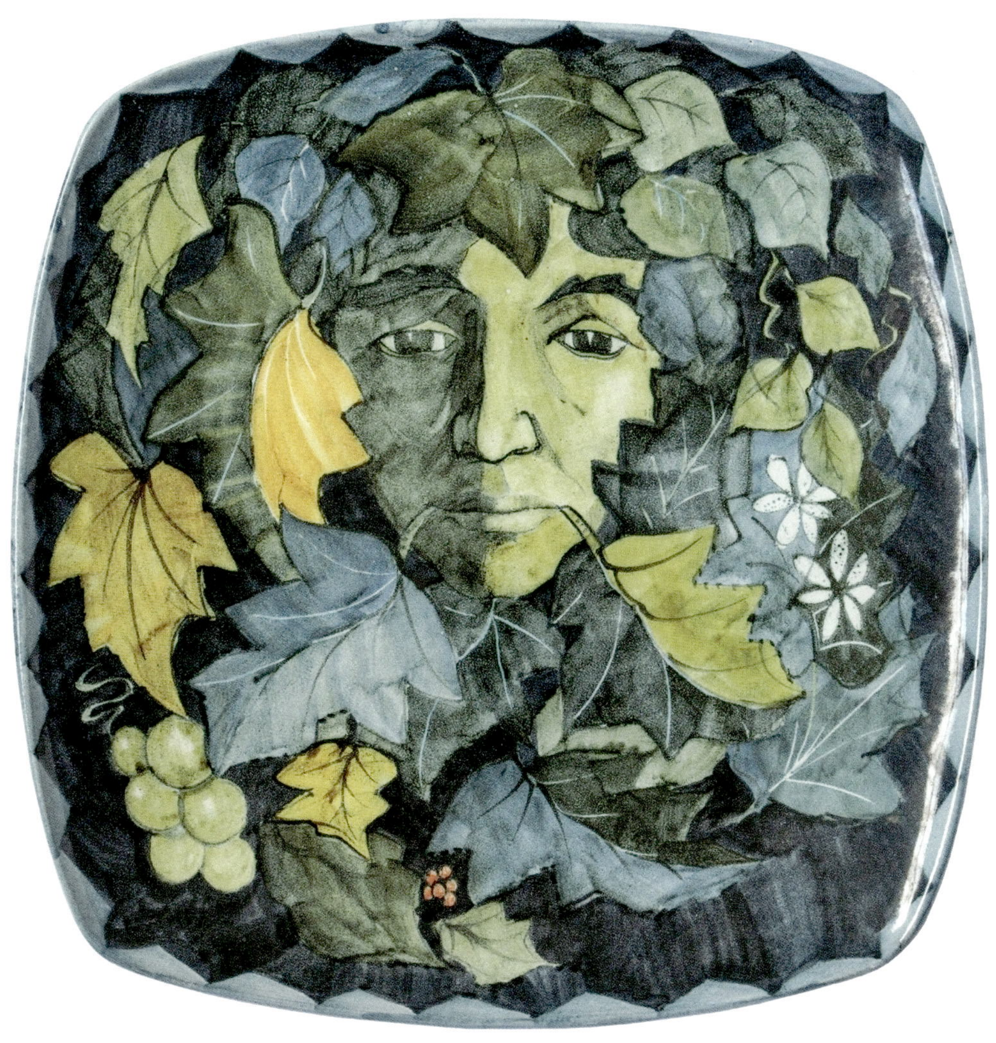

'Green Man' square dish by Alan Caiger-Smith, 1987, w. 33 cm
Collection Alan Caiger-Smith

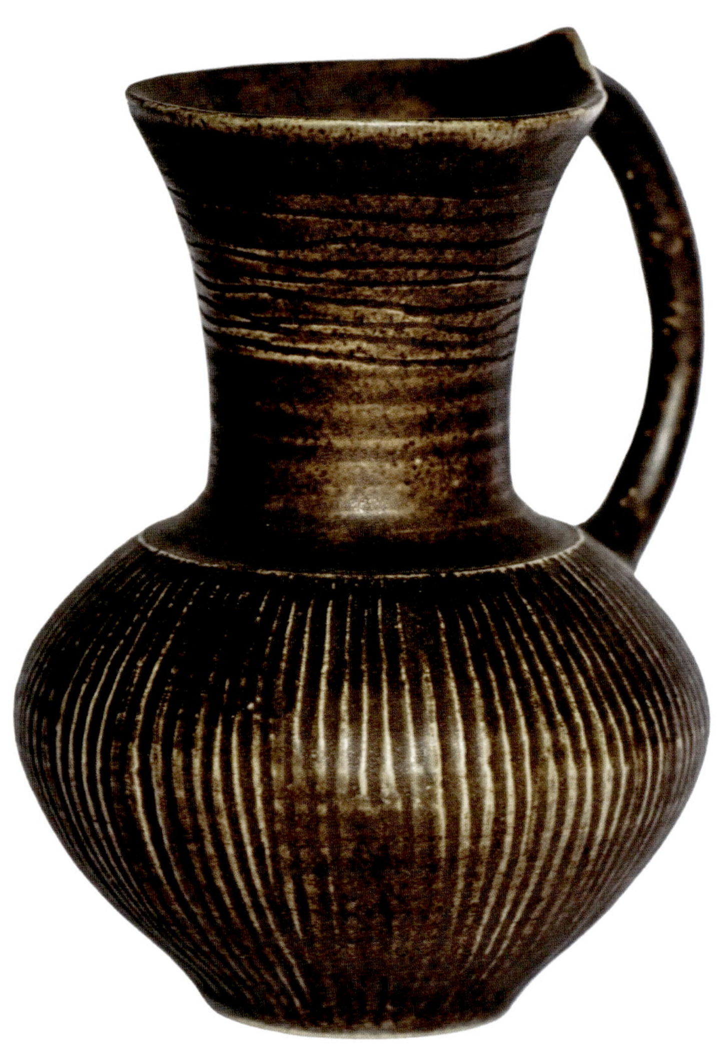

Handled vase made in porcelain by Alan Caiger-Smith, 1988, h. 15.25 cm, w. 8 cm
Collection Alan Caiger-Smith

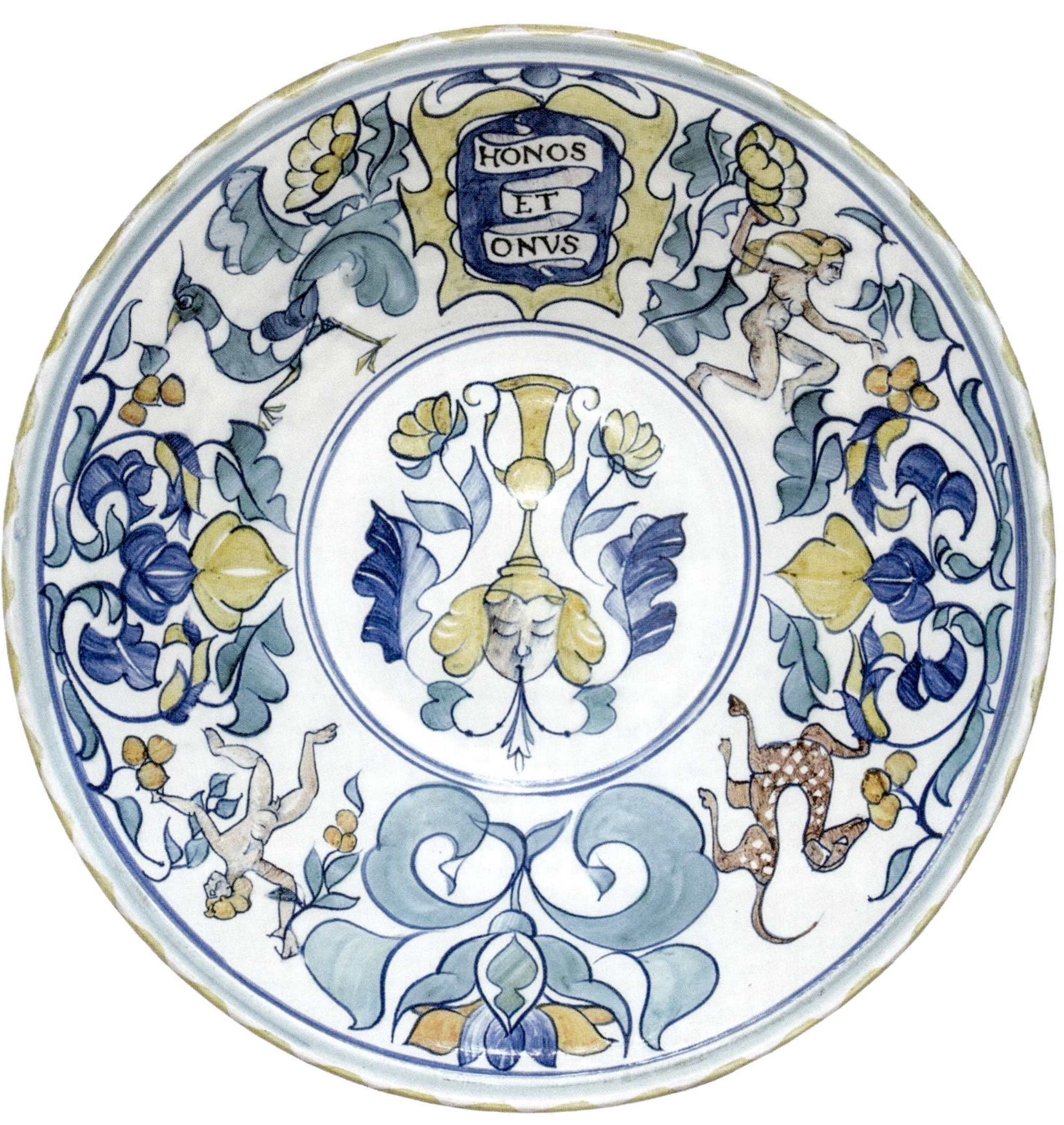

Presentation plate in Renaissance style by Alan Caiger-Smith, 1990, made to
commemorate Timothy Wilson's departure from the British Museum, diam. 36 cm
Collection Timothy and Jane Wilson

135

— 7 —

People and Places
1979–1983

In 1979 Caiger-Smith took on another local young person, Martin Wright; he had been at school with Jaki Rothery and, like Rothery, started with a Saturday job at the Pottery. He had previously trained as a chef and a shepherd, and after becoming a full-time assistant at Aldermaston would often cycle from his home in nearby Brimpton Common, arriving at the Pottery at 5 a.m. to do piece work before the day started, as he was saving up for a small flock of sheep and a few acres of land. Laurence McGowan taught him the skills of throwing: he described McGowan as a wonderful teacher with lots of patience, and a very nice person.[1] Gill Bent remembers that when Wright first came to work at the Pottery he was quite shy and withdrawn, but that he soon came out of himself and showed his intelligence and skill as a potter. As with many of the assistants, including Bent herself, the Pottery was the making of him: during his seven years there he became an excellent potter, made many friends and met his future wife.[2]

Towards the end of 1979 Jason Shackleton and Laurence McGowan moved on to set up potteries of their own. Both have had very successful careers. Shackleton had been left a small inheritance by his grandparents; it had been sitting on his piano for a year amid a pile of music before he decided that the time was right to set off on his own. He and his future wife, Jessica (a weaver who had been living with him in Aldermaston), headed for Scotland. They settled on a semi-derelict farmhouse in the hills 12 miles north-west of Dumfries, with 9 acres of land, a walled garden, fruit trees and a resident pig, as well as plenty of outbuildings for workshops. Full of enthusiasm for the future, Shackleton recalls: 'We loaded the Land Rover and trailer with our worldly belongings, pottery wheel, clay and tools, and last but not least, the produce from the garden, and then we drove north with the "Bonza Bute" (Catherine Bennett) riding shotgun, to start a new life.'[3]

For Shackleton one of the key attractions of becoming a potter had always been the wood-fired kiln, and one of the first things he did after moving to Scotland was to use 3 acres of the land to plant 2,000 trees to ensure that he would always be self-sufficient in wood for firing his kiln. He also put in 500 fruit trees and started keeping sheep, pigs and goats. With John Seymour's iconic *Complete Book of Self-Sufficiency* always to hand, he even produced his own bacon. After a year of arduous work the old dairy had been converted into a pottery workshop with a 30-cubic-foot wood-fired kiln, the house was habitable, and Laurieston House

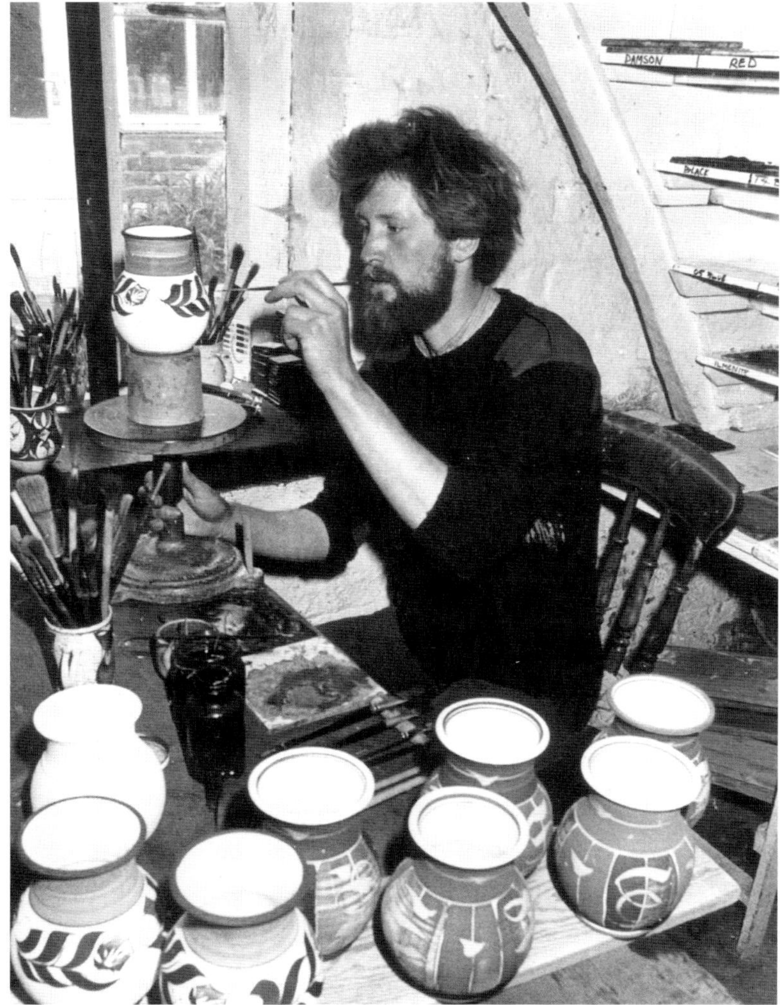

Martin Wright painting, 1986

Pottery was open for business. The first pots made at Laurieston were hand-thrown, a combination of slip-decorated and sgraffito earthenware, and painted tin-glaze maiolica. To start with Shackleton took part in about 35 shows a year, and soon found himself with an order book that was filled for the next four years. He took on his first assistant, Stephen Johnson, who proved himself a hard worker and a good potter, and together they built a 160-cubic-foot wood-fired kiln. The kiln used approximately 3 tons of wood for each firing, and could fire extremely large pieces safely and evenly because of its size. This was the first kiln Shackleton had built that never needed any adjustments, although the quality and quantity of well-seasoned wood used at every stage of the firing was crucial to achieving an even temperature and a clean burning atmosphere.[4]

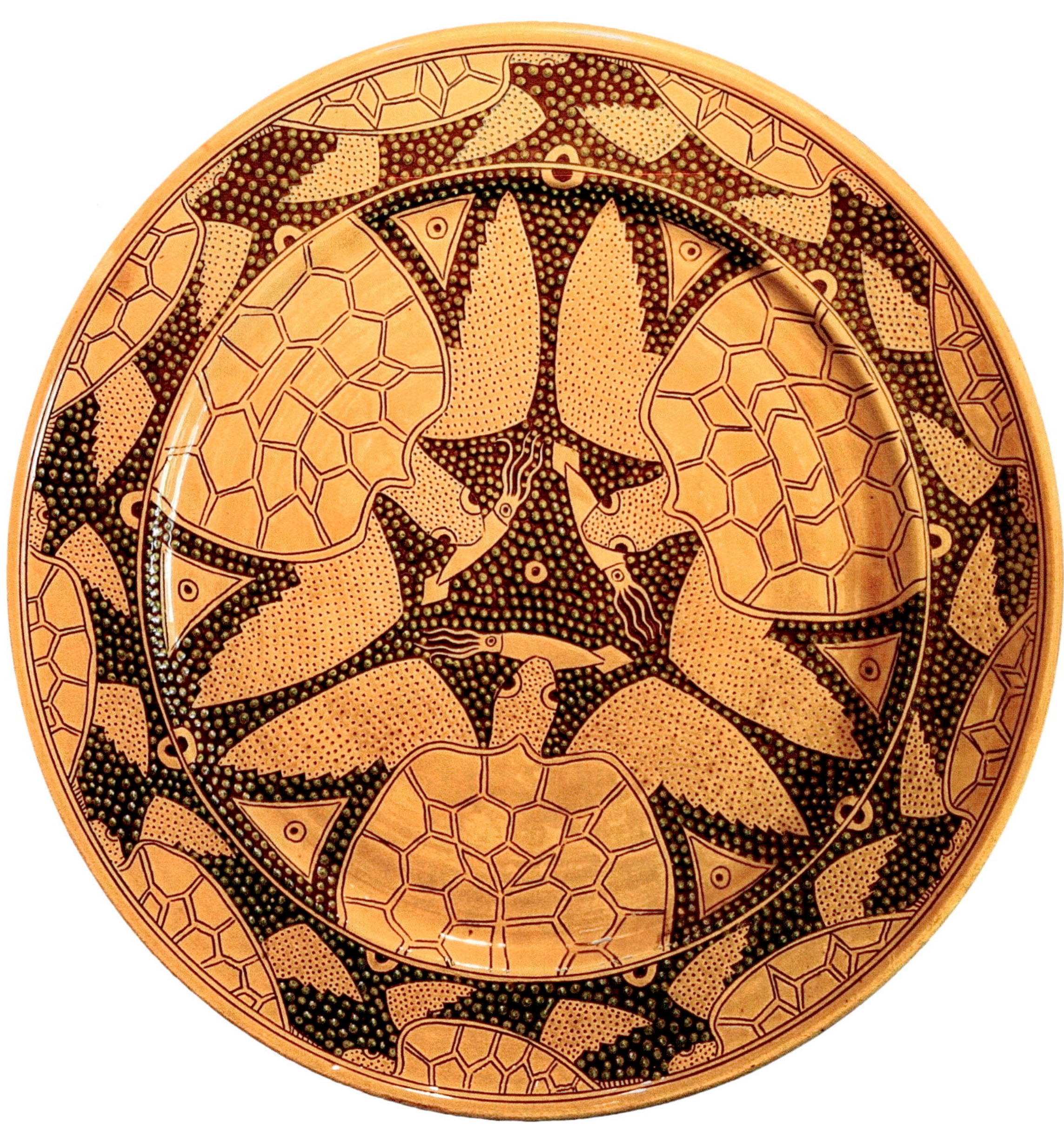

'Turtle Platter' by Jason Shackleton, *c.* 1992, diam. 60.96 cm
Collection Jason Shackleton

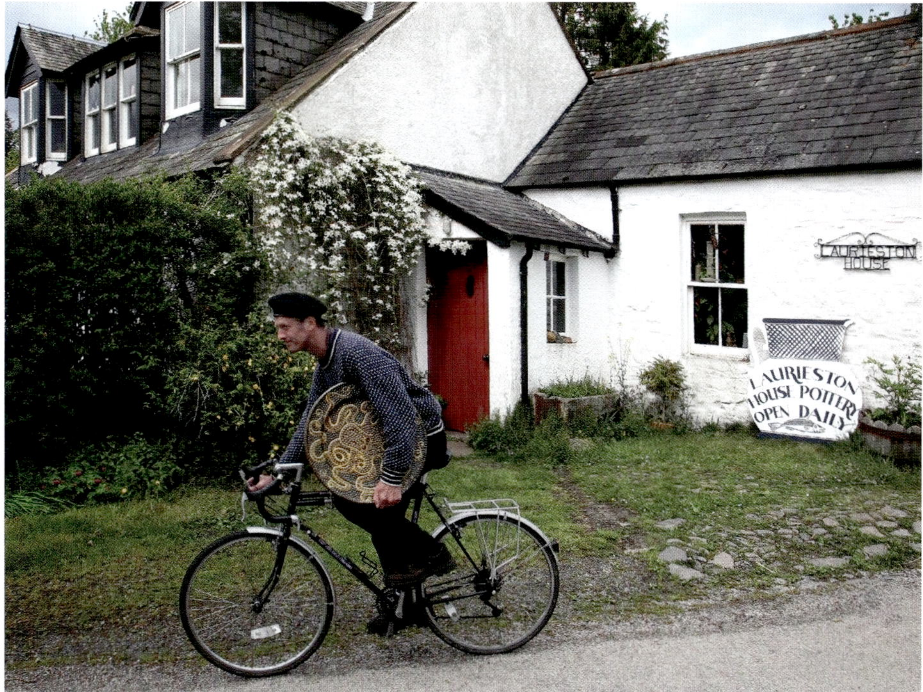

Jason Shackleton with a large platter outside Laurieston House Pottery, 1994

Ten years after opening the pottery Shackleton was becoming bored with making repeat orders for small items, and reduced his number of shows to five a year, all in Edinburgh, Glasgow and London. He also stopped taking private orders, apart from commemorative ware and tile murals, which had always constituted over half of his work. With time to concentrate on his more personal work he now began producing some of his most unique and individual ceramics and exhibiting at the Holland Gallery in London, where he soon attracted the attention of serious collectors.[5]

In 2011 Shackleton reflected that his most significant influences were Caiger-Smith and European and South American pottery,[6] but that the hardest thing was to develop an individual style. He had turned to diverse sources for inspiration, including his unusual upbringing, travelling with his father and snorkelling on reefs in the Seychelles, Africa and the Bahamas. He began to develop ceramics with a distinct narrative, decorating plates and bowls on the theme of pollution: a clear blue sea with sea snakes and an oil slick; 'Oil Fire', depicting burning oil-wells, sand and sky; 'Avenger Exhausts', with fumes signifying the end of our civilisation. When scud missiles were fired by Saddam Hussein's forces during the First Gulf War, Shackleton depicted these in his ceramics, with the missiles disappearing into a black hole in the centre of the piece. He also made a collection of work following a space theme: planets passing other planets and stars, rockets, spacemen and satellites, which he said tested his skills as a painter in new

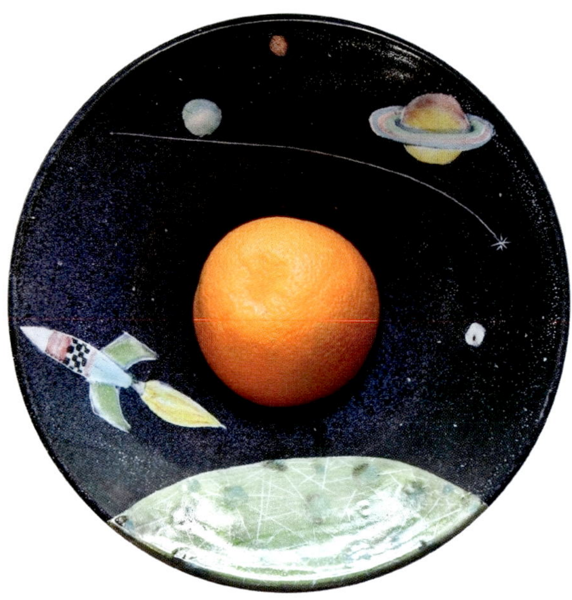

'Space Dish' by Jason Shackleton, 1994, diam. 25.4 cm
Collection Jason Shackleton

directions; he always painted an orange in the centre of these pieces, as his father
had used an orange to symbolise the planets.[7]

Shackleton's 'Predator Ware' featured the New York skyline, fish, teeth, and
all the 'bad people' of the world snapping at each other. On a 'Predator Plate' he
illustrated turtles eating squids; when his father told him that turtles don't eat
squids, his reply was that just because no one had ever seen them eat squids it didn't
mean they never had. (Five years later a German photographer captured a turtle
eating a squid!) Shackleton believes that all successful designs must have a 'lead-in'.
He ponders a blank shape, imagining 10–20 designs; if one seems exciting he just
goes with it, the design evolving as he works. He finds that hardest designs to get
right are usually the best: it takes time to get them right and to look balanced and
resolved, looking from all angles to check progress.[8] Although today's economic
climate is difficult for craftsmen, Shackleton has always believed that 'potters are
great survivors, because all they need is clay and a working kiln. Inspiration comes
from the land and sea around them, with the help of their imagination. Long may
their fingers work.'[9]

Not many of the assistants at Aldermaston found themselves in a position to
employ anyone after setting up on their own, but the great importance of passing
down the legacy of knowledge to the next generation is illustrated by Hannah
McAndrew, who came to work as an apprentice potter with Jason Shackleton in
October 2001. By this time it was becoming extremely difficult to gain workshop
experience with any working potter, as McAndrew found out. However, since

leaving Laurieston House Pottery her valuable training has enabled her to forge a successful career using traditional methods, against the tide of contemporary and conceptual ceramics that dominates the field today. She acknowledges the important legacy that she has inherited as a result of Shackleton's generosity:

In 2000 I had just graduated with a degree in Three-Dimensional Design and a passion for ceramics. I was determined to be a potter but knew that I didn't have the skills to be able to go it alone, so I spent the next six months writing to over ninety potters to try to find an apprenticeship, all to no avail.

On a visit home to my parents in Dumfries and Galloway, a stroke of good fortune led me to the door of Laurieston House Pottery, which was opened by a tall, animated man, bespectacled and dressed in a boiler suit and beret. It was Jason. I nervously explained why I had come, and my wish to pursue a life in clay, and to my surprise and delight, he couldn't have been more enthusiastic and encouraging, and immediately invited me to work with him at the pottery.

Jason shared every aspect of the process with me, making tin-glazed, painted maiolica and slipware. We threw, turned, handled and slipped pots. We weighed, prepared and sieved slips. We packed and fired the huge wood kiln, stacking and sorting tons of wood in preparation, cleaning and batt washing kiln shelves. We mixed glazes, glazed pots and prepared painting pigments for use on the tin-glazed wares. Fired pots were inspected, priced and packed.

I worked at Laurieston House Pottery for two extraordinary, invaluable years. It was such a time of learning, of practising skills and developing techniques, and of beginning to find my own stylistic, creative voice. I wanted to build a wood-fired kiln of my own. Jason kindly offered me a stack of firebricks, and with his help I set about building my first kiln. All these years later Jason is still always there for me with words of encouragement and praise, and his support and nurture have never wavered. I take great pride in the lineage that I have inherited and it is important to me that I should continue to pass forward the legacy of skills and knowledge that I was so generously given.[10]

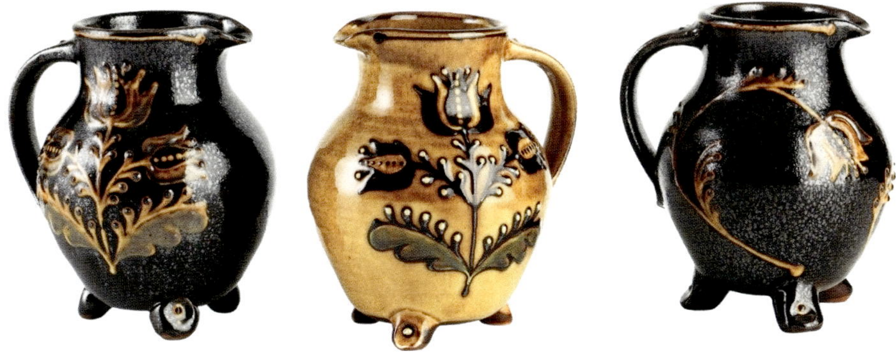

Slip-trailed tripod jugs by Hannah McAndrew, 2015, each h. 18 cm
Private collection

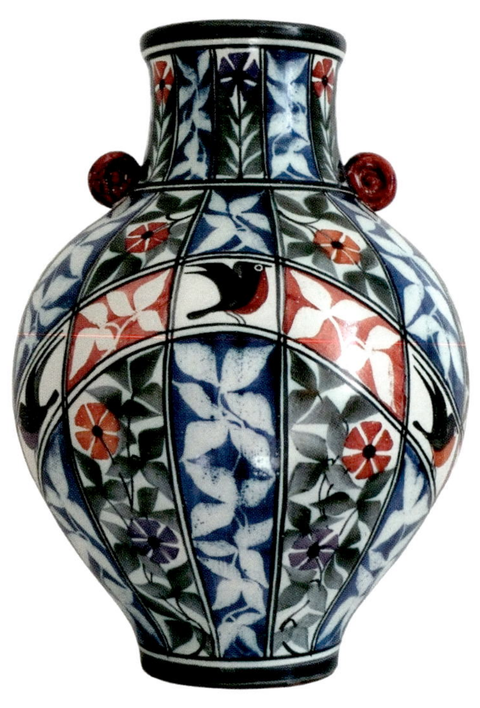

Vase with lugs by Laurence McGowan, 1997, h. 29 cm
Collection Laurence and Jackie McGowan

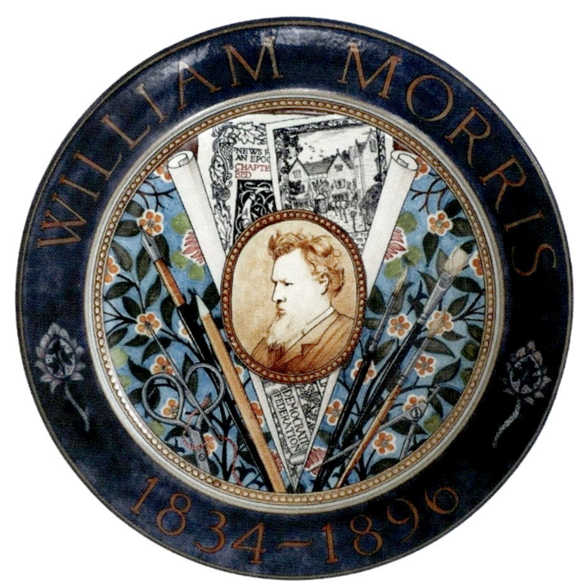

William Morris commemorative plate by
Laurence McGowan, 1992, diam. 34 cm
Collection Laurence and Jackie McGowan

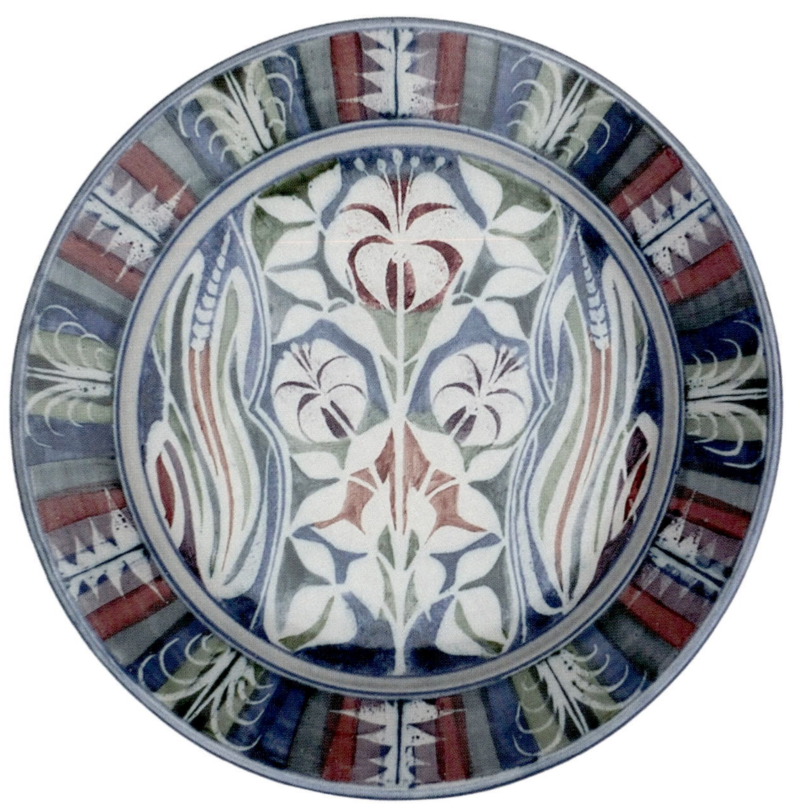

Stoneware charger by Laurence McGowan,
2014, diam. 40 cm, h. 6 cm
Private collection

Like Shackleton, Laurence McGowan also left Aldermaston in 1979 and set up his own studio in Collingbourne Kingston, Wiltshire, where he continued working until his semi-retirement in 2016. For nearly forty years he has produced functional domestic ware and commemorative pieces in his distinct calligraphic style, reflecting his love of Islamic art and architecture, his days at Aldermaston, and the Arts and Crafts influence unconsciously absorbed from his childhood home. He has never used a wood-fired kiln, preferring instead to fire to 1260°c in an electric kiln using a stoneware clay. McGowan uses a Cornish stone/dolomite-based glaze, substituting zirconium silicate for the tin oxide used in the Aldermaston glazes, but still decorates his work using the maiolica technique. Firing at higher temperatures produces work that is more durable, and in an era when functionality and the ability to put pieces in a dishwasher has become increasingly desirable, he feels that this is important. McGowan intends his ceramics to be used, pricing them so that everyone can afford them and derive pleasure from using handcrafted objects. In doing so he reflects one of William Morris's founding principles: 'Have nothing in your houses that you do not know to be useful or believe to be beautiful.'

McGowan has a deep admiration for Caiger-Smith and acknowledges the debt he owes him for passing on a legacy not only of skills, but also of an 'Aldermaston consciousness', a set of standards or aspirations that remain 'tantalisingly in the mind's eye, but … stubbornly just beyond grasp, making the daily pursuit worthwhile'. To this day McGowan keeps Caiger-Smith's essence with him in the workshop, in the form of a rejected lustre tankard, rescued unbroken from the dustbin at Aldermaston. From its position in the workshop it looks down on him while he's decorating, keeping a critical and encouraging eye on him as he works. [11]

It was significant for McGowan that Caiger-Smith recommended him to the organisers of the *Art in Action* show. Although Caiger-Smith had demonstrated and exhibited there himself with some of the potters, he found that five days away from the Pottery, plus the preparation and the aftermath, was too disruptive. But for McGowan the introduction was life-changing:

> Bar a couple of years out, I went on to be invited almost continuously for the next 25 years. *Art in Action* was what really enabled me to become a self-employed potter, and with Jackie at home doing all the selling, accounts etc., it enabled me to support my family entirely on the proceeds. [12]

One of the most unexpected outcomes of McGowan's time at Aldermaston was his extensive travelling with Jackie to the Near East, from Istanbul to Iznik, to Damascus, and even to Raqqa, where they have sought out beautiful tin-glazed and lustreware ceramics in museums. McGowan had developed a deep interest in Islamic art and culture following a spell working in Iran and a visit to Istanbul in the 1960s, but it was the influence of Caiger-Smith and his *Tin-Glaze Pottery in Europe and the Islamic World* (1973) that encouraged him and Jackie to explore the subject further.

McGowan says regrettably his finances did not allow him to employ anyone; but conscious of his heritage and passing on the legacy of skills and knowledge, for ten years he was a visiting tutor at VITA, the post-graduate Visual, Islamic and Traditional Arts School (a branch of the Prince's School of Traditional Arts). Here he says he tried to pass on something of Caiger-Smith's bequest, his way of looking and discerning, and his sensitivities. [13] McGowan's work is in many private and public collections across Britain, including the Ashmolean Museum in Oxford and the Potteries Museum and Art Gallery in Stoke-on-Trent. But more importantly to McGowan, his pottery is used and enjoyed in people's homes throughout the world.

With the dawn of the new decade Caiger-Smith faced another problem. The inflation of the 1970s had left the Pottery in financial straits, and his old friend Oliver Roskill once again offered to step in and examine the Pottery's business activities. Jenny Jowett explains:

> It is at times like this that artists realise that they are not businessmen, and for Alan it must have been hard; we had never done stock-taking, nor worked out the

prices against time, etc. Following Oliver's appraisal Alan put up the prices and all the wages and introduced a 'Gold Label' to highlight the better pieces. This rise in prices made absolutely no difference to sales. I think most artists need help with the business side.[14]

They also carried out an appraisal of their range of work and, with the help of Roskill's knowledge of time and motion studies, they reconsidered the shapes and designs they made, not only with economics in mind but also allowing for the abilities of the apprentices.[15]

Once their finances were more secure, and never needing an excuse for a celebration, in February 1980 the potters organised a small party for Caiger-Smith's 50th birthday, as Doreen Campden recalls:

Martin Wright had made a most beautiful birthday cake with fifty candles. He came in through the pottery door all the candles lit, and handed the cake to Alan. Alan gazed in awe at the wonderful glow of light from the candles that lit up his face. The glow picked out his red neckerchief and rust corduroy jacket and yellowed the bundles of reeds drying on the beams above his head. Someone had given him a lovely silk scarf, and that had been draped across the horns of the ram's head that hung on the wall over the wedging bench. I still have the sketch I did from memory that evening, but I never got around to painting it. Maybe I will yet![16]

It was around this time that a young Australian with 'a passion for brush-decorated ceramics and a developing interest in history'[17] sent a letter of introduction to Caiger-Smith. His name was Peter Pilven. He was offered a position, and soon found himself sharing morning tea with the man whose work and writing he had admired for many years. Although Pilven was at first slightly intimidated by Caiger-Smith's scholarly intellect and knowledge of the world, his accommodating manner, gregarious as well as generous, soon put him at ease. He enjoyed the harmonious and supportive atmosphere at Aldermaston, with Caiger-Smith and Edgar Campden as the elder and wiser statesmen, and Gill Bent and Catherine Bennett the thoughtful, gentle souls balancing out the three younger boisterous men, Julian Bellmont (who started later that year), Martin Wright and Pilven himself.[18]

Pilven was already a skilled production thrower when he arrived at Aldermaston, and was able to throw large pieces as well as long runs of identical shapes,[19] but he had to take a severe cut in his wages (from 350 Australian dollars to £28 a week) to come to England to train. Nevertheless, he describes his two years at Aldermaston as 'one of the most influential and inspiring periods of my life'.[20] Although a more senior member of the team gave each trainee direction, it was Caiger-Smith who introduced the nuances and brush sequence of each new pattern, a skill that Pilven was keen to learn:

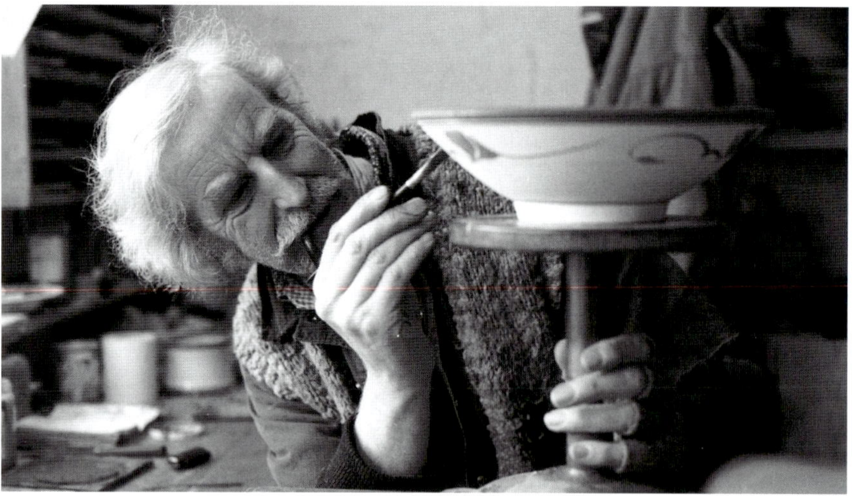

Edgar Campden painting, 1990

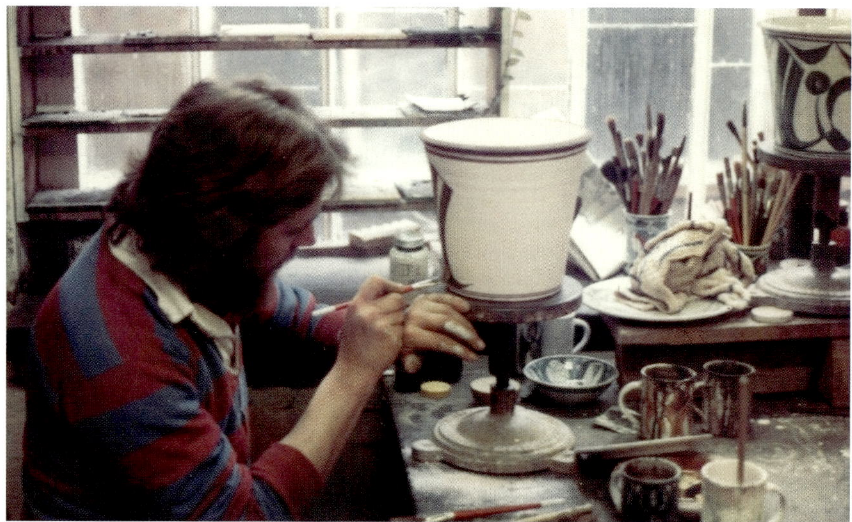

Peter Pilven decorating, 1981

I vividly remember having a minor anxiety attack the night before I was to be given a lesson in brush decoration. From memory, the 'Owl Pattern' consisted of 72 brushstrokes that relied on a reasonably precise application of the strokes, on pots that had been made specifically for that pattern. The 'Owl Pattern' was the foundation for many of the other studio brush patterns. As a trainee's skill developed they were introduced to a range of increasingly difficult patterns that included further embellishments and arabesque variations. Alan was an incredibly patient and calm teacher, who encouraged with a pipe-filled smile or a knowing nod of approval.[21]

During these demonstrations Pilven became aware of Caiger-Smith's vast knowledge and comprehensive understanding of world ceramics and art, and his acute awareness of the cultural, political and environmental circumstances that supported such rich cultures as the Italian and the Hispano-Moresque, and their ceramic traditions. He felt that Caiger-Smith's Cambridge education had fostered an intense and restless curiosity, which had seemingly never dissipated over the years; his agile intellect left an indelible mark on Pilven, which fuelled his own interest in history. Later in his career, when he became a full-time lecturer at the University of Ballarat (now Federation University Australia), his teaching practice, particularly in ceramics, 'was liberally laced with a range of healthy historical and global cultural references, as well as a very methodical technical research approach that I observed at Aldermaston'.[22]

The morning and afternoon coffee and tea break were important parts of the daily routine at the Pottery, and mentioned by almost every potter who came to work there. Pilven said that it was 'something of a ritual':

> the unwritten rule was that everyone took turns in making sure the fire was well fed, and the kettle full for the morning cuppa. Alan was a wonderful raconteur, a master of story-telling and, depending on which story he was relating (and it was always Alan relating), morning tea could extend for up to 45 minutes, something that astonished me, as when I had worked in a production pottery in Australia you were allocated just seven minutes for tea breaks.[23]

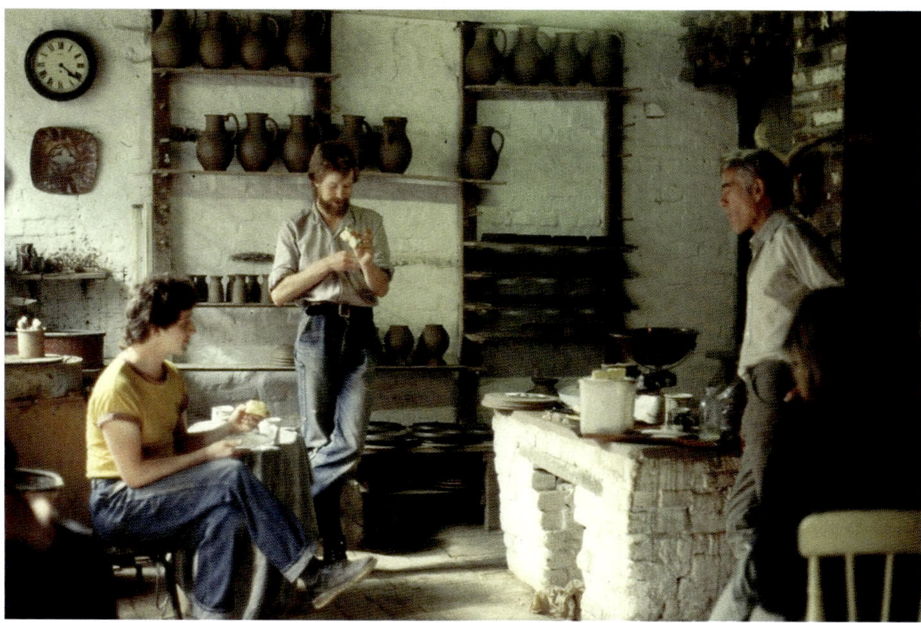

Monday teatime, 1981: left to right, Julian Bellmont,
Martin Wright, Alan Caiger-Smith and Jenny Jowett

In midwinter the potters would all 'huddle around the wood-burning stove, which was next to the wedging bench, which also doubled up as a good seat, listening to Alan's stories, many of which were about his experiences in Egypt and other foreign lands'.[24] In summertime they would all sit on tree stumps in the back garden. One of the potters remembers team efforts to draw Alan into telling us one of his long stories quite close to the end of the break, and that he almost always started by saying 'I think it was probably a Wednesday…'.[25]

Real coffee was made in one of the coffee pots designed by Alan, and everyone drank from a mug made by one of the other potters. Pastries, sticky buns or lardy cakes from the village shop would be warmed on the stove-top and consumed as the potters sat and shared ideas and ideals. In the words of Catherine Bennett,

> It was often at these times that I gradually gained some idea of Alan's philosophies, his strong belief in the value of small workshops and making work enjoyable, the importance of passing on skills, the pleasures of making beautiful things by hand, and his need to combine those things with the economics of keeping such a workshop viable. It was a delicate balance.[26]

Jane Follett remembers that 'These times were rich too, with talk about firings coming up, orders placed, pots bought during the day, problems, pleasures and leg pulling. Alan was very sociable and enjoyed the time to chat with his team. He was warm, outgoing and enthusiastic, and he laughed easily.'[27] Mohamed Hamid notes that 'the fact that many of the potters had come from different backgrounds and had different types of experience, meant that these times were a great hothouse for ideas, and these all fed into the great institution and school that Aldermaston was'.[28]

During the summer of 1980 there were more celebrations for the potters, with the weddings of Jane O'Connor and Gill Bent. O'Connor married Paul Follett in July, and although she had only been at the Pottery for two years, it was a mark of Alan's generous nature that he presented them with a beautiful lettered lustred jar as a wedding present. She treasures it to this day, alongside the couple's other lustre pots, bought with the proceeds of hundreds of hours spent doing overtime making 'owl' mugs on the jigger and jolley machine, to pay for their developing 'lustre habit'.[29] Earlier in the year Caiger-Smith had allowed Gill Bent to stay behind at the end of the day so that she could make her own work for a joint exhibition with the painter Peter Bartlett. The show opened in September, in her hometown of Taunton, just before she was married to her partner Allen Careless. She was delighted that most of the potters, including Alan and Anne-Marie, drove to Somerset for their wedding.[30]

After her marriage Jane Follett left Aldermaston, first gaining employment as a full-time pottery teacher in a secondary school, where she gained the confidence to use industrial lustre with her pupils. She built a wood-fired raku kiln and taught numerous quite challenging children how to throw during the lunch hour. Having stopped work to raise her own family, she returned to teaching in primary schools and enjoyed teaching the joys of working with clay to younger children. After building a studio at her home ten years ago Follett returned to making her own work, while also teaching individuals the skills of throwing. She works mainly in stoneware, making thrown domestic ware decorated with over-glaze colour and oxides, and sometimes using wax-resist and sgraffito. She also makes thrown and coiled garden pots, often to commission and incorporating text, and uses a large Laser gas kiln to fire her work.[31] She speaks fondly of her time at Aldermaston:

> the legacy of working for Alan at Aldermaston has been a rich and enduring one. It was such a happy and life-shaping time, which I have treasured these last 36 years, and although it was such a short time, in my life it fills a space that is out of all proportion to those two years. It was a time when I developed as a potter, but so much more than that. It was a time of great joy, of laughter, of growth, of warmth and of learning. Also a time of routine, repetition, learning disciplines, and of being part of a community of purpose headed up by the delightful Alan Caiger-Smith.[32]

Soon after Jane Follett left, Julian Bellmont joined the team; he was to work at the Pottery for the following 13 years, until it stopped employing assistants in 1993, and played a major part in some of its most exciting commissions. As a student of Multidisciplinary Design at the North Staffordshire Polytechnic, Bellmont had been inspired by Caiger-Smith's demonstration of the 'Dagger Pattern' on the BBC television series *The Craft of the Potter*, and decided to write his final-year

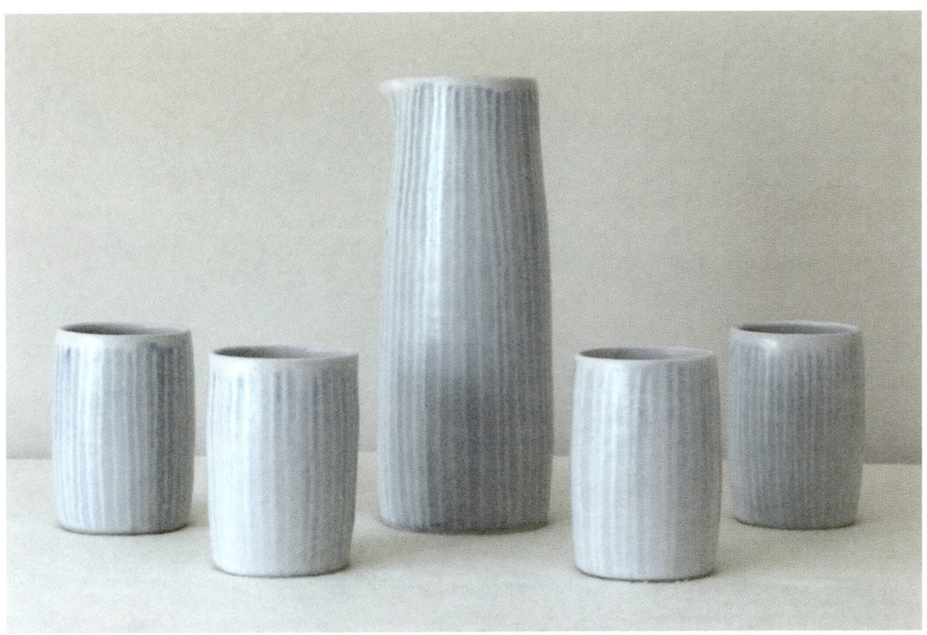

Group of vessels by Jane Follett, wax resist, grey underglaze decoration
and opaque white glaze, 2016, max. h. 23 cm, min. h. 9 cm
Private collection

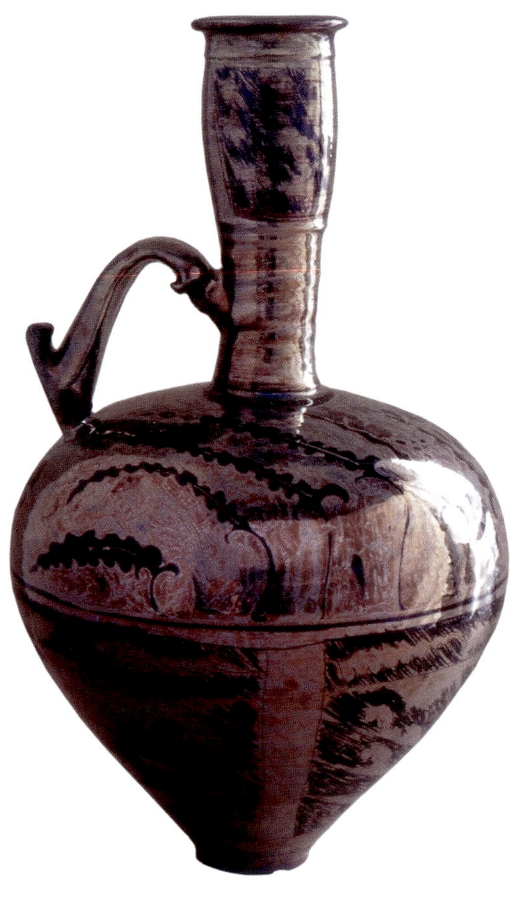

Sculptural vessel with silver, copper and mercury lustre
by Alan Peascod, 1983, h. 57 cm, w. 23 cm
Alhambra Museum, Granada, Spain

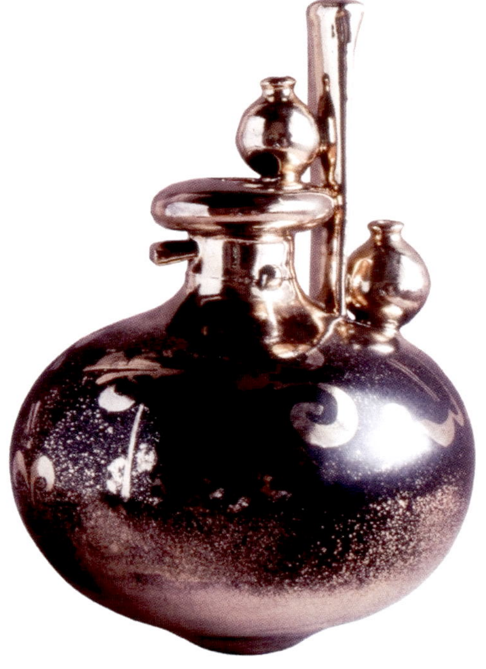

Sculptural vessel with copper and silver lustre
by Alan Peascod, 1990, h. 30 cm, w. 20 cm
Alhambra Museum, Granada, Spain

thesis on 'The tin-glaze ware of Alan Caiger-Smith'. Like others before him, he was captivated by the atmosphere and ambience of the Pottery when he arrived to interview Caiger-Smith for his dissertation. He soon found himself writing an addendum on the bottom of his thank-you letter asking if there was any possibility of a job. On 4 August 1980 he started his first working day at the Pottery; he was to be paid £40 a week and charged £6 rent for a seventeenth-century cottage in the village. He recalls details of his first day:

> It all started with an old Leach kick wheel and sugar bowls. I was shown the 'Bible' that had all the weights and measurements of everything the pottery made, and when I asked how many I would be expected to make the reassuring answer was 'make as many as you can make well'. By the end of the day I had made 36 bowls as far as I can remember. We threw pots for three weeks and then painted for the next three. During the first throwing session I made sugar bowls, cider tankards, 'swallow' bowls, quart jugs and some 'string' bowls; I also packed the big wood kiln for biscuit firing with Martin. Within a few years I was finishing the biscuit firings.[33]

During 1980 the potters had helped to build a second, smaller wood-fired kiln, to be used for reduction porcelain and lustre, and for more experimental firings. In 1981 Caiger-Smith was invited to exhibit at the Craft Centre in Melbourne and at the Blackfriars Gallery in Sydney. In Sydney he demonstrated and gave a lecture at the National Art School, which was received with great acclaim. He also met Alan Peascod again, after a 14-year break. They renewed their friendship and the following year Peascod came to England to work briefly in Aldermaston, firing lustre in the newly built experimental kiln. Caiger-Smith describes their shared experience as 'unforgettable': Peascod's inventiveness made him realise that a living tradition must continuously break its own boundaries.[34]

In the intervening years Peascod had been greatly influenced by an Egyptian potter, Said el Sadr. They had first met in August 1972, when el Sadr was in Australia visiting his family having recently retired as Dean of the Faculty of Ceramics at the College of Applied Arts in Cairo. Peascod was teaching at the School of Art in Canberra at that time, and he engaged el Sadr for a two-month short-term teaching job, and helped him prepare for an exhibition of his lustre-wares. Kindred spirits, they got on well from the start. El Sadr was a gifted teacher and greatly enjoyed sharing knowledge, especially as in his lifetime of teaching very few students in his own country had taken on the challenge of lustre. The following year Peascod spent some time with el Sadr, working with him and the traditional craftsmen and artisans in Fostat, an ancient pottery district on the outskirts of Cairo, where potters had been working for 2,000 years, and where el Sadr had chosen to have his studio. Together they tested lustre pigments and fired them in el Sadr's mud-brick kiln, fuelled with sugar cane and reduced with scraps of leather – 'sandshoes worn by Egyptian soldiers in the 1973 war with Israel', el Sadr had told Peascod; 'pitifully inadequate, the young men who wore them were probably killed in the Sinai'. The time he spent with el Sadr and the potters of Fostat gave Peascod a deep appreciation of the Middle East and Islamic art. He describes it as an awakening: their chance meeting entirely altered the direction of his creative life.[35] Caiger-Smith, too, had great respect for the Egyptian potter, whom he had first met on a visit to Cairo in May 1969. He visited Fostat several times over the following decades, and published a biography of el Sadr in 2010.[36]

Later in the summer of 1981 Peter Pilven had to return to Australia, much to Julian Bellmont's disappointment, as they had become firm friends and keen members of the local cricket team – although according to Pilven their weekly participation in the matches was primarily motivated by 'the sponges, cup cakes and trailer-loads of fresh white bread cucumber sandwiches being served up by the players' mums, sisters and girlfriends (feminism having not quite reached the Aldermaston Cricket Club in 1980)!' On his return to Australia Pilven initially recommended contract throwing, while setting up a small studio of his own, where he began making saggar-fired stoneware and neutrally glazed mid-temperature-range functional ware. Aware of the significance of the Aldermaston experience, having observing other potters who had worked there before him, like Shackleton he wanted to develop his own style. But before long he was yearning to use the brush and colour in his work once more. Colourful glaze stains and under-glaze colours were not readily available in Australia at that time, and he became obsessed with developing a palette of colour that could be used at high temperatures, tirelessly researching the glaze chemistry, learning about spinels, calcination and endless grinding in his quest to gain an understanding and knowledge of ceramic colour.[38]

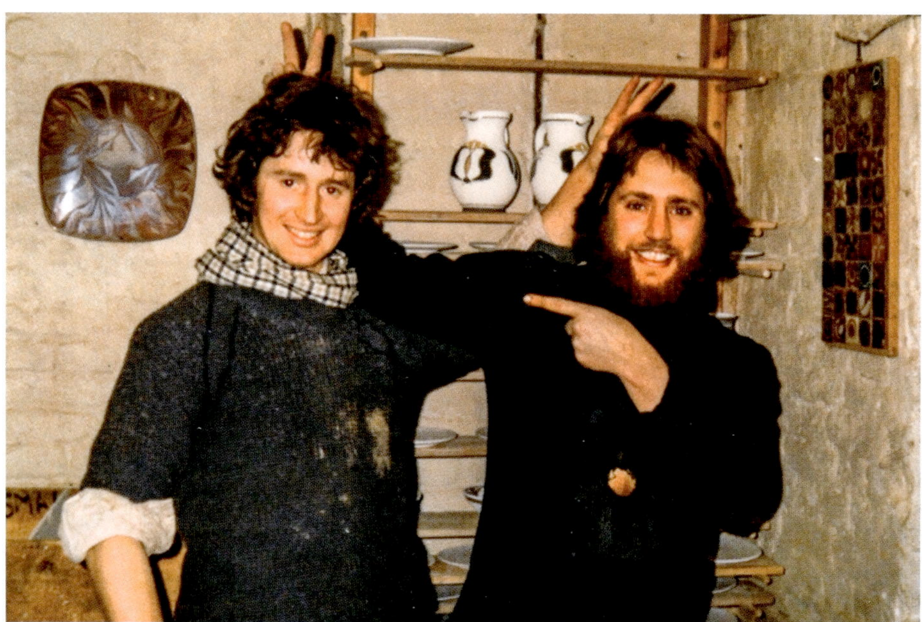

Julian Bellmont and Peter Pilven, 1980

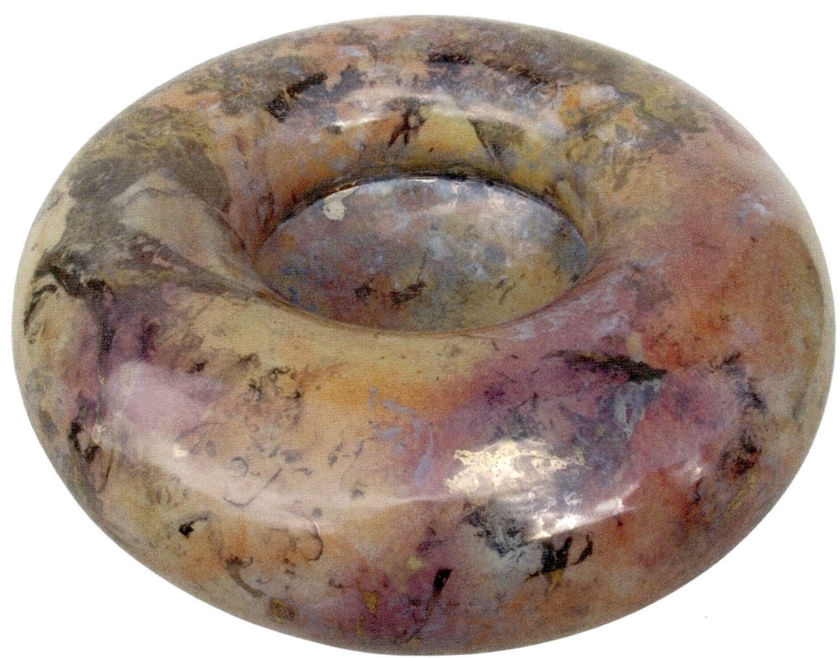

Porcelain 'Cushion Bowl' by Peter Pilven, 1996, diam. 45 cm, h. 16 cm
Collection Peter Pilven

Pilven built a 50-cubic-foot kiln designed to fire in an even, neutral atmosphere, a specific requirement to avoid burning out the glaze stains or under-glazes, whether fired at 1060°C (as at Aldermaston) or 1300°C (as at his studio in Ross Creek). At first his decoration was a mix of arabesque and a looser broad-brush application based on what he had learnt at Aldermaston. He applied the colours over industrial porcelain that he sourced locally, and which was extremely hard. By 1988 he had built a house and a large studio, equipped with two gas kilns and a wood-fired kiln, on 10 acres of land at Ross Creek. For about ten years Pilven and his wife Janine worked in the studio making high-quality wheel-thrown functional ware from white clays, decorated with under-glaze slips, in-glaze painting, and lustre.[39]

In 1985 Pilven was appointed as a full-time ceramics lecturer at Ballarat University, where he was able to contribute to a vigorous ceramics course that equipped graduates with a range of skills, understanding and aesthetics. He continued teaching full-time at the university for over thirty years, during which time he was awarded three significant teaching awards, whilst still maintaining a busy schedule making and exhibiting his pottery. In 1996 he had made the decision to concentrate totally on firing with wood, and took long-service leave to build an anagama kiln.[40] Anagama kilns are fired solely with wood, and are a Japanese version of the climbing dragon kilns of South China: they were brought over

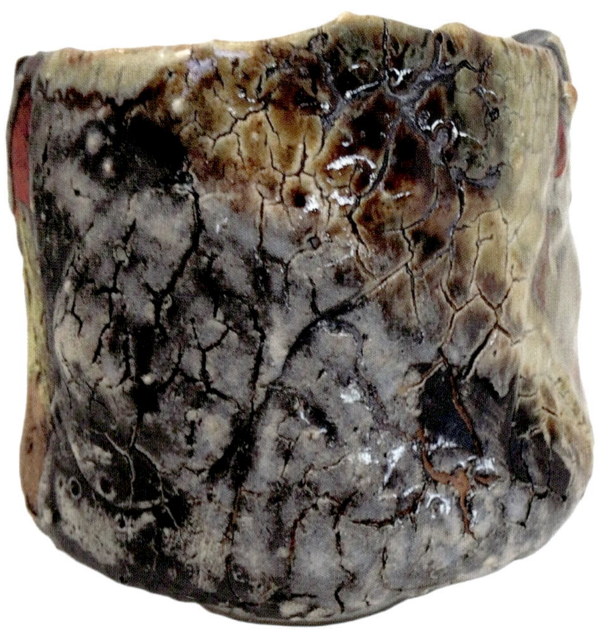

Stoneware vessel by Peter Pilven, 2017, h. 9 cm, w. 10 cm
Collection Peter Pilven

to Japan from China, via Korea, in the fifth century. Like Caiger-Smith, Pilven believed that the development of more than a superficial 'wood-fire' aesthetic is something that can only be absorbed and partially understood over a long period of time.[42]

His work was gradually evolving, and although he continued to use colour, its application became more and more abstract and esoteric. His research interests at the university became focused on the pre- and post-goldmining era of the Ballarat district, stimulated by his earlier training in the 1970s at the Ballarat School of Mines. He began looking particularly at the degradation and transformative effect that the mining industry had had on the topographical and geological landscape; this in turn began to inform his work, which was further defined by the firing in the anagama kiln.[43] His work now showed the effect of time on objects: although some were readily recognisable as a bottle or bowl, other enclosed forms appeared as human artefacts or relics, suggesting an ambiguity of function.

Pilven has won a number of awards for his ceramics and participated in numerous solo and group exhibitions, his work appears in public collections across Australia and Japan, and he has passed on his legacy of knowledge to generations of students. His daughter, Ruby Pilven, continues the family tradition as a full-time ceramic artist, and her work can be seen in galleries and museums throughout Australia, as well as in the United Kingdom, the USA and Canada.[44]

During the summer of 1981 Miranda Thomas, a young graduate of West Surrey College of Art and Design, joined the team at Aldermaston; she had spent the previous year training with Michael Cardew at Wenford Bridge in Cornwall. Born in New York but brought up mostly in Australia, Italy and England, Thomas was introduced to pottery at the age of 16. During her apprenticeship with Cardew she became proficient in throwing and glaze calculation, and developed a knowledge of wood-firing, but all at high stoneware temperatures; like Pilven, she was keen to find a pottery where she could develop her brushwork skills. Cardew told her that he considered Caiger-Smith 'the master of decoration', so together they hatched a plan that she should go and learn from him. Cardew believed that with Caiger-Smith's training in brushwork and decoration, coupled with the training in shape and form that she had received at Wenford, she would be able to make beautiful pots in both decoration and form:

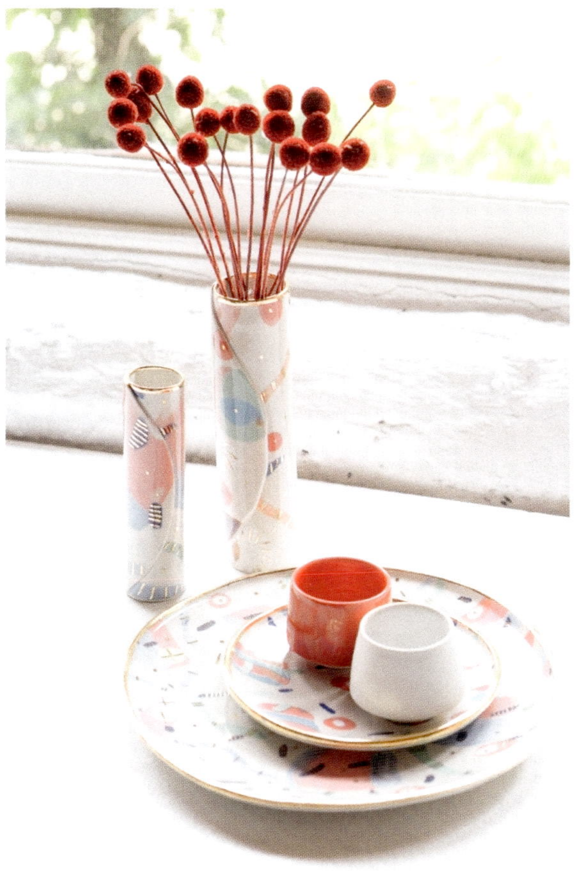

Stoneware and porcelain with gold lustre by Ruby Pilven, 2015, small vase h. 13 cm, large vase h. 18 cm, large plate diam. 30 cm, small plate diam. 15 cm, beakers h. 5 cm
Ruby Pilven 2015 summer collection

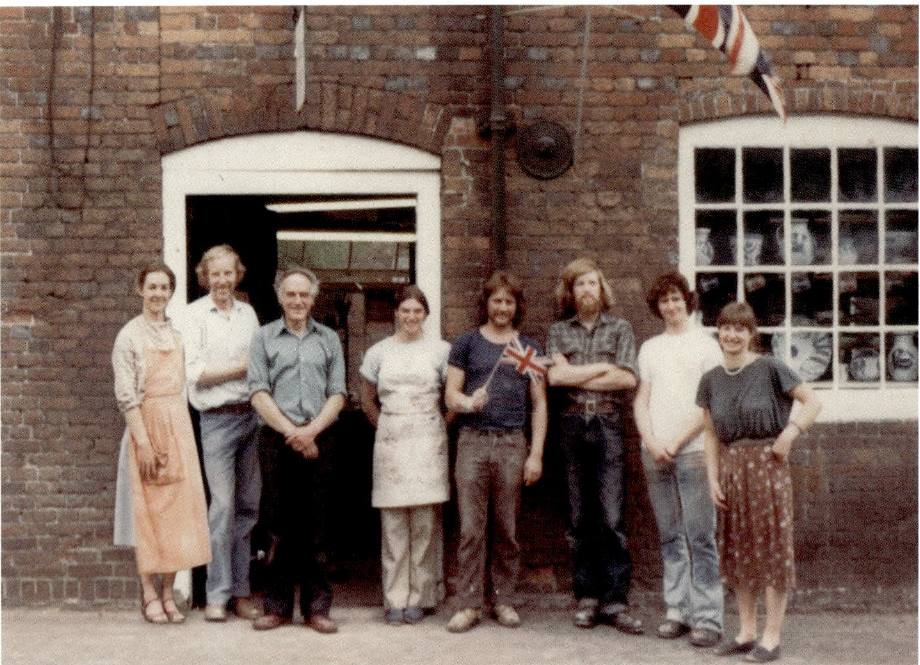

The Aldermaston Pottery team, 1981: left to right, Catherine Bennett, Edgar Campden,
Alan Caiger-Smith, Miranda Thomas, Peter Pilven, Martin Wright, Julian Bellmont, Gill Bent

unlike other Cardew students I was having a further experience beyond Wenford,
a different experience, and one that was supported by Michael himself. This lib-
erated me beyond indoctrination … Also, working at Aldermaston was my first
proper full-time 'paying job' as a potter, and I was very proud of it!

I was learning to work to hours, as one of a team in an organised, systematic
way, quite unlike Wenford. We also only worked five days a week at Aldermaston,
compared to every day at Wenford. I loved working with a team of young people,
and enjoyed getting a pay cheque every two weeks. However, I must have been a
pain to work with, because I was struggling to get to know a foreign material to
me, earthenware. We didn't use slips at Aldermaston, and at Wenford we hadn't
biscuit-fired the pots because we raw-glazed. I had to give up many of the ways
that I had learnt and had felt was the 'only way' while at Wenford. It felt more
'commercial', and I had to learn to throw to size and measurement to exacting
shapes, all of which was new to me. At Michael's I had done it purely by feel and
interpretation.[45]

During Thomas's first year at the Pottery, Michael Cardew died; she says that in
many ways Aldermaston was pivotal in her getting over it, and in making her see
the Cardew doctrine in perspective.[46] She greatly enjoyed the new experience of
painting in bright joyful colours, so different from the rustic tones of stoneware,
but she found that mastering the decoration presented a huge learning curve.
Through practice and repetition she gradually began to acquire the skills and says:

I remember the thrill of doing precise banding lines after chiseling out my brush. Learning to master the 'Dagger' stroke on the bowls, and the long, sweeping fish-shaped strokes. These were all done with a long, superbly made Japanese brush of horse and dog hair. I still covet those brushes. A family in Japan, which Alan had learnt about from Bernard Leach, made these brushes and we each were given one.

When Alan used them it was like watching a beautiful dancer, as he bounced around on the brush's tip, and he could make it do the most incredible tricks! We used chisel-shaped sable brushes, which gave satisfying crescent shapes, and these brushes gave the signature 'Aldermaston style', and a sixties feel to the decoration. There were also the sublime long, thin, zero-sized riggers, which we used for interpretive squiggling dancing lines; these brushes were our chance to inject our own touch or style into the decoration. I loved how you could easily tell one person's decoration from the others just by how they held and used their brushes. One of the biggest skills I acquired while I was there, which remains the backbone of my business today, is the hand-painted lettering on commemorative pieces.[47]

In September 1983 Helen Caiger-Smith passed away. Catherine Bennett had returned home to Australia and Nicola Werner joined the team as an assistant. The following year Mohamed Hamid arrived, and Gill Bent left Aldermaston to set up her own workshop in the nearby village of Beenham. In this Edgar Campden was enormously helpful to her:

He always had a 'trick' up his sleeve to put things right, or he knew a better way to get around a problem, and he was a big inspiration. For many years after I left the pottery I would always be hearing Edgar's words in my head telling me the right way to do things. He had a lovely gentle manner and a very keen eye. I will always

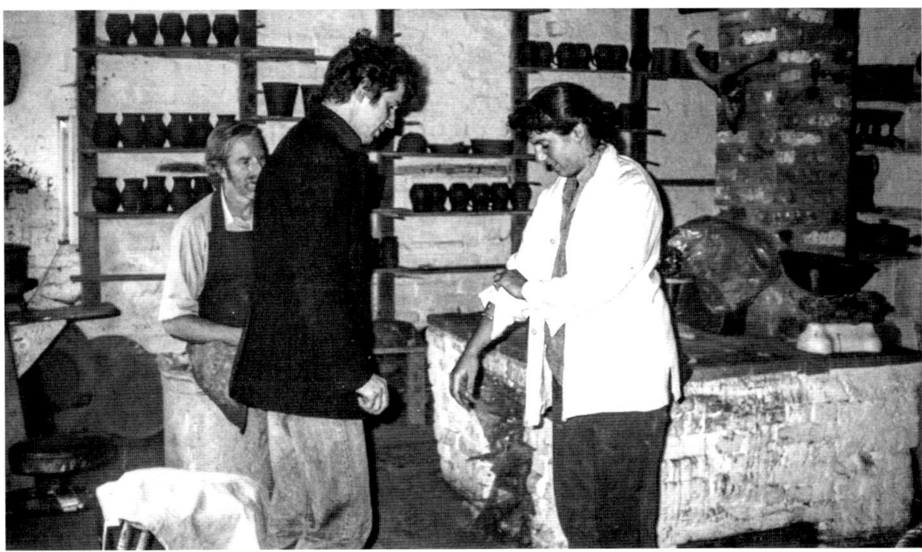

Edgar Campden, Julian Bellmont and Miranda Thomas at coffee time, 1982

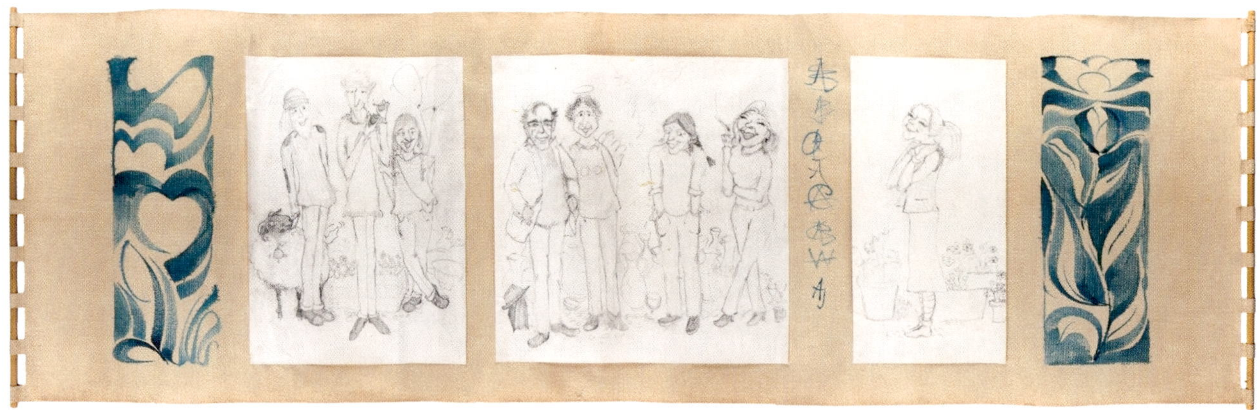

Catherine Bennett's leaving scroll, 1981: drawn by Miranda Thomas, it depicts the potters who worked with Catherine at the Pottery. Left to right, Martin Wright, Edgar Campden, Gill Bent, Alan Caiger-Smith, Julian Bellmont, Miranda Thomas, Jenny Jowett and Catherine Bennett.
Collection Catherine Bennett

remember painting opposite him in the back workshop. He would notice so much that was going on in the garden. He seemed to have exceptionally good eyesight and would always remark on what birds were around; he was a great nature lover.[48]

By 1984 she was regularly selling work to Primavera in Cambridge and to a gallery in Lewes, Sussex; three years later she moved house and set up a new workshop in a village a few miles away. She has been a regular participant over the years in the Newbury Open Workshop Scheme set up by Pat Eastop.

Bent works in red earthenware with clay slips and sgraffito, and for many years, in common with many of the Aldermaston potters, she continued using the same Fremington clay as the Pottery. When the suppliers of the clay, Brannam's of Barnstaple, ceased production in 2005 it left many of the potters with a conundrum. Some tried other earthenware clays but none met their expectations, so several of them changed direction entirely. Jason Shackleton even bought the last 8 tons of Fremington from the clay works, hoping it would last his lifetime. Eventually a solution came from Caiger-Smith himself. Around the time that Brannam's closed, he travelled to Italy and met potters there who recommended a buff-red clay from San Sepolcro for maiolica. He had always taken a keen interest in the subsequent careers of the potters from his 'Pottery family', so on his return he informed them all of his discovery. Bent, along with many of the others, began importing this clay, sometimes blending it with other, redder earthenware clays until they achieved a satisfactory mix; many of them still use it today.

Both Nicola Werner and Mohamed Hamid had been formally trained before they arrived at Aldermaston, Werner in Fine Art at the Central School of Art and Hamid at the West Surrey College of Art and Design. Hamid came straight to Aldermaston from college, as he needed to find employment fairly quickly to

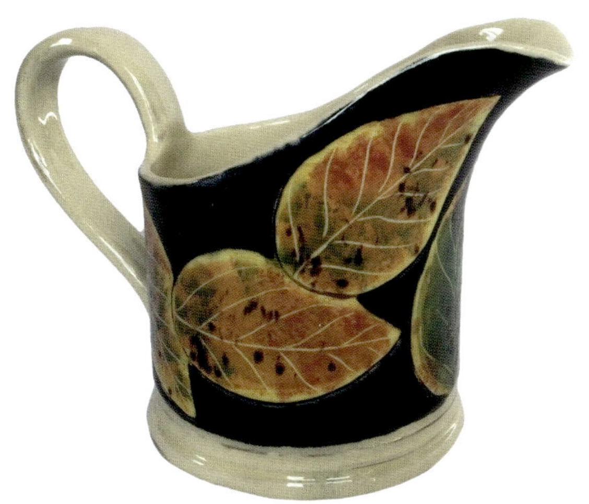

Slip-decorated jug by Gill Bent, 2016, h. 13 cm
Collection Gill Bent

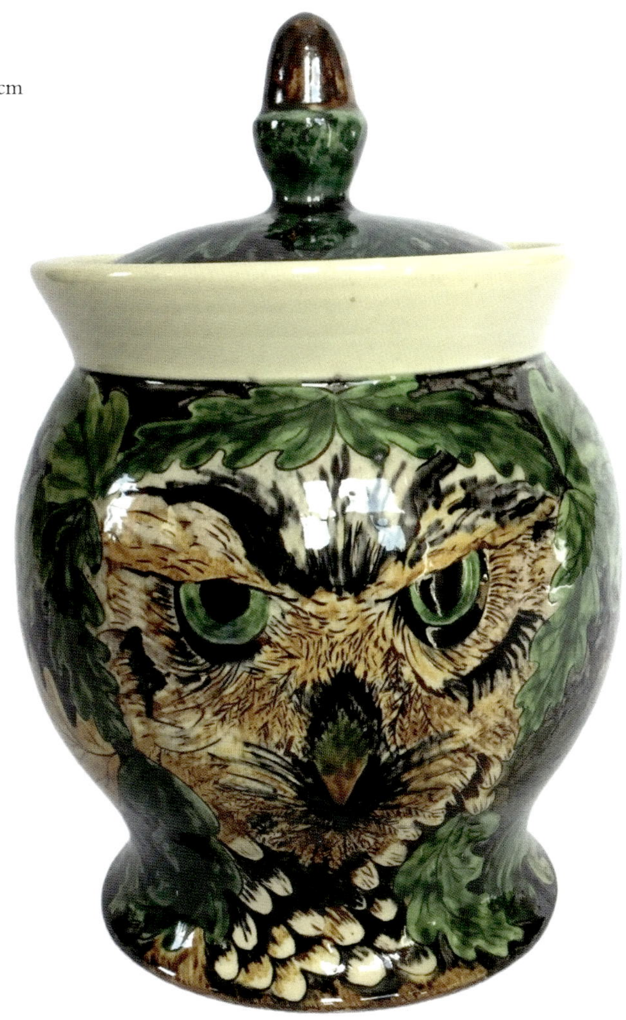

Slip-decorated lidded jar by Gill Bent, 2009, h. 23 cm
Collection Gill Bent

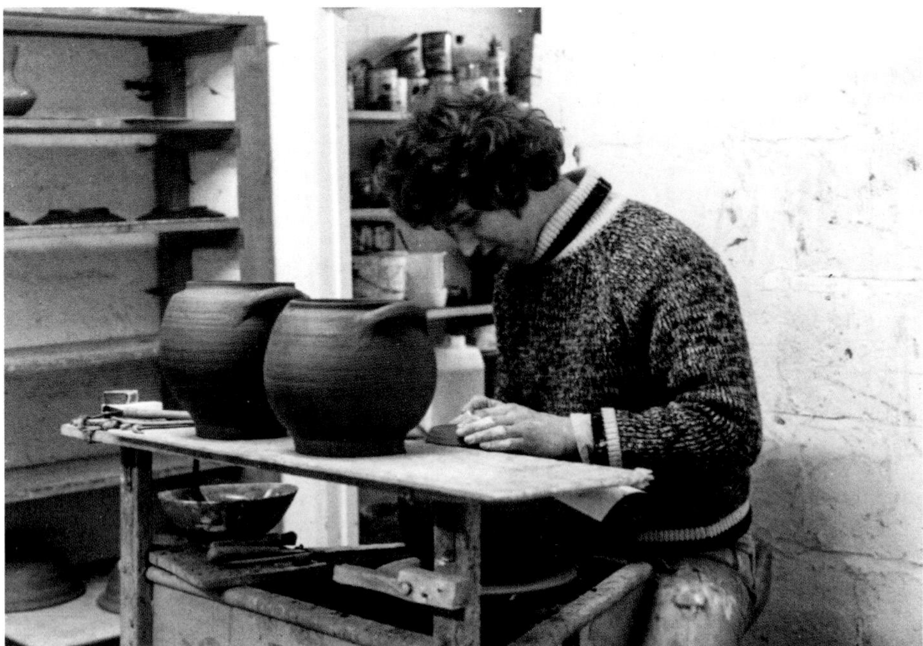

Julian Bellmont turning soup tureens, 1981

help support his mother, a single parent. Werner, on the other hand found herself drawn to ceramics while travelling, in her quest to make a practical living out of art. Thus they both found their way to Aldermaston, and the training they received there would set each of them up for a lifetime career making tin-glaze maiolica. Although Werner went on to work primarily on her own, Hamid passed on his skills to a succession of apprentices in his very busy co-operative workshop in Lewes, Sussex, as well as teaching both children and adults.

Werner moved into Pottery Cottage and Hamid lived opposite her, at No. 22b. He remembers his time at Aldermaston as 'pretty idyllic', with an emphasis on quality rather than rushing the work. They were even asked to throw away biscuited work if they felt the quality was not high enough, so there were very few 'seconds', much to the frustration of the customers. According to Werner, this emphasis on high quality meant that the potters were not under pressure, and were given time to improve and hone their work, resulting in a happy working environment. The fact that they came from very different backgrounds made for a very vibrant atmosphere, and they had a lot of fun. Having worked for over thirty years as a professional potter, Hamid recognises this as an unusual situation. At the time when he and Werner started at Aldermaston the Pottery was well established and Caiger-Smith was very much at the peak of his fame, concentrating on his lustreware work and major commissions for special customers, so they saw little of him. Consequently Edgar Campden, the most senior assistant, was primarily responsible for the day-to-day running of the workshop and for overseeing and teaching the learners.[49] Werner learned many of her skills from Campden, and his phrase 'economy of movement' has stayed with her, guiding her through her working life:

> a mantra for life, not fussing and faffing, but stating an intent and following through: i.e. place the pot carefully on the banding wheel, decide on your colour, choose the correct brush and paint the best stroke you possibly can each time, immediately and confidently. There is no second chance with painting on tin glaze unless you start scratching bits off with a knife, and that often shows – it is a spontaneous activity and requires quiet concentration without pretentious flourish.[50]

By this time Caiger-Smith had also become more relaxed about allowing the potters to make work that they had designed themselves, with their own variations. Hamid says 'this was very satisfying and pleasing, and meant that we didn't feel we were drones in any way'.[51] Julian Bellmont explains:

> we were all encouraged to develop ideas for different patterns and shapes. I had been painting some albarellos and I had been thinking of how flags and ribbons flap about in the wind. I tried to replicate this in one of the jars, and when the next wood kiln was emptied Alan came through to the pottery with a small albarello asking if this was my design, I said it was, and he asked me to develop the idea. It was one of those lucky patterns that work well on the outside and inside of shapes, and so the 'Ribbon Pattern' was born.[52]

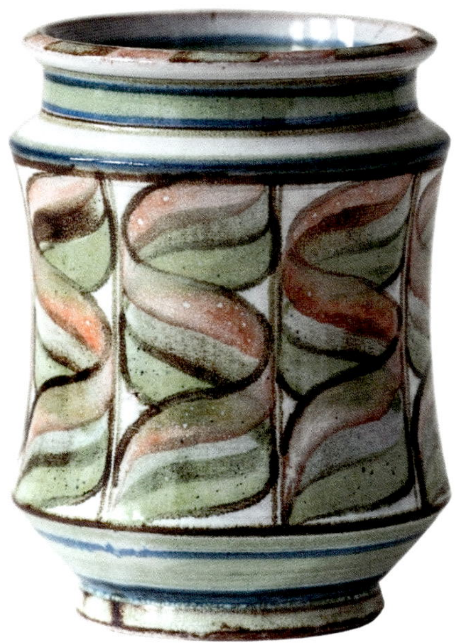

The original ribbon pattern albarello, designed by
Julian Bellmont, 1981, h. 11.5 cm, w. 9 cm
Collection Julian Bellmont

Miranda Thomas saw this freedom to express themselves as one of the great benefits of working at Aldermaston; another was that they were allowed to make their own work in their own time:

> Making our own design ideas was an incredible boost, and this also led to a great exchange of ideas amongst us potters. If Alan liked a particular pattern, he allowed it to go into production. Julian Bellmont's 'Ribbon' pattern was a good example. He also allowed us to take up supremely valuable spots in the kiln.[53]

In 1983 Caiger-Smith purchased a very small 1-cubic-metre fibre gas kiln; this proved very useful for test-firing, as well as for firing stoneware 'owl' mugs at porcelain temperature to produce better colours. It was around this time that some students in Australia, where Caiger-Smith had been demonstrating and lecturing, discovered completely by accident that the W/A92 glaze used for lustre at Aldermaston could also be used at high temperature, and it worked well at 1260°C in the electric kiln. On learning this, Bellmont carried out his own set of tests and found that the colours stayed the same in the electric kiln but not in the gas kiln. He also found out that the glaze reacted well to the low temperatures used in the reduction firings, and produced very high-key copper lustres at the top of the kiln and smoky reduction colours at the middle and bottom. Bellmont was later to use this the W/A92 glaze fired at high temperature in his own studio work after leaving Aldermaston.[54]

Miranda Thomas left Aldermaston at the end of 1983 and moved to America in search of 'a sort of last land', a place where people lived as they used to live. She went to Vermont and started working for the Irish glass blower Simon Pearce, who had a workshop in an old mill building on the Ottauquechee River in Quechee. Her future husband, Charles Shackleton, whom she had first met while they were both studying at Farnham, had moved out to the USA in 1981 to work for Pearce, first as a glass blower and later designing furniture for him. Like Pearce, he had been attracted to Vermont as it reminded them both of the west coast of Ireland, where they had both grown up.[55]

When Thomas started working for Pearce she began as a thrower, but she was soon designing her own lines. Over the following years she built up a team of ten potters making her fish, rabbit, grape and bird brushwork designs, which stayed in continuous production for 15 years after she had left to set up her own pottery.[56] But Pearce's business was based on the economies of efficiency, and with that came the division of labour and specialisation, and both Thomas and Shackleton were determined to create a different kind of workplace, in which almost everything would be created by hand and each piece would be made from start to finish by the same person, following the same ideals that Thomas had observed at Aldermaston:

> From my working experience at Aldermaston I was also hell bent on creating a working pottery, not just an artistic studio. The pottery in my mind was for the customer, the people who wanted to give a gift to themselves or others to celebrate

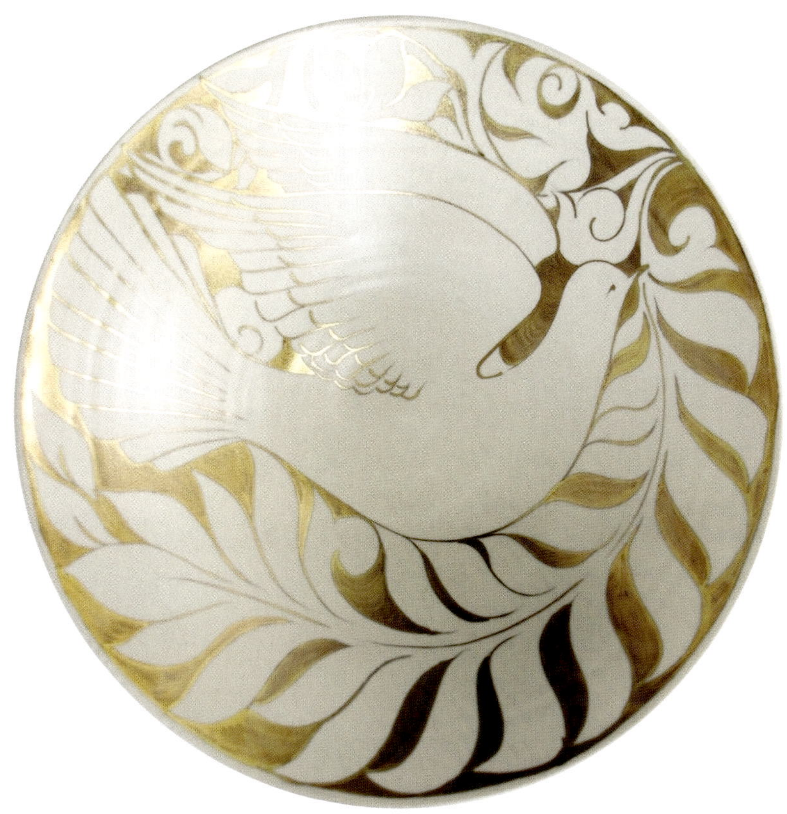

Gold lustre 'Peace Bowl' by Miranda Thomas Shackleton, 2017, diam. 46 cm, h. 18 cm
Smithsonian Institution, Freer Gallery of Art

the cherished moments in their lives, births, deaths, marriages and anniversaries. The pottery then becomes part of their fabric, their shared experience; it becomes part of their families and traditions. I believe this is what has made my own pottery successful and a mainstay in Vermont.[57]

Charles Shackleton and Miranda Thomas were married in 1986, and decided to set up on their own and put into practice their shared feelings about the importance of handwork. By 1987 Shackleton had his own workshop where he made and sold furniture. In 1990 Thomas also started working independently, setting up a basement studio at her home while she was bringing up their two small children; here she built up a team of four potters producing carved designs.[58] As Shackleton's business became more successful he needed to expand, so in 1991 he moved to the small town of Bridgewater, and began developing workshops in an old mill. In 1995 the couple bought a wing of the mill, which was on the same river that had inspired Pearce, converting four floors into their workshop. Their company, ShackletonThomas Inc., was born. The following year Thomas joined

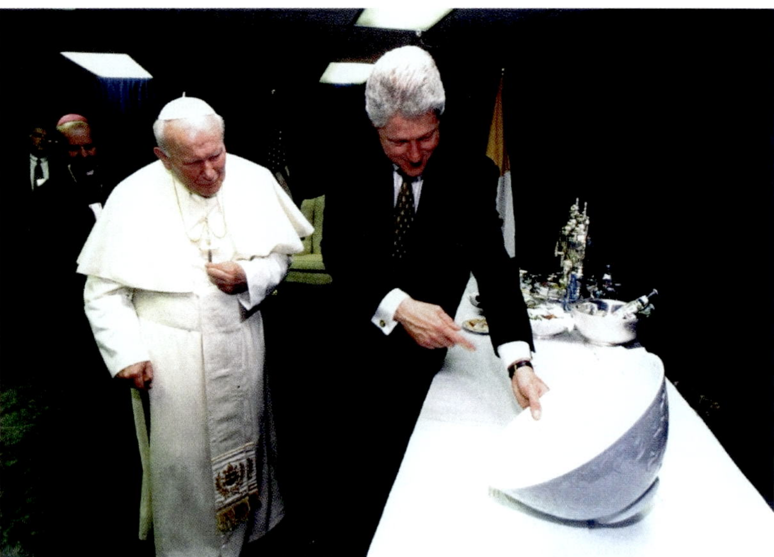

The 'Peace Bowl' is presented to Pope John Paul II by President Bill Clinton, 1999

her husband and set up a larger workshop adjacent to the mill, and four years later the family moved into a house they had built on a hill above the town.[59]

For the first 12 years their work was sold mostly wholesale to 15 shops around the country, although they preferred selling directly to the customer. 'We really liked our customers', Thomas says, 'and we wanted to know them, to be able to picture where our pieces would be used and by whom.'[60] So the main floor of the mill was made into a retail store, featuring a showroom, furniture workshop and pottery studio, enabling them to connect directly with their customers and also creating a space where customers can still see work being made in the traditional manner.

In their working practice Thomas and Shackleton have adopted an aesthetic philosophy that they call the 'Fourth Dimension' – which is to give life and soul to the inanimate object. The first three elements are design, materials and craftsmanship, and the fourth is the result of an object being made by the human hand and the inevitable inability to control the outcome perfectly. They encourage and highlight these variations, believing that imperfections enhance the design, the material, and the craftsmanship, and 'define our individuality'.[61]

Employees of ShackletonThomas are part of a small family business that values artistry, hard work, creativity, collaboration and quality of life. True to these ideals, each piece of furniture or pottery is made solely by one person and bears the date and the maker's name alongside that of ShackletonThomas. The studio model they brought over from England is not cheap and profit can be elusive, but the need to remain flexible and the ability to respond to the moment is vital if a business is going to remain sustainable – which was exactly what Caiger-Smith found out over 51 years of running the pottery at Aldermaston.

Over the last four decades Miranda Thomas Shackleton has built up a following across the USA and completed a large number of prestigious commissions. Notably in 1998 President Bill Clinton commissioned her to make 16 pieces as gifts to Heads of State for presentation on his Middle Eastern Tour, and a carved porcelain 'Peace Bowl' which he presented to Pope John Paul II as a personal gift the following year. From 2000 onwards Thomas has been commissioned by the United Nations Association to make gold lustre and carved pieces for presentation at their annual Humanitarian Awards, and a large bowl decorated with a dove carrying an olive branch was presented to the UN's Secretary General Kofi Annan on his retirement. In 2009 President Obama commissioned her to make a 'Blue and Gold Lustre Bowl' for presentation to the Yad Vashem Museum in Israel. But her greatest pleasure comes from work celebrating the daily lives of her customers.[62]

Looking back at her time with Caiger-Smith in the early 1980s, she says:

I have used and grown from everything I learnt at Aldermaston. The brushstrokes are the foundations to much of my work. The knowledge of glazes, firings, team building, humour, story telling, understanding of symbolism, and especially of movement and form in decoration, which is just as important as the pots form and shape. But most of all it is attitude of work. That it is an evolving process, rarely perfect, but the goal is a happy work environment, as that is what makes the best pots.[63]

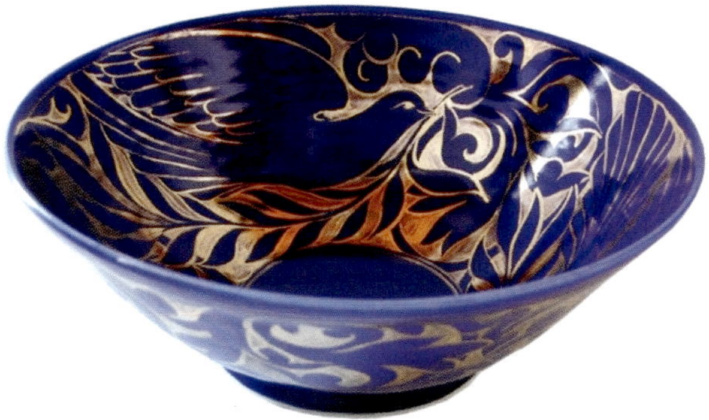

'Blue and Gold Lustre Bowl' by Miranda Thomas Shackleton,
commissioned by President Obama and presented to the
Yad Vashem Museum, Israel, 2009, diam. 38 cm, h. 12.7 cm
Yad Vashem Museum, Jerusalem

— 8 —

Commissions and Exhibitions
1983–1993

In the late summer of 1983 serendipity once again played a part in changing the course of another potter's life, as Harriet Coleridge relates:

> Alan Caiger-Smith did not so much influence my life as entirely alter its course. One day in 1983 I paid a fortuitous visit to Aldermaston in order that my mother might buy a wedding present. I had never made a pot and had not even attended an art lesson since primary school. I had embarked on postgraduate studies (Theology) and assumed that I would probably become an academic of some sort. But that day in 1983 was sunny, and the pottery hummed with a good energy as seven or eight potters threw or trimmed, glazed or painted a variety of tin-glazed earthenware pots. Wink (Miranda Thomas) showed us the garden, and it looked like a lovely life, I remarked on this, and Wink suggested I become an apprentice, she was soon to leave and they would be short of a potter. She was an extremely good potter and I had never made a pot – but I could type, and I hoped I could learn. It seemed to me then – and, indeed it still does – purely miraculous that Alan should even have considered taking me on. I always thought that my surname – Coleridge – might have been the catalyst; Alan, who had read English Literature at Cambridge, is a Romantic, and I felt my connection to Samuel Taylor might just have prompted him to take a risk. He had, though, taken on very green apprentices before and had found that as long as they were enthusiastic they could learn from scratch. For all that, he had no reason to believe that I would ever be able to make – or decorate – a pot, but he took a punt and my life changed course.[1]

Coleridge was offered temporary accommodation in Helen Caiger-Smith's house, which was now empty, while she looked for somewhere to live nearby. She was one of the most inexperienced assistants Caiger-Smith had ever taken on, and found learning to master all the skills required to be a member of the team very hard:

> Alan was incredibly generous with his time, giving me frequent demonstrations, and encouraging me to stay at the end of the day to watch him throw. I'm sure he was right, that one simply absorbs a sense of how to make a pot from seeing someone do it; the rhythms and repetitions pass silently from the maker to the companion. In the end, anyway, it came – fits and starts and frustrations, and an astounding tolerance of my incompetence on the part of the other potters – and

166

gradually the little triumphs multiplied. And as I learned to make, I learned to look – curves and concavities that I had never seen before absorbed my waking hours. A vase could sit like a sack of vegetables or spring from the table like a dancer.[2]

Soon after she arrived Coleridge came up with a simple suggestion that made an immense difference, as Caiger-Smith recalls:

> From the word go, orders and commissions had always been written down in a notebook, which inevitably became grubby and hard to decipher. She advised me to print out a card with spaces allocated to the buyer and their address, the description of the order and the estimated price, and the date for its completion. It was a simple administrative suggestion, and long overdue, but I would never have thought of it myself, nor had anyone else done so.[3]

The following year, in September 1984, Andrew Hazelden joined the team. Hazelden had studied at Epsom Art School, and subsequently spent four weeks that summer working at Mary Wondrausch's pottery now located at her home, Brickfields, in Compton, Surrey. While Hazelden was working with her,

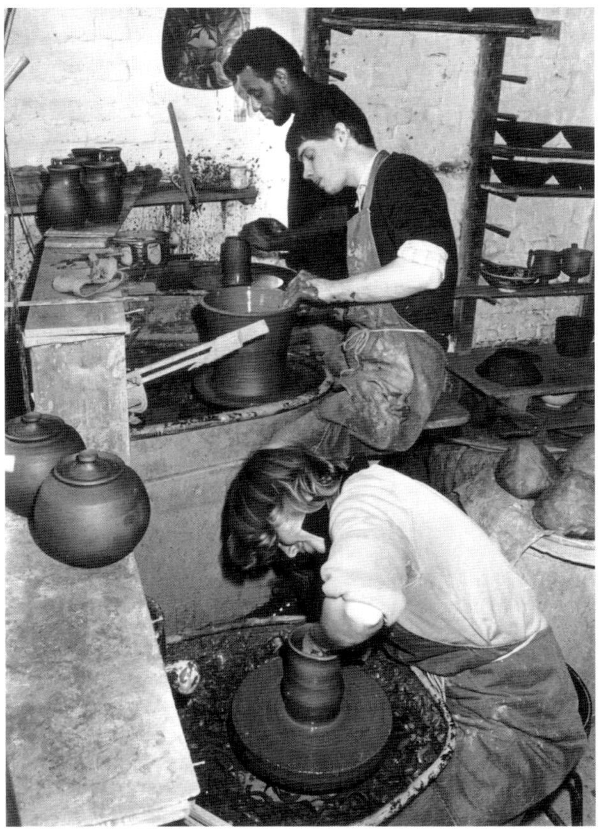

Mohamed Hamid, Andrew Hazelden and
Nicola Werner throwing pots, *c.*1985

Wondrausch had written to Caiger-Smith suggesting that he might fit in well as part of the team at Aldermaston. After a very informal interview and a trial period of four weeks, he moved to Aldermaston. At first he lodged with Dolly Saunders in the village for two years, before moving into No. 22, the cottage opposite the Pottery, when Mohamed Hamid left. He worked at the Pottery for 24 years, until its final closure in 2006.[4]

The same year Caiger-Smith received a most unusual request from a man named Edward Bramah, to make the world's largest teapot to commemorate the history of tea. The intention was to honour the memory of the people and events that were important in the world of tea growing and marketing through the centuries. Bramah had spent his life travelling the world in the tea and coffee industry, and he had a reputation as a slightly obsessive enthusiast – while recognised as probably the prime world authority on tea and coffee.[5]

The potters were all enthusiastic about the challenge, so in January 1985 they embarked on the first stage. The enormous teapot was thrown in six stages over nine days. In total it used 135 lb of Fremington clay mixed with 15% fine sand and grog, which after the firing weighed 90 lb. It was made larger than the required finished size, to allow for 9% shrinkage during the firing. The wide bowl which formed the base rising up to the widest part of the belly used 40 lb of clay, the lower half of the body 30 lb, the upper half of the body 25 lb, the upper part and the collar 20 lb, and the spout and handle 15 lb each. The four sections of the body were partially dried and stiffened with a gas burner before being luted together on the wheel and re-thrown to the intended size. The handle was in two strap-like lengths joined at the highest point, and a spine-like rib was added, giving a T-section so that it appeared thicker than it really was – otherwise the contraction during drying and firing would have distorted the pot or pulled away at the joining points. Even so, a repair had to be made at these positions after the firings.

It took three months to dry the teapot before it had contracted sufficiently to fit through the door of the kiln, and three people were needed to position it in the kiln. It was fired very slowly to minimise the risk of cracking; initially the temperature rose by only 15°C per hour, which meant adding one 7-in long stick to the firebox every 20 seconds, through the first six hours of the night and the early hours of the morning. The firing took 36 hours to reach a top temperature of 960°C.

The glazing, with opaque white tin glaze, took a day and a half to complete, and was applied using a spray gun normally used for car bodies, with a petrol-driven air compressor. The backdraught of escaping air made it difficult to glaze the inside; the outside was rubbed down with fingers after spraying to make it as smooth as possible for painting. Caiger-Smith decided that most of the detailed decoration would be painted in a cobalt-ilmenite blue pigment, because it was the least likely to run during the firing, and the painting took nine days to complete. The decoration was designed to commemorate people who brought fame to the world of tea, and included the names of the 18 tea-producing countries.

In the summer of 1985 the teapot was finally ready for its glaze firing. On 18 July the firing was begun, starting with a low temperature rise of 30° per hour, and reaching a top temperature of 1040°c – the maturing temperature of the Fremington clay; the firing lasted for 28 hours. Because of its size it was impossible to enclose or cover the teapot, so the wood-fired kiln was fired exceptionally gently to avoid lifting any ash into the draught as the flames passed around the pot. Periods of light reduction occurred during the later stages of the firing, deepening the white of the glaze and adding quality to the colours, especially the blues, and the kiln was allowed to cool for 60 hours before the teapot was taken out. Apart from a light repair at the lower part of the handle where it joined the body, all was well, much to everyone's relief.[6]

In 1992 Edward Bramah opened the world's first museum completely devoted to the history of tea and coffee at Butler's Wharf in London, where the enormous teapot was a popular exhibit. In the late 1990s the museum was relocated to Southwark Street, near the newly opened Tate Modern, a popular area for tourists. In 2003 Bramah was delighted when, during a visit to the museum, the Japanese ambassador posed with him beside the Bramah Teapot.[7] By this time the world's largest teapot had become famous, now acknowledged as having

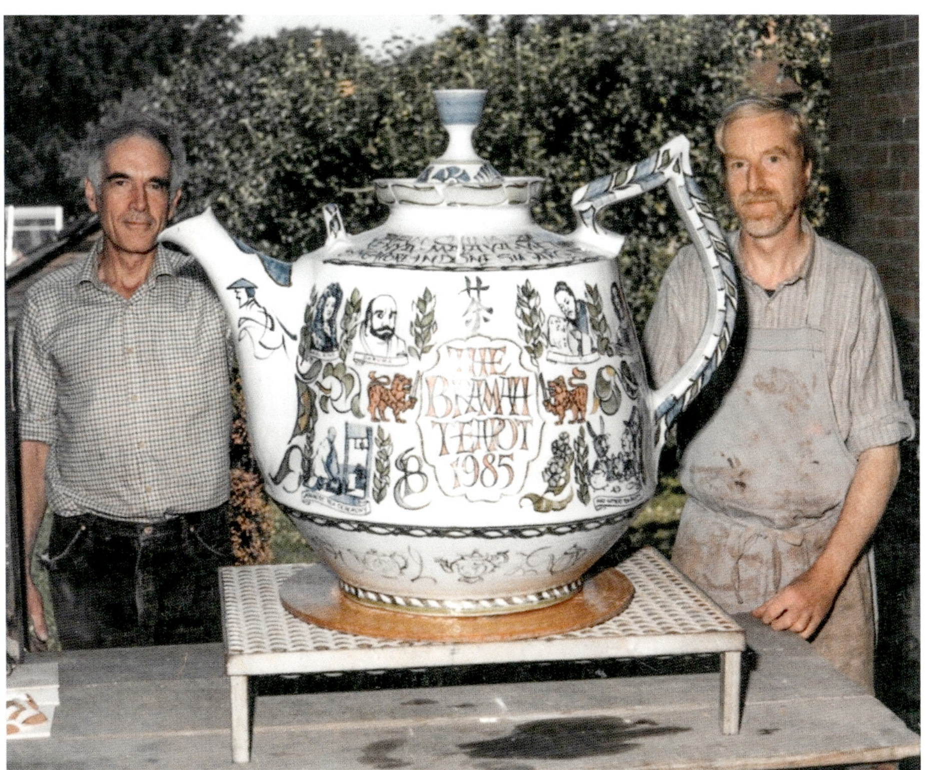

Alan Caiger-Smith and Edgar Campden with the Bramah Teapot, 1985

broken the record held by the giant teapot made for the Great Exhibition of 1851. Although this was a similar height (2 ft 6 in), the Victorian teapot only held 13½ gallons, whereas the Aldermaston teapot could hold 25 gallons, or 800 cups of tea.[8] As it weighed 153 kg it was difficult to pour, but Caiger-Smith said that tea was actually brewed in it on special occasions.[9]

Special commissions such as the Bramah Teapot often presented new problems, many involving more work than had been foreseen. But there was always a tremendous sense of satisfaction when they ended well, and of course many things were learned along the way, whose benefits might not be felt for some time. Although the teapot project seemed daunting at first, the lessons learned from it were to prove invaluable. Without the experience of making the largest teapot in the world, the potters might never have undertaken the project to make the 26 large lustre pots for Pearl Assurance just over five years later.

At the beginning of 1985 a young Irishwoman, Mary O'Gorman, arrived at Aldermaston. O'Gorman was a colourful, free-spirited character, a graduate from Harrow who, like so many before her, had come to Aldermaston to hone her decorating skills. She soon endeared herself to the other potters, including one of Edgar Campden's three sons, Mark, whom she later married. She stayed at Aldermaston for five years, eventually leaving because she yearned for a workshop of her own in Ireland.

Mary O'Gorman's arrival coincided with Nicola Werner's departure to spend six months painting and sketching in the Lake District. In July Werner returned to Aldermaston for a final six months. The following year she set up her first workshop at her parents' house in rural Kent, with the help of the Enterprise Allowance Scheme. In 1987 she bought a terraced house in Milverton, Somerset, on a 100% mortgage, establishing a workshop on the ground floor where she

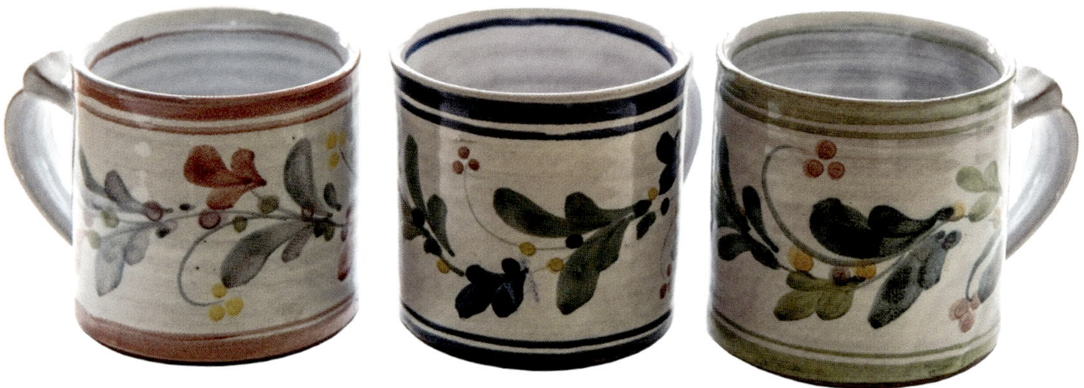

Maiolica mugs by Nicola Werner, 2012, h. 6.5 cm, w. 7 cm
Collection Jane and Bob White

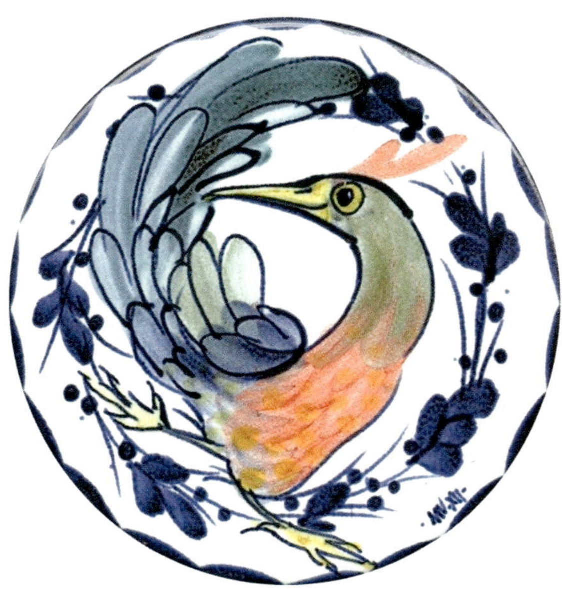

Maiolica plate by Nicola Werner, 2012, diam. 15 cm
Collection Nicola Werner

worked 12-hour days for the first five years and lived in the kiln heat above. The hard work paid off and she became established, with commissions including pots for the Victoria and Albert Museum. Now a highly successful potter, she says of her craft: 'I have made a living solidly by throwing and painting pots and tiles. It is my career and I owe everything to my training at Aldermaston.'[10]

Werner's painterly style is ideally suited to the maiolica medium and she is inspired by the natural world – leaves, flowers and birds, mainly in a softened palette for our climate's light, with no pure cobalt or copper but a small addition of ilmenite and softened industrial tints. She describes her pots, which are practical and made for use, as 'the everyday made as pleasurable as possible, in a very William Morris way'. Now on her fourth (and largest) West Country workshop, she gets help with glaze-mixing, a little throwing, and with lamp fitting. She uses an alsager wheel and a Cromartie kiln, and is another of the potters now using the San Sepolcro clay that Caiger-Smith discovered in Italy in 2005:

> I am never happier than when throwing – it is a grounding and pure magic, that I see first hand in my day courses for beginners. I lead a charmed life making my living as a potter, helped by a natural tenacity and a huge love of particularly earthenware pottery.[11]

All through the 1980s Caiger-Smith and his assistants had been kept busy sending work to exhibitions across the globe, including Sweden, Canada, Ireland, Scotland and the USA, with a successful solo exhibition of Caiger-Smith's work

171

in the Middle East, at the Arts Centre in Dubai. In 1984 and 1986 he had exhibitions at the Medici Gallery in London, and another important exhibition of lustre at the Oxford Gallery in 1984. The same year there was a show of work from the Aldermaston Pottery at the Craftsmen Potters Shop in Marshall Street, London. But the most important exhibition at this time was the 30-year retrospective, *Aldermaston Pottery 1955–1985* at the Potteries Museum and Art Gallery, Stoke-on-Trent, curated by Kathy Niblett. This opened in the summer of 1985 and in the autumn it went on tour in England and Scotland, ending at the Geffrye Museum in London in 1987.

Preparations for the retrospective had begun in 1983, when the Hanley Museum proposed a touring exhibition celebrating thirty years of the Aldermaston Pottery. Julian Bellmont recalls that the two-year lead-up required a lot of planning, but like everything the potters got involved with at Aldermaston, it had been very exciting and great fun.[12] A film was made of a lustre firing to accompany the exhibition, and several of the potters – Geoffrey Eastop, Edgar Campden, Laurence McGowan, Martin Wright, and Julian Bellmont – were invited to show their personal work. A couple of days before the private view everything was driven to Stoke-on-Trent by Bellmont in his MG sports car. The first time Caiger-Smith saw the display was when he arrived for the private view, having been driven all the way up there by Andrew Hazelden, who was learning to drive; Caiger-Smith thought it would be good practice for him.[13] Bellmont recalls: 'the display looked fantastic and was beautifully presented. It was an Aladdin's cave of pots, and every pot looked as if it had had its own special display stand made just for it.'[14] There were lectures organised to accompany the exhibition, where the film was also shown, and Caiger-Smith and Bellmont gave demonstrations of brushwork and patterns. When the exhibition came to the Geffrye Museum in London for its last showing, it was Bellmont and Hazelden who gave the demonstrations.[15]

It seemed that 1985 was a year of celebrations, as it was the same year that finally saw the publication of Caiger-Smith's book, *Lustre Pottery*, the definitive volume on the subject. He wrote:

> Years ago I searched high and low for a book of this kind, but it didn't seem to exist, and after working with lustre for about twenty years it occurred to me to try and write it myself. There were at that time many excellent publications about Italian lustre, a smaller number about lustre in the Middle East, relatively few about Spanish lustre and not many about lustre made in more recent times.... These various phases of lustre expressed different aesthetic ideals and were differently motivated, but there was a deep-seated relationship between them because the ideas and technical methods had been transmitted from master to master and from place to place over the centuries. Yet it seemed that no-one had considered the lustres as members of an extended family, nor given credit to the unusual technical skills that lay behind them.[16]

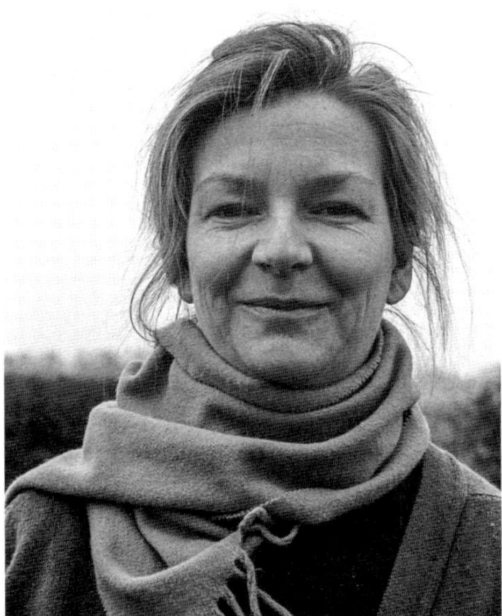

Myra McDonnell, 1992

The book included four chapters on materials and technical methods, as well as chronicling the cultures in which lustre flourished. It has since been published in Arabic, the culture in which lustre began, so in many ways the story of lustre has now gone full-circle. In his text Caiger-Smith wrote that he hoped to convey not only his wonder at this intriguing branch of ceramics, but also his deep admiration for the masters who produced works of great beauty long before we were born, but who are in a sense still very close to us.[17]

During the 1970s Caiger-Smith had begun lecturing, usually giving one or two lectures a year. Occasionally, as on his lecture tour to New Zealand in 1975, he would give a series. He would never repeat a lecture, revising the content for each audience.[18] It was after one of his lectures at the Royal College of Art in 1985 that he first met Myra McDonnell. She had just closed her factory-based business and was looking to set up a studio producing blue and white tin-glaze ware; she was also very interested in Caiger-Smith's lustre work. He invited her to Aldermaston and during the visit asked her if she would like to work at the Pottery on Saturdays, helping him with glaze development and making plates on the industrial jolley machine. McDonnell had been trained for industry and knew the technical processes well, so this seemed a happy marriage of skills and minds. Also, the Aldermaston potters disliked using the jolley and the preparation of glazes, both of which McDonnell enjoyed.[19] McDonnell remembers her time at Aldermaston:

> I drove down from London every weekend and worked across the road from the main workshop, behind Tile Cottage. Edgar and Doreen Campden lived there with a lovely donkey and several dogs. I spent several years there, plate-making or press-moulding, making up the '057 glaze' for the potters to use, or manning the gallery if plate-making wasn't required. I worked alongside Jenny Jowett for years, as she too would often come in on Saturdays to paint 'owl' mugs. I would go across the road for coffee with the potters, and chat with Alan at Shalford over lunch, and over the years I got to know the potters well, but I was essentially an outsider. I didn't live in the village but in a small bedsit in London, and I came there for the experience and to get out of the city. I still continued my own studio work, Delft tile panels, working for Dart Pottery in Devon and in Finland, and for the British Council in Pondicherry, India. I went back to Aldermaston whenever I could, homing in on the peace and quiet of the pottery environment. Alan generously gave me this freedom.[20]

McDonnell started to learn the basic patterns of the Aldermaston brushstrokes, how to use the calligraphy brushes and the techniques of mixing oxides. But she was stylistically quite different, her techniques based more on the Dutch/Italianate tradition of tin glaze. Nevertheless, Caiger-Smith allowed her the freedom to continue in her own style, even giving her some space to sell her own work in the Pottery's final exhibition.[21]

The variety of earthenware clays available for thrown pottery in the mid-1980s was surprisingly small, and Caiger-Smith felt that ideally a pottery should be able to prepare its own material. To this end in 1986 he purchased and installed a filter press and made a large number of trials of natural clays. McDonnell remembers:

> there was a digging expedition to Devon, and afterwards there was all the cleaning, slipping and pugging. Sometimes it would take weeks to make the clay usable. Adrian, the local car mechanic, and Campden, shrouded in smoke from his pipe, would spend hours with their heads bowed over the antiquated machinery, teasing it to make it work. Caiger-Smith would search for interesting earthenware clays, which might be used after the beloved Fremington clay ran out.[22]

During the process they learned a great deal but also encountered many difficulties. The filter press was eventually used to refine crude Fremington clay, adding to it 7% dolomite, which lightened the colour and stabilised the clay during firing. The clay slurry was passed through screens of 30, 40 and 60 mesh, and for ovenware and the very large pots made some four years later, they added 20% of fine silver sand; the resulting clay was normally biscuit-fired at 1020°C and glaze-fired at 1050°C. The potters found the clay a delight to work with, as well as being strong and durable, and it proved excellent for painted tin-glaze and lustre.[23]

During 1986 Mohamed Hamid left to work with Jonathan Chiswell-Jones for three years at his pottery in Alfriston, East Sussex, where he was allowed to develop his own designs.[24] Chiswell-Jones had never worked at Aldermaston but he was influenced by Caiger-Smith. In the 1980s he was working in stoneware, with glazes in brown or white, although he changed to brush-decorated porcelain during the 1990s. He later became known for his work with reduced-pigment lustre in a gas kiln,[25] where the results are more predictable but different from the lustreware produced in a wood-fired kiln.

In 1989 Hamid was awarded a Crafts Council Grant, which he used to establish a workshop in the old Star Brewery building in Lewes, Sussex, where he has worked ever since, as part of a bohemian community of artists with studios in the building. He enjoys the sound and activity of all the other artists and craftspeople working around him, and revels in the fact that he is engaging in a traditional craft and keeping skills alive. Over the past 28 years he has trained a succession of craftspeople at his workshop, equipping them with the skills associated with being a potter; many have gone on to have successful careers of their own. Hamid also exhibits the work of his students and professional associates alongside his own, in the Gallery Shop at the front of the workshop. He runs a full programme of pottery classes and courses for children and adults, and encourages visitors to come and see the potters working, throwing, glazing and decorating the pots; he also fires pieces of work for local potters and sculptors. He works with the maiolica technique, citing his inspiration as Islamic art, Continental maiolica and Dutch delftware. He makes some low-fired work using a tin glaze which he fires to 1040–1060°C, but also uses a zircon-based glaze which he fires to 1280°C. Hamid works with simple classical forms and produces approximately 15 standard pattern

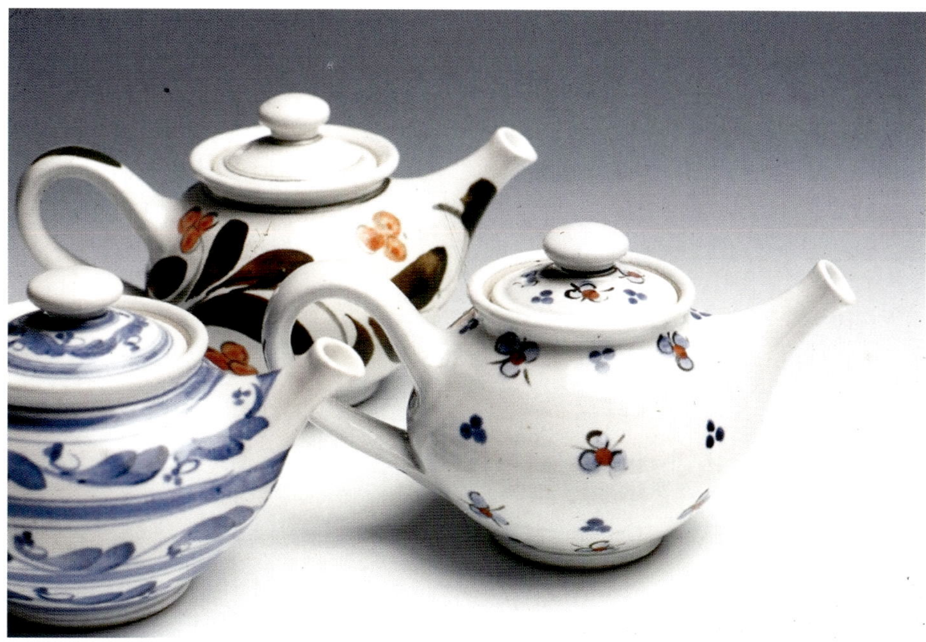

Stoneware decorated teapots by Mohamed Hamid at Star Pottery, 2018, h. 12 cm
Private collection

designs on about 30 different forms and sizes. As well as his range of domestic pottery and his commissions for special commemorative pieces, he also makes a small range of 'one-off' reduced-pigment lustreware, which he fires to 720°c in an 18 cubic foot Laser gas kiln, using techniques developed from his time at Aldermaston.[26]

Ursula Waechter had to wait two years to join the Pottery, until Hamid's departure in the summer of 1986 made a space available for her. She had first met Caiger-Smith when he came to give a brushwork demonstration while she was studying in 1979–81 for a degree in Three-Dimensional Design at the Bath Academy of Art at Corsham. She had been so inspired that in 1984 she applied to join the Pottery as soon as there was a vacancy. After her degree in 1981 she was awarded a fellowship at the Academy to study kiln building, following which she set up a workshop, where she worked in the intervening years before coming to Aldermaston. After leaving Corsham she went on learning about kiln building, wood-firing, tin glaze and brushwork, and also used this time to go on study tours: looking at faience ware in France, maiolica in Italy, Moorish architecture and Hispano-Moresque ceramics in Andalucia, and visiting art and craft workshops in China.

Waechter spent five years at Aldermaston, working mostly with Campden, Bellmont, Hazelden, and O'Gorman, and also with a young man who joined the following year, Sam Davies. He was studying for a ceramics degree at Hornsey College of Art, and as part of his year out on his four-year sandwich course he had been running a schools' pottery workshop for Ironbridge Gorge Museums. He had also worked in a shanty town in Kenya, where he had built a kiln for an arts group working with street children, and nearly died of malaria. He arrived at the Pottery, a long-haired, guitar-playing idealist with a thick Shropshire accent. He was not sure how well he would fit in, but he recalls that the other potters, and Alan in particular, always treated him as an equal: 'although it was no utopian collective Aldermaston certainly was a meritocracy, and if you were a good potter you did well'. He remembers feeling totally at home from the minute he arrived, and that there were many great discussions over coffee about human rights, ecology, and politics, as well as about the pots.[27]

Caiger-Smith offered Davies a permanent job at the Pottery providing he finished his degree. So he returned to London for six months before coming back to Aldermaston and moving into one of the cottages, where he had his first foray into self-sufficiency: his first vegetable garden at 34 The Street. His efforts not only kept him in vegetables while he was living there, but he was also able to feed all the other potters with the surplus, and he has remained an enthusiastic grower ever since.[28]

In July 1989, during Davies's time at the Pottery, he became something of a local celebrity when he appeared on the BBC morning news during the Great Aldermaston Flood, caused by a torrential rainstorm and exacerbated by the non-porous tarmac of the Atomic Weapons Establishment above the village. The retaining ponds there were overwhelmed and sent water gushing through the village. Although the flood fortunately did not affect the Pottery, which was higher up The Street, it swamped Davies's cottage:

> My house was at the bottom of the village and had 2 ft of water in it by the end of a very frantic day trying to get the furniture upstairs. When we finally gave up we all went up to Mary's house and downed some of her home-brewed ale. By 4 a.m. or so I was still awake from the adrenalin and rather worse for wear from the home brew, so I went to check on the house. It was then that a reporter approached me from the BBC morning programme, delighted to have found a 'Flood Victim', as he put it. He got me to hold his umbrella whilst he fixed his make-up; I was now drenched by the rain. The interview went out on national television the next day. I never saw it – but it was seen by my mother, who rang me. 'Are you alright?' she asked, 'you looked awful, and you were so tired you were slurring your words.' I think the slurring was mostly the effect of Mary's legendary home brew![29]

In 1988 Caiger-Smith was awarded an MBE for Services to Ceramics. In the same year Martin Wright and Harriet Coleridge were married, and she set up her first studio, Cherry Tree Pottery, in Headley, Hampshire, making tin-glaze maiolica. Unfortunately their marriage did not last, and Wright went on to pursue a career making furniture and building barns. Coleridge fulfilled the time invested in her by Caiger-Smith, continually expanding her ceramic processes over the following 30 years. In 1994 she and her second husband moved to America, where they lived for six years on a farm near the Delaware River. Here she set up Spindletop studio and began collaborating with local potters, and together they built a wood-fired salt kiln in one of the fields. In 1995 she became a founder member of the Covered Bridge Artisans; the group held twice-yearly exhibitions in cities in the states surrounding New Jersey, which still continue today. She found it liberating and exciting to be using stoneware and firing it with wood and salt, after years of working with a strictly controlled and largely predictable electric kiln, and when she returned to England in 2001 she continued to explore these processes.[30]

Coleridge now works from her Ewelme Pottery in Oxfordshire, also spending some of each summer working with local potters in France, firing Limoges porcelain and a local blue stoneware clay from St Amand, in a shared anagama kiln. In Ewelme she has two gas kilns, one of which she uses for experimental soda firings. She uses celadons and copper-red glazes, and a variety of ferociously reduced carbon-trapped shino glazes, and also decorates some pieces with liquid gold lustre brushwork, sparingly applied, and fired on in a third firing. She continues to make some decorated maiolica. Her work is exhibited in galleries around Britain, and each year she takes part in the Oxfordshire Artweeks/Open Studios event. As a maker, she says: 'whether I am throwing or firing, I am always seeking that point of balance between the knowable, which I can determine, and the unexpected, which gives the work life.'[31]

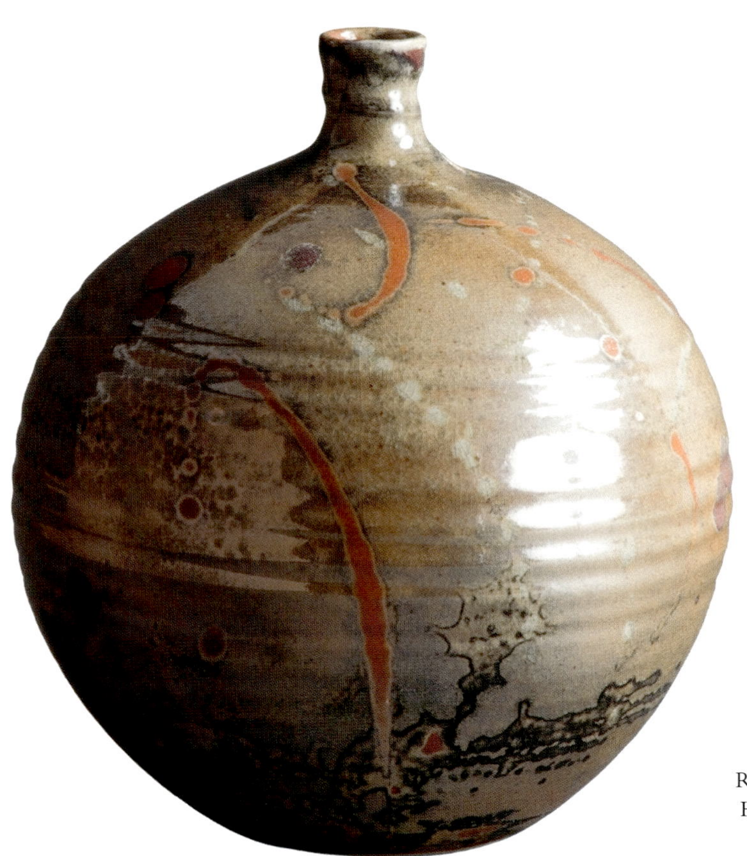

Round soda-fired stoneware vase by
Harriet Coleridge, 2017, h. 25.5 cm
Collection Nigel Hills

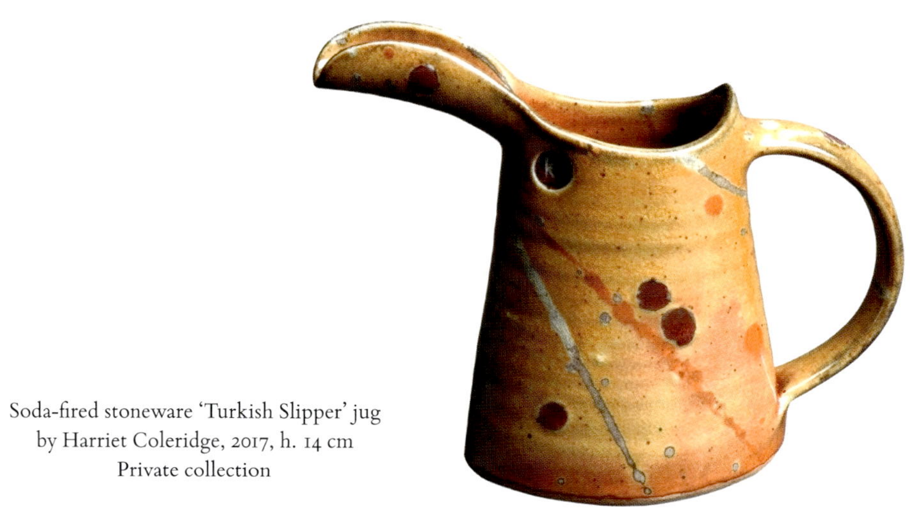

Soda-fired stoneware 'Turkish Slipper' jug
by Harriet Coleridge, 2017, h. 14 cm
Private collection

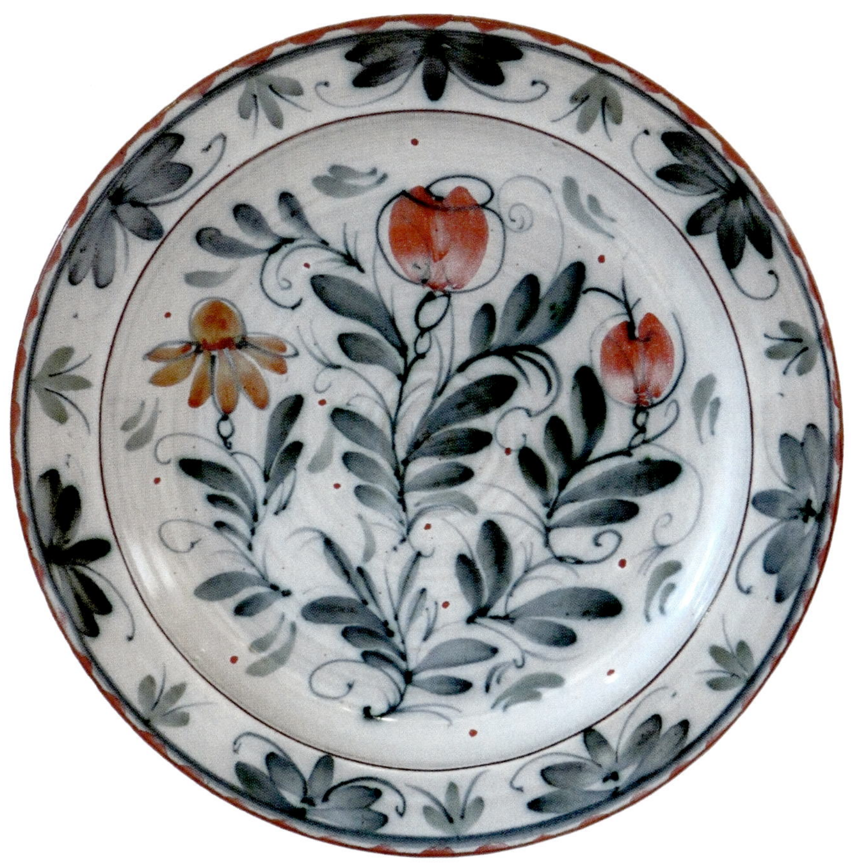

Small maiolica platter by Mary
O'Gorman, 2004, diam. 35 cm, h. 4 cm
Collection Anthony O'Brien

Mary O'Gorman left for Southern Ireland in 1989 to join a new Start Your Own Business Course funded by the Crafts Council of Ireland in the old Kilkenny Design Workshops. The following year Mark Campden joined her, and together they started looking for a studio to set up a pottery. Eventually they found a tiny building with no windows in the village of Bennetsbridge, which was to be the home of Mary O'Gorman Studio Pottery for the next few years.[32]

The unique set-up at Aldermaston and Caiger-Smith's reputation as a master of lustre pottery meant that vacancies at the Pottery were short-lived. The gap left by O'Gorman was soon taken by Louise Bashall, a young woman eager to learn more about what she describes as the 'dark art'.[33] She had acquired a shard from one of Caiger-Smith's large yellow-gold lustre bowls while she had been studying at the West Surrey College of Art and Design. The shard had fascinated her and had drawn her to visit Aldermaston on a couple of occasions. Alan was always welcoming to her, and generous with his knowledge. He offered her a job at the

Pottery on graduating, but she had already secured a year-long position working with Henry Hammond. However, shortly after she started work with Hammond he died of a heart attack on his way to a Buddhist retreat. So once again she found herself on the doorstep of the Pottery at Aldermaston.

Caiger-Smith's patience with his young assistants, and his wish never to stand in their way if an opportunity arose, was tested twice with Bashall. Soon after joining the Pottery she was offered two-week lecturing post at the Art School in Cork. On her return from Ireland she then received a phone call from Nigel Wood, her glaze technology tutor at Farnham, offering her a month in Nepal helping develop glazes for a group of potters, as he had too many lecturing commitments to take up the position himself. Once again Caiger-Smith selflessly let her go, saying 'I don't want to get a phone call from you in four weeks' time saying that you're staying on'. So Bashall joined the Nepal Leprosy Trust in Patan, just outside Kathmandu:

> the potters were from families that had had leprosy, and in that culture there was a huge stigma attached to leprosy. They had been given some basic glazes, so I worked on developing a wider range of colours and slips, as well as forms and patterns for them to produce. It was a very busy and intense four weeks, and I have very happy memories of the warmth of the Nepalese people, and the relief of a good firing, which was celebrated by drinking tea with thick, thick coagulated yak milk that I had to politely force down.[34]

On her return she happily settled into life at Aldermaston. She said it was a steep learning curve: 'there's nothing like sitting on a wheel and throwing swallow bowls all day to really learn how clay moves. Watching Edgar was a lesson in mastery, as he would effortlessly and efficiently produce rack after rack of bowls'. Her favourite time of day, however, was after everyone had gone home and Alan would stay behind to work an extra hour; Bashall would 'watch quietly from the side-lines as he was throwing big bowls in the back workshop, or decorating one of his stunning large lustre bowls … with that in mind, I think one of Alan's greatest legacies to me is his patience, confidence and the presence in his work'.[35]

During the Pottery's last years as a collaborative workshop the potters faced their biggest challenge yet. This was an unusual request from the architects Chapman Taylor, who were building and furnishing a new headquarters for the Pearl Assurance Company at Lynch Wood, near Peterborough. No one knew that these would be their last few years working together, the commission ultimately proved a fitting climax to 38 successful years of prolific and historically significant production.

The seemingly impossible request for some sixty pots, 6 ft and 5 ft high, was initially turned down politely as the size and quantity they required would pose excessive problems both in the making and firing. However, Julian Bellmont had recently acquired a new photographic enlarger and, eager to try it out, he produced some enormous highly coloured prints of the two large vases made for the British Embassy in Washington, to demonstrate what the pots might look like; these were enclosed with the reply. Expecting to hear nothing more, normal work resumed. Then one day the telephone rang: the architects wanted to meet at the Pottery to discuss the idea further. Obviously the photographs had made the project look far too realistic an option.[36]

In the intervening weeks Caiger-Smith started to make some enquires about subcontracting out the production of the pots to factories specialising in large-scale production, working to his drawings and prototypes, since this seemed the only feasible way of overcoming the technical obstacles. However, his enquires to factories in the UK and Germany drew a blank, apart from one British company, which gave a verbal estimate for a 4-ft-high pot. This was much higher than Caiger Smith had expected, and proved helpful in preparing an estimate.

The meeting with the architects took place on a cold winter's evening in the unflattering lamplight of the loft showroom. In spite of Caiger Smith's protestations about the impossibility of the whole idea, they managed to persuade him to at least 'have a go', having revised their demands to 'only' 26 pots, 4 ft high and decorated with reduced-pigment lustre, like the pots on the photographs they had been sent. It seemed that they wanted the impossible, but eventually it was agreed that a pilot project to produce six prototypes would be run the following summer, with an undertaking to share the financial risk if it proved impossible.[37]

So work began in the summer of 1990, using the experience gained from making the 25-gallon teapot six years earlier. As the pots were going to be so large, the potters used plans that Caiger-Smith designed and Anne-Marie had drawn up. These showed the profile of the pot at 1:1 scale, and the corresponding width at certain heights. It was agreed that the pots would be made mostly in groups of three, one pot 4 ft high, one 3 ft high, and a planter-form 2 ft high and at least 27 in wide – the largest sizes they thought they could manage. The youngest potters, Davies, Bellmont and Hazelden, were the principal throwers for this monumental project; Bellmont threw all the 4-ft-high pots. Two wheels were needed, each with a large but easily removable disc on the wheel-head, one for the bottom section and one for all the other sections.[38] A low wheel was specifically purchased for the bottom section, but unfortunately the first one had a malfunctioning pedal, so when Hazelden was using it for the first time some 30 lb of clay flew off the wheel at top speed and ended up coiled around his feet.[39]

A pot 4 ft high required 200 lb of wet clay. Using the low wheel, the base was thrown first, resembling a very large bowl with walls ¾ in thick and using 40 lb of very soft clay. Then additional sections were thrown on the second wheel, using 30 lb of clay for each section. These were then partially dried with a plumber's blowtorch and left to cool. Then two people would remove the disc from the wheel, turn it upside down, and join it to the previous section, rim to rim, before re-throwing it. This process was repeated until the desired height was reached. For the large pots this took two to three days, planned so that the pot would be finished on a Friday, dry over the weekend and be turned the following Monday.

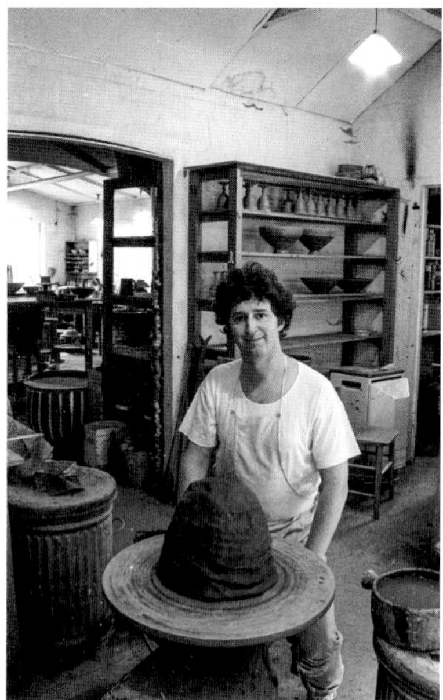

Julian Bellmont about to start
work on a large pot, 1990

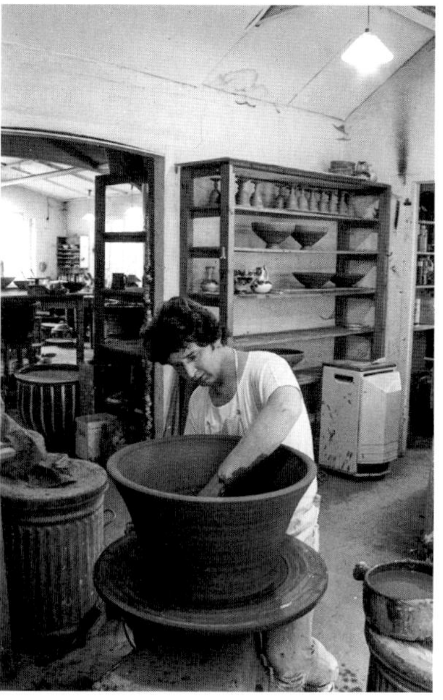

Julian Bellmont throwing the first
section of the large pot

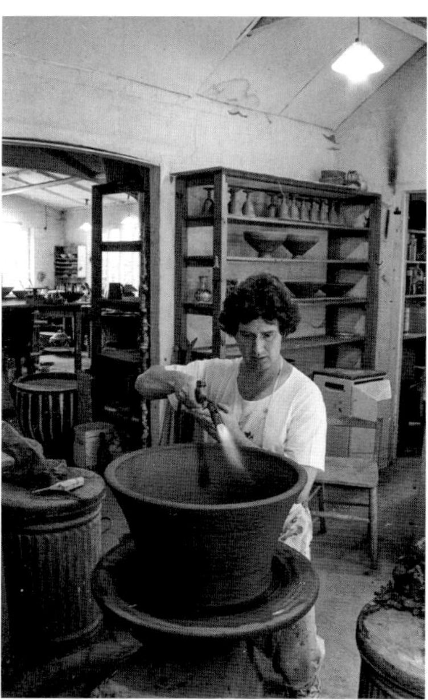

Julian Bellmont drying the first
section of the large pot

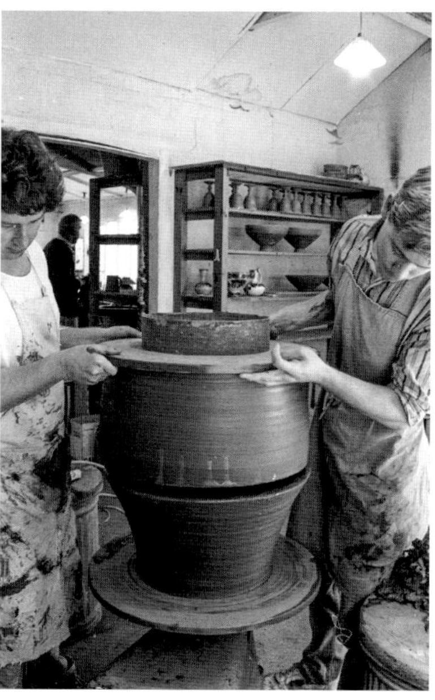

Julian Bellmont and Andrew Hazelden
presenting the second section to the first

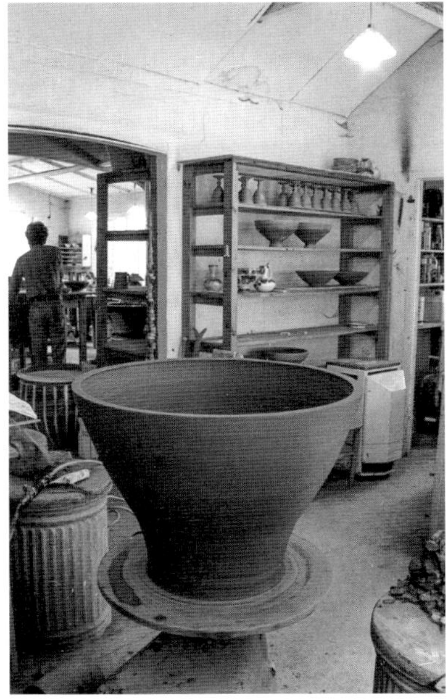

The second section thrown

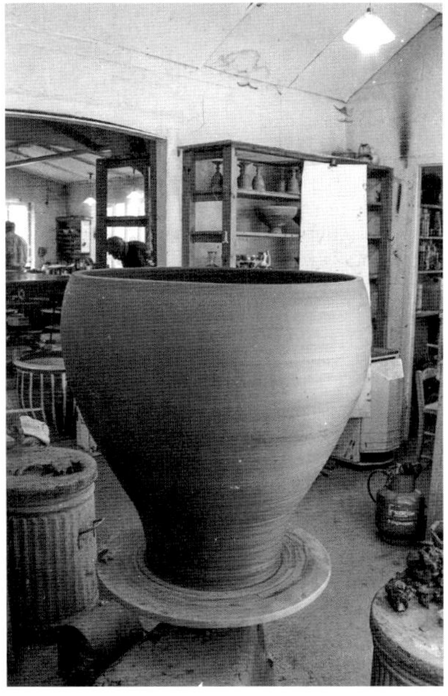

The third section thrown

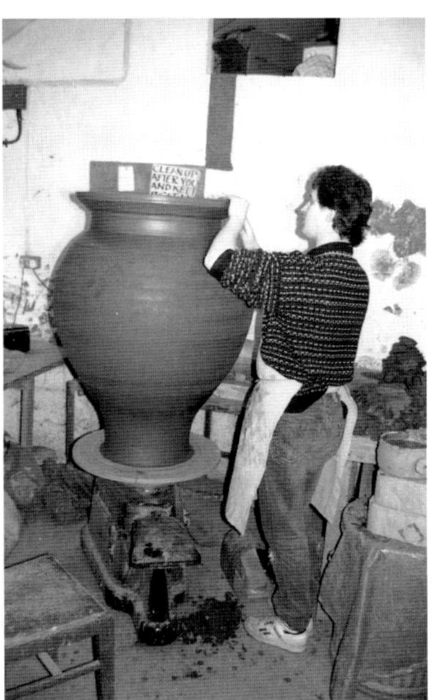

Julian Bellmont finishing a large pot

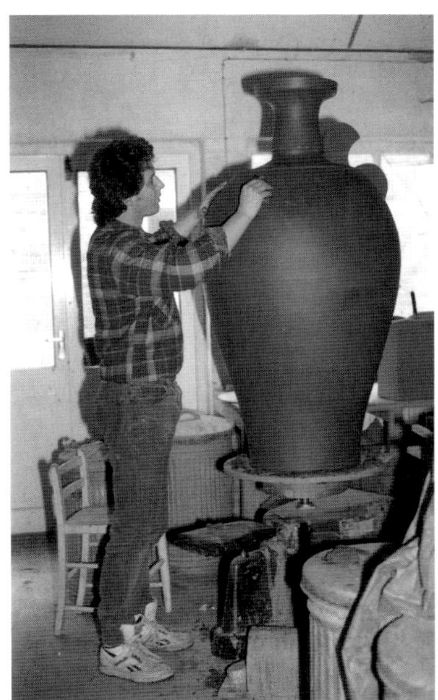

Julian Bellmont finishing a 4-ft pot

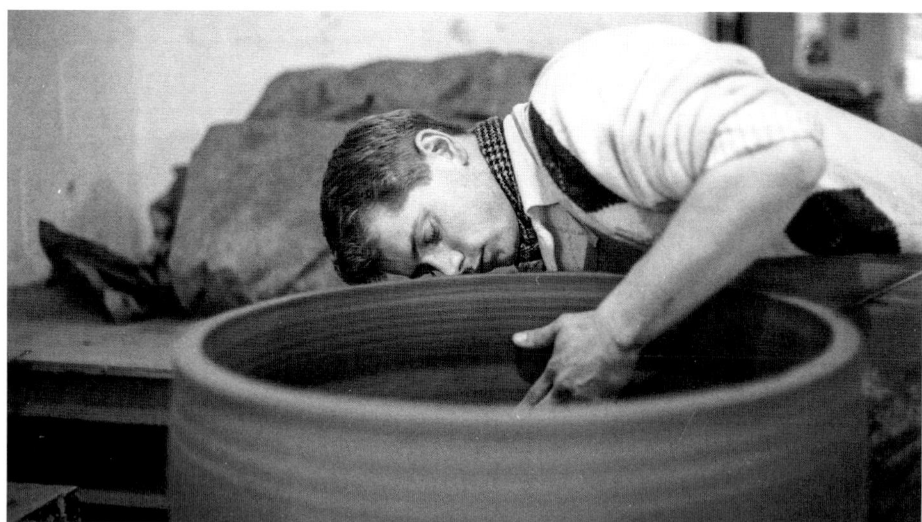

Andrew Hazelden throwing a section of a large pot, 1990

Three people, using a double bed sheet wrapped around its belly, were needed to lift the pot off the wheel. Turning the pots was almost as difficult as throwing them, mindful of the thickness of the walls and the bottom – which was almost impossible to check on a 4-ft pot. When this stage was finally finished the pot was left to dry.[40]

To avoid the laborious and exhausting process of firing with wood, a decision was made to take up the generous offer of a friend, Rupert Spira, to fire the pots in his new computer-controlled gas kiln with ceramic fibre insulation. Although meticulous care was taken during the firing, the team had not allowed for the fact that although ceramic fibre is an excellent insulation material, it has little mass and does not retain its heat. The pots therefore cooled too quickly for their size, causing dunting-cracks to develop, so four months' work had been wasted.[41]

A long, apologetic letter to the architects followed, explaining that there was now no possibility of completing the pots by the required date. Undaunted, the architects revised their completion date and agreed that as long as some of the pots were ready by the end of 1991 then that would be fine. Work began again. The potters decided to add 20% fine sand as well as 7% dolomite to the clay to strengthen it further, and to fire it in the Aldermaston kiln, bringing the pots very slowly to red heat before finishing off with wood in the usual way. Edgar Campden pointed out that being built of solid brick, the kiln would cool very slowly, so there was less risk of dunting. He then enlarged the doorway to accommodate the largest pots, ingeniously severing the girders holding the sides of the kiln together and re-welding them to form a pointed archway high enough to allow the pots to pass through.[42] Some were still too big to fit in the large wood kiln, so these were made with detachable necks to be fixed into place after firing. Campden and Bellmont also converted part of the long shed into a drying room, with a paved floor and metal ventilating grids. The following winter insulated walls and heating were also added, to protect the pots from frost.[43]

The firings in the wood kiln for the big pots differed from the usual firings, as Julian Bellmont explains:

> Normally the firing of the wood kiln would start at around 10 p.m., when Edgar Campden would light a gas poker and place it in the fire chamber of the kiln to warm the whole thing up. Then at around 4 a.m. myself, Martin Wright, or Andrew Hazelden would arrive, and start adding small slithers of willow into the fire chamber, eventually turning off the gas so the kiln started to be fuelled by wood alone. We had some tried and tested methods for firing the kiln and we kept to a graph, so we would feed the kiln to maintain temperature to a given timeline. We would then go on to using larger pieces of wood, and the firings would normally finish at around 6 p.m. that evening.
>
> However for the firing of the big pots for Pearl Assurance the poker was put in at around 5 p.m., and either Andrew or I would come to work at midnight and slowly feed the chamber with the small slithers of willow, paying attention so the temperature would only rise by ten or twenty degrees per hour. The whole process was slowed down so we didn't cause the pots to crack, and the firing would finish sometime the following evening.
>
> Looking after the kiln during an all-night session was wonderful; I used to bring my faithful hound, Owen, with me. He was sensible and went to sleep on the lawn, but occasionally he would come to see if I was OK. The evening would start off noisily, with the birds chirping away, people returning home from the pub, and cars driving through the village. At about 2 a.m. everything went very quiet and still; all you could hear was the crackling of the burning willow. This would last until around 5 a.m. when the birds would wake up, the traffic would begin, and the sun would rise. At around 8 a.m. the other potters would arrive for work with comments like: 'Still awake then?' 'Hasn't gone out yet?' 'Fancy a cuppa?' For me it was time to go home for some well-deserved sleep.[44]

In the late summer of 1991 a young Indian potter, Padma Rajagopal Joshi, joined the team and was delighted to find herself basking in temperatures often as hot as Bombay. This was perfect for drying the pots, and by the late autumn the potters were congratulating themselves on the successful biscuit firing of three large pots. However, with 23 still to be made, and more crucially, two more risky firings for each pot, they still had a long way to go.[45] In spite of this the potters still managed to find the time to have fun, as Louise Bashall recalls:

> we had some great parties during the summer in the Pottery garden, especially with the Indian potters – Padma, and later Kristine Michael (who came the following year). Sam was a lovely guitar player, and Ursula was very keen on medieval music – we used to play recorder duets at a number of the parties, and the wonderful thing was that we could borrow beautiful serving bowls from the showroom to serve all the delicious food.[46]

The next big challenge for the potters was glazing the enormous pots. As they had found with the giant teapot, the backdraught of escaping air made it impossible to use a spray gun. The problem was solved by lying each 200 lb pot on its side and throwing in two buckets of thin glaze; it was then rolled back and forth by two people kneeling on the table on either side of it, until the inside was completely covered. Then, keeping a firm grip on the pot, it was upended to remove the surplus glaze, with a good deal of splashing and laughter. The outside was then sprayed by Campden using a spray gun. Once again the double bed sheet came in handy, as the pots, covered with powdery glaze, had to be placed inside the kiln and accurately positioned without disturbing any of the glaze. So two people enveloped the pot with the sheet and used it to manoeuvre the pots into position.[47]

By this time the pots had contracted by 9% and shrunk by nearly 5 in during the bisque firing, so the second glaze firing posed less of a risk than the first; nevertheless, the potters were very relieved when the pots emerged from this firing still intact. The final challenge of painting a design on these magnificent enormous white pots lay entirely in Caiger-Smith's hand. He had envisaged the pots in groups of three, each with a distinct colour and design. He decided to paint one pot in each group in red lustre, one in silver-gold, and one with lustre on blue (clear glaze over blue slip). Each group included three different themes: a strong structural theme, a softer, cursive design, and an emblematic theme. After struggling for a couple of days with painted dyes he was ready to begin, and working not only with brushes but also sprayed pigment, which he then wiped away with a sponge to define the contours. Gradually gaining confidence, by the time he was on the seventh pot he had become master of his technique. The final problem, of placing the painted pots in the kiln, was eventually solved by spraying car-body lacquer over the pigment to protect it while the pots were moved; this would then burn away during firing.[48]

The first pots were fired to lustre temperature extremely slowly, taking 14 hours instead of the usual seven, and everyone held their breath. When they emerged from the lustre firing no one dared hope that the lustre would have developed as they wanted. But as they began to rub away the scorched and blackened ochre they could soon see the glorious, rich red iridescence lying just below the surface of the glaze. Soon they had two magnificent pots before them; all that remained was to repeat the process a dozen more times.[49] As it was not possible to store more than six pots of such size, they were removed at intervals by fine art movers Rees Martin Ltd, until at last in April 1992 the project was completed, exactly two years after it had first begun.[50]

The successful completion of the Pearl Assurance commission was a major achievement, but was to be the Pottery's swan song after 38 years as a place of learning and production. Nothing could have prepared the team for the breathtaking impact of the 26 huge lustre pots installed in the cathedral-like space of the company's vaulted glass atrium. Not since the majestic winged lustre pots were installed in the Alhambra Palace in fourteenth-century Granada had such large

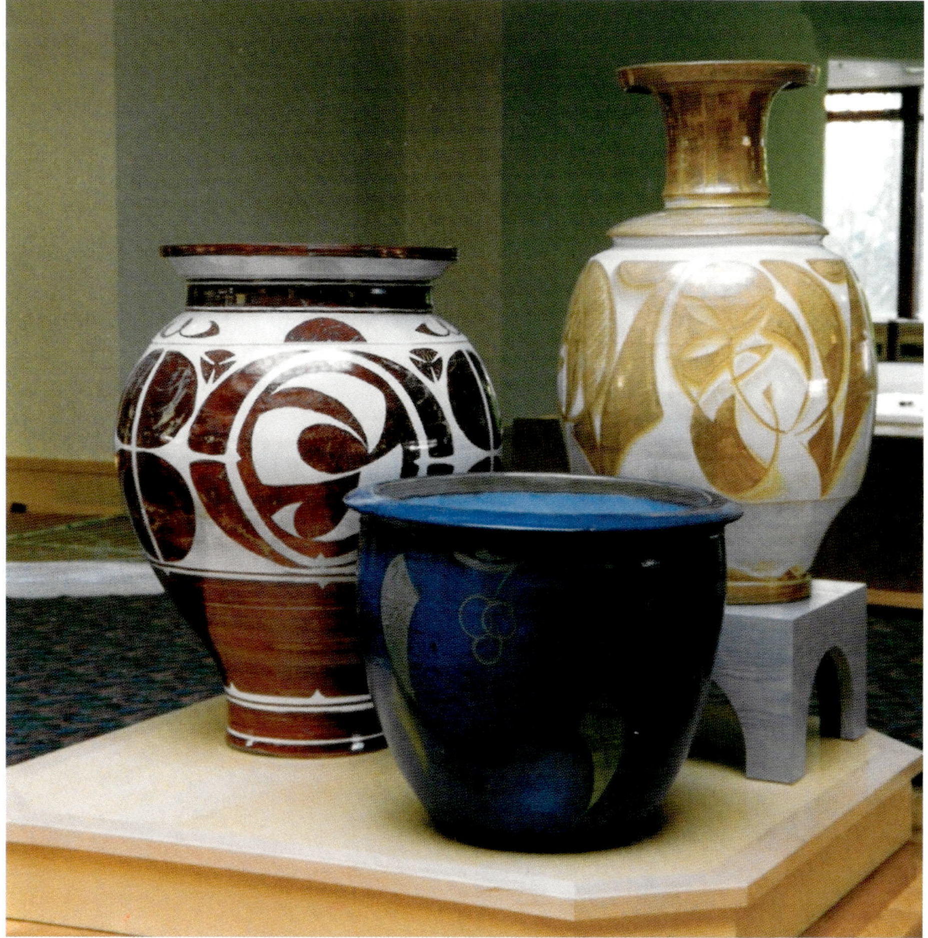

A group of three large pots at the Pearl Assurance Head Office, 1992

pieces in reduced-pigment lustre been made. The magnificent sentinels were an awe-inspiring sight, and represented the culmination of years of hard work, perseverance and endeavour. Time stood still as sunlight streamed down in golden shafts from above, and the iridescent lustre shimmered with a luminous intensity, just as it must have done in the great palace centuries ago.

In 1991 Ursula Waechter had left Aldermaston to go on a study tour of Southern India, and on her return she went back to Germany to set up a workshop in Bremen, where she worked for the next six years. Although Bellmont, Hazelden, Davies and Campden were principally involved with making the big pots at this time, the everyday orders and commissions still had to be fulfilled, so a new assistant, Silke Nerger, was taken on to replace Waechter. Nerger, who had received a thorough training in Germany, worked at the Pottery for nearly two years. Caiger-Smith remembers her as one of the most gifted throwers he ever engaged, equally impressive on a large or a small scale, her every movement

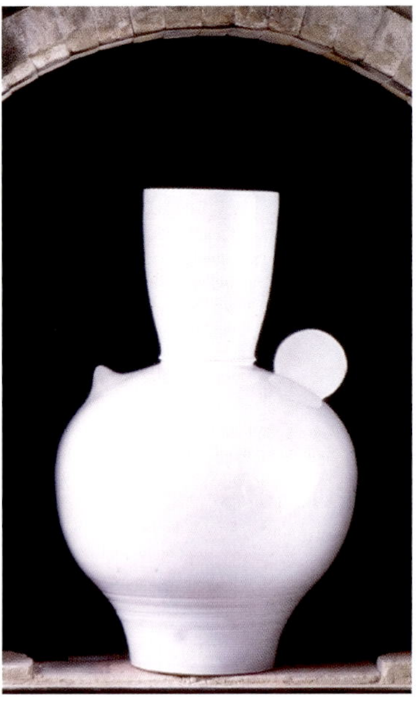

Large pot thrown by Andrew Hazelden,
1990, h. 100.5 cm

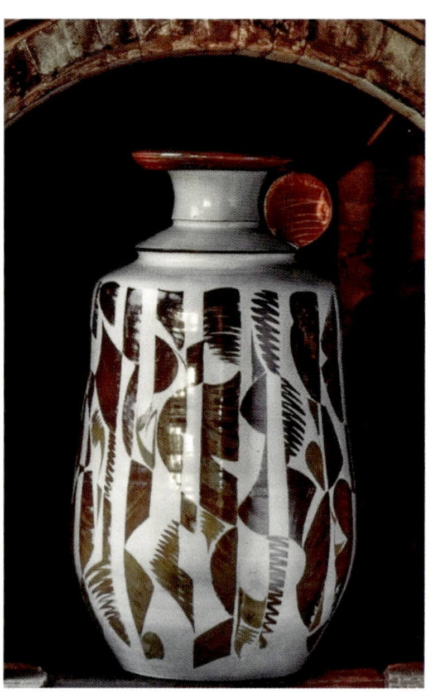

Pot thrown by Julian Bellmont and
decorated by Alan Caiger-Smith, 1991,
h. 112 cm

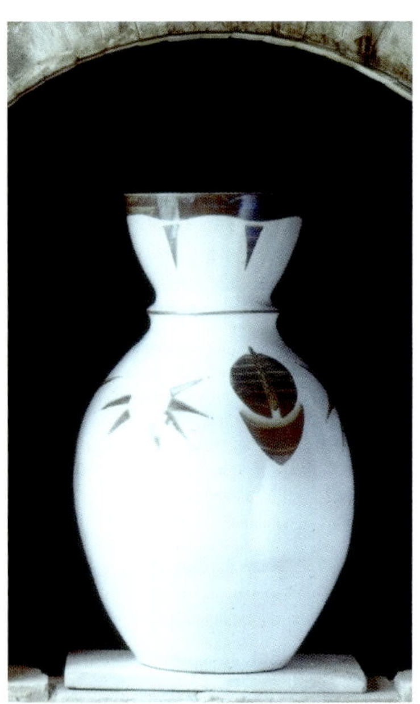

Pot thrown by Andrew Hazelden and
decorated by Alan Caiger-Smith, 1991,
h. 99 cm

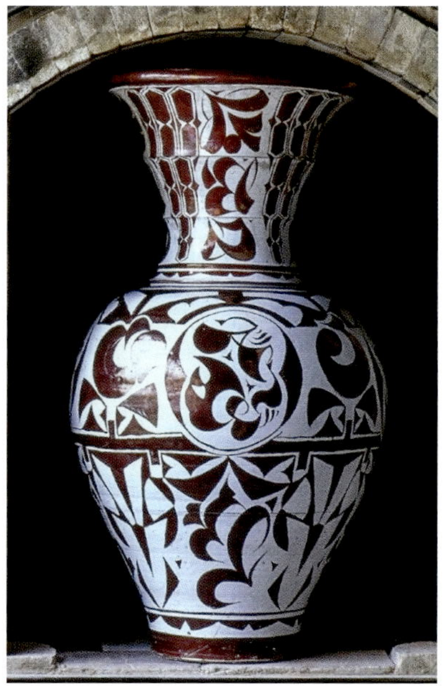

Pot thrown by Julian Bellmont and
decorated by Alan Caiger-Smith, 1991,
h. 128 cm

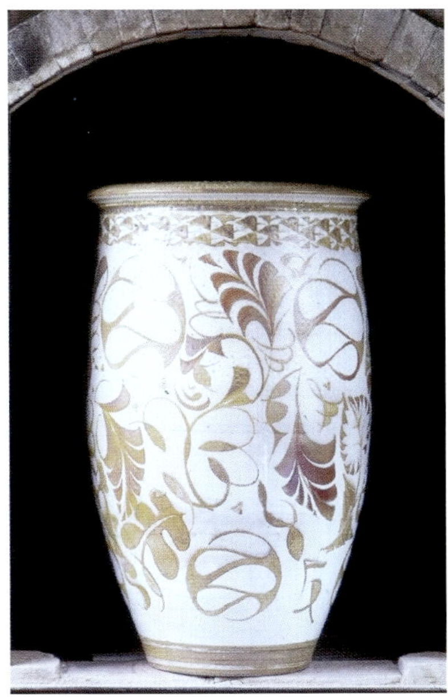

Pot thrown by Julian Bellmont and
decorated by Alan Caiger-Smith, 1991,
h. 105 cm

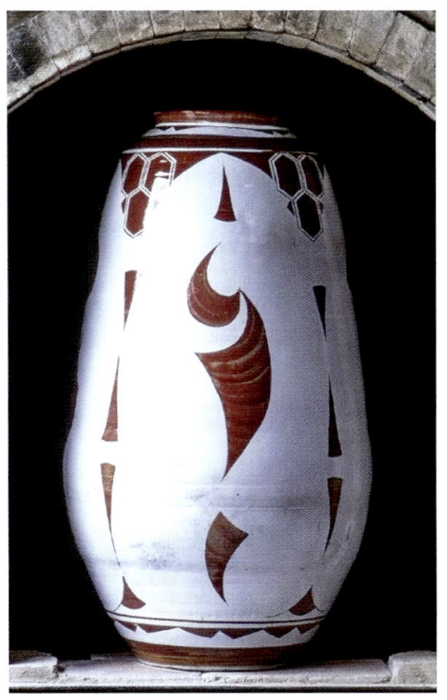

Pot thrown by Julian Bellmont and
decorated by Alan Caiger-Smith, 1991,
h. 118.5 cm

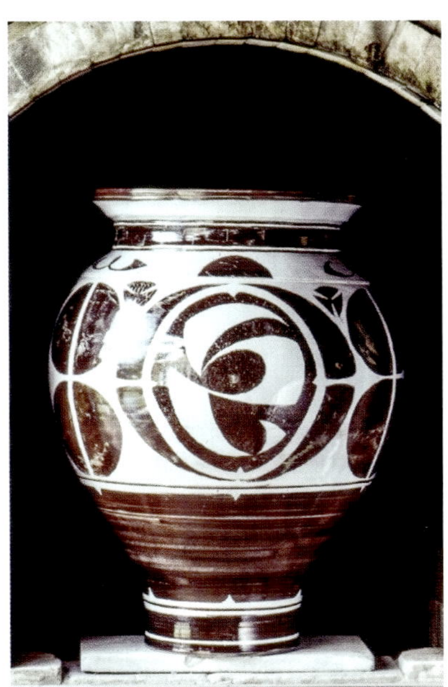

Pot thrown by Julian Bellmont and
decorated by Alan Caiger-Smith, 1991,
h. 100.5 cm

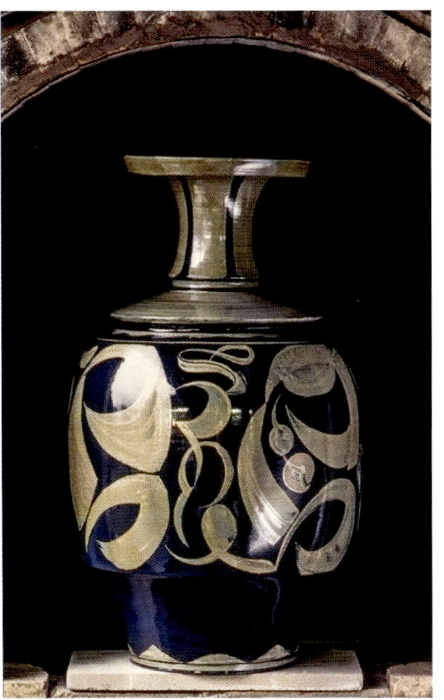

Pot thrown by Julian Bellmont and
decorated by Alan Caiger-Smith, 1991,
h. 105 cm

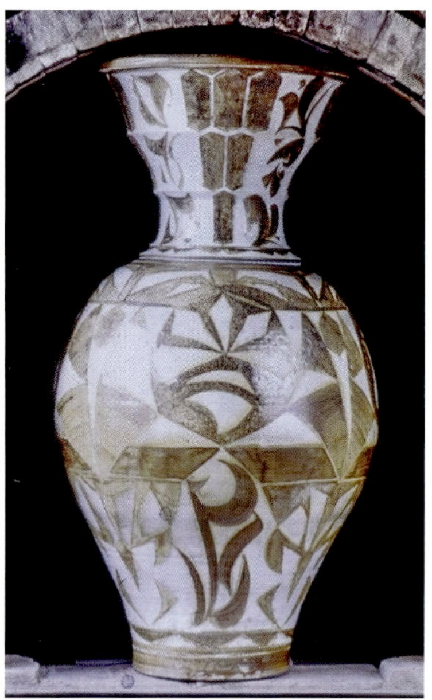

Pot thrown by Julian Bellmont and
decorated by Alan Caiger-Smith, 1991,
h. 128 cm

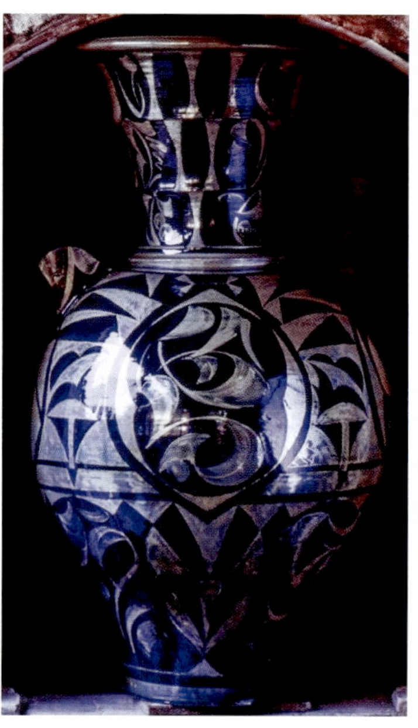

Pot thrown by Julian Bellmont and
decorated by Alan Caiger-Smith, 1991,
h. 128 cm

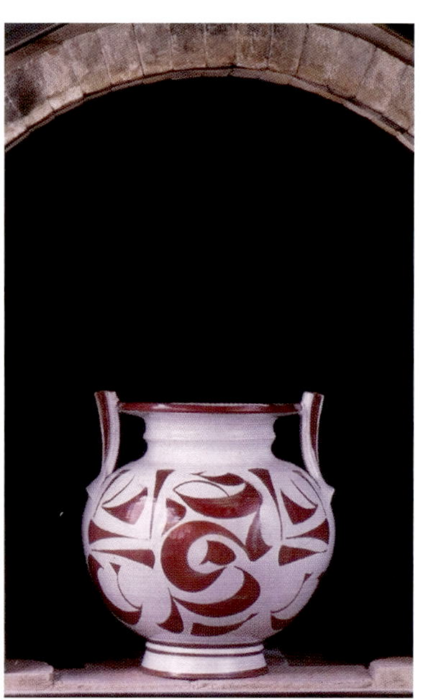

Pot thrown by Julian Bellmont and
decorated by Alan Caiger-Smith, 1990,
h. 60 cm

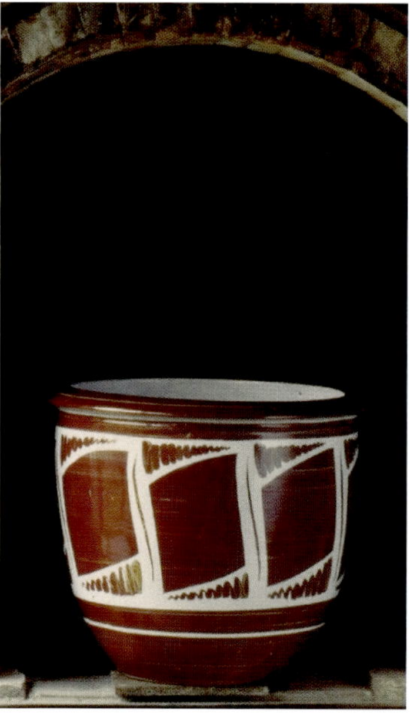

Pot thrown by Andrew Hazelden and
decorated by Alan Caiger-Smith, 1991,
h. 60 cm

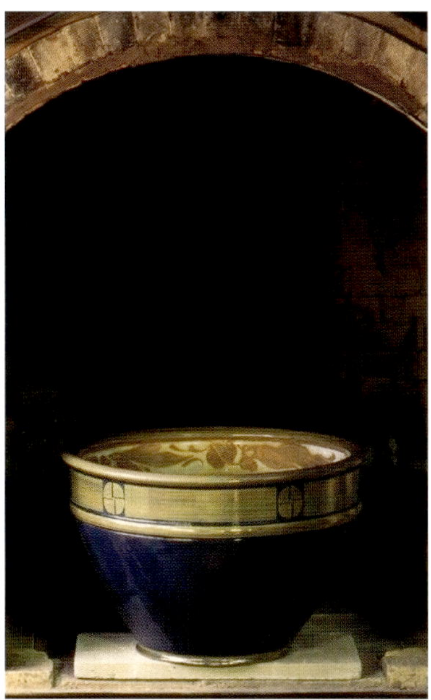

Pot thrown by Andrew Hazelden and
decorated by Alan Caiger-Smith, 1991,
h. 40 cm

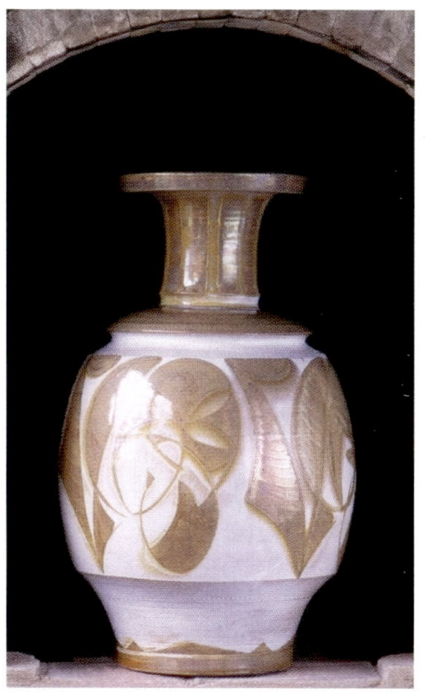

Pot thrown by Andrew Hazelden and
decorated by Alan Caiger-Smith, 1991,
h. 103.5 cm

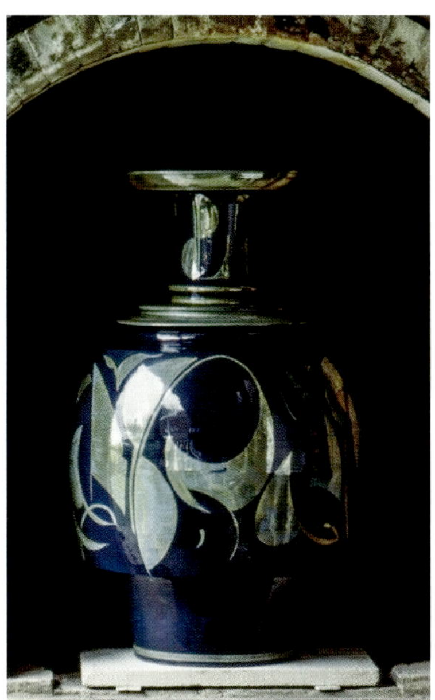

Pot thrown by Julian Bellmont and
decorated by Alan Caiger-Smith, 1991,
h. 102 cm

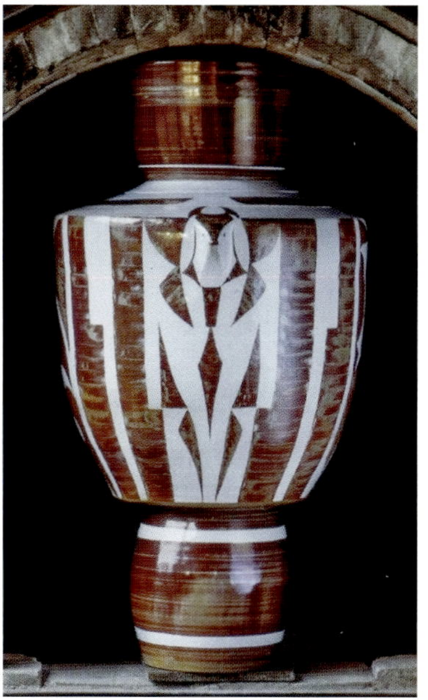

Pot thrown by Julian Bellmont and
decorated by Alan Caiger-Smith, 1991,
h. 130 cm

precise and seemingly effortless.[51] She was also a talented musician. Soon after leaving Aldermaston in 1993 to set up her own studio in Wiltshire, however, she was struck by multiple sclerosis. She carried on potting and playing music as her condition worsened, and soon after the birth of her daughter in the summer of 2000 she had a major relapse and was unable to continue. Caiger-Smith considered it a great tragedy that her full potential could never be realised.[52]

During 1991 an opportunity arose for Sam Davies to teach ceramics at the University of the Andes in Merida, Venezuela, and so he left Aldermaston 'with the confidence I needed to make my way in the world'. An attempted military coup the following year forced the university to close for a time, so Davies used the time to go to Guatemala to work with local potters, an experience he wrote about in an article for *Ceramic Review*.[53] He also became involved with human rights work, both in Guatemala and in Colombia, before returning to the UK in September 1992 for the birth of his son.[54]

On his return Davies taught ceramics and craft skills to people with disabilities before completing a teacher training course. He became a lecturer in Learning Difficulties at Worcester College of Technology, where he was eventually appointed head of the Department for Special Needs. Having taken voluntary redundancy, he now devotes his time to running an organic smallholding in the wilds of Shropshire with his wife, Kate. They are largely self-sufficient, producing their own wine, honey, eggs and cheese. But Davies says if he ever gets time he'll build the raku kiln he has been thinking of ever since he left Aldermaston.[55]

One winter morning in January 1992 Kristine Michael arrived at Aldermaston from India. She found the shock of the cold immediately countered by the warmth she received from Alan and Anne-Marie, who 'had opened their home and hearts to me, for which I was infinitely grateful'.[56] Louise Bashall recalls: 'I remember her cycling in from Shalford in the morning and her being so cold that her beautiful Indian face was frozen, so she'd come in and hover over the wood-burning stove to get warm, saying, "my face is so frozen that I can't smile".'[57] Michael became particularly fond of Anne-Marie: she could identify with her Scandinavian sense of design and aesthetics, having received a Bauhaus-style design education at The National Institute of Design in Ahmedabad, set up by Charles and Ray Eames in 1961.[58]

Michael had come to serve a six-month apprentice at the Pottery under the Charles Wallace Trust, Festival of India Arts Award for 1992; she was the first Indian potter to win the prestigious British award. She had spent six years studying industrial ceramic design at the National Institute of Design during the 1980s, but found that her main passion remained the non-industrial craft object and the aesthetics of objects of everyday use. She then spent four years apprenticed to Ray Meeker and Deborah Smith at their renowned Golden Bridge Pottery in Pondicherry, where she gained experience in wood-firing, stoneware and salt glazes. On being awarded the scholarship she says she made the decision to come specifically to Aldermaston, because

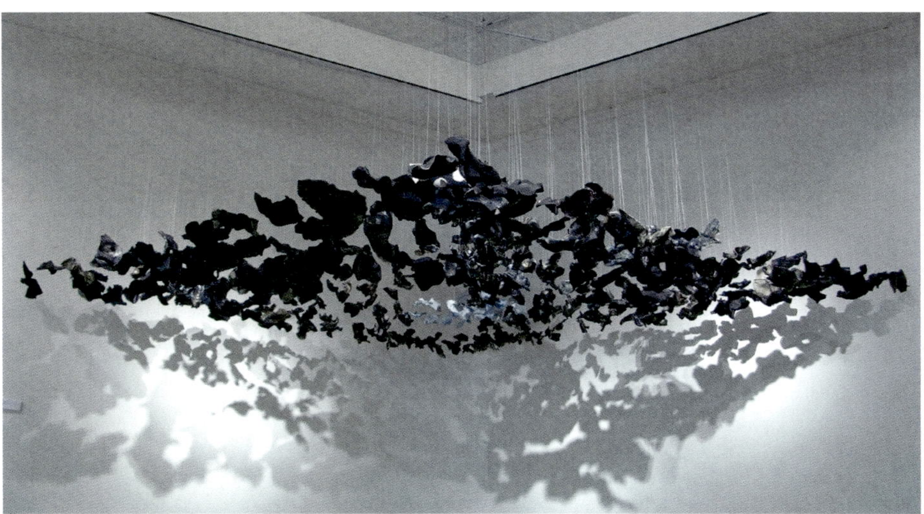

'Rites of Passage' raku-fired installation by Kristine Michael, 2007, w. 460 cm
Private collection

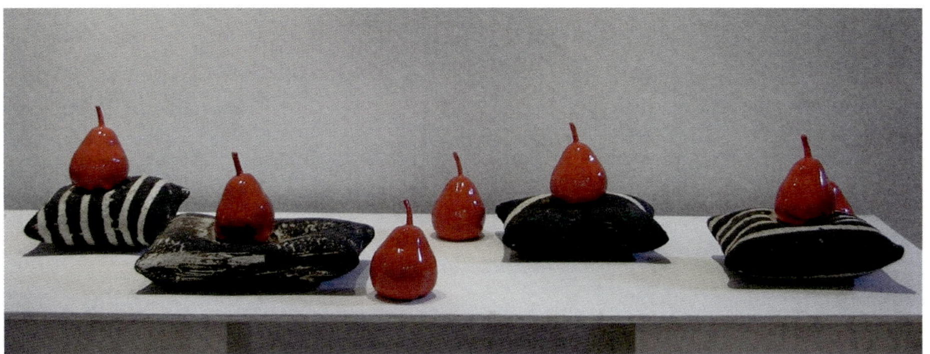

'Cradle Song' installation stoneware with low temperature overglaze
by Kristine Michael, 2006–8, max. h. 30 cm, length 180 cm (variable)
Private collection

the work Alan was doing in red clay, using low temperature tin glazes with
reduced lustre, based on Spanish and Arab techniques, was of great interest to me.
I had been working with rural traditional potters in various parts of India, and
trying to inject new ideas and designs of glazed ware to a rapidly fading market,
and I hoped to learn new techniques for low temperature as well as expand my
own artistic practice. The firing was also of special interest, as I'd had experience
of doing stoneware wood-reduction downdraft firings in Pondicherry, but to see
his kiln based on the old Piccolpasso design, and the intricacies of the firing cycle
was a revelation.[59]

During her short time at Aldermaston Michael was given a whirlwind course in
all aspects of the Pottery and she loved every moment:

It always struck me that Alan had an Indian soul with his endless fascination for the East. Its cultures and idiosyncrasies were often discussed during long Shalford dinners around their table, which was always graciously set out with an array of goblets, bowls and plates with delicious food. Often, as I cooked Indian dinners for them, and sometimes also for the other potters, the aroma of garlic and turmeric would waft beyond the Aga and out into the surrounding lawns. Conversation ranged from Indian spirituality and Bahai to aesthetics and the Arts and Crafts movement. It was a great learning experience for me to see some of those values of the early Morris and Ruskin movement in practice – small workshops with a master potter and apprentices who varied in skills, learning the intricacies of a common craft. Teaching came naturally to Alan, and he gathered around him like-minded, loyal students who were the backbone of the running of the Pottery. He had a capacity to inspire strong team ethics, and he always challenged us to go beyond our expectations.[60]

Before returning to India later that year Michael spent the last months of her Charles Wallace Award with Peter Cook, Steve Course and Janice Tchalenko at the Dart Pottery in Devon. She set up her first ceramic studio in 1994 at the Sanskriti Kendra, Anandgram in New Delhi, where she ran intensive pottery courses alongside making her own work.

Michael uses her sculptural pieces to explore the symbolism of forms drawn from nature, and how different groups relate to each other. She often works on a series of art pieces based around a particular theme, each piece distinct but in harmony with the group. She has also experimented with digital imagery. Her work is part of important collections in England, Korea, the USA and Austria.

In the 25 years since leaving Aldermaston, Michael has enjoyed a distinguished career as a sculptural ceramic artist, writer, researcher, and independent scholar, and she has participated in numerous conferences and workshops across the world. She is currently Curriculum Leader of Visual and Performing Arts at the British School, New Delhi.

Louise Bashall left Aldermaston in the summer of 1992 to train as a chiropractor, having suffered recurring problems with her back while she had been working at the Pottery. However, her training at the Pottery had given her a solid foundation as a potter, which she has used throughout her life, including setting up a studio producing tin-glazed earthenware to subsidise her studies while she was at college doing her chiropractic training.[61]

In March 1992 Myra McDonnell had returned to work full time at Aldermaston after spending a year in Finland:

I took Dart stoneware reduction pottery techniques/decoration out to a Finnish pottery, Jusssi Keramiks, that had bought them under a trial 'franchise' system. Janice Tchalenko had been my tutor at the RCA and knew I could pick up techniques, so I spent a couple of months at Dartington, then went out to a Finnish island called Aland to train up their potters.[62]

When she finally came to work at the Pottery as a full-time assistant, many of the potters she had known from the mid-1980s had left and the new assistants were unaware of what she had been doing before. So she started as a beginner, and 'a lesson in humility and patience followed, doing the menial tasks that the throwers didn't like'. In retrospect McDonnell feels that it was an unfortunate time to join the Pottery, with its disparate personalities, and it felt very different. Within the year the Pottery had closed.[63]

The Pottery had continued to thrive until the financial recession of the 1990s. The Pearl Assurance commission for 26 giant pots had been a major achievement but had taken up a lot of their time, and had diverted the potters' attention. During the summer of 1992 Caiger-Smith noticed that the ordinary business of the workshop was shrinking and none of the usual invitations to exhibit were forthcoming. By November he decided that he should look through the account books properly with his son Nick, who exclaimed: 'my goodness Pa, you have left this a bit late haven't you?' when he discovered that they were in fact running at a serious loss. As income for the first three months of the year never covered their costs anyway, he could see that they would have to close before the following spring.[64]

Julian Bellmont recalls the moment that Caiger-Smith broke the news to the potters:

> At the end of 1992 the economy was not good and sales were beginning to suffer, and then one afternoon Alan asked us all to stay back for a while after work. He started by letting us know that there would be good bonuses that year as the previous financial year had been good, however this year had not been so good. He said that things were not going well, and he did not want the Pottery to slowly slip away and grind to a halt. Instead he wished to have the Pottery's final exhibition in six months' time, and then close the doors. We could all go out with a 'bang'. He said that he would make sure we were all compensated financially as much as he could afford, but this came as a big shock to us all; at the time my second son was only a month old.
>
> As soon as the news was out, the newspapers and television stations started to arrive. It was quite an ego boost shooting a TV interview and then seeing it broadcast later on that day. Friends got in touch after reading the news, articles appeared in *Crafts*, and people seemed genuinely interested in what everyone was doing. Alan was very keen to talk to each of us alone at Shalford about our thoughts for the future, and he explained he would go as far beyond normal redundancy payments as was feasible. In reality life continued as usual, and as news of the imminent closure began to spread the orders increased, as did sales from the showroom.[65]

Caiger-Smith explained the situation to the customers and gallery contacts, asking them to support the Pottery for the next five months so that the following May they could end with a final exhibition. He says the effect was stupendous and people responded in the most staggering way: sales increased dramatically, and he had never made so much money in his entire working life. Furthermore, 'we had gained time to think ahead and to prepare for a splendid exhibition, which was a massive success. After that the potters had to be dispersed, but they had at least been given time to prepare for their futures, and it turned out well for everyone.'[66]

So work began to prepare for the final exhibition, which was to include both regular stock items and special exhibition pieces. Everyone worked extremely hard, often staying on into the evenings to make special pieces. The firings were all very good, and after each one the best pots would be set aside for the exhibition. Over the following months the Pottery produced an amazing collection of pots and some impressive commissioned work. The final show was to include a few large pots similar to those for the Pearl Assurance commission: a pair of tall vases and a 4-ft-high blue-slipped vase. Bellmont was also asked to photograph the work for the exhibition catalogue:

> those final months were very busy, and along with preparing for the exhibition, completing orders, and stocking the showroom, my other task was to plan what I was going to do when I left the pottery. When it was time to move on Alan stuck to his word, and we all received good redundancy settlements.[67]

The final exhibition was a tremendous success: of all the exhibitions Caiger-Smith had ever had, this was the one of which he was most proud. He said its success was also due in large part to Anne-Marie, who reorganised the back workshop and arranged the display, as well as masterminding the catalogue and photographing many of the illustrations.[68]

At 1 p.m. on Saturday, 29 May the sign that had hung above the door for 38 years was taken down and Aldermaston Pottery closed. Alan and Anne-Marie hosted a wonderful party at Shalford; Alan thanked everyone for all their hard work and then presented each of the potters with a personalised chalice, inscribed inside the foot-ring with the potter's own mark and 'from AC-S, May 1993'.[69]

Kristine Michael came back from India for the final exhibition and the formal closure of the Pottery. In an article she wrote for *The Economic Times* on her return, she says:

> My apprenticeship with the Aldermaston Pottery in 1992 opened up many areas for me technically, artistically, and spiritually. If the workshop experience did with others as it did with me, generate a new creative impulse and make me self-reliant, then no one is going to disappear. Everyone working there has plans for the future, and Aldermaston Pottery will live on as a philosophy and a shared experience which, in turn, can be shared.[70]

So ended 38 years of convivial working, learning and friendship, which had seen nearly sixty full-time assistants and many occasional students pass through the Pottery doors. Caiger-Smith recalls:

we ended with a highly successful exhibition, the profits were shared out and the potters dispersed, most of them setting up successful studios of their own. In countless ways every person who spent any length of time at the Pottery contributed something of lasting value. Everyone's input was unique, and altogether they enlivened the pulse of whatever we undertook.[71]

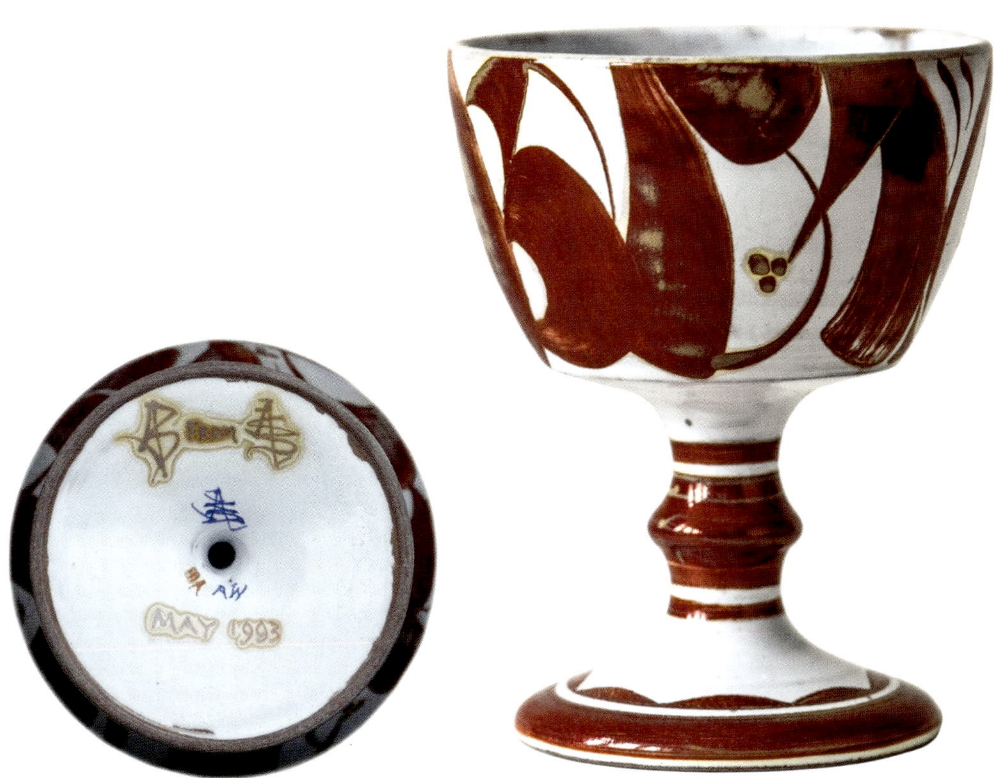

Lustre chalice with copper and silver decoration
by Alan Caiger-Smith, 1993, h. 15.5 cm, w. 12 cm
Collection Julian Bellmont

One of these chalices was given to each of the final team. Inside the footring is inscribed: '[initials of potter] from AC-S, Alan Caiger-Smith's signature, IOA [the lustre used], AW [the glaze used], May 1993'

197

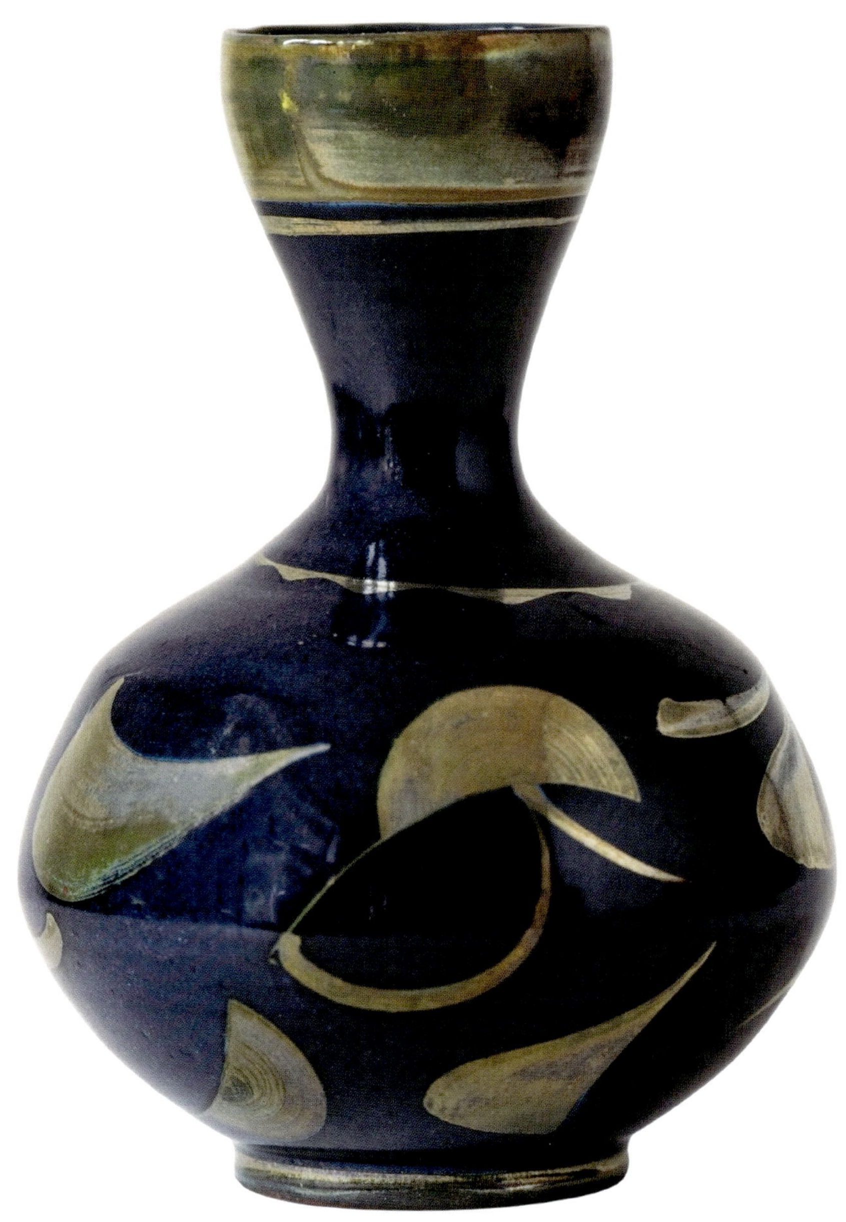

Small blue vase with silver lustre decoration
by Alan Caiger-Smith, 1992, h. 26 cm, w. 10 cm
Collection Julian Bellmont

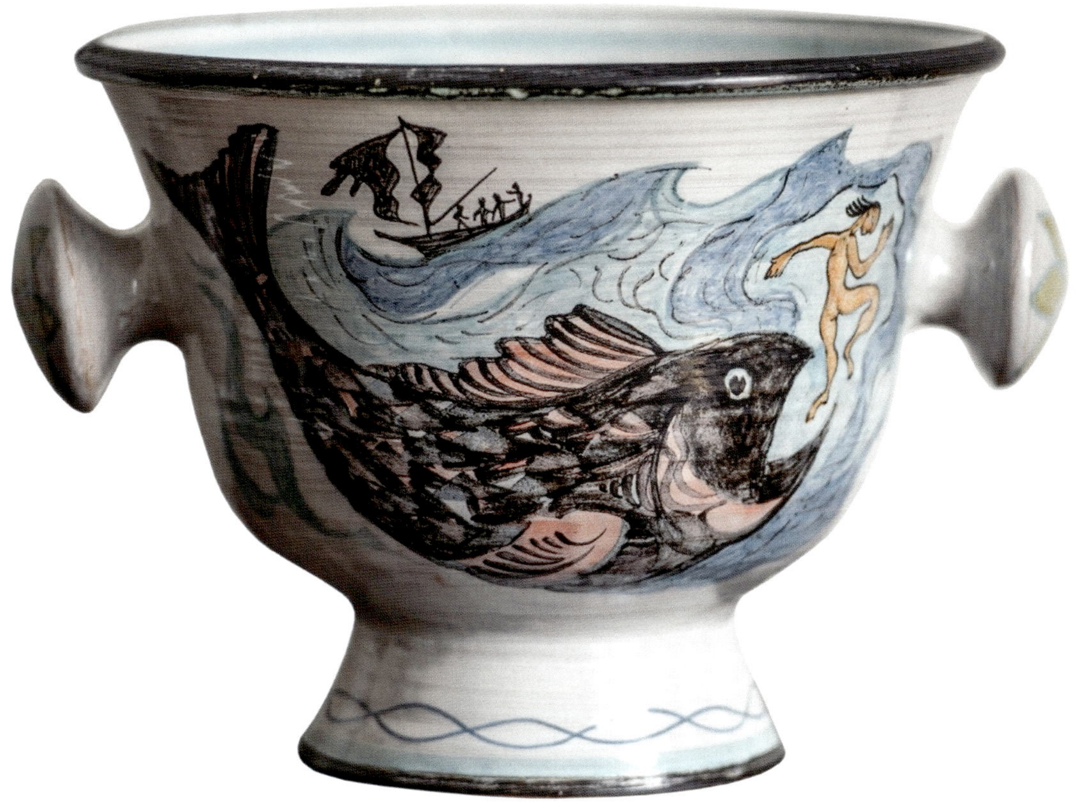

'Jonah & the Whale' by Alan Caiger-Smith,
1992, h. 36 cm, w. 38 cm
Collection Peter and Sally Dolphin

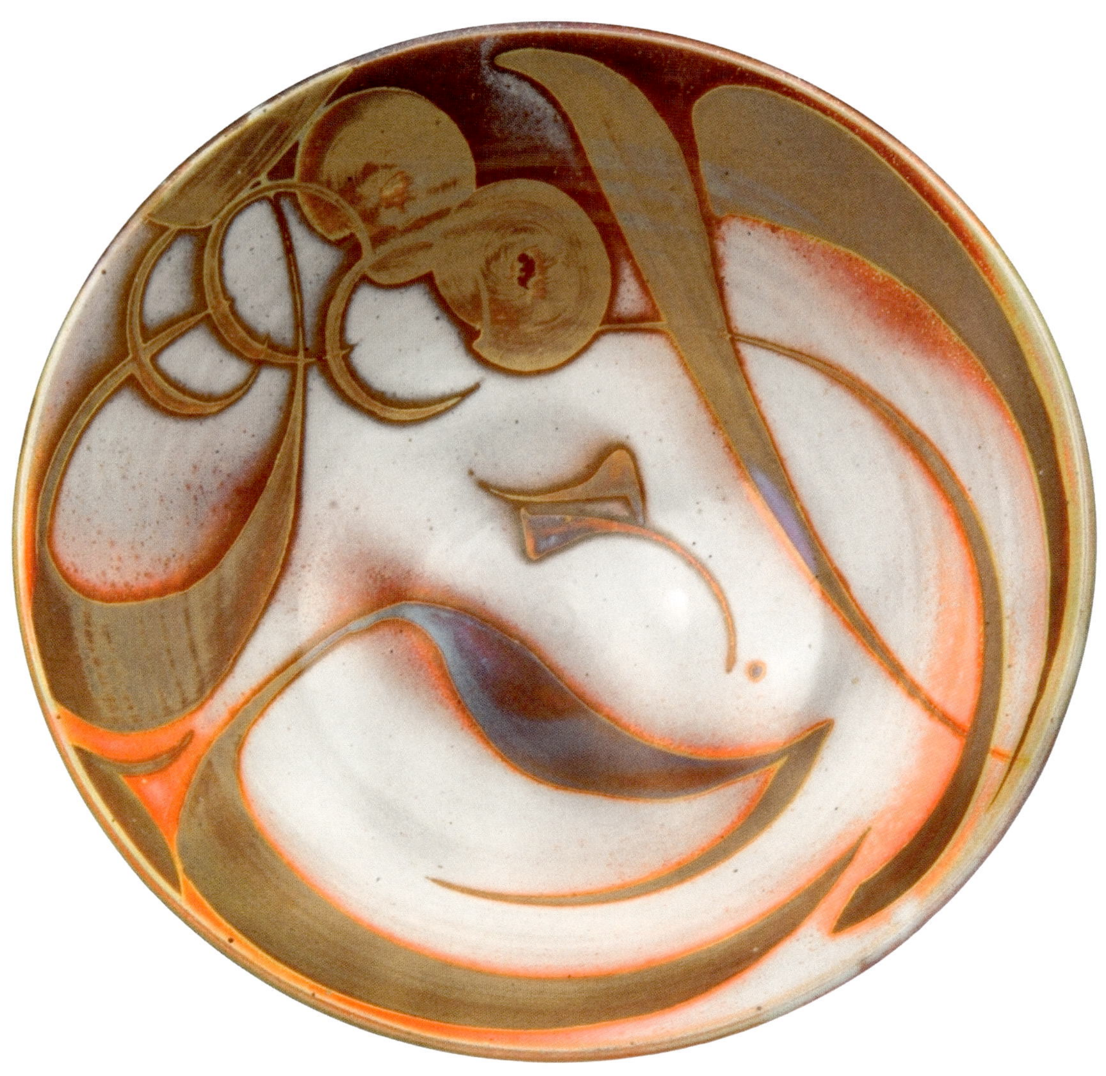

Medium bowl with copper lustre by
Alan Caiger-Smith, 1993, diam. 28 cm, h. 9 cm
Collection Alan Caiger-Smith

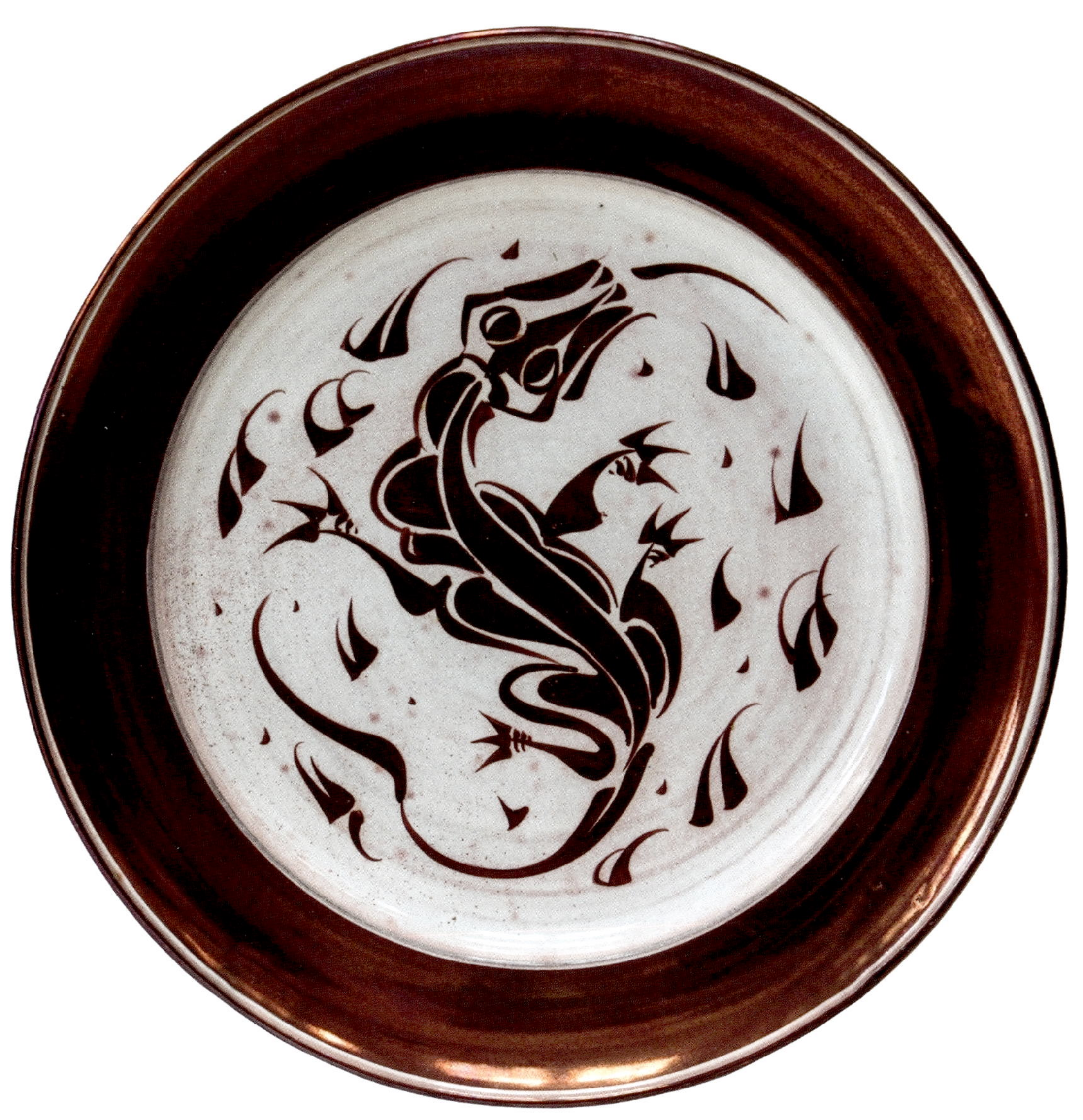

Copper lustre, 'Salamander' platter by
Alan Caiger-Smith, 1991, diam. 35 cm, h. 2.5 cm
Collection Sarah and Adrian Dixon

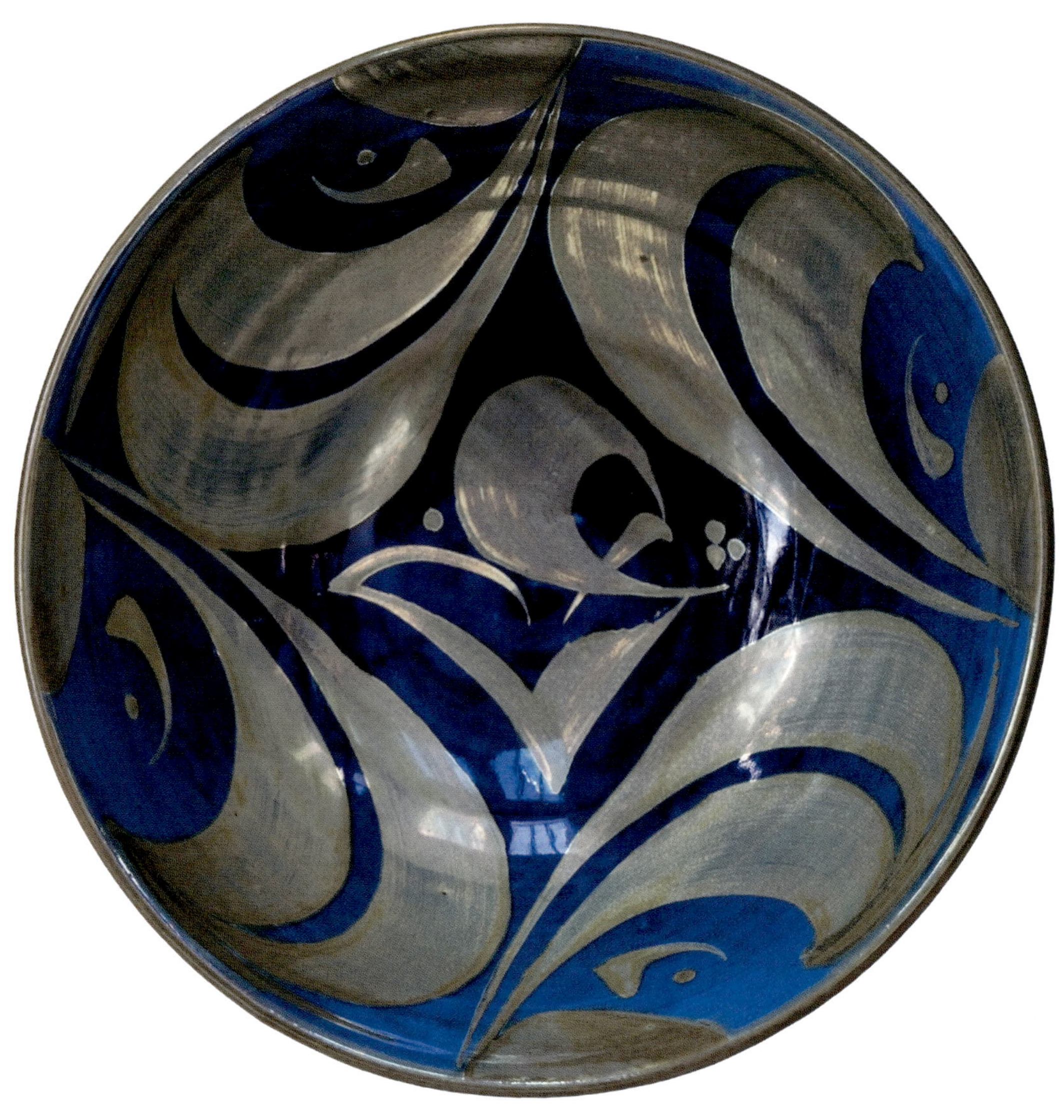

Serving bowl, silver lustre on blue glaze, by
Alan Caiger-Smith, 1996, diam. 23 cm, h. 8 cm
Collection Sarah and Adrian Dixon

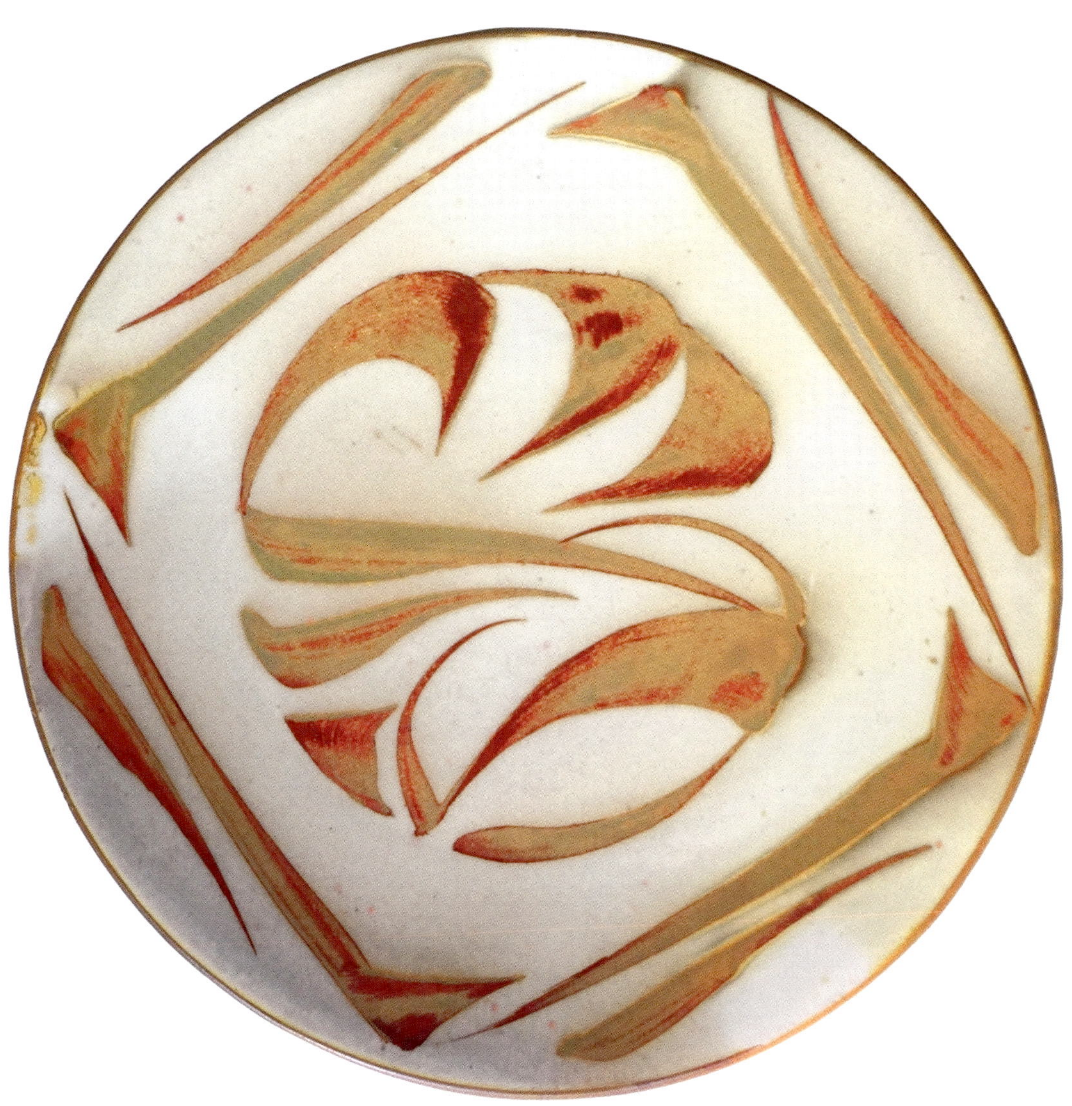

Red lustre plate, by Alan Caiger-Smith,
2005, diam. 26.8 cm, h. 3 cm
Collection Jane and Bob White

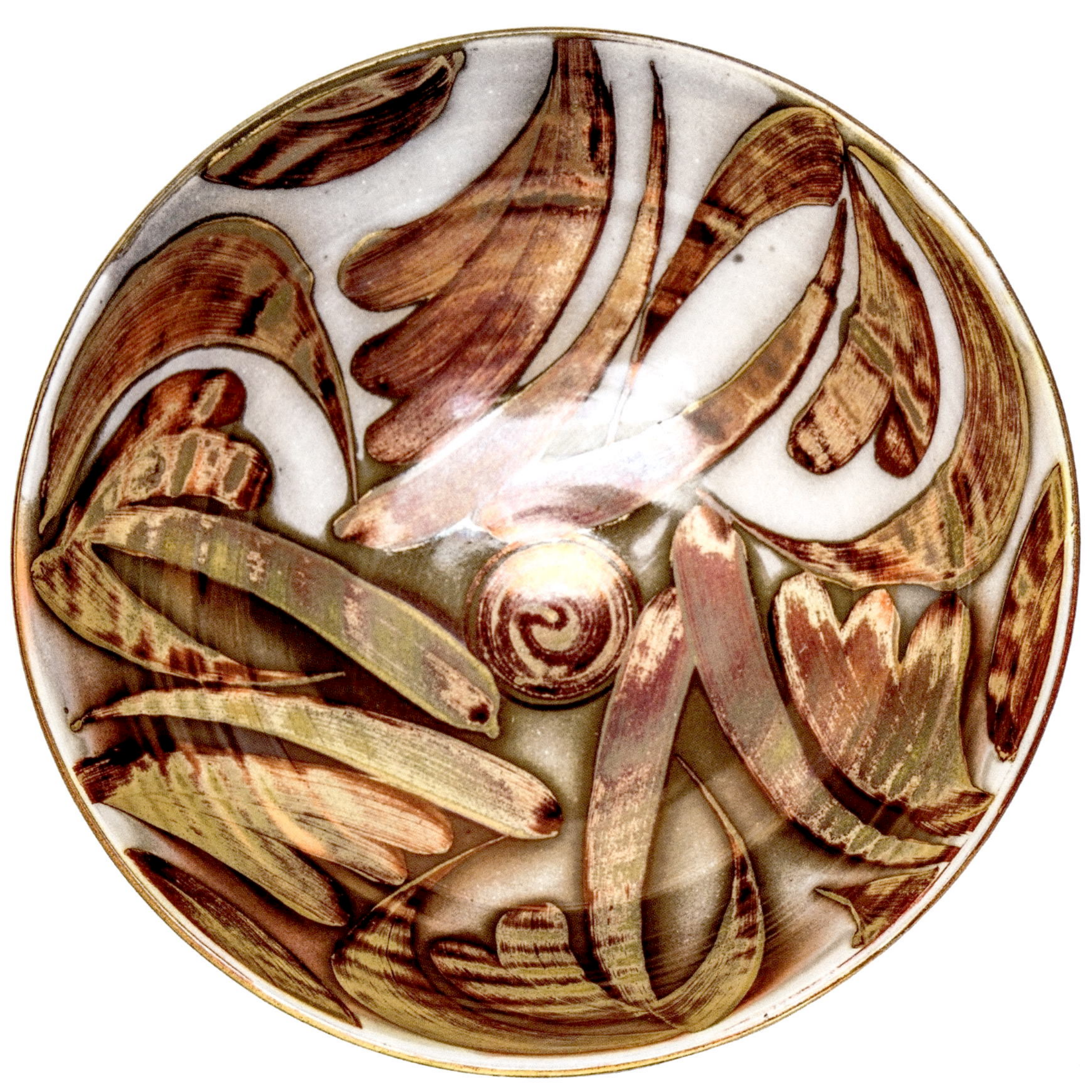

Medium lustre bowl, vapoured golden red, by
Alan Caiger-Smith, 2005, diam. 24.7 cm, h. 9.4 cm
Collection Jane and Bob White

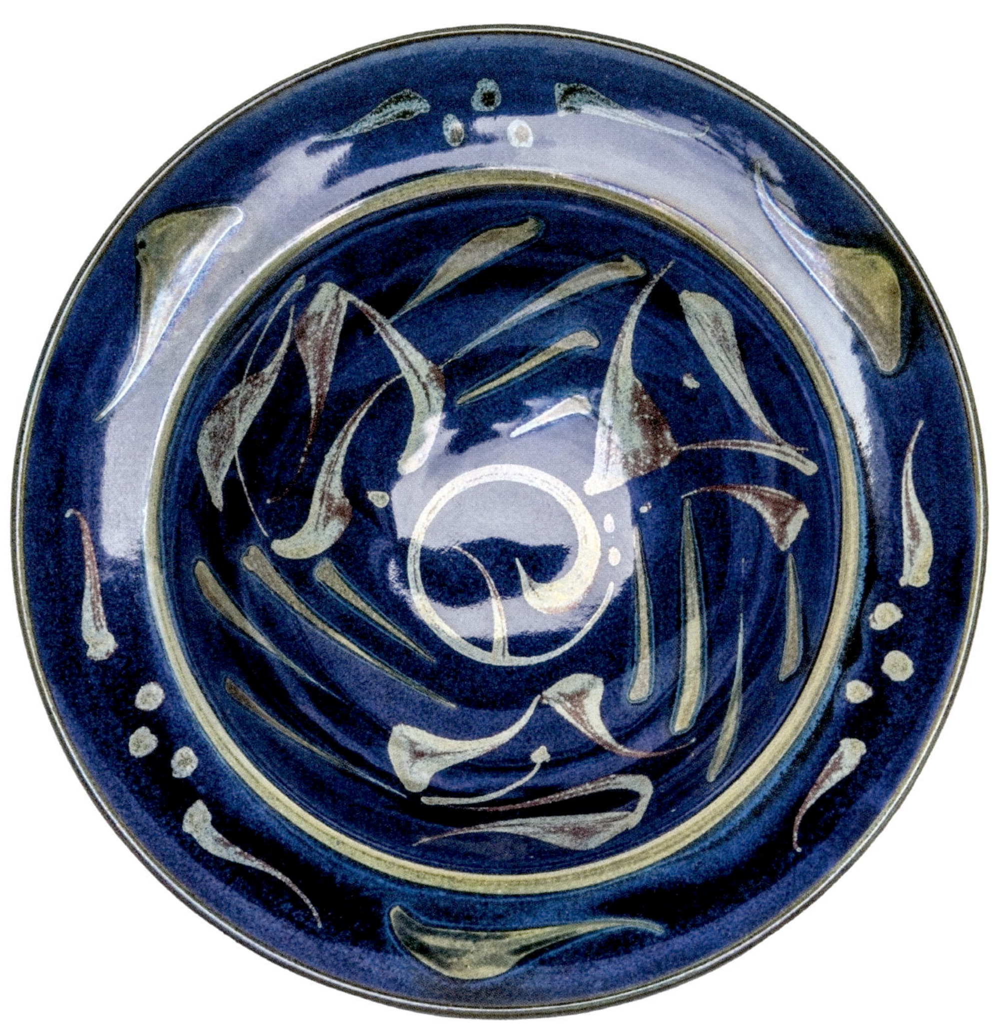

Small blue glazed bowl with silver lustre, by
Alan Caiger-Smith, 2006, diam. 17.7 cm, h. 5 cm
Collection Jane and Bob White

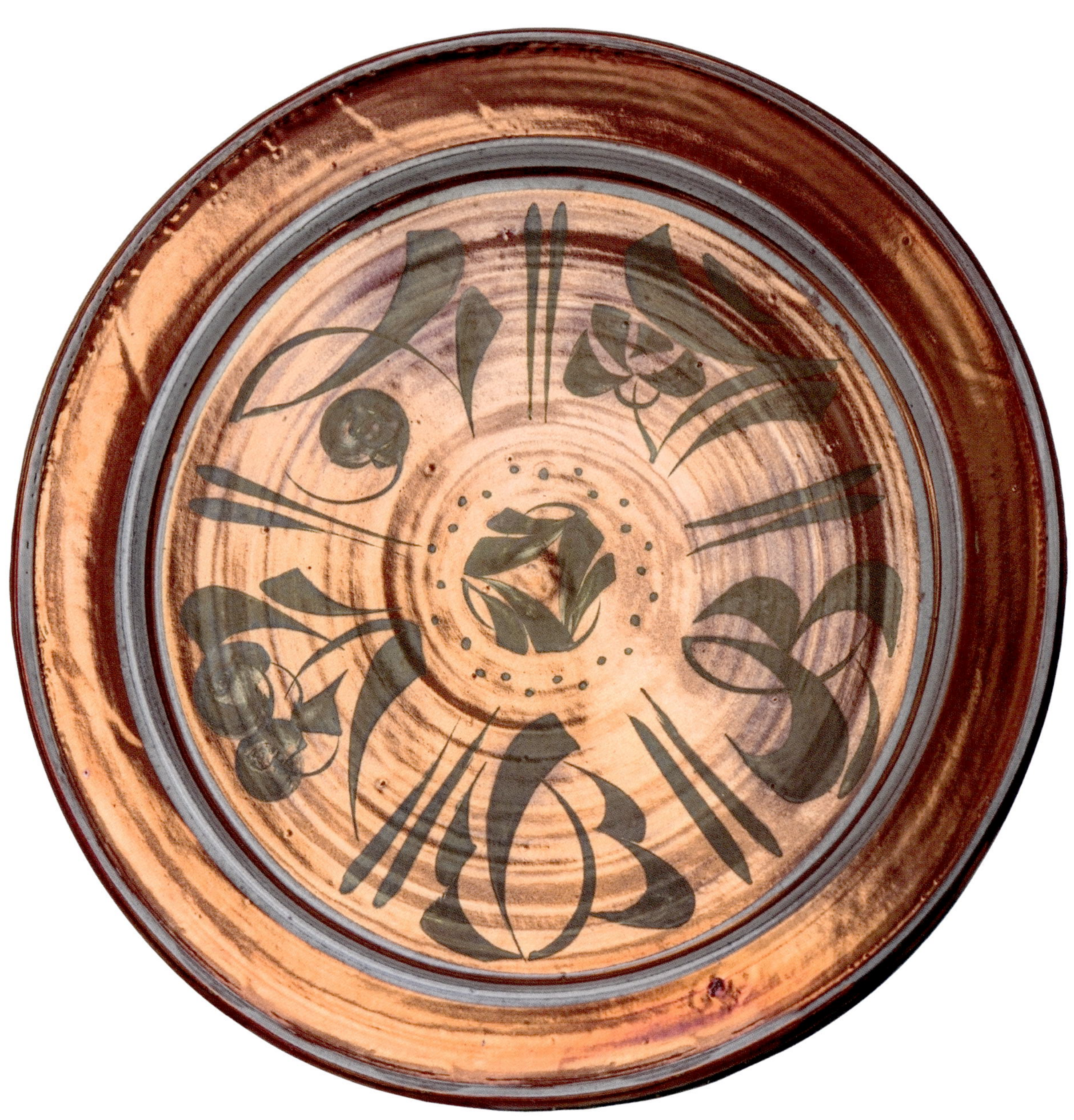

Large copper lustre platter by Alan Caiger-Smith, from the final firing
of the wood kiln at Aldermaston Pottery, 2006, diam. 61 cm, h. 7.5 cm
Collection Sarah and Adrian Dixon

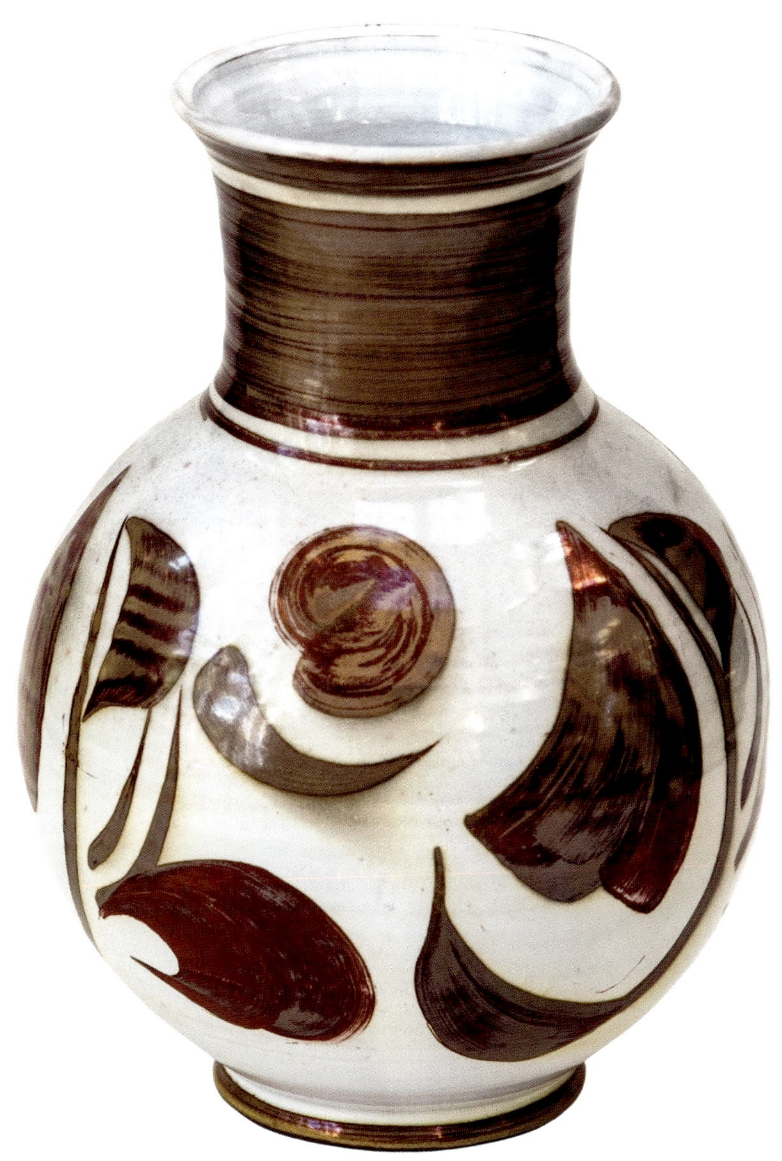

Round vase, copper and silver lustre, by
Alan Caiger-Smith, 2006, h. 30 cm, w. 21 cm
Collection Sarah and Adrian Dixon

A Different Way of Working
1993–2009

When Aldermaston Pottery closed in 1993, Julian Bellmont and Edgar Campden were its longest-serving potters. As soon as he knew that the Pottery was closing Bellmont started looking for premises locally, where he could move with his family and set up a workshop with space for a gallery. He already had a small studio on the side of his house in Tadley, where he had been developing his work since 1983, mostly in porcelain, with Caiger-Smith's encouragement. He had started selling to a few galleries and had had two exhibitions in Scotland. In May 1993 he found the perfect house, an old bric-a-brac shop in the High Street in Kintbury, about 15 miles from Aldermaston. It seemed the ideal place to start a pottery and

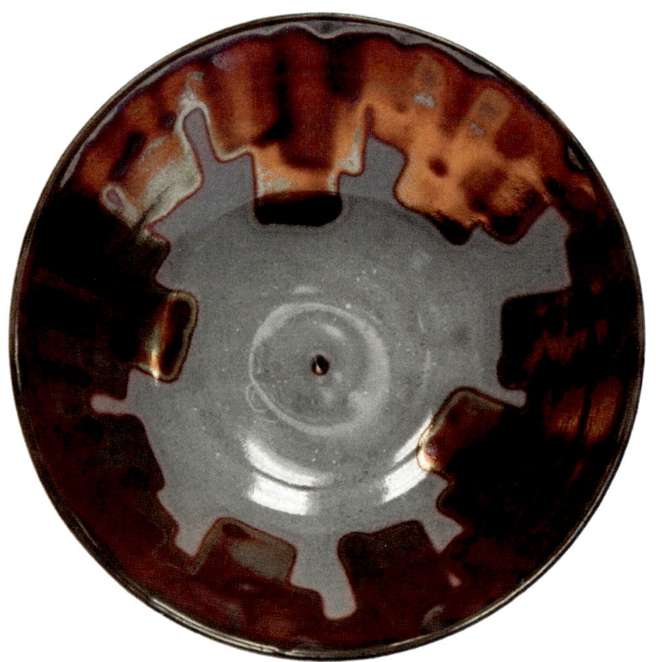

'Manhattan Pattern' bowl made by Julian Bellmont at the High Street Pottery,
Kintbury, copper lustre on white, high reduction, 1998, diam. 18 cm, h. 11 cm
Collection Sarah and Adrian Dixon

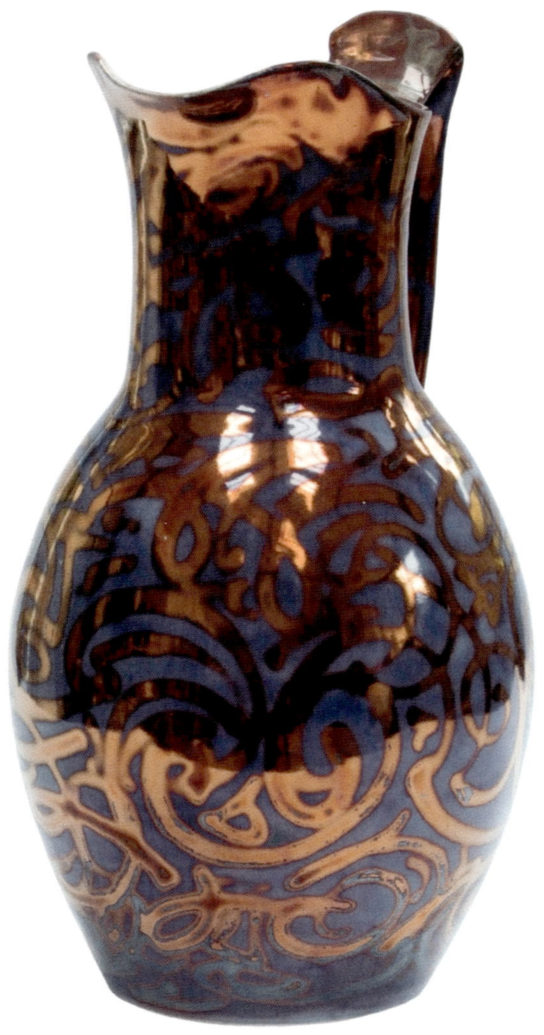

Ewer made by Julian Bellmont at the High Street Pottery, Kintbury,
blue with copper lustre, high reduction, 2002, h. 38 cm, w. 17 cm
Collection Sarah and Adrian Dixon

to raise a family. The house was about three hundred years old and needed considerable restoration, but by October the High Street Pottery was ready to open.[1]

During Bellmont's session at Shalford to discuss his future, Caiger-Smith had agreed to let him have the Pottery's customer list. So several hundred personalised letters were sent out, the local press, radio and television contacted, and on the last Sunday in October 1993 High Street Pottery opened its doors to a showroom full of newly made pots. The place was packed and the pots flew off the shelves, and for the next 14 years the pottery had an almost continuous stream of customers. It was open five days a week and took commissions, including many commemorative

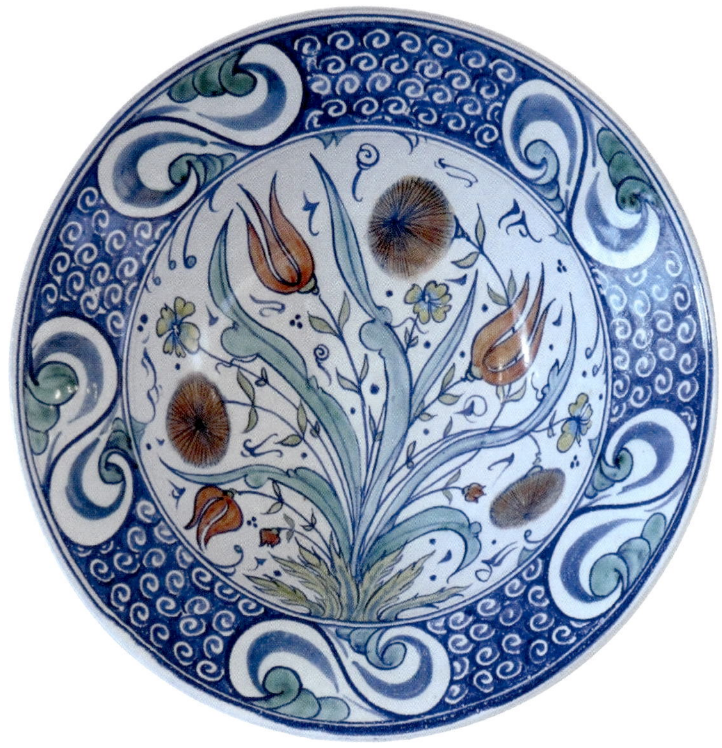

Rimmed maiolica bowl by Edgar Campden,
1995, diam. 30 cm, h. 3 cm
Collection Doreen Campden

pieces. Among these was a set of limited edition plates to celebrate 400 years of Newbury's Royal Charter; plate no. 1 was presented to the Queen when she visited Newbury during its 400th anniversary celebrations. High Street Pottery was one of the first potteries to have a website, which drew in many new customers. Bellmont also employed an assistant for a short time, Justine Jenner, who eventually set up her own pottery studio in Hampshire. Throughout his working life Bellmont says he has always remembered Caiger-Smith's words to him on his very first day at Aldermaston – one of the most influential things ever said to him: 'Make as many as you can make well'.[2]

After working with Caiger-Smith for 32 years Edgar Campden was also keen to make a fresh start, but was unable to find affordable premises in the UK. By this time his son, Mark, and Mary O'Gorman had been working in Ireland for a few years, and by chance saw a house advertised nearby as 'a dwelling suitable for livestock'. Mark remembers:

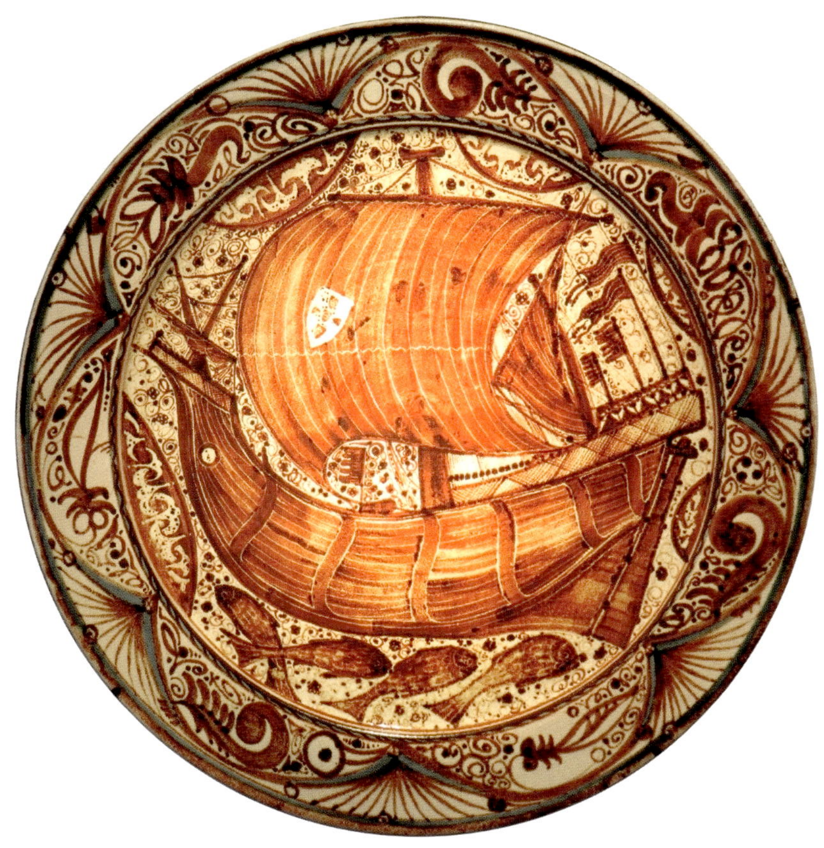

Large wood-fired charger with Portuguese sailing
boat by Edgar Campden, 1973, diam. 60 cm
Collection Doreen Campden

one half was a derelict shell, the other a pre-electrification time warp. There were broken spongeware cups amongst fertiliser bags and baling twine, giving clues as to when it was last a home. It had a barn with a hayloft, and a small cart house with a stable, which were all suitable for workshops.[3]

Edgar had exactly enough redundancy money to purchase it:

Edgar and Doreen moved to Ireland and lived in a small caravan in the courtyard while making the house habitable. While the house was progressing Edgar was asked by a local potter, Michael Jackson, to help with brush designs on his range of stoneware. Edgar's skills were also recognised by the Craft Council of Ireland's Pottery Skills Course Director, Gus Mabelson, who asked him to give the students a two-day masterclass in brush decoration. Teaching was something Edgar enjoyed very much, and he is still remembered with great affection by Gus and the students who were lucky enough to have been on the course at this time. He would also come to Mary's workshop and paint pots and sell to maintain a small income.

211

Edgar was enjoying the freedom of painting his own designs and they were many and varied, always experimental and searching. He was experimenting too in his own workshop; different clays, glazes and pigments were tried and tested.

In the cruelest way, just as Edgar was embarking on his own solo career, he was struck down with an aggressive form of multiple sclerosis. Without remission the disease steadily robbed him of all his wonderful skills. The sense of injustice and frustration was overwhelming. Try as he did to continue to make pots, the disease soon prevented Edgar from making at all. Confined to a wheelchair, he produced some wonderful tile commissions and found some comfort in drawing and painting, but this too was soon taken from him. Cancer further compounded his ill health and he died in November 1998, just a few days after his sixtieth birthday.

His death was a huge loss to the family. The real tragedy is that his full potential was never realised. The ceramic world would never know what could have been produced if he had lived another twenty years. Edgar's work will probably remain largely unrecognised, but should rank amongst all the other great potters of his era.[4]

He was also loved and respected by many of the potters who had been fortunate enough to work with him at Aldermaston, as Nicola Werner acknowledges:

> Edgar was a fine craftsman in so many fields, clay, metal, leather, wood, paint, and I often think of his dexterous hands at the end of long ginger-haired arms, demonstrating how to throw a certain shape with barely a fleck of clay on himself, deftly and beautifully done, often ending with a sharp high-pitched laugh. He was a true artist [and] an amazing teacher…[5]

Meanwhile Andrew Hazelden had asked Caiger-Smith whether, if the Pottery was not going to be sold immediately, he might stay on and work there independently. Caiger-Smith readily agreed: he was still helping the potters who remained prepare for their new futures, and was not ready to decide what should happen to the Pottery. Sadly, the retirement he and Anne-Marie had planned was not to be: in March 1994, just ten months after the final exhibition, Anne-Marie died from cancer at Shalford: 'her death changed everything'.[6] He decided to return to the Pottery and to continue working part-time and semi-retired, sharing the premises with Hazelden. No longer needing to run the Pottery, he was free to concentrate on his own personal work and on exhibitions and occasional lectures; it was during this period that he made some of his most accomplished work.

Caiger-Smith invited Myra McDonnell to share the facilities with him and Hazelden, which she describes as an unexpected joy to her; she was stylistically quite different and had a great deal of technical expertise, so together they would make a good team. By this time she had moved to Hampshire and was renting out her London studio, so she came to Aldermaston three days a week, including Saturdays, while continuing to work at Selbourne and Dart Potteries. She offered Andrew and Alan the use of her kiln for biscuit firing, as it was smaller and more convenient than the big electric one, and the three of them worked convivially and quietly together for several years. They were later joined by Charlotte Davis,

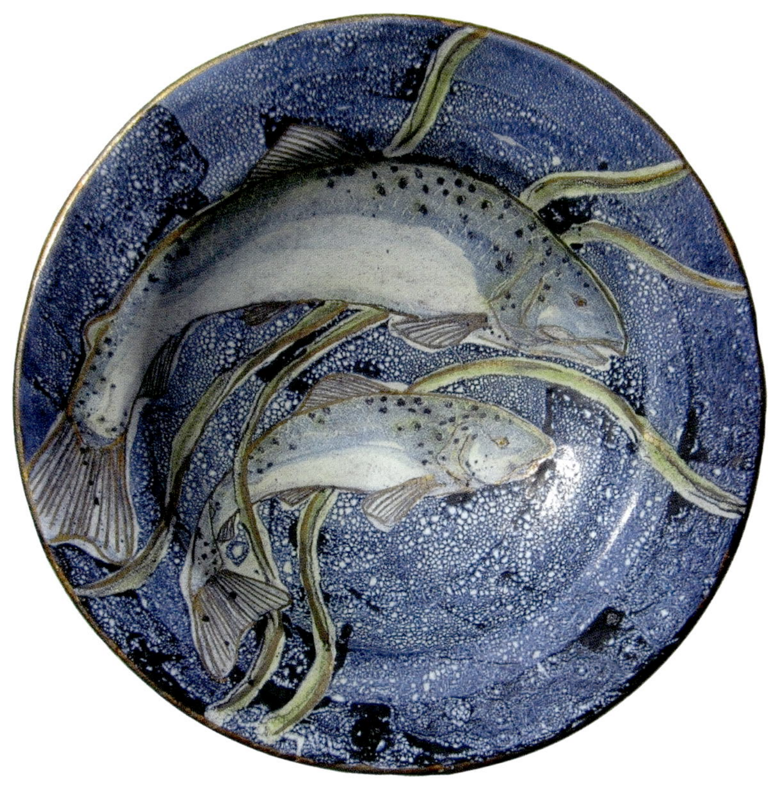

'Tondino' plate by Myra McDonnell, 1990s, diam. 40 cm
Collection Myra McDonnell

who had first worked at the Pottery as a student one summer over thirty years ago, and in 2001 Ursula Waechter returned to spend the last five years with them all, before the final closure of the Pottery in 2006.

Hazelden describes the new arrangement as a 'loose co-operative'. They all worked independently but shared the general running of the workshop, the firings in the wood kiln and the costs. When they decided to open more regularly, Hazelden had a new sign made 'with the agreed name, "The Pottery Aldermaston". Alan stressed that this was very different from "Aldermaston Pottery", and soon customers started to visit again.' Hazelden continues:

After Ursula had rejoined the Pottery in 2001 we decided on two wood kiln glaze-firings a year, which I coordinated and Ursula helped me pack. We also agreed to have two exhibitions a year in the showroom, at Christmas and in the spring. Alan was able to concentrate on the lustre firings, which took two days to pack, and which he always packed himself, and I helped with the crucial reduction period. Although Alan didn't come in everyday any more, and we turned up at 9 a.m. rather than 8 a.m., the place still had the same prevailing atmosphere.

After bagged Fremington clay became hard to get hold of we decided the only solution was to collect five tons of raw clay from Barnstaple. So Daniel Adamson, who lived in Pottery Cottage, and I, rented a seven and a half-ton truck and went down to collect it. We stored it in a shed and employed local schoolboys to crush and sieve the clay using the filter press. I had a love-hate relationship with that old press, as although it made three quarters of a ton of beautiful clay, it also leaked clay and oil regularly, and I will not forget having to mop up three inches of clay from the workshop floor. We used that press right up to the closure in 2006.[7]

It was during this time that the only one of Caiger-Smith's sons to take up their father's mantle worked for a short time at Aldermaston. Nick Caiger-Smith had a career hiatus between 1997 and 2000 and started making a wide range of tableware and lustreware at Aldermaston and at his nearby home, ably partnered by his wife, Jane. Nick Caiger-Smith had acquired basic pottery skills in his early teenage years, and he used the familiar clay and tin-glaze recipes, as well as extending into white earthenware and stoneware clays and new glaze and pigment variants. Wonderful lustre pieces came out of the wood-fired kiln, and he also experimented successfully with gas-fired lustre. He decorated with vigorous brushwork, often inspired by historical pieces from Egypt where he had lived for two years. His creative capability was at times transformed, at others ruined, by the vagaries of the kiln, which he found exciting, challenging and frustrating all at once. It was a steep

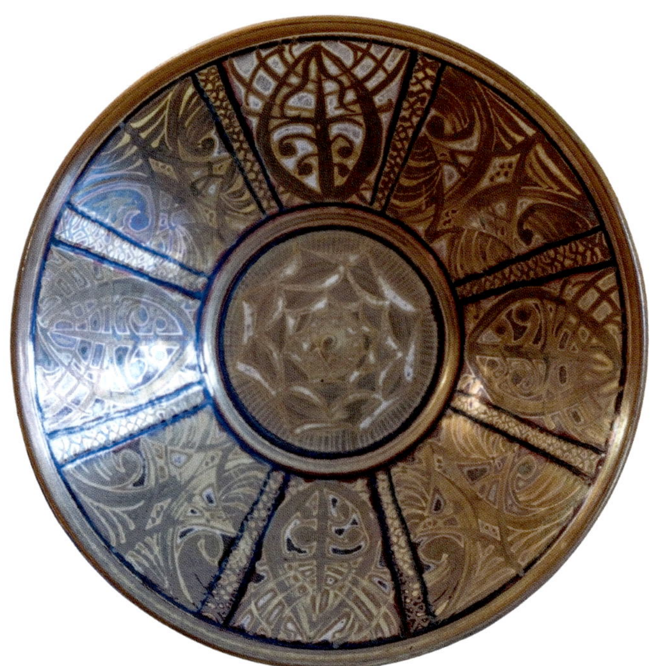

Bowl by Nick Caiger-Smith, silver
lustre and blue decoration, 1997, diam. 24.5 cm
Collection Jane and Nick Caiger-Smith

214

learning curve, but he had rapid success selling work privately, in exhibitions and through galleries.[8]

Caiger-Smith visited India, as he had always planned to do, in January 1996, as Kristine Michael recalls:

> We had often planned a trip for Alan and Anne-Marie to visit India for a few weeks, but sadly when it materialised Alan had to come alone. We planned an interesting schedule. First in Delhi with Devi Prasad. Then to Jaipur to meet Kripal Singh Shekhawat of the Jaipur Blue pottery. To Banaras, to meet Kalindi Jena at the MFA Fine Arts department of Banaras Hindu University. And on to Mysore to stay with Padma Rajgopal, and then to Pondicherry to meet Ray Meeker and Deborah Smith of the Golden Bridge Pottery. While in South India, we travelled to Pudukottai to see the making of the giant Ayyanar clay horses, and to visit the temple town of Tanjore and others. Alan lectured everywhere to rapt audiences, and he absorbed India, its sights, people and ways of looking at the world, with wonderful openness and receptivity.[9]

In November 2005 Caiger-Smith was invited to attend a symposium in Gubbio, Italy, where Maestro Giorgio Andreoli had developed his ruby lustre in the early sixteenth century, making his family's fortune and enriching his adopted city. The symposium, entitled 'The art, science and technology of lustred maiolicas', was organised by Gubbio Town Council and the National Research Council's Institute for the Study of Nanostructured Materials, and attended entirely by potters, scientists and art historians. Caiger-Smith gave two of the lectures, 'A historical introduction to the lustre technique' and 'Research and experimentation in lustre production'. One of the attending scientists had written that 'ceramic reduction lustre is the first reproducible nanostructured metallic film ever made by humans' and that such metallic films are 'promising materials for switching, routing, and signal processing devices able to work in optical fibre communications at much higher speeds than electronics'.[10] It was a revelation to Caiger-Smith that all the years he had been struggling to produce lustre he had in fact been making nano-structures. He also discovered that the test rings he withdrew from the kiln at intervals during a lustre firing could provide valuable information about the way in which nanocrystals develop high density in a glassy matrix. What surprised him even more is that the thickness of the lustre layer amounts to about one thousandth of the thickness of the glaze in which it is held. The particles of pure silver and copper in the lustre film are almost unimaginably tiny, between five and fifty millionths of a millimetre in diameter. It had always been assumed that the lustre film lay on the extreme surface of the glaze, but this is not so: during the periods of reduction, a very fine layer of colourless glaze develops on the outermost surface, above the lustre film. This may explain why ceramic lustre tarnishes so little, and why it is possible to refire it as much as 30° beyond the temperature of the lustre firing without losing the sheen. This previously unrecognised glassy layer makes ceramic lustre possible.[11]

After the symposium one of the finest Gubbio lustre potters, Giampietro Rampini, invited Caiger-Smith to his workshop. Working together on lustre techniques, they made, decorated and fired several dishes at Rampini's studio.[12]

The following year Caiger-Smith decided that the time had come to finally close the Pottery:

> I had carried on at the Pottery with Andrew, and occasionally Charlotte, Myra and Ursula until 2006, and we had several good exhibitions. By then I was 76, and it was obviously soon time to stop. We had had some excellent firings, and it was best to end on a high. The pottery came to an end at Christmas 2006. Two days earlier I had been diagnosed as having an aggressive lymphoma cancer, and I spent the next four months successfully receiving chemo and radiotherapy.
>
> The whole place, together with the adjoining cottage, was offered for sale. Several pottery people came to look at it, but they all said it was too big for them to take on. This wasn't surprising, since the whole activity was labour intensive. It had grown over the years, and what with the wood-fired kiln and the clay filter press, the showroom and the packing arrangements, it needed seven or eight people to run it.
>
> Before it could be sold, however, it had to be cleared of all the pottery and equipment and materials that had been built up over the years. Coming on top of four months of cancer treatment I never felt so tired, but eventually Charlotte and I managed it. In the end it was sold to a local couple, and they converted it into a private house. I was sad that the one building in the village that had been built as a working place should become residential, but there was no alternative, and in July 2007 it passed out of my hands.[13]

The final exhibition and sale at the Pottery took place on Saturday 2 December 2006. Afterwards the sign was taken down once again and 51 years of potting history finally came to an end. Doreen Campden sums up the sentiments of that historic day:

> Many of the people of Aldermaston were sorry to see the place close. Time moves on of course, and the new inhabitants of the village would hardly have guessed that such a lively, creative and famous workshop had existed there. Judging by the wonderful letters I received from people in the village at the time of Edgar's death, I would say that not only Edgar but the pottery itself meant a great deal to them, and it goes without saying Alan has always been part of the fabric of local life and still is. I bet there isn't one house or cottage in the village that doesn't have at least one piece of Aldermaston Pottery in it.[14]

Myra McDonnell continued her career as a freelance designer for Froyle Tiles, consultant at Grayshott Pottery, and as Senior Ceramics Technical Lecturer at the University for Creative Arts in Farnham. Among her many commissions she has designed ceramics for Raymond Blanc at Soho House and for the furniture and lighting company Porta Romana. Of Caiger-Smith she says:

the influence of Alan on me has been profound. Not so much the style of the pots, as his philosophy of potting and life. It is this that I treasure…. In past times he would be called a guru. He is a charismatic teacher, never pushing your understanding beyond what it could cope with. The way of life, the respect for traditional skills, calm measured working, sympathy for the quiet introspective aspect of creation, and a love of the beauty of the environment, all these things he taught over the years to a whole parade of potters, the wheat and the tares. He needed to teach, pass on to us what we could take in, and in turn we must pass it on.[15]

Ursula Waechter set up a workshop at her home in Aldermaston, where she continues making ceramics in the 'Aldermaston style', regularly exhibiting in the Hampshire and Berkshire Guild exhibitions as well as attending shows and fairs. Following a visit to an International Arts and Craft Fair in Burkina Faso in 2011 she became involved with setting up microcredit projects here and in neighbouring Mali, mostly training programmes for women to become potters or to acquire other skills. In 2013 she was involved with a project to teach women how to raise sheep in Dogon, Mali. On one of her visits she also made a special trip to an

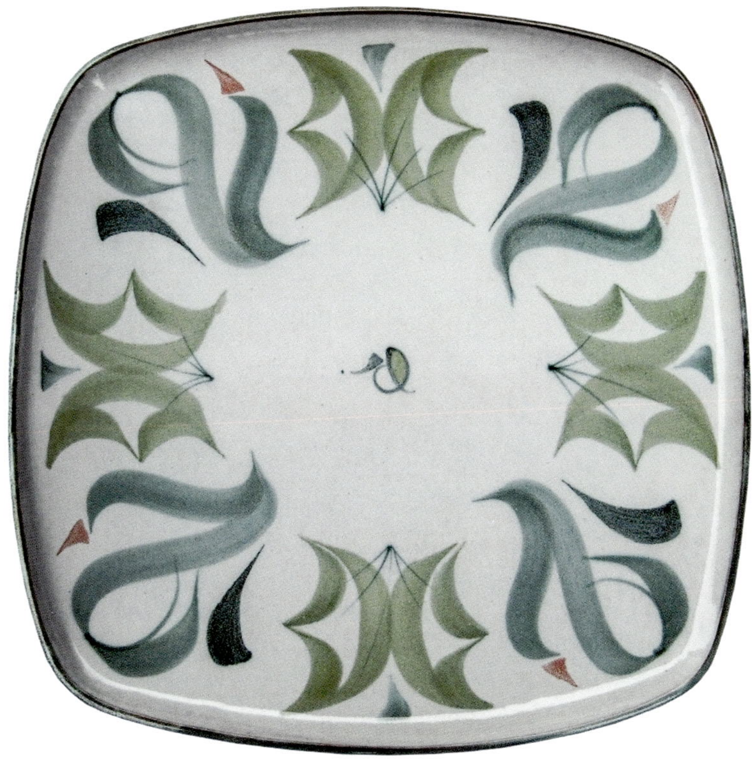

Square maiolica dish by Ursula Waechter, 2013, w. 34.29 cm
Private collection

elderly and very skilled potter in Lobi country in south Burkina, where she was able to observe the processes and the tools used to make the beautiful stackable kitchen storage pots on circular bases.[16]

Andrew Hazelden stayed on for a short time after the final closure, while making plans to start his own workshop in Yarnton, Oxfordshire. His move to Yarnton Pottery was made possible by his friends Ray and Veronica Williams, who had bought a blacksmith's thatched house with a derelict stable. From the autumn of 2006 Hazelden would travel to Yarnton at weekends to transform the stable into a pottery,

> designing the windows to look similar to the Aldermaston pottery windows, and putting in a stable door which was made by my father, which again reminded me of Aldermaston.
>
> After the final closure of the pottery Alan had wanted to share out materials and equipment and I took one of the wheels and the pug mill to Yarnton, as well as the old pottery clock that now hangs on the wall at Yarnton Pottery. I also took the blacksmith's brass tap that had been on the standpipe in the front workshop.

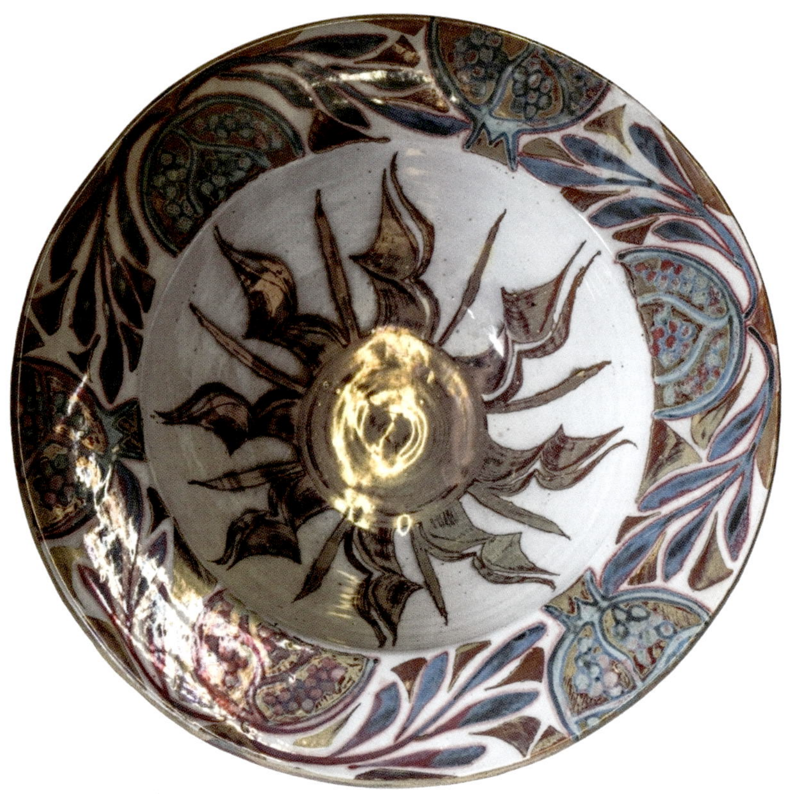

'Tondino' dish made by Andrew Hazelden at Yarnton
Pottery, lustre and oxides, 2012, diam. 40 cm, h. 12 cm
Collection Andrew Hazelden

218

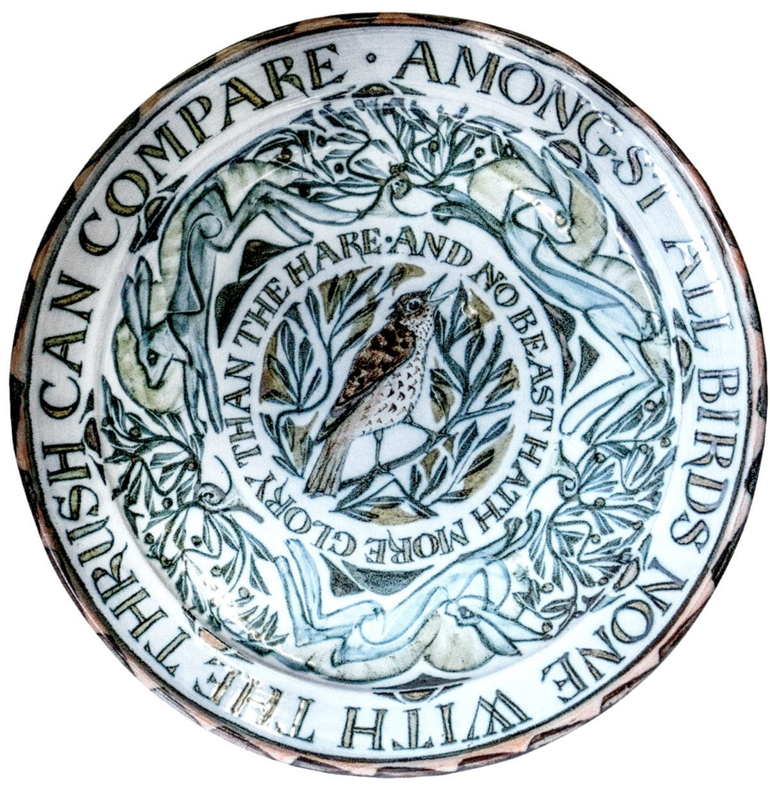

Maiolica platter made by Andrew Hazelden
at Yarnton Pottery, 2017, diam. 42 cm
Collection Andrew Hazelden

We had to take the tap off 'live' as only the deceased blacksmith knew where the stopcock was! That tap is now being used every day at Yarnton, as are the shelves and racks from Aldermaston.

Yarnton Pottery officially opened in March 2007 and many potters and friends came, and Alan gave a speech, so a new pottery was started from the old. Yarnton Pottery has now passed its tenth anniversary, and because of the skills I had learnt under Alan at Aldermaston I have been able to make a good living…

On Alan's suggestion I now use Italian clay from San Sepolcro.… I haven't got the luxury of a wood-fired kiln here but look back with fond memories of those 24 years firing the Aldermaston kiln. With the knowledge acquired at Aldermaston I now produce lustre in the gas kiln, but it is difficult to fire it as we did at Aldermaston. I still have regular phone calls with Alan, troubleshooting glaze problems etc. and he is always glad to help. I also visit him at Shalford Farm House with examples of recent work.

To make a successful living as a potter one has to create a market, and one aspect of this has been making bowls for the old fonts in churches. I have to date made ten bowls, which are now in churches from St Austell in Cornwall to Barcheston in Warwickshire. I have also made a bowl for Yarnton church. Through the skills

219

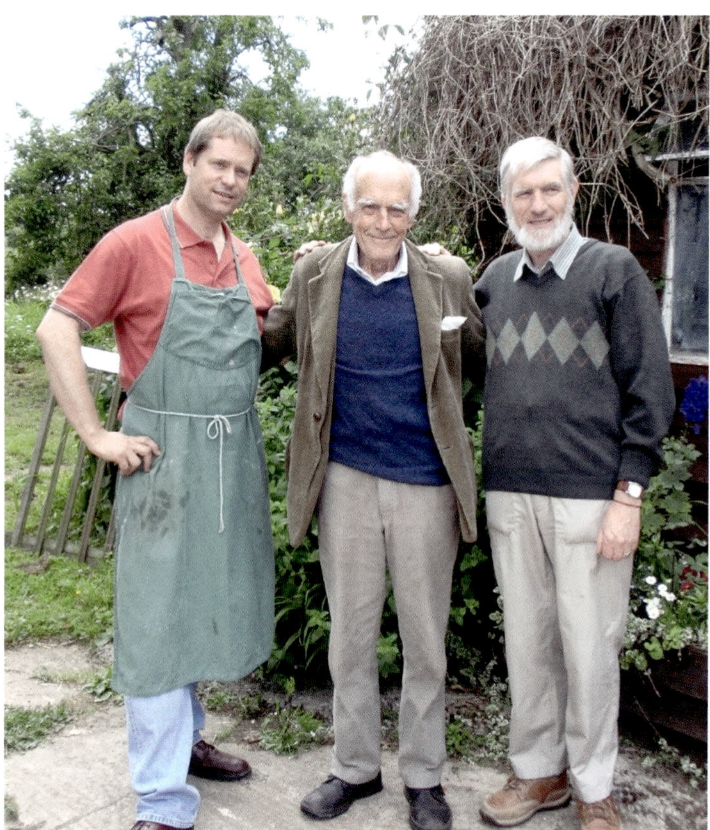

Andrew Hazelden, Alan Caiger–Smith and Laurence McGowan, June 2010

learnt at Aldermaston I have been able to carry on as a potter. I still have visitors from Aldermaston days, and children who remember growing up surrounded by Aldermaston pots now visit me and carry on the tradition of their parents.[17]

After Edgar Campden died, Mark and Mary continued to make their living from their pottery while raising a family; Mary also made a good living from selling her paintings in galleries around Ireland, where her free style became popular. They moved to premises at the other end of Bennetsbridge by the River Nore, The Bridge Pottery. The business grew and, needing more space, they decided to build a workshop and gallery at their own home in Burnchurch, Kilkenny, where they employed a part-time thrower to keep up with the demand. After several years of working happily in the new workshop Mary suffered a return of the cancer she had several years earlier. A courageous and tenacious person, she continued working in the pottery, and even experimenting with different techniques, until a month before her death. She died peacefully at home on Easter Sunday 2008.[18]

Mary had been the principal maker at The Bridge Pottery, and Mark reflects that without the help and support he received after her death he might well have given up. However, he continued in the pottery and was eventually joined by

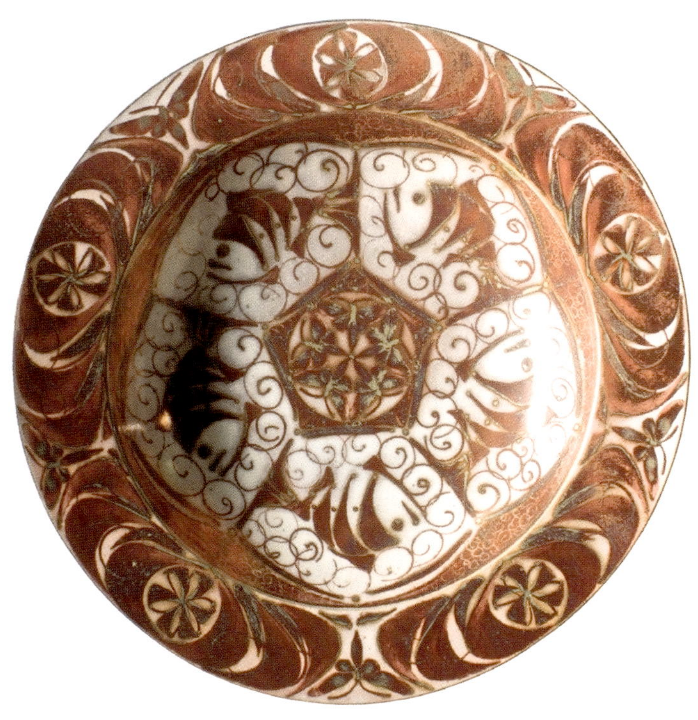

Large lustre bowl made by Mark Campden at the Bridge Pottery,
Bennetsbridge, Ireland, 2014, diam. 55 cm, h. 14 cm
Collection of Ballysallagh House

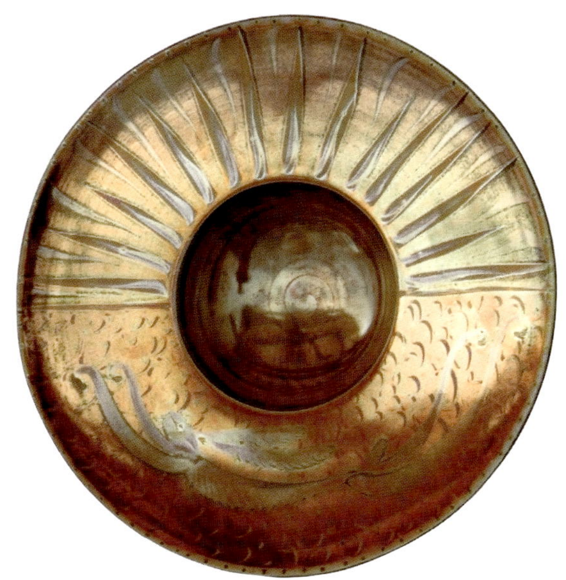

Lustre 'Sunset Hare Bowl' by Mark Campden,
2016, diam. 30 cm, h. 7 cm
Private collection

local potter Caroline Dolan. It was Caroline's encouragement that led him on a journey to rediscover the practice of reduced-pigment lustre and to carry on the tradition from where his father left off; he is now making some of the most significant lustre pieces to have been produced since Aldermaston Pottery closed:

It was around 2012 when my mother gave me a folder of my father's notes. Amongst them was an old photocopy of a list of all the lustre pigment recipes used at Aldermaston Pottery from the mid-1980s, many amended by Edgar to his preferred preparation. There was also a diagram of the best positions to place these pigments in the kiln. It was this list of pigments, and a re-reading of the chapter 'The technique of reduced-pigment lustre' in Alan's book *Lustre Pottery*, that started me down the path of lustreware. It is not an easy path, and I can only imagine the difficulties that Alan faced in the 1970s. There is still very little information published on the technique. Alan's book is still the most complete and informative available.

My first few tests were in a converted top-loading kiln. I pulled all the electrics out and made a wood/gas hybrid test kiln. The first few tests were promising. I started with various glaze recipes and only a few pigments. The glaze that worked best was Alan's W/A recipe used at Aldermaston, it fired well to 1120°C and was a good fit on the body I was now using. With my tests improving I wanted to try a larger firing and asked to use a friend's wood kiln … It was a bit of a disaster struggling with a kiln I didn't know. It was always going to end badly, most of the pots were pink and dull but there were a few good effects on some pots; enough to keep me interested. I fired the same kiln again a few months later with some minor alterations to improve the reduction. The firing was a big improvement but all the large pieces dunted as the kiln cooled. The effects however were very good.

It was clear that I needed to build my own lustre kiln and improve my kiln-firing technique. Caroline encouraged me to take the logical step and go and see Alan, and we visited him in March 2013 at Shalford, spending a wonderful afternoon talking lustre pots and reminiscing. He was very generous with his time, his invaluable information, and his encouragement. It was a particular treat to see the sample room at the back of Tile Cottage (the house I grew up in) where many of the lustre pots from Aldermaston were still stored. Some of Alan's personal favourites still remained there, and it was a real privilege to have them shown and explained by him. At the time he was seeking a home to which he could donate the large collection of Aldermaston Pottery samples. They are now comfortably housed at Great Dixter.

Returning home, I got on with building the kiln, and although the wood kiln at Aldermaston was long gone and so could not be studied, the plans were readily available as they are printed at the back of the final exhibition catalogue from 1993 [see pp. 50–51]. I reduced the size to one third that of the Aldermaston kiln, and recalculated the firebox flues and chimney using guidelines from Fred Olsen's *The Kiln Book*. So far the kiln has performed well and given me some wonderful pots but, because of the many variables in the technique, success is never guaranteed, so I have also had the odd disaster. Hopefully with practice my firings will improve, and one day I might get close to the level of technical and decorative skill achieved at Aldermaston.[19]

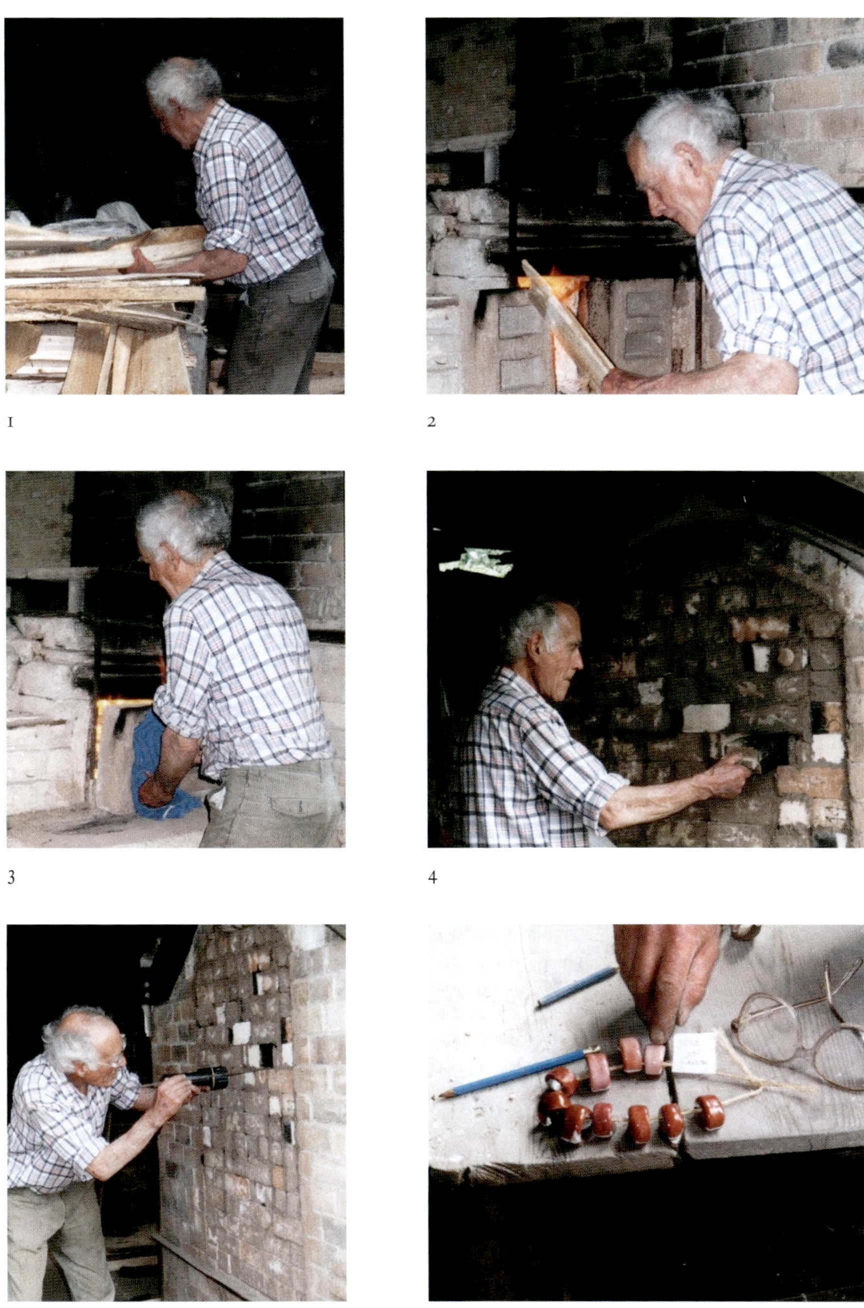

Alan Caiger-Smith and the lustre-firing process, June 2002. From top: 1) preparing bundles of willow for the reduction phases of firing; 2) stoking through the side door of the firebox; 3) closing the firebox to exclude secondary air and prevent the temperature from rising; 4) removing a brick to look inside the chamber; 5) removing a test ring with a light metal rod; 6) a loop of test rings

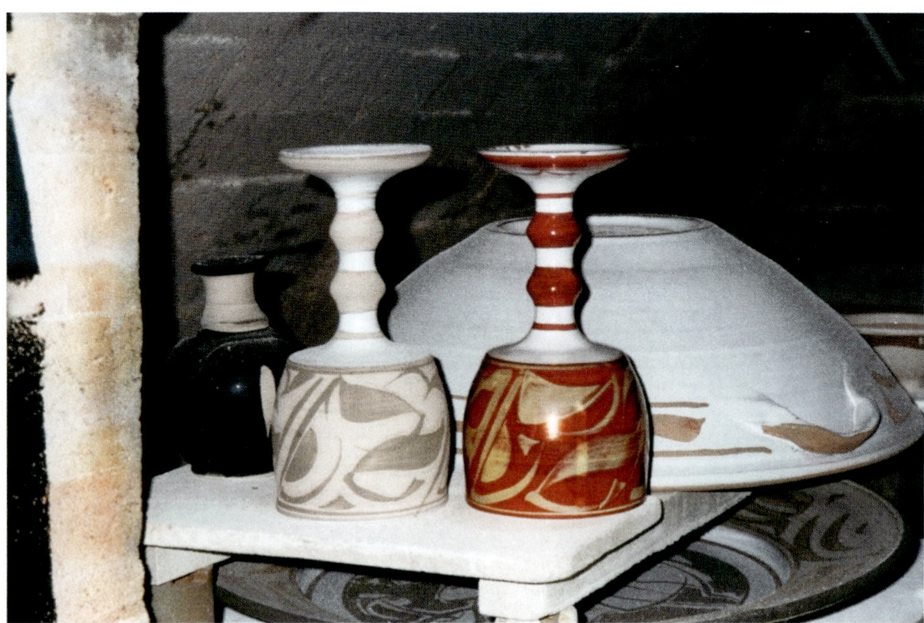

Inside the kiln after firing: the chalice on the right has been rubbed clean;
the other is still covered with the ochre that carried the pigment

After the difficult year that followed the final sale at the Pottery in December 2006, Caiger-Smith's Italian friends in Umbria proposed an exhibition of his work in the Palazzo dei Consoli in Gubbio in September 2008 to honour his lifetime work with reduced lustre. Described as 'an extremely significant cultural event', the exhibition was dedicated to Alan Caiger-Smith, 'an internationally famous artist, with strong ties to Gubbio', and was the culmination of a decade of celebrations in honour of Maestro Giorgio Andreoli, the 'unsurpassed and unsurpassable inventor of metallic lustre',[20] who unlocked the secret to the reduced lustre technique in Gubbio early in the sixteenth century.

The exhibition, entitled *Gubbio Honours Alan Caiger-Smith*, ran from 6 September 2008 until 1 January 2009 and featured 25 pieces from the last lustre firing at Aldermaston in 2006 and also some 30 pieces representing his artistic evolution. Characteristically, Caiger-Smith suggested that his pieces should be complemented by the works of Umbrian lustre potters, so 27 works by three artists were included from each of the three towns where the lustre technique predominated. These potters were Giulio Busti, Patrizio Chiucchiù and Marino Ficola (from Deruta), Graziano Pericoli, Maurizio Tittarelli Rubboli and Ceramica 'Vecchia Gualdo' (from Gualdo Tadino) and Lucia Angeloni, Katia Baldelli and Giampietro Rampini (from Gubbio).[21] There was also a section of the exhibition honouring the British-born Australian ceramicist Alan Peascod, Caiger-Smith's friend, who had died in January 2007. This featured Peascod's tin-glazed ceramics, most of which had been made in Gubbio in the workshop of Giampietro Rampini. Caiger-Smith

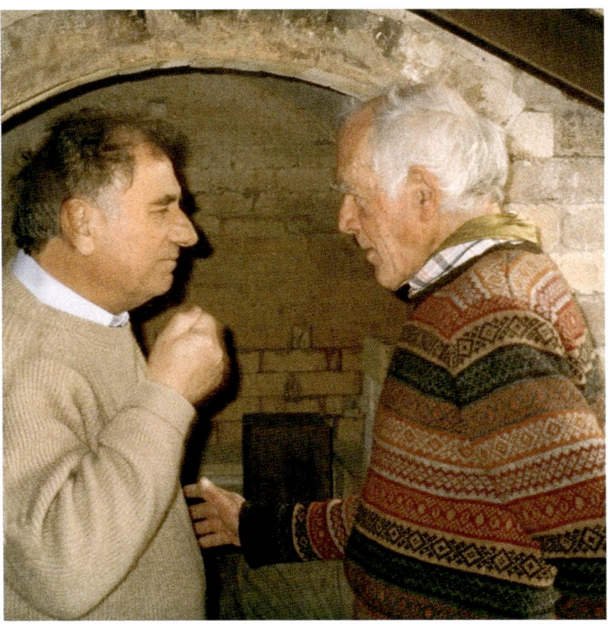

Master potter Giulio Busti of Deruta with Alan Caiger-Smith
at the Aldermaston Pottery, March 2004

had included photographs of Peascod's work in his book *Lustre Pottery*, and recalled that while the book was in preparation the two of them had had many enjoyable exchanges of knowledge and working methods; he also acknowledged Peascod's dynamic approach to new possibilities of lustre technique and design.[22]

The Gubbio Exhibition was a great success, and led to a warm friendship with Maurizio Tittarelli Rubboli. In July 2010 Rubboli invited Caiger-Smith to open an exhibition of the Rubboli Collection in Gualdo Tadino. Afterwards they returned to the family house and workshops, soon to become a museum, which Caiger-Smith had first visited with Anne-Marie many decades ago when he was researching *Lustre Pottery*, just before the Alberto Rubboli production came to an end.[23]

The exhibition in Gubbio in 2008 had been a glorious finale to Caiger-Smith's 53-year career, and marked the end of a period that had produced some of the most outstanding lustre pots to be made in over a century. So much had been learned during that time, and so many had benefited from the knowledge gained. The voyage had come round full circle when it ended, very fittingly, in Umbria. Here the great age of Renaissance lustre had come into being, not far from Castel Durante, where Cipriano Piccolpasso had written his famous treatise, and where for Caiger-Smith in some ways it had all begun. In Umbria he was in a country he loved, among the potters whose work he admired, and who in turn acknowledged and respected his own work. He had found his spiritual home.

— IO —

The Aldermaston Legacy

The thing that I loved was he went beyond Japanese, Korean, and Chinese influences. And in my mind was a Byzantium man. He loved colour, dance, mysticism, poetry, music, but was functional and practical enough to run a successful business that never compromised his vision.

Miranda Thomas Shackleton[1]

What made working at Aldermaston so enjoyable was the creativity that emanated from all the potters, it was a wonderful warm, caring environment in which to work and grow. Alan gave his own time to teach very new potters the skills and disciplines required to produce a vast selection of pottery. He also encouraged people to develop their own artistic interpretation of working with tin glazes and lustre, using the colours and shapes that best defined Aldermaston Pottery. He always had time and energy to discuss his work and aspirations with all his employees, and to listen to theirs; he had a sympathetic ear, masses of empathy and a warm heart. He is one of those people that light up a room.

Sheen Sinclair[2]

Today I spent the day stacking and splitting oak and acacia for the kiln here in France, along with the eight or nine other people, French, Canadian, Latvian, Czech, and English, all involved with the present firing. I was reminded of those early days when we split and stacked the cricket bat willow for the wood kiln at Aldermaston. Moreover, next week, while the kiln cools, I will go, by chance, to Seville and Vejer and visit the very parts of Moorish Spain that originally inspired Alan to make pots and, later, to reintroduce to England the tradition of lustreware that he made his own. I never gave back to Aldermaston even a portion of what I gained from it, but as the years pass I become more acutely aware of Alan's legacy – not just the pots, but also the potters he brought to life; so many of us went on to set up our own studios.… Alan was very much a member of the international ceramic 'family', travelling and working with potters in Spain, Morocco, Egypt, India and Iran, as well as in Europe and North America, Australia and New Zealand.

Harriet Coleridge[3]

Daniel Silas Adamson lived in Pottery Cottage for six years before the workshop finally closed in 2006. A journalist,[4] Adamson never worked at the Pottery but he spent hundreds of hours talking to Caiger-Smith and watching him work; although Caiger-Smith taught him to throw on the wheel, he did no more than dabble. But the time he spent with him had a profound effect on his life, and a deep influence on his own understanding and perception of things.

Adamson writes about what Aldermaston Pottery meant to all those who had even the smallest part in its history. The experience of being there was in nearly every case life-changing and profound.

I never saw Aldermaston in its heyday. By the time I met Alan in 1999, the pottery had ceased to be a place of employment and had settled into a quieter rhythm as a workshop that Alan shared with one or two other independent potters. Still, the place functioned much as it always had, and the pots that Alan made in the first years of the twenty-first century were the culmination of four or five decades' artistic and technical experimentation at Aldermaston. The subtleties of the firing process had been mastered, the glazes and pigments perfected. Alan was free from the responsibilities of being a manager and able to spend more time on his own work. Those years produced some of the finest pots to emerge from the kiln, and I feel fortunate to have witnessed that last phase of the pottery's life.

No one who spends any time with Alan could fail to notice his unusual alertness to the beauty of the world. He loved the textures and colours of the workshop, of course – the cords of willow in the yard, the cypress trees guarding the kiln, the iron-hard oak board that had been the blacksmith's bench – but these were things that anyone of an artistic temperament would have appreciated. More striking is the entirely spontaneous way in which Alan pays attention to objects that are usually outside the range of our appreciation. I remember him looking up at the cobwebs hung between the beams in the old workshop, watching them as they caught the faintest currents of air, and remarking on how beautiful they were.

This was one of many instances in which I saw in Alan the kind of freshness of vision that you often see in young children, but which usually seems to cloud over with adulthood. He notices things – bricks, straw matting, the weave of blanket – that most people simply overlook. And although there is a childlike aspect to this seeing, I can think of many occasions where Alan would combine this kind of close, appreciative observation with a more analytical turn of mind. He will comment on the architecture of Aldermaston, for example, or on the geometries of the Alhambra palace, in ways that deepen your appreciation and enjoyment of the world. This made an impression on me because critical intelligence is so often used to deconstruct or denigrate things, and so rarely brought to the task of appreciation. It is hard to witness Alan's unforced delight in the material world, and his informed appreciation of it, without starting to share them in some measure.

Alan's way of seeing profoundly influenced my own: the warmth and liveliness of his aesthetic sensibility. This human warmth is the quality that, for me, shines through Alan's pottery more clearly than any other, and that sets it apart from so much of the ceramics made in the twentieth century. Why, at a time when almost all western potters were making pots that inclined towards the spare, monotone minimalism of the East Asian tradition, did Alan strike out alone towards the colour and warmth of Middle Eastern and Mediterranean tin-glazed earthenware? I don't think this was a deliberate attempt to be contrary, or to find a less crowded niche in the market. It was simply that the spontaneity and expressive joyfulness of that tradition rhymed with Alan's own way of seeing the world, setting him off on an artistic trajectory that produced pots that you want to touch, to fill and pour and eat from, to wash up and to hold in both hands. Not all of Alan's pots are successful, but none is cold.

An appreciation for pattern and colour, for functionality and purpose, and for objects that emerge from a particular cultural tradition (rather than from a rootless, uncompromising artistic individualism) is among the many things that I absorbed from Alan's way of seeing. He pointed me towards an elusive but unmistakable quality – a kind of 'current of liveliness' – whose presence or absence I often notice in the objects of everyday life. This liveliness is often present in objects of fairly robust or spontaneous manufacture, but one of Alan's achievements as an artist is that he has brought this vividness and spontaneity over into pottery of real ambition and refinement.

One special attribute that Alan had, that made Aldermaston so successful as a place of learning, was his encouragement of others. This encouragement was never indiscriminate; Alan was too perceptive and honest to dole out insincere praise. But his basic attitude towards other people's work was one of positivity and confidence. Assured of his own gifts, he didn't feel threatened by other people's talents and did everything he could to foster them. I don't think Alan ever saw the hours spent teaching as a sacrifice. Of course he could have spent that time on his own work, but it was perfectly obvious, even to a bad apprentice like me, that he delighted in the process of sharing his knowledge.

Another reason for Aldermaston's success as a training ground is that even the manual work felt like a meaningful part of the process of making pots. One of the jobs I did often was processing clay: taking a mass of clodded earth, mixing it in the crude and lethal blunger, and then forcing it through the rusting dinosaur of a filter press until it emerged as a beautiful creamy clay that was ready to be formed on the wheel, fired, and transformed again by the shine and colour of the glaze. There was no commercial justification for this, which is why no other pottery of comparable size attempted it. The value, for Alan, was in following the sequence of transformations from raw formless mud to rows of finished pots, quietly shining with light and colour. You did not need any special artistic sensibility to sense that there was something magical about this. It was pure alchemy. The knowledge that you were participating in this chain of transformation produced a transformation of its own: it turned the often cold and boring work of shovelling, filtering and pressing the clay into a task you could do with real pride and pleasure.

Alan's insistence that each potter should share in the entire process of manufacture was clearly among the main reasons that Aldermaston produced so many potters who were later able set up on their own. It also demonstrated Alan's commitment to work that was meaningful, even when this meant a loss of profit. He was not blind to the need for hard-headed pragmatism, and always understood that Aldermaston would disappear the moment it stopped being profitable. But he wasn't going to press his employees into drudgery, or deprive them of the magic of participating in the great chain of transformation that, for Alan, was at the heart of the whole endeavour.

It is hard to overstate how rare that kind of attitude had become by the end of the twentieth century. By putting people rather than profit at the centre of the thing, Alan created one of the few spaces in which young people without any private wealth were able to learn a craft, to participate in a community, and to live a lifestyle that allowed them the time and freedom to mature as people and to develop their own interests and ideas. There was a breadth of outlook to Aldermaston that went far beyond the making of pots. For me (and, I suspect, for many other young people), spending time around Alan felt like a general broadening of the horizons of knowledge and perception. He would talk about the Book of Kells, about the prehistoric avenue of yew trees at Shalford, or about a Sufi shrine he had visited in rural Iran. He would quote Yeats from memory ('the blue and the dim and the dark cloths / Of night and light and half-light'), and also find the poetry in the most everyday things. All of this rubbed off, even on those of us who did not end up as potters.

One special memory I have of the time I spent at Aldermaston was the annual firing of the kiln in the weeks before Christmas, an important event in the calendar of the Pottery. I remember this because it was so intensely atmospheric – the wood smoke in the sharp air, the autumn darkness beyond the glow of the bricks, the blaze and crackle of the willow as it met the heat of the firing chamber, the liquid curl of the flame as it reached and vanished into the kiln. I also remember these occasions because they had the feel of a celebration or ritual that brought together so many of the qualities that defined Aldermaston – the seriousness and professionalism of the pottery, the care and craftsmanship with which the whole process was handled, the sense of friendship and collaboration amongst those who helped with the firing, and, most of all, the beauty and mystery of the process by which formless mud is transformed into warm, useful, beautiful pots.

These firings were so vividly atmospheric that you couldn't help but feel privileged to be a participant – and much of the magic came from Alan himself, who was so utterly in his element. In my mind's eye I can see him there, bending to feed the splintery willow to the flame, checking the temperature graphs, stepping out onto the frozen grass to watch the sparks from the chimney flee into the darkness. His contagious delight in the work of the firing, and his appreciation of the whole process of pottery, from its technical and scientific basis to its human and historic and even mystical dimensions, lent a sense of celebration to the occasion that was just a delight to be a part of.

The pots that emerged from those firings are the product not just of Alan's exceptional artistry and technical expertise, but of his whole disposition and temperament. I have three of four of them at home – bowls and jars which remind me of the years I spent at Aldermaston and which represent a set of attitudes and a standard to which I aspire in my own work, even though that work has nothing to do with pottery. The pots speak about the discipline needed to master a craft; about the value of making ordinary, everyday things with care; and about the kind of confidence and imagination required to make ambitious and lasting work. More importantly, they remind me to try and be generous, to remain alert to the beauty and mystery of this world, and to listen out for the stillness from which the pots themselves have emerged.

The firing ceremony brought these qualities into sharp focus, but in truth Alan brought a sense of enchantment and purpose to everything to do with the pottery. To be a part of that, to share in the work and to absorb the spirit of the place, was a privilege for which I, and many others, will always be grateful.[5]

Postscript

In the course of compiling this book Jane White has come to know more than I ever did about many of the people who worked in the Pottery. I am intrigued to learn what they expected to get from it and how they fared once they had left to set up on their own, as most of them did, and about the public positions that several of them held. How fortunate I was to have people of such quality as assistants.

Almost everyone who worked with me came on their own initiative and asked if they could join the set-up. Some of them had already received good training but many had not, and only a few had any knowledge of brush decoration. What really counted was their eagerness to come, in spite of the low wages that were the best I could offer. I chose people who seemed likely to become effective members of the team within a few months, and in almost every case my hunch was proved right.

The potters came from very different backgrounds. Some were from established families, others from homes with limited means or none at all. A well-known crafts writer said that she could not believe that such a mixed bag of people could possibly get on well together, but she was overlooking the unifying effect of the work itself. Our trust in it, our enjoyment of it and the demands it made transcended differences of background or temperament and drew us together with remarkably little friction, and everyone could be themselves. You cannot invent such people: you can only find them, or better still, be found by them.

The village of Aldermaston, where I spent much of my boyhood, was itself an attractive asset, and the Pottery, situated right in the middle, was easy for visitors to locate. Almost everyone in the village took an interest in what went on at the Pottery and a good many local people would regularly call in to have a look. No one seemed to object to the vehicles that sometimes occupied too much of the street; in fact, when Mick Casson came with his BBC television team in the 1970s, everyone was thrilled. No-one with washing on the line ever complained about the clouds of smoke issuing from the kiln chimney in a wood-firing, nor did anyone mind the hubbub of a Pottery party. These things were all part of the life of the place. When the Pottery closed for good in 2006, villagers said they missed the buzz it used to generate in the middle of the village.

Another vital element was the visiting public. Artist-craftsmen are generally self-motivated, but not entirely. Our visitors did much more than buy: they also commented on what they saw, sometimes to suggest improvements, sometimes with generous praise. That kind of support is golden: it is a return of creative energy and it establishes a bond. It makes the good times brighter still and helps everyone through doubts and setbacks. As one of the potters said, 'I enjoy making things for people who really want them. In college we were more or less isolated.'

Some of our visitors introduced new ideas and their commissions often involved challenges that we would never have thought of or imposed on ourselves. One of the first was a cross and candlesticks for an East Anglian church whose brass and silver had been stolen. Earthenware equivalents, having no intrinsic value, were a simple solution, and several similar commissions followed. Another commission was a leaving present for a theatre director, representing scenes from some of the plays he had put on – difficult but delightful to do – and still treasured today. Another challenge was the collection of 65 illustrative dishes for the Roanoke Foundation in Virginia, commemorating various aspects of the establishment of the first colony in 1585. Then came the 25-gallon teapot, decorated with stories from the history of tea. Firing it was a daunting challenge, lasting 40 hours, and the painting took a full fortnight. A pair of large jars, about 45 in high, for the British Embassy in Washington, took us into hand-building. Before we got them right we had to construct them several times over, but they worked in the end and we learnt a lot. They in turn led to the massive commission for 26 lustre-painted jars made for the Pearl Assurance headquarters near Peterborough. Eight of them were about 4 ft high. They were thrown section by section, each section being luted on to the one below before the vessel was finally shaped. They had to be fired extremely slowly in the wood kiln, and the third firing (for lustre) was nerve-racking. The commission took two years to complete and in one way or another everyone in the Pottery played a part in it.

Personal commissions usually reflect things of importance in someone's private life. One in particular stays clearly in my mind. Our visitor asked for an inscription on a tile, which he said would mean a great deal to him. Having been given the wording, I said I would be more than willing to do it. He looked relieved. 'I was afraid you might think it silly', he said. How could I possibly have done? It said 'In loving memory of Pluto, a gentleman, born a Labrador'.

I would like to acknowledge the inspiring advice of David Castillejo, whose collection is the foundation of the long-term display in Reading Museum. I shall always be grateful to him for his generous interest in all we did and for his unexpected suggestions about what we made, or might make, as well as for his help in the research for my writings, which led to our travels in Spain and Morocco. He has been a resolute friend, challenging and always supportive, a constant source of original ideas and insights.

Only when her text was almost completed did Jane White reveal that she had at one time hoped to join the Pottery herself. Some years later she wrote an outstanding dissertation about it for her degree, which led Timothy Wilson to invite her to undertake this book. I am deeply grateful to Tim for promoting an idea that means so much to me, and to Jane for painstakingly assembling the potters' recollections and for weaving them into a sustained narrative. She has devoted much of her personal working time to this project, visiting many of the potters and coaxing written records from several people who were normally averse to putting words on paper. I thank her for the wholehearted way she has persevered in a long drawn-out project and brought it to fruition, working in close contact with Julian Bellmont. Starting in 1979, Julian spent 13 very active years in the Pottery, becoming a valued friend as well as a tireless and loyal colleague in all kinds of circumstances. He has my warmest thanks for his superb photographic illustrations. He has given a lot of his time and insight to this undertaking and no one else could have matched it.

I should like also to record the indispensable contribution made by my dear wife, Anne-Marie (who died in 1994) to every aspect and every phase of the Pottery's existence, her loving trust and understanding, and the professional skills through which she helped it to develop. She cared so perceptively for everyone and everything. I also acknowledge gratefully the many years of support and the rewarding company of the potters who worked alongside me, never forgetting the ten who are no longer living. Altogether the team included a good many people of exceptional quality. Each person contributed in some special manner to the enterprise, either in experience or practical skill or inventiveness or joie-de-vivre or commercial acumen, or in good-humoured perseverance when things went wrong, and sometimes in each one of these ways. We were all in it together.

Alan Caiger-Smith

Notes

Introduction

1 Alan Caiger-Smith, 'Foreword', in Ostermann 1999, p. 7.
2 Caiger-Smith 1973, p. 21.
3 French 1984, p. 6.
4 Caiger-Smith 1993b, p. 31.
5 Alan Caiger-Smith, 'Time and change' (letters), *Ceramic Review* 221, September/October 2006, p. 17.

Chapter 1: Early Life

1 Alan Caiger-Smith interviewed by Hawksmoor Hughes, *National Life Stories: Crafts Lives*, British Library Sounds, parts 1 and 6, 15 September 2004.
2 Ibid.
3 Alan Caiger-Smith in conversation with the author, 2016.
4 Alan Caiger-Smith interviewed by Hawksmoor Hughes (see note 1), part 6.
5 Caiger-Smith 1995, p. 7.
6 Dr Anthony Wallersteiner, headmaster of Stowe School, in a review for the American Worthies Award 2015.
7 Caiger-Smith 2012, p. 91.
8 Alan Caiger-Smith interviewed by Hawksmoor Hughes (see note 1), part 14.
9 Caiger-Smith 1995, p. 12.
10 Ibid.
11 Alan Caiger-Smith interviewed by Hawksmoor Hughes (see note 1), part 13.
12 Caiger-Smith 1973, p. 17.
13 *English Medieval Mural Paintings*, Oxford 1963.
14 Alan Caiger-Smith, 25 May 2016.
15 Ibid.
16 Caiger-Smith 1995, p. 13.
17 Billington 1955, p. 18.
18 Robert Fournier interviewed by Hawksmoor Hughes, *National Life Stories: Crafts Lives*, British Library Sounds, 2005, track 1 (of 2). Also quoted in Marshall Colman, 'Dora Billington: from Arts and Crafts to Studio Pottery', *Interpreting Ceramics*, 16.

19 Emmanuel Cooper, obituary of Walter Vivian Cole in the *Independent*, 29 January 1999.
20 Alan Caiger-Smith 25 May 2016
21 Caiger-Smith 1993a, p. 7.

Chapter 2: Early Days at Aldermaston

1 Alan Caiger-Smith, 25 May 2016.
2 Alan Caiger-Smith, 25 November 2017.
3 Ibid.
4 Caiger-Smith 1993a, p. 5.
5 Alan Caiger-Smith, 25 May 2016.
6 Niblett 1985, p. 28.
7 Ibid.
8 Eastop 2011, p. 9.
9 Jonathan Blatchford (www.http://www.johnlewismemorystore.org.uk/page/gradual_demise_and_sudden_tragedy?path=0p317p329p333p), accessed January 2016.
10 Pat Eastop, biography of Geoffrey Eastop in Eastop 2011, p. 80.
11 Geoffrey Eastop, unpublished memoirs, quoted by kind permission of the Eastop family.
12 Alan Caiger-Smith interviewed by Hawksmoor Hughes, *National Life Stories: Crafts Lives*, British Library Sounds, part 22, 2004.
13 Alan Caiger-Smith, May 2016.
14 Alan Caiger-Smith, 25 May 2016.
15 Graham Adamson, 1 July 2016.
16 Jane Follett (née O'Connor), 30 March 2016.
17 'Alan Caiger-Smith and Geoffrey Eastop', in *Housewife Magazine*, September 1961.
18 Miranda Thomas Shackleton (née Thomas), 2016.
19 Niblett 1985, pp. 7–8
20 Murray Fieldhouse, 'Aldermaston Pottery', *Pottery Quarterly*, 20, winter 1958, quoted in Niblett 1985, p. 8.
21 Geoffrey Eastop, unpublished memoirs.
22 Pat Eastop, biography of Geoffrey Eastop (see note 10), p. 81.

23 Ibid.
24 Spalding 2009, pp. 456–7.
25 Eastop 2011, pp. 28–9.
26 Ibid., pp. 22, 23
27 Spalding 2009, p. 457–9.
28 Pat Eastop in Eastop 2011, p. 81.
29 Ibid., pp. 47–8.
30 Anne, Lady Hallifax (née Blakiston-Houston), in conversation with the author, 2016.
31 Anne, Lady Hallifax, 2016.
32 Alan Caiger-Smith 1995, pp. 44–5.

Chapter 3: Turning Point
 1 Caiger-Smith 1985, p. 17.
 2 Wilson 2017, p. 29.
 3 Ibid., pp.11, 29.
 4 Caiger-Smith 1973, p. 65.
 5 Ibid., p. 70.
 6 Ibid., pp. 79–80.
 7 Caiger-Smith 1995, p. 45.
 8 Ibid., p. 46.
 9 Alan Caiger-Smith in conversation with the author, 2016.
10 Hanssen Pigott 1990, p. 21.
11 Australian Pottery at Bemboka.
12 Tanya Harrod, obituary of Gwyn Hanssen Pigott in the *Independent*, 16 July 2013.
13 Hanssen Pigott 1991 (www.studiopotter.org/autobiographical-notes, accessed 15 March 2017).
14 Ibid.
15 Ibid.
16 Ibid.
17 Tuckson 1984, p. 26.
18 Hanssen Pigott 1991 (see note 13).
19 Niblett 1985, p. 29.
20 Caiger-Smith 1995, p. 24.
21 Niblett 1985, p. 30.
22 Caiger-Smith 1995, p. 45.
23 Alan Caiger-Smith interviewed by Hawksmoor Hughes, *National Life Stories: Crafts Lives*, British Library Sounds, part 21, 2004.
24 Caiger-Smith 1993b, pp. 28–31.
25 Ibid., p. 26.
26 David Whiting, obituary of Gwyn Hanssen Pigott in the *Guardian*, 11 July 13.
27 Tuckson 1984, p. 28.
28 Hanssen Pigott 1991 (see note 13).

29 Tuckson 1984, p. 28.
30 Hanssen Pigott, 1991 (see note 13).
31 Caiger-Smith 1995, p. 11.
32 Victor Margrie, foreword to Gwynn Hanssen Pigott exhibition at the Galerie Besson, London, 1992.
33 Quoted by Steve Dow in the *Sydney Morning Herald*, 7 July 2013.
34 Harrod 2015, p. 283.
35 Caiger-Smith 1993a, p. 7.
36 Ibid., p. 41.
37 Alan Caiger-Smith, May 2016.
38 Ibid.
39 Ibid.
40 Emmanuel Cooper, obituary of Derek Emms in the *Independent*, 7 November 2004.
41 Alan Caiger-Smith, May 2016.
42 Ibid.
43 Niblett 1985, p. 28.
44 Doreen Campden, 4 June 2017.
45 Gill Bent, 4 April 2016.
46 Alan Caiger-Smith, May 2016.
47 Alan Caiger-Smith interviewed by Hawksmoor Hughes, *National Life Stories: Crafts Lives*, British Library Sounds, parts 1 and 6, 15 September 2004.
48 Judith Partridge, letter from Thomastown, Kilkenny, Republic of Ireland, 30 March 2015.
49 Ibid.
50 Blog by Joy Georgeson, former Melbourne State College student (joygeorgeson.blogspot.com.au/p/blog-page.html, accessed in winter 2016).
52 Alan Caiger-Smith in conversation with the author.
53 Alan Caiger-Smith, 25 May 2016.

Chapter 4: A Co-operative Workshop
 1 Alan Caiger-Smith, 12 October 2017.
 2 Niblett 1985, p. 29.
 3 Caiger-Smith, 'The pottery workshop', in Niblett 1985, p. 34.
 4 Caiger-Smith 1993a, p. 37.
 5 Alan Caiger-Smith, 'Working in the Pottery', 24 March 2017.
 6 Simon Rich, 28 August 2017.
 7 Niblett 1985, p. 30.
 8 Alan Caiger-Smith interviewed by Hawksmoor Hughes, *National Life Stories:*

Crafts Lives, British Library Sounds, parts 21 and 22, 2004.

9 Alan Caiger-Smith, 'Working in the Pottery', 24 March 2017.

10 Jason Shackleton interviewed by the author, January 2016, at Laurieston House Pottery, Wallaceton Dunscore, Dumfries.

11 Alan Caiger-Smith interviewed by Hawksmoor Hughes, *National Life Stories: Crafts Lives*, British Library Sounds, part 9, 2004.

12 Peter Haynes, Canberra, 1985 quoted in Mansfield 2008.

13 Alan Caiger-Smith, 'Working in the Pottery' 24 March 2017.

14 Niblett 1985, p. 27.

15 Cardew 1969, p. 123.

16 Alan Caiger-Smith, 'The pottery workshop', in Niblett 1985, p. 34.

17 Caiger-Smith 2012, p. 91.

18 Caiger-Smith 1970, p. 4.

19 Caiger-Smith 1993b, p. 29.

20 Dormer 1994, p. 26.

21 Ibid., p. 104.

22 Ibid., p. 14.

23 Caiger-Smith 1981, p. 27.

24 Harriet Coleridge, 24 May 2017.

25 Myra McDonnell, 30 March 2016.

26 Juliet Harkness (née Wilson), 10 May 2016.

27 Caiger-Smith 1995, p. 35.

28 Caiger-Smith 1970, pp. 4–5.

29 Gill Bent, 4 April 2016.

30 Alan Caiger-Smith, 'The Pottery Workshop', in Niblett 1985, p. 34.

31 Smith, Adam, *An Inquiry into the Nature and Causes of the Wealth of Nations*, 2 vols, London 1776.

32 Graham Adamson, 1 July 2016.

33 Niblett 1985, p. 32.

34 Caiger-Smith 1970, p. 6.

35 Juliet Harkness (née Wilson), 10 May 2016.

36 Niblett 1985, p. 29.

37 Caiger-Smith 1970, p. 6.

38 Juliet Harkness (née Wilson), 10 May 2016.

39 Ibid.

40 Michael Cardew, Book Reviews, *Ceramic Review*, 25, January/February 1974, p. 20.

41 Jenny Jowett, 10 July 2016.

42 Alan Caiger-Smith, May 2016.

43 Ibid.

44 Ibid.

45 Graham Adamson, 1 July 2016.

46 Ibid.

47 Jane Follett (née O'Connor), 30 March 2016.

48 Jenny Jowett, 10 July 2016.

49 Doreen Campden, 4 June 2017.

50 Graham Adamson, 1 July 2016.

51 Caiger-Smith 1993a, p. 10.

52 Graham Adamson, 1 July 2016.

53 Caiger-Smith 1970, pp. 4–6.

54 Dunning 1970, p. 18.

55 Ibid.

56 'Association news', *Ceramic Review*, 5, October 1970, p. 2.

57 'Faenza success', *Ceramic Review*, 12, November/December 1971, p. 9.

58 Jenny Jowett, 10 July 2016.

59 Alan Caiger-Smith, May 2016.

60 Simon Rich, 28 August 2017, and information supplied by Bryony Rich, email 28 August 2017.

61 Information supplied by Bryony Rich, 28 August 2017.

62 Alan Caiger-Smith, May 2016.

63 Ibid.

64 Harriet Owen in conversation with the author, 2016.

65 Ibid.

68 Myra McDonnell, 30 March 2016.

69 Gill Bent, 2016.

70 Jaki Rothery, 22 March 2016.

71 Rungwe Kingdon interviewed by the author, 17 March 2016.

72 Ibid.

73 Catherine Bennett, 23 March 2016.

74 Niblett 1985, p. 33.

75 Jenny Jowett, 10 July 201.

76 Ibid.

77 Juliet Harkness (née Wilson), 10 May 2016.

78 Graham Adamson, 1 July 2016.

Chapter 5: New Beginnings and Discovering Lustre

1 Established just after the Second World War, the British Crafts Centre was set up to support and encourage the making of fine crafts in Britain, and to keep them in the public eye. It was later renamed Contemporary Applied

Arts (CAA), and through its exhibitions and activities it has continued to highlight the important and often unnoticed role that the applied arts play in our domestic lives and in the wider environment.

2 Alan Caiger-Smith, 'Working in the Pottery', 24 March 2017.

3 Caiger-Smith 1985, p. 185.

4 Caiger-Smith 1973, p. 80.

5 Ibid.

6 Graham Adamson, 1 July 2016.

7 Ibid.

8 Caiger-Smith 1995, p. 51.

9 Lightbown and Caiger-Smith 1980, p. 90.

10 Caiger-Smith 1995, pp. 51–2.

11 Cooper and Lewenstein 1974.

12 Jonathan Griffiths, apprentice potter at Cregiaeu Pottery, c.1976–9.

13 Catherine Bennett, 23 June 2016.

14 Schumacher 1973; see Caiger-Smith 1995, p. 43.

15 Caiger-Smith 1995, p. 43.

16 See www.ryepottery.co.uk/about/history/ history-the-cole-brothers-wally-and-jack (accessed 25 May 2018).

17 Jaki Rothery, 22 March 2016.

18 Caiger-Smith 1995, pp. 21, 24.

19 Jason Shackleton, 2016.

20 Alan Caiger-Smith, 24 March 2017.

21 Graham Adamson, 1 July 2016.

22 Caiger-Smith 1995, p. 21.

23 Ibid., p. 24.

24 Caiger-Smith, Alan, *Aldermaston Pottery: The Last Lustre and Glaze Firings*, produced by Tony Booth (DVD), 2006.

25 Graham Adamson, 1 July 2016.

24 Jaki Rothery, 22 March 2016.

27 Ibid.

28 Ibid.

29 Ibid.

30 Caiger-Smith 1995, p. 37.

31 Niblett 1985, p. 33.

32 Alan Caiger-Smith interviewed by Colin Martin (Martin 2016, p. 46).

33 Sheen Sinclair, 3 May 2017.

34 Ibid.

35 Ibid.

36 Caiger-Smith 1995, pp. 203–4.

37 Ibid., pp. 205–8.

38 Caiger-Smith 1993a, p. 39.

39 Jane Follett (née O'Connor), 30 March 2016.

40 Miranda Thomas Shackleton (née Thomas), 16 March 2016.

Chapter 6: Community and Friendship

1 Doreen Campden, 4 June 2017.

2 Jane Follett (née O'Connor), 30 March 2016.

3 Gill Bent, 4 April 2016.

4 Ibid.

5 Obituary of Keith Shackleton, *Daily Telegraph*, 24 April 2015.

6 Jason Shackleton, interview at Lauriston House Pottery, Wallaceton Dunscore, Dumfries, January 2016.

7 Ibid.

8 Ibid.

9 Caiger-Smith 1995, p. 36.

10 Gill Bent, 4 April 2016.

11 Jason Shackleton, 7 April 2016

12 Ibid.

13 Ibid.

14 Ibid.

15 Ibid.

16 Ibid.

17 Michael Mosse, 29 June 2016.

18 Organisation that maintained and serviced government buildings.

19 Caiger-Smith 1995, p. 109.

20 Ibid., p. 110.

21 Michael Mosse, 29 June 2016.

22 Caiger-Smith 1995, p. 113.

23 Ibid., p. 65.

24 Ibid., p. 67.

25 Catherine Bennett, 23 March 2016.

26 Blog, ARThive (an artist-run initiative in Hunters Street Mall, Newcastle, New South Wales, Australia).

27 Laurence McGowan, 2 March 2016.

28 Ibid.

29 Michael Mosse, 29 June 2016.

30 Ibid.

31 Ibid.

32 David Lyon (Managing Director, Redland PLC 1985), 'Industry and the Arts', in Niblett 1985, p. 63.

33 Ibid.

34 Ibid.

35 Gill Bent, 4 April 2016.

36 Ibid.

37 Ibid.

38 Miranda Thomas Shackleton (née Thomas), 16 March 2016.

39 Jane Follett, 30 March 2016.

40 Gill Bent, 4 April 2016.

41 Caiger-Smith 1985, p. 16.

42 Gill Bent, 4 April 2016.

43 Ibid.

44 Jane Follett, 30 March 2016

45 Gill Bent, 4 April 2016

46 Jane Follett, 30 March 2016.

47 Jason Shackleton, 7 April 2016.

48 Obituary of Duncan Grant, *Daily Telegraph*, 8 August 2007.

49 Jason Shackleton, 7 April, 2016.

50 Gill Bent, 4 April 2016.

51 Laurence McGowan, 2 March 2016.

52 Collins 1984.

53 Caiger-Smith 19 October 2017.

54 Catherine Bennett interviewed by Terry Colhoun at Cowra, 19 March 2003 (Australia War Memorial S03079) for 'Cowra – Japan conversations' (www.ajrp.awm.gov.au/ajrp/ajrp2.nsf/trans-print/4D27F5F97F456D21CA256D56001B51CC?OpenDocument, accessed winter 2016).

55 Ibid.

56 Catherine Bennett, 26 March 2016.

57 Ibid.

58 Ibid.

59 Ibid.

60 Ibid.

61 Ibid.

62 Ibid., and Catherine Bennett interviewed by Terry Colhoun (see note 54).

63 Catherine Bennett, 26 March 2016.

Chapter 7: People and Places

1 Martin Wright, in conversation at Ewelme Pottery, 2016.

2 Gill Bent, 4 April 2016.

3 Jason Shackleton, 7 April 2016.

4 Shackleton, 'Man and mud', *Debrett's International Collection 1994*, eds Rex Berry and Anna McCorquodale, London 1994, pp. 24–8.

5 Jason Shackleton, interviewed in January 2016 at Laurieston House Pottery, Wallaceton Dunscore, Dumfries, Scotland.

6 Nichola Hunter, 'United Artists', *Dumfries and Galloway Life*, May 2011, pp. 70–72.

7 See note 4.

8 Ibid.

9 See note 4.

10 Hannah McAndrew, 4 August 2017.

11 Laurence McGowan, 2 March 2016.

12 Ibid.

13 Ibid.

14 Jenny Jowett, 10 July 2016.

15 Catherine Bennett, 23 March 2016.

16 Doreen Campden, 4 June 2017.

17 Peter Pilven, March 2016.

18 Ibid.

19 Catherine Bennett, 23 March 2016.

20 Peter Pilven, March 2016.

21 Ibid.

22 Ibid.

23 Ibid.

24 Gill Bent, 4 April 2016.

25 Louise Bashall, 28 January 2018.

26 Catherine Bennett, 23 March 2016.

27 Jane Follett (née O'Connor), 30 March 2016.

28 Mohamed Hamid, 6 May 2016.

29 Jane Follett, 30 March 2016.

30 Gill Bent, 4 April 2016.

31 Jane Follett, 30 March 2016.

32 Ibid.

33 Julian Bellmont, 4 August 2017.

34 Caiger-Smith 2008.

35 Alan Peascod, 'Recollections of Said el Sadr from the years 1972–1975, in Caiger-Smith 2010, pp. 79–83.

36 Caiger-Smith 2010.

38 Peter Pilven, March 2016.

39 Ibid.

40 Ibid.

42 Peter Pilven, www.sidestoke.com/Pilven/work1.html (accessed 20 April 2016).

43 See www. federation.edu.au/arts-academy/research/researchers/Peter-pilven (accessed 20 April 2016).

44 See www.rubypilven.com (accessed 20 May 2016).

45 Miranda Thomas Shackleton (née Thomas), 16 March 2016.

46 Ibid.

47 Ibid.

48 Gill Bent, 4 April 2016.

49 Mohamed Hamid, 6 May 2016.

50 Nicola Werner, 7 April 2016.

51 Mohamed Hamid, 6 May 2016.

52 Julian Bellmont, 4 August 2017.

53 Miranda Thomas Shackleton, 16 March 2016.

54 Julian Bellmont, 4 August 2017.

55 Susan Salter-Reynolds, 'Success made from scratch', *Los Angeles Times*, 29 May 2010, p. 32.

56 Miranda Thomas Shackleton, 14 July 2017.

57 Miranda Thomas Shackleton, 16 March 2016.

58 Ibid.

59 Rosie Doyle, 'Shackleton explores Craft of Furniture in US', *Irish Times*, 21 July 2007.

60 Miranda Thomas and Charles Shackleton quoted by Susan Salter-Reynolds (see note 55).

61 See www.shackletonthomas.com/page/286/ the_fourth_dimension/ (accessed 20 August 2017).

62 Ibid.

63 Miranda Thomas Shackleton, 16 March 2016.

Chapter 8: Commissions and Exhibitions

1 Harriet Coleridge, 24 May 2017.

2 Ibid.

3 Alan Caiger-Smith, 24 March 2017.

4 Andrew Hazelden, 7 July 2017.

5 Leigh Hatts, obituary of Edward Bramah, *Independent*, 8 February 2008.

6 Alan Caiger-Smith, unpublished notes recording the making of the biggest teapot in the world, written in 1985.

7 Leigh Hatts, 8 February 2008.

8 *The Bramah Teapot*, n.p., n.d.

9 Alan Caiger-Smith in conversation with the author, March 2016.

10 Nicola Werner, 7 April 2016.

11 Nicola Werner, 'The everyday made as pleasurable as possible', http:// contemporaryceramics.blogspot.com/2018/07/ nicola-werner-everyday-made-as.html (accessed 15 July 2018).

12 Julian Bellmont, 4 August 2017.

13 Andrew Hazelden, 3 August 2017.

14 Julian Bellmont, 4 August 2017.

15 Ibid.

16 Alan Caiger-Smith, 'Biographical notes by the writer', in Caiger-Smith 2012, pp. 91–2.

17 Ibid., p. 92.

18 Kathy Niblett, 'Aldermaston Pottery', in Niblett 1985, p. 33.

19 Myra McDonnell, 30 March 2016.

20 Ibid.

21 Ibid.

22 Myra McDonnell, 30 March 2016.

23 Caiger-Smith 1993a, p. 41.

24 Mohamed Hamid, 6 May 2016.

25 http://www.jcjpottery.co.uk/ (accessed 25 August 2017).

26 Mohamed Hamid, 6 May 2016.

27 Sam Davies, 28 August 2017.

28 Ibid.

29 Ibid.

30 Harriet Coleridge, 24 May 2017.

31 http://www.studiopottery.co.uk/profile/ Harriet/Coleridge (accessed 10 January 2016).

32 Mark Campden, 5 June 2017.

33 Louise Bashall, 28 January 2018.

34 Ibid.

35 Ibid.

36 Caiger-Smith 1995, p. 114.

37 Ibid., pp. 115–16.

38 Julian Bellmont, 4 August 2017.

39 Andrew Hazelden, 12 July 2017.

40 Julian Bellmont, 4 August 2017.

41 Caiger-Smith 1995, p. 117.

42 Ibid., p. 118.

43 Julian Bellmont, 4 August 2017.

44 Ibid.

45 Caiger-Smith 1995, p. 118.

46 Louise Bashall, 28 January 2018.

47 Caiger-Smith 1993c, pp. 21–2.

48 Ibid., p. 22.

49 Caiger-Smith 1995, p. 121.

50 Caiger-Smith 1993c, p. 22.

51 Alan Caiger-Smith, 25 September 2017.

52 Ibid.

53 Sam Davies, 'Pottery and community in Guatemala', *Ceramic Review*, 148, July/August 1994, pp. 12–13.

54 Sam Davies, 28 August 2017.

55 Ibid.

56 Kristine Michael, 26 March 2017.

57 Louise Bashall, 28 January 2018.

58 Kristine Michael, 26 March 2017.

59 Ibid.

60 Ibid.

61 Louise Bashall, 28 January 2018.

62 Myra McDonnell, 12 August 2018.

63 Myra McDonnell, 30 March 2016.

64 Alan Caiger-Smith interviewed by
Hawksmoor Hughes, *National Life Stories:
Crafts Lives*, British Library Sounds, part 41,
2004.

65 Julian Bellmont, 4 August 2017.

66 Alan Caiger-Smith, 25 May 2016.

67 Julian Bellmont, 4 August 2017.

68 Alan Caiger-Smith interviewed by
Hawksmoor Hughes, *National Life Stories:
Crafts Lives*, British Library Sounds, part 41,
2004.

69 Ibid.

70 Kristine Michael, 'The cruel spoke in the
potter's wheel', *The Economic Times, New Delhi*,
4 July 1993, p. 12.

71 Alan Caiger-Smith, 24 March 2017.

Chapter 9: A Different Way of Working

1 Julian Bellmont, 4 August 2017.

2 Ibid.

3 Mark Campden, 5 June 2017.

4 Ibid.

5 Nicola Werner, 7 April 2016.

6 Alan Caiger-Smith, 25 May 2016.

7 Andrew Hazelden, 12 July 2017.

8 Nick Caiger-Smith, 15 September 2017.

9 Kristine Michael, 26 March 2017.

10 J. Perez-Arantegui et al., quoted in 'Ceramic
lustre', *Ceramic Review*, 219, May/June 2006,
pp. 51, 52.

11 Caiger-Smith 2006, pp. 51–2.

12 E.A. Sannipoli, 'Alan Caiger-Smith and
Gubbio', in Sannipoli and Wilson 2008, p. 33.

13 Alan Caiger-Smith, 25 May 2016.

14 Doreen Campden, 4 June 2017.

15 Myra McDonnell, 30 March 2016.

16 Ursula Waechter, 30 August 2017.

17 Andrew Hazelden, 12 July 2017.

18 Mark Campden, 5 June 2017.

19 Ibid.

20 Goracci, Orfeo, Mayor of Gubbio, in Sannipoli
and Wilson 2008, p. 7.

21 E.A. Sannipoli, 'Nine Umbrian potters', in
Sannipoli and Wilson 2008, p. 34.

22 E.A. Sannipoli, 'Tribute to Alan Peascod', in
Sannipoli and Wilson 2008, p. 37.

23 Caiger-Smith 2012, p. 92.

Chapter 10: The Aldermaston Legacy

1 Miranda Thomas Shackleton (née Thomas),
16 March 2016.

2 Sheen Sinclair, 3 May 2017.

3 Harriet Coleridge, 24 May 2017.

4 Adamson worked for many years in the Middle
East, as an independent writer and campaigner
in Syria, Lebanon and the West Bank,
contributing to *The Guardian* and the BBC. He
now works as a producer and journalist with
the BBC World Service, focusing on Africa.

5 Daniel Silas Adamson, December 2016.

Glossary

batt-wash/kiln wash
A refractory powder mixed with water and
painted on kiln shelves to prevent ware and
accidental glaze drips from sticking during firing.

biscuitware/bisque ware
Ware that has been fired once and has no
chemically bonded water left in the clay. It is a
true ceramic material, although usually the clay
body has not reached maturity, which it will
achieve in the second glaze/glost firing.

Continental kick wheel/momentum wheel
Potter's wheel that relies on the build up of
speed of a heavy flywheel and using the falling
momentum to throw the pots. These wheels are
cheap, use no power, have no vibration, and allow
the user to be more connected with their work
without the need to constantly kick.

Delftware
Tin-glazed earthenware decorated with cobalt blue
designs, produced mainly around the city of Delft.
Its main period of manufacture was between 1600
and 1780, after which it was succeeded by white
stoneware and porcelain.

dolomite
Material used in ceramic glazes as a source
of magnesia and calcia – a uniform calcium
magnesium carbonate. When used in glazes
melting over 1170°C it will produce a silky matt
surface.

fettling
Tidying up rough clay edges prior to bisque firing.
Can also refer to smoothing out the surface of a
dry glaze prior to painting or firing.

filter press
Press used to remove excess water from liquid
clay/slip prior to putting it through the pug mill.

glazes

057 glaze
The tin glaze used most often at Aldermaston.
A reliable glaze with an unusually wide colour
range. Fires 1020–1080°C:
61 Lead bisilicate
5 China clay
11 Cornish stone
9 Calcium-borate frit
2 Zinc Oxide
10 Tin oxide

W/A 92 lustre glaze
The glaze used most often for lustre at
Aldermaston Pottery. Fires 1040 – 1260°C:
35 Lead bisilicate
38 F Calcium-borate frit
5 Zinc oxide
2 China clay
7 Flint
3 Zirconium silicate
10 Tin oxide

Haban wares
The Habans were originally a Swiss community
of Anabaptists who converted to Catholicism
during the eighteenth century. Mainly artisans
who were famous for their pottery, they moved
from Switzerland through Austria to Bohemia,
before migrating to northern Hungary and then
to Translyvania. Their pottery reflected all these
influences, and their art gradually merged into
Hungarian and Slovakian folk culture.

jigger and jolley
A machine for mass producing ceramic hollow
shapes such as bowls and plates by scraping the
clay with a profiled cutter while it rotates on the
wheel. Jiggering is a method to form the outside
of the piece while jolleying forms the inside.

pug mill /pugging
A machine that mixes/recycles clay that has been dried out, slaked in water and then had the water removed from it, either by using a filter press or by evaporation. When it is the right consistency for pugging it is churned through an auger and emerges as a sausage of workable clay.

raku
Pottery made by a process by which it is heated quickly to a high temperature and then removed while red hot; it may then be placed in a closed container containing combustible material such as sawdust, which then ignites and causes a reaction creating surface colours and patterns. Alternatively, it may be instantly cooled in water to stop and fix the glaze reaction, or slowly cooled in the open air – the traditional Japanese method of raku.

reduced-pigment lustre/ lustreware
A technique that depends on heavy reduction (starvation of oxygen) at around 540°c, when the glaze is beginning to soften. Metallic compounds of silver and copper contained in pigments, and usually mixed with a clay medium to dilute them, are applied in brushstrokes to the already glazed surface. During the firing these break down and become deposited as a thin metallic film on the surface of the pot.

saggar
A fireclay container used to protect pottery from flames or smoke during firing.

sgraffito
Decorating technique in which layers of colour – either underglazes or coloured slips – are applied to leather-hard pottery and then scratched off to create contrasting patterns prior to firing.

slipware/slip decorated/slip trailed
Pottery decorated with liquid clay of contrasting colours applied to a leather-hard surface, either by dipping or painting. Slip-trailed decoration uses clay applied in a device similar to a piping bag to create a design or lettering.

soak/soaking
Maintaining the kiln at the same temperature for a period of time to allow proper formation or maturation of clay and glaze effects.

spinel
A hard, glassy mineral occurring as octahedral crystals of variable colour and consisting mainly of magnesium and aluminium oxides.

terra sigillata
A very fine colloidal slip made by mixing dry clay with a deflocculant, this is left to settle and the very fine middle layer is siphoned off, painted onto pots and polished, before firing within the low-temperature range to give a shiny and glossy surface.

tin-glaze maiolica
Earthenware pottery covered with a glaze containing tin oxide, which gives a shiny white opaque surface. The decoration of metallic oxides is applied to the unfired glaze surface by brush, which then melts into the glaze during the firing to give a unified surface.

wax resist
A waxy substance used to prevent slips or glazes from adhering to the clay body prior to applying a slip or glaze. Can also be used as a decorative technique. The wax will burn off during the firing.

wedging bench
A robust workbench used for wedging and kneading clay to a workable consistency.

Timeline of Potters and Assistants
at Aldermaston Pottery

1956–61
Alan Caiger-Smith with
 Geoffrey Eastop

1957–59
Maura Pender

1960–61
Gwyn Hanssen Pigott

1961–2
Anne Blakiston-Houston –
 Homer Street

1961
Edgar Campden (–1993)
David Tipler (–1975)
Noel Flood
Judith Partridge (–1962)

1962–3
Sally Newton (–1964)
Edgar Campden
David Tipler

1964
Elizabeth Frith-Powell (–1968)
Edgar Campden
David Tipler

1965–7
Simon Rich (–1969)
Edgar Campden
David Tipler
Elizabeth Frith-Powell

1968
Clare Cherrington
Oldrich Asenbryl (–1970)
Ben Wilson (–1969)

Simon Rich
Edgar Campden
David Tipler

1969
Juliet Wilson (Harkness) (–1972)
Graham Adamson (–1973)
Suzanne Gabriel (–1971)
Oldrich Asenbryl
Ben Wilson
Simon Rich
Edgar Campden
David Tipler

1970
Suzanne Gabriel
Oldrich Asenbryl
Juliet Wilson
Graham Adamson
Edgar Campden
David Tipler

1971
Harriet Owen (Smith) (–1974)
David Anthony (Pratt) (–1975)
Janet Green
Jenny Jowett (–1993; part-time,
 1 day/week)
Juliet Wilson
Graham Adamson
Edgar Campden
David Tipler

1972
Angela Monkton (–1975)
Joanna Morland (–1974)
Bill Mehornay (–1973)
Harriet Owen
Juliet Wilson
David Anthony

Graham Adamson
Edgar Campden
David Tipler
Jenny Jowett

1973
Angela Monkton (–1975)
Joanna Morland (–1974)
Bill Mehornay (–1973)
Harriet Owen
David Anthony
Graham Adamson
Edgar Campden
David Tipler
Jenny Jowett

1974
Bernard Cass (–1975)
Teresa Plumb
Sheen Sinclair (–1977)
Harriet Owen
Angela Monkton
Joanna Morland
David Anthony
Edgar Campden
David Tipler
Jenny Jowett

1975
Jaki Rothery (–1978)
Jason Shackleton (–1979)
Venetia Seiveking
Christopher Bayley (–1977)
Sheen Sinclair (–1977)
Angela Monkton
Bernard Cass
David Anthony
Edgar Campden
David Tipler
Jenny Jowett

1976
Michael Mosse (−1978)
Laurence McGowan (−1979)
Jaki Rothery
Jason Shackleton
Christopher Bayley
Sheen Sinclair
Edgar Campden
Jenny Jowett

1977
Michael Mosse (−1978)
Laurence McGowan (−1979)
Jaki Rothery
Jason Shackleton
Christopher Bayley
Sheen Sinclair
Edgar Campden
Jenny Jowett
Stella Biggage

1978
Gill Bent (Careless) (−1983)
Jane O'Connor (Follett) (−1980)
Susan Cooke-Smith
Simon Middleton (−1980)
Michael Mosse
Laurence McGowan
Jaki Rothery
Jason Shackleton
Edgar Campden
Jenny Jowett

1979
Catherine Bennett (−1981)
Laurence McGowan
Gill Bent
Jane O'Connor
Simon Middleton
Jason Shackleton
Martin Wright (−1986)
Edgar Campden
Jenny Jowett

1980
Julian Bellmont (−1993)
Peter Pilven (−1981)
Martin Wright
Catherine Bennett
Gill Bent
Jane O'Connor
Simon Middleton
Edgar Campden
Jenny Jowett

1981
Miranda (Wink) Thomas
    (Thomas Shackleton)
Catherine Bennett
Gill Bent
Peter Pilven
Martin Wright
Julian Bellmont
Edgar Campden
Jenny Jowett

1982
Nicola Werner (−1985)
Gill Bent
Miranda (Wink) Thomas
Martin Wright
Julian Bellmont
Edgar Campden
Jenny Jowett

1983
Mohamed Hamid (−1986)
Miranda (Wink) Thomas
Nicola Werner
Martin Wright
Julian Bellmont
Edgar Campden
Jenny Jowett

1984
Harriet Coleridge (−1987)
Andrew Hazelden (−1993)
Nicola Werner
Mohamed Hamid

Martin Wright
Julian Bellmont
Edgar Campden
Jenny Jowett

1985
Mary O'Gorman (−1989)
Harriet Coleridge
Mohamed Hamid
Martin Wright
Andrew Hazelden
Julian Bellmont
Edgar Campden
Nicola Werner (July to
    December)
Jenny Jowett

1986
Ursula Waechter (−1991)
Mary O'Gorman
Harriet Coleridge
Mohamed Hamid
Martin Wright
Andrew Hazelden
Julian Bellmont
Edgar Campden
Jenny Jowett

1987–8
Sam Davies (−1991)
Michael Willey (−1989)
Ursula Waechter
Mary O'Gorman
Andrew Hazelden
Julian Bellmont
Edgar Campden
Jenny Jowett

1989
Louise Bashall (−1992)
Sam Davies (−1991)
Michael Willey (−1989)
Ursula Waechter
Mary O'Gorman
Andrew Hazelden

Julian Bellmont
Edgar Campden
Jenny Jowett

1990
Padma Rajagopal Joshi
Louise Bashall
Sam Davies
Ursula Waechter
Andrew Hazelden
Julian Bellmont
Edgar Campden
Jenny Jowett

1991
Silke Nerger (−1993)
Louise Bashall

Sam Davies
Ursula Waechter
Andrew Hazelden
Julian Bellmont
Edgar Campden
Jenny Jowett

1992
Kristine Michael
Myra McDonnell (−1993)
Lieselotte Harrer (−1993)
Silke Nerger
Louise Bashall
Andrew Hazelden
Julian Bellmont
Edgar Campden
Jenny Jowett

1993
Myra McDonnell
Lieselotte Harrer
Silke Nerger
Andrew Hazelden
Julian Bellmont
Edgar Campden
Jenny Jowett

Aldermaston Potters' Marks

Alan Caiger Smith

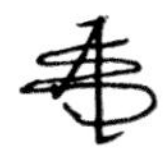

1955–92 Made at Aldermaston

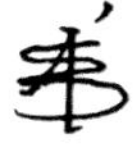

1956–63 Made at 32 Homer Street, London

Since 1959 Alan Caiger-Smith's personal mark is usually accompanied by a symbol for the year. Year marks were originally marked on the base of his pots in order to keep track of changes to the glaze compositions and the firing temperatures. Since they were of general interest, Caiger-Smith continued to use them. The 1969 symbol remained in use throughout 1970.

Year		Year		Year		Year	
1959		1971		1983		1995	
1960		1972		1984		1996	
1961		1973		1985		1997	
1962		1974		1986		1998	
1963		1975		1987		1999	
1964		1976		1988		2000	
1965		1977		1989		2001	
1966		1978		1990		2002	
1967		1979		1991		2003	
1968		1980		1992		2004	
1969		1981		1993		2005	
1970		1982		1994		2006	

The Aldermaston Potters

Most of the potters used personal marks, incorporating
A for Aldermaston and one of their initials.

Graham Adamson
1969–73

David Anthony
1971–5

Oldrich Asenbryl
1968–70

Louise Bashall
1989–92

Christopher Bayley
1975–7

Julian Bellmont
1979–93

Catherine Bennett
1979–81

Gill Bent (Careless)
1978–82

Stella Bigage
1977–8

Anne Blakiston-Houston
1961–2

Edgar Campden
1961–93

Bernard Cass
1974–5

Clare Cherrington
1968

Harriet Coleridge
(Akoulitchev)
1984–6

Susan Cooke-Smith
1978

Sam Davies
1987–91

Geoffrey Eastop
1956–60

Noel Flood
1961

Elizabeth Frith-Powell
1964–8

Suzanne Gabriel
1969–71

Janet Green
1971–2

Mohammed Hamid
1983–6

Lieselotte Harrer
1992–3

Andrew Hazelden
1984–93

Padma Rajagopal Joshi
1990

Jenny Jowett
1971–93

Myra McDonnell
1992–3

Laurence McGowan
1976–9

Bill Mehornay
1972–3

Kristine Michael
1992

Simon Middleton
1978–80

Angela Monckton
1972–5

Joanna Morland
1972–4

Michael Mosse
1976–8

Silke Nerger
1991–3

Sally Newton
1962–4

Jane O'Connor (Follett)
1978–80

Mary O'Gorman
1985–9

Harriet Owen (Smith)
1971–4

Judith Partridge
1961–2

Maura Pender (Hyde)
1957–9

Gwyn Hanssen Pigott
1960–61

Peter Pilven
1980–81

Teresa Plumb
1974

Simon Rich
1965–9

Jaki Rothery
1975–8

Jason Shackleton
1975–9

Venetia Sieveking
1975

Sheen Sinclair
1974–7

Miranda Thomas (Thomas Shackleton)
1981–3

David Tipler
1961–75

Ursula Waechter
1986–91

Nicola Werner
1982–4

Michael Willey
1987–9

Ben Wilson
1968–9

Juliet Wilson (Harkness)
1969–72

Martin Wright
1979–86

Principal Exhibitions

★ Special Aldermaston Pottery exhibition
Solo exhibition

1956
The Padworth and Aldermaston Group, Parsons
Gallery, London

1957
British Artist Craftsmen (travelling exhibition, USA)
The Crafts 1957, Arts and Crafts Exhibition Society
show, Victoria and Albert Museum, London
(USA tour 1958–60)

1958
Aldermaston Pottery, Craftsman's Market, Heal's,
London ★ #
British Art and Craftsmanship Tour of the USA,
1958–60

1960
Four Modern Potters, National Museum of Wales,
Cardiff
Victoria and Albert Museum travelling exhibition
of British studio pottery
Under Thirties, Craft Centre of Great Britain,
London
Made in the Country, Rural Industries Board
Exhibition, Tea Centre, London
Design Centre, London

1961
Modern Potters (Victoria and Albert Museum
exhibition), Abbot Hall, Kendal
The Aldermaston Pottery, Reading Museum and Art
Gallery #
Artist Potters, Turner House, Penarth, Wales
Glynn Vivian Art Gallery, Swansea, Wales
*Tin Glaze Ware by Alan Caiger Smith and Geoffrey
Eastop*, Aldringham Craft Market, Leiston,
Suffolk #

1962
Teapots, Craftsmen Potters Association, London
British Industries Fair, Stockholm, Sweden
Crafts Centre of Great Britain, London

1963
Alan Caiger-Smith, Primavera Gallery, London ★ #
Ideal Home Exhibition, London
The Mark of the Maker, Swyre, Gloucestershire

1964
Alan Caiger-Smith, Primavera Gallery, Cambridge
★ #
10 Modern Potters, Victoria and Albert Museum
travelling exhibition (touring for several years)
Casseroles, Craftsmen Potters Association, London

1965
Studio Pottery, Society of Designer Craftsmen
Exhibition, City Museum and Art Gallery,
Stoke-on-Trent

1967
International Ceramic Exhibition, Istanbul
British Council Exhibition of Modern British Pottery,
Ankara
Crafts Council of Great Britain exhibition, Bristol
Monza, Italy

1968
Matsuya Gallery, Tokyo ★ #
International Exhibition of Ceramics, Victoria and
Albert Museum, London
Alan Caiger-Smith, Primavera Gallery, Cambridge
★ #

1969
British Potters '69, Quantas Gallery, London

Ceramics, Primavera Gallery, London
Oxford Gallery ★ #

1970
*Alan Caiger-Smith and Members of Aldermaston
    Pottery*, Peter Dingley Gallery, Stratford-on-
    Avon ★ #
25 Years in Association with Primavera, Primavera
    Gallery, London
International Exhibition of Ceramics, Faenza, Italy
    (Lion's Club Prize)
Bondgate Gallery, Alnwick ★ #
British Studio Pottery, Design Centre, London
Crafts for Ceremonies, Society of Designer
    Craftsmen Exhibition, All Hallows on the
    Walls, London
Five Modern Potters, Victoria and Albert Museum
    travelling exhibition (touring until 1974)

1971
Aldermaston Pottery, Bedford Crafts Centre #
Aldermaston Pottery, British Crafts Centre, London
    #
Twenty British Potters, Kettle's Yard, Cambridge
International Ceramics, Faenza, Italy (Ballardini
    Prize)
Sturt Workshops, Mittagong, New South Wales,
    Australia #

1972
International Ceramics Exhibition, Victoria and
    Albert Museum, London (touring until 1977)
International Ceramics, Faenza, Italy
Wessex Design Workshops, Winchester ★ #

1973
The Craftsman's Art, Victoria and Albert Museum,
    London
Craft Centre, South Yarra, Melbourne, Australia #
*Tin-Glazed Earthenware: Alan Caiger-Smith
    and Aldermaston Potters*, Craftsmen Potters
    Association, London #

1974
Ceramic Boxes, Craftsmen Potters Association,
    London
New Ceramics, British Crafts Centre, London
Craft Centre, South Yarra, Melbourne, Australia #

New Ceramics, Ulster Museum, Belfast (toured to
    Cork, Dublin and Limerick)

1975
New Zealand Touring Exhibition, sponsored by
    Queen Elizabeth II Arts Council ★ #
Henschel Gallery, Houston, Texas, USA #
Candlesticks and Candleholders, Craftsmen Potters
    Association, London
Rich and Rare, Arts Centre, Bampton, Oxfordshire
Ceramics Alan Caiger-Smith and Aldermaston Potters,
    Yew Tree Cottage Gallery, Ingleby, Derbyshire
    #
*Alan Caiger-Smith Painted Tin-glaze Earthenware and
    Smoked Lustre*, Salix, Windsor #
The Potters Choice, Aldringham Craft Market,
    Leiston, Suffolk
New Zealand Potters' Society, Hastings, New
    Zealand #
Crafts Centre, South Yarra, Melbourne Australia
Goblets, Bohun Gallery, Henley-on-Thames #

1976
The Craft of the Potter, British Crafts Centre,
    London ★
Tin-Glaze and Smoked Lustre Pottery, British Crafts
    Centre, London #
Craft Centre, South Yarra, Melbourne, Australia #
*Crafts Advisory Committee Exhibition of Craftsmen on
    the CAC Index*, Design Centre, London
Potters on Pottery, Casson Gallery, London
Best of the Lot, Yew Tree Cottage Gallery, Ingleby,
    Derbyshire #

1977
Canterbury Society of Arts, Christchurch, New
    Zealand ★#
Alan Caiger-Smith Recent Lustre and Earthenware,
    Oxford Gallery, Oxford #
Potters and Ceramic Artists, Abbot Hall Art Gallery,
    Kendal
Contemporary British Ceramics, Prieto Gallery,
    Oakland, CA, USA
Around Summer, Yew Tree Cottage Gallery,
    Ingleby, Derbyshire #
Leisure Centre, Bridgnorth, Shropshire
Small Pots, Bohun Gallery, Henley-on-Thames

1978

Permanent Collection Exhibition, Shipley Art Gallery,
    Gateshead
*Ceramics by Full Members of the Craftsmen Potters
    Association*, Wolverhampton Art Gallery
The Bowl, World Crafts Council, New York, USA
Alan Caiger-Smith: Lustre Decorated Ware, Century
    Galleries, Henley-on-Thames #
Society of Designer Craftsmen: 14 exhibitions
    shown simultaneously in England and Scotland
Rothschild Exhibition, Eckenforde, West Germany

1979

Blackfriars Gallery, Sydney, Australia ★#
Gallerie de Proen, Amsterdam, Netherlands ★#
Ceramics by Alan Caiger-Smith, Museum and Art
    Gallery, Bolton
Ceramics by Alan Caiger-Smith, National Museum
    of Wales, Cardiff #
*Alan Caiger-Smith: Pottery and Potters at Aldermaston
    Pottery*, Black Horse Crafts Centre, Norwich #
Museum of Applied Arts, Bergen, Norway
Lustreware, Usher Gallery, Bishop Grosseteste's
    College, Lincoln
*Artist Craftsmen of Quality: Objects from the Crafts
    Council Collection*, Castle Museum, Norwich
Lustrous and Rare, Yew Tree Gallery, Ellastone,
    Staffordshire
Ceramic Lustre by Alan Caiger-Smith, Oxford
    Gallery, Oxford ★#

1980

Ceramics at Sudbury, Sudbury Hall, Derbyshire
21st Birthday Exhibition, Bluecoat Display Centre,
    Liverpool
Crafts by the Month: November, South Hill Park Arts
    Centre, Bracknell, Berkshire

1981

Blackfriars Gallery, Sydney, Austalia #
Crafts Centre, Melbourne, Australia
Living Letters, Craft Study Centre, Bath
Alan Caiger-Smith and Edgar Campden, Barclaycraft,
    Brighton #
Alan Caiger-Smith and the Aldermaston Pottery, Cider
    Press Centre, Dartington #
Big Pots, British Crafts Centre, London
Handmade in Britain: The Crafts Council Collection,
    Stoke-on-Trent City Museum and Art Gallery

The New Ceramics, Rufford Crafts Centre,
    Nottinghamshire

1982

*Painted Tin-glaze and Lustre Pottery by Alan Caiger-
    Smith*, The Arts Club, London #
The Maker's Eye, Crafts Council Gallery, London
Potter's Pots, Craftsmen Potters Association,
    London
Recent Work by Alan Caiger-Smith, Bluecoat Display
    Centre, Liverpool #
Ceramics by Alan Caiger-Smith and Edgar Campden,
    Falcon House Gallery, Boxford, Suffolk #
Prophecy and Vision, The Fabric of the Church, City
    of Bristol Museum and Art Gallery; urham
    Light Infantry Museum; Campden Arts Centre,
    London (September 1982–March 1983)
Alan Caiger-Smith, The Gallery, Worksworth,
    Derbyshire #
British Contemporary Crafts, Houston, Texas, USA
International Ceramics, Cork, Eire

1983

Contemporary Glass and Ceramics, Katherine House
    Gallery, Marlborough
The Granary, Newbury
Thirty-Seven Potters return to Kettles Yard, Kettles
    Yard, Cambridge
Lustreware, British Crafts Centre, London
Arts Centre Dubai, United Arab Emirates #
Studio Ceramics, Craftsmen Potters Association,
    London
*Studio Ceramics Today: 25 years of the Craftsmen
    Potters Association*, Victoria and Albert Museum,
    London
Candlesticks and Silks, Mirrors and Boxes and Bowls,
    Katherine House Gallery, Marlborough
Recent Pots, Open Eye Gallery, Edinburgh,
    Scotland
Dulwich Picture Gallery, London

1984

Alan Caiger-Smith, Medici Gallery, London ★
Fireworks, David Canter Fund exhibition,
    Craftsmen Potters Association, London
Alan Caiger-Smith: New Developments in Lustre,
    Oxford Gallery, Oxford ★#
Pottery by Alan Caiger-Smith, Broughton Gallery,
    Lanarkshire, Scotland #

Contemporary Decorated Pottery, Katherine House
    Gallery, Marlborough
The Granary, Newbury
Pots and Potters, The Suffolk Craft Society
    Exhibition, Aldeburgh, Suffolk
Contemporary British Pottery, Fireworks Gallery,
    Seattle, USA
Alan Caiger-Smith and Aldermaston Pottery,
    Craftsmen Potters Association, London

1985
Parnham House, Dorset ★
*Tin-Glaze and Smoked Lustre Pottery by Alan
    Caiger-Smith and Aldermaston Pottery 1955–1985:
    Thirty-Year Retrospective Exhibition*, Stoke-on-
    Trent City Museum and Art Gallery # (toured
    1985–7 to: Andover Museum; Cleveland
    Gallery,
Middlesborough; Abbot Hall, Kendal; Norwich
    Castle Museum; Holbourne
Museum, Bath; Lotherton Hall, Leeds; Glasgow
    Art Gallery and Museum;
Geffreye Museum, London) ★

1986
Medici Gallery, London ★
Crafts Study Centre, Bath

1987
Gallerie Munken, Stockholm ★
Open Eye Gallery, Edinburgh ★
Gardiner Museum, Toronto ★

1988
Bohun Galllery, Henley-on-Thames ★
Crafts Classics, Craft Council, London

1990
Open Eye Gallery, Edinburgh ★
Scottish Gallery, Edinburgh

1991
Colours of the Earth, British Council Exhibition
    (toured 1992 to India and Malaysia)

1992
British Ceramics, Barcelona

1993
Biennale de la Faience, Nevers, France
*Alan Caiger-Smith and Aldermaston Pottery 1955–
    1993*,(final exhibition) Aldermaston Pottery

2004
East Meets West: Then and Now, De Morgan
    Centre, London

2005
Golden Jubilee Exhibition, The Pottery, Aldermaston

2006
Closing exhibition and sale, Aldermaston Pottery

2008–9
*Tribute to Alan Caiger-Smith: Master of Lustred
    Pottery*, Palazzo dei Consoli, Gubbio, Italy

2013
*Alan Caiger-Smith and The Aldermaston Pottery: A
    Retrospective Display at Great Dixter*, Great Dixter
    House, Northiam, East Sussex

Select Bibliography

Billington, Dora, 'The New Look in British Pottery', *The Studio*, 149, no. 742, January 1955, p. 18

Caiger-Smith, Alan, *English Medieval Mural Paintings*, Oxford 1963

Caiger-Smith, Alan, 'Workshop/Aldermaston Pottery', *Ceramic Review*, 5, October 1970, pp. 4–6

Caiger-Smith, Alan, *Tin-Glaze Pottery in Europe and the Islamic World: The Tradition of 1,000 Years in Maiolica, Faience and Delftware*, London 1973

Caiger-Smith, Alan, 'Why decorate pots?' *Crafts*, September/October 1981, pp. 27–30

Caiger-Smith, Alan, *Lustre Pottery: Technique, Tradition and Innovation in Islam and the Western World*, London 1985

Caiger-Smith, Alan, *Alan Caiger-Smith and Aldermaston Pottery, 1955–1993: Selective Catalogue of the Final Exhibition 1993 with a Brief Survey of the Pottery over 38 Years*, exh. cat., Aldermaston 1993a

Caiger-Smith, Alan, 'Ending with a flourish', *Crafts*, 122, May/June 1993b, pp. 29–31

Caiger-Smith, Alan, 'Big pots', *Ceramic Review*, 141, May/June 1993c, pp. 21–2

Caiger-Smith, Alan, *Pottery, People and Time: A Workshop in Action*, Ilminster 1995

Caiger-Smith, Alan, 'Ceramic lustre', *Ceramic Review*, 219, May/June 2006, pp. 51–3

Caiger-Smith, Alan, *Times and Seasons: Umbrian Writings*, Perugia 2012

Cardew, Michael, *Pioneer Pottery*, London 1969

Collins, Judith, 'Roger Fry and Omega Pottery', *Ceramic Review*, 86, March/April 1984, pp. 29–31

Cooper, Emmanuel, and Eileen Lewenstein, *Potters: An illustrated Directory of the Work of the Full Members of the Craftsmen Potters Association*, London 1974

Dormer, Peter, *The Art of the Maker: Skill and its Meaning in Art, Craft and Design*, London 1994

Richard Dunning, exhibition review, 'Alan Caiger-Smith and members of Aldermaston Pottery, Peter Dingley Gallery Stratford upon Avon 7–28 March 1970', *Ceramic Review*, 2, April 1970, p. 18

Eastop, Geoffrey, *The Piper Years: A Memoir*, Zingaro 2011

French, Neal, 'Lustre and light', *Ceramic Review*, 90, November 1984, pp. 6–8

Frost, Abigail, 'Omega Anonymous', *Crafts*, 66, January/February 1984, pp. 40–44

Hanssen Pigott, Gwyn, 'Clarity of intention,' *Ceramic Review*, 124, July/August 1990, pp. 20–22

Hanssen Pigott, Gwyn, 'Autobiographical notes', *The Studio Potter*, 20, no. 1, 1991

Harrod, Tanya, *The Real Thing: Essays on making in the modern world*, London 2015

Lightbown, Ronald, and Alan Caiger-Smith (eds and trans.), *The Three Books of the Potter's Art*, London 1980

Mansfield, Janet, 'Technical innovator', in *Alan Peascod: Influences and Dialogue*, exh. booklet, Woolongong City Gallery, NSW, 2008

Martin, Colin, 'The potter and the plantsman', *Ceramic Review*, 277, January/February 2016, pp. 42–7

Martin, S.A., R. Braithwaite, P. Jeffcoate, T. Girling and C. Moore, *Memories of Life in an English Country Village*, Aldermaston 2005

Niblett, Kathy, *Tin-Glaze and Smoked Lustre: Pottery by Alan Caiger-Smith and Aldermaston Pottery 1955–1985*, exh. cat., Stoke-on-Trent City Museum and Art Gallery 1985

Ostermann, Matthias, *The New Maiolica*, London 1999

Sannipoli, Ettore A., and Timothy Wilson (eds), 'Alan Caiger-Smith and Gubbio', *A Tribute to Alan Caiger-Smith: Master of Lustred Pottery*, exh. cat., Palazzo dei Consoli, Gubbio, 2008

Shackleton, Jason, 'Man and mud', *Debrett's International Collection 1994*, eds Rex Berry and Anna McCorquodale, London 1994, pp. 24–8

Schumacher, E.F., *Small is Beautiful: A Study of Economics as if People Mattered*, London 1973

Spalding, Frances, *John Piper, Myfanwy Piper: Lives in Art*, Oxford 2009

Tuckson, Margaret, 'Gwyn Hanssen Pigott: seeking perfection', *Ceramic Review*, 89, September/ October 1984, pp. 26–31

Wilson, Timothy, *Italian Maiolica and Europe: Medieval and Later Italian Pottery in the Ashmolean Museum*, Oxford 2017

Index

Page numbers in *italics* refer to illustrations

Photographic Credits

All photographs in this book were taken by Julian Bellmont,
with the exception of the following:

Graham Adamson p. 79
David Anthony (Pratt) p. 81
Oldrich Asenbryl pp. 67, 68
Ashmolean Museum, University of Oxford p. 9
Catherine Bennett pp. 74, 98, 99, 102, 112, 118, 121, 146,
    152, 160
Gill Bent p. 159 (above and below)
© Ange Boott pp. 49, 56, 57 (above and below), 72, 73,
    75 (above and below), 113
Ben Boswell p. 6
Alan Caiger-Smith p. 24 (left)
Anne-Marie Caiger-Smith pp. 2, 24 (right), 37, 41, 44,
    50–51, 65, 137, 167
Mark Campden pp. 179, 210, 211, 221 (below)
Marshall Colman p. 45
John Daly p. 120 (above and below), 158
Ansel Dickie p. 163
Ben Eastop p. 28
Courtesy of Erskine, Hall & Coe Ltd p. 41
Teagan Glenane 155
Courtesy of Great Dixter House and Gardens p. 48
    (photo: Jane White)
Peter Greenland p. 178 (above and below)
Juliet Harkness p. 78
Gerald Hunt p. 23
Hali Issente (Yad Hassan) p. 165
Zvonko Kracun pp. 138, 139, 140
Howell Lambert p. 200
Peter Liepins p. 149
Myra McDonnell p. 213
Jackie McGowan p. 142 (above and below), 143
Courtesy of Mallams Auctioneers p. 40
Kristine Michael p. 193 (above)
Peter Pilven pp. 153, 154
© Piper Estate, courtesy of Seb and Mary Piper p. 29
    (photo: Seb Piper)
Courtesy of Redland Roof Tiles Ltd p. 111
Les Reed p. 221 (above)
Bryony Rich pp. 69, 70
Jaki Rothery pp. 92, 94 (above and below)
Gift of Dolly Saunders p. 20
Siddharth Photographics p. 193 (below)
Leigh Simpson p. 175

Miranda Thomas Shackleton p. 147
Shannon Tofts p. 141
Ursula Waechter p. 217
Peter Waugh p. 18
Nicola Werner p. 171
Jane White pp. 48, 220
White House issued photo p. 164
Angi Wiesner p. 157
Timothy Wilson pp. 223, 224, 225